Krista Lynes, Tyler Morgenstern, Ian Alan Paul (eds.)
Moving Images

Media Studies | Volume 64

Dedicated to all those who resist and oppose the global bordering regime.

Krista Lynes is Canada Research Chair in Feminist Media Studies and Associate Professor in Communication Studies at Concordia University (Montreal, Canada) where they also founded and direct the Feminist Media Studio.

Tyler Morgenstern is a PhD candidate in the Department of Film & Media Studies at the University of California, Santa Barbara, and a doctoral fellow of the Social Sciences and Humanities Research Council of Canada. His work focuses on the imbrications between information and communication technologies and the racial and territorial politics of empire. He is also a contributing member of the Media Fields editorial collective at UCSB.

Ian Alan Paul is a transdisciplinary artist and theorist and is Assistant Professor of Emerging Media in the Department of Art at Stony Brook University. Their projects examine instantiations of power and practices of resistance in global contexts, and have been exhibited and published internationally.

Krista Lynes, Tyler Morgenstern,
Ian Alan Paul (eds.)

Moving Images

Mediating Migration as Crisis

[transcript]

This project is made possible with the support of numerous institutions and funding agencies: the Social Sciences & Humanities Research Council of Canada, the Canada Research Chair program, the Feminist Media Studio, and Stony Brook University. The project is also published with the important support of Fondation IMéRA of Aix-Marseille University, and the French Agence Nationale de la Recherche, as part of its "investissements d'avenir" program (ANR-11-LABX-0027-01).

Bibliographic information published by the Deutsche Nationalbibliothek

The Deutsche Nationalbibliothek lists this publication in the Deutsche Nationalbibliografie; detailed bibliographic data are available in the Internet at http://dnb.d-nb.de

© 2020 transcript Verlag, Bielefeld

Cover layout: Maria Arndt, Bielefeld
Cover illustration: Zineb Sedira, SeaPath, 2017
Layout: Jan Wenke, Leipzig
Typeset by Jan Wenke, Leipzig
Printed by Majuskel Medienproduktion GmbH, Wetzlar
Print-ISBN 978-3-8376-4827-0
PDF-ISBN 978-3-8394-4827-4
https://doi.org/10.14361/9783839448274

Contents

Section Two. Mobile Positions

Afterword

Lies of the Land

Bibliography

Acknowledgements

It seems fitting that the recursive, iterative and circulatory dynamics of mediation at the heart of this anthology are matched in pace and connectivity by the processes that brought it to fruition. The project has advanced haltingly but collaboratively over the course of many years, taking a multiplicity of forms and interpellating a number of audiences and participants along the way. Our editorial efforts, moreover, have been matched unevenly by the rapid tempo of the unfolding "migrant crisis," a temporality that made various forms of analysis impossible, even as it pushed us to generate new modes of thinking and academic engagement.

Some of our initial thinking was incubated at the Hemispheric Institute's *Encuentro* in 2014 in Montréal/Tio'tiá:ke, which helped flesh out the possibilities and limitations of the concept "trespass" (a modality for us to think bodily crossings and mediated borders). We are grateful also to participants in a workshop at the National Women's Studies Association Annual Conference in 2016 that sought to critically examine the representational regimes that frame and instantiate the European "migrant/refugee crisis" and consider the decolonizing potentials of various strategies of counter-mapping, critical reading, and collaborative knowledge production.

The anthology would not have been possible without the generous and generative participation of Farah Atoui, Allan deSouza, Corinn Gerber, Bishnupriya Ghosh, Adi Kuntsman, Suzana Milevska, Thomas Nail, and Veronika Zablotsky at the Trespassing Europe Summer Institute, hosted by the Feminist Media Studio in Montréal/Tio'tiá:ke in June 2017. We extend gratitude to Maya Youngs-Zaleski, whose labors as a research assistant were absolutely vital to the Institute's success.

We are grateful also to the participants in this project who joined along the way—Abdessamad El Montassir, Charles Heller and Lorenzo Pezzani, Thomas Keenan and Sohrab Mohebbi, Banu Cennetoglu, LGBTQIA+ Refugees in Greece, Sandro Mezzadra, Zineb Sedira, and Lonnie van Brummelen and Siebren De Haan. The project is infinitely richer with their participation.

We are particularly indebted to the Social Sciences and Humanities Research Council of Canada for the Connection Grant that made possible the Trespassing Europe Summer Institute, and an Insight Grant that buoyed the exchanges and this anthology which results from it. Much of the project materially depends on the Canada Research Chair in Feminist Media Studies (Lynes) and the *Feminist Media Studio* at Concordia University supported through it. We are also grateful to the *Fondation IMéRA—Institut d'Etudes Avancées* for supporting this project in multiple ways, and concretely through a publication grant. This support was vital to making the anthology Open Access, a key political decision for us as editors. We also thank Transcript Verlag, and Jakob Horstmann particularly, for receiving this manuscript so warmly and for working with us to both honor the visual contributions so vital to the anthology and to make the anthology accessible. We thank also Fanny Gravel-Patry, our research assistant who indeed assisted indefatigably throughout the editorial process.

Finally, we feel it important to acknowledge how profoundly this project has been informed by the various sites at and across which it has taken shape. Though our analytic focus has for years now been trained on the European context, our thinking has been nourished by the places in which we have written, taught, and thought (together and apart) over the course of this book's creation. Humbly, we have learned, and continue to learn, from the struggles for migrant justice currently unfolding at and around the borders of Canada, the United States, and Mexico; from the struggle for Palestinian liberation in the West Bank and Gaza; from the decolonial aspirations and sovereign enactments of Indigenous peoples and movements across Turtle Island from Tio'tiá:ke to Chiapas, and in all places between and beyond; and from the insistent, insurgent, and indefatigable demands of Black Lives Matter. Our thinking is quite impossible without the spaces of imaginative, political, and ethical possibility such projects, among innumerable others, manage to hold open amidst and against the relentless forces of enclosure. We acknowledge our deep intellectual and political debts to this movement work, which is always knowledge work, and always theory.

Preface

Sandro Mezzadra

Labels matter. To speak of a "migrant crisis" with respect to what happened in Europe in and since the summer of 2015 is not neutral, as readers of this book will soon realize. It has deep political implications and it also requires and nurtures specific forms of visualization—or a specific set of "image operations," to employ a notion that figures prominently in this book. Shipwrecks at sea and corpses on a beach, ungovernable bodies in motion and scenes of destitution in informal camps: a whole humanitarian visual culture has developed around such images of crisis, with the aim to nurture compassion and engagement from afar. There was no shortage of such images in the summer of 2015. The point is of course not to downplay their relevance as iconic representations of the events, nor is it to simply articulate once again a critique of humanitarian reason. Nevertheless, it is clear that the selection of those images obscures other aspects of the migratory turmoil at the borders of and in Europe in 2015/16. What if we take as guiding thread other images, for instance snapshots of the "march of hope" from Budapest to the Austrian border on September 4, 2015, or of the elementary force with which tens of thousands of women, men, and children on the move swept away border fences and walls from Macedonia to Hungary, across the "Balkan route" during that summer? A different picture of the events emerges. What strikes in those images is not so much "crisis," as rather the sense of an uncontainable movement, of a radical challenge to Europe's borders, of an even joyful practice of freedom. In emphasizing such images, activists and critical migration and border studies called the events of 2015/16 the "long summer of migration."[1]

It is important to recover the insurgent character of the movements of migration in Europe in the summer of 2015. A shift in migrants' routes from the Central to the Eastern Mediterranean as of May of that year made the crossing of the European maritime "external borders" significantly safer for the first time in the recent history of trans-Mediterranean migration.[2] Needless to say, this does not mean that there would be no deaths at sea in the following months. But thousands of migrants were able to get to the European shore of the Greek islands and continue their travel further North across the "Balkan route." I am not proposing a naive celebration or even a romanticization of the "summer of migration." Migratory routes at sea and on land were plagued by any kind of obstacle, threat, and violence; hunger, thirst, and death were continuing to

---

1   See Kasparek and Speer, "Of Hope."

2   Heller and Pezzani, "Ebbing and Flowing."

haunt migrants. But the subjective dimensions of migration, the search for freedom, and the desire for a better life that so often sustain the dynamics of migration were particularly apparent in the long summer of 2015. The passage across the Mediterranean and the "Balkan route" clearly took the characteristic of a *political* movement, and at least for a moment it was understood in such terms by wide sections of the European public, which mobilized to welcome migrants in countries like Greece, Austria, and Germany.

The encoding of the events as a "migrant crisis" did not merely happen in the framework of a humanitarian discourse sincerely responding to the perceived predicament and pain of migrants. It quickly became the mainstream reaction of EU institutions, national governments, and global media. While the events in the summer of 2015 had manifested a crisis of the European border regime, the discourse surrounding the "migrant" (or "refugee") crisis dramatically shifted the responsibility toward a threat coming from the outside of a supposedly stable and ordered European space. The political dimension of the movements and struggles of migration was thus *neutralized*, and the image of the crisis—with its affective resonances and its visual instantiations—began to be mobilized against the challenges posed by the "summer of migration." Far from responding to those challenges—envisaging a democratization of borders and taking the opportunity for imagining a different Europe as well as different relations between Europe and its multiple outsides—the institutions of the EU and national governments began to work in tandem to reinforce the border regime. The enhanced deployment of Frontex in Greece, the establishment of the hotspot approach of the European Commission, and the crackdown on so-called "secondary movements" of migrants and refugees were among the main steps of a strategy that was crowned by the EU-Turkey deal in March 2016. The externalization of European borders, underway since the 1990s, thus reached a further stage, leaving thousands of migrants and refugees stranded in Greece while maritime crossing shifted again toward the Central Mediterranean, definitely the most lethal border in the world.[3]

"Mediating migration as crisis is a global affair," the editors of this book write in their introduction. Over the last years we have witnessed such a global scope in many parts of the world, in a political conjuncture that is characterized by the rise of old and new nationalisms, as well as by various degrees of combination between authoritarianism and neoliberalism. As far as Europe is concerned, the increasing nationalization of political discourse and processes have led to multiple conflicts and tensions between the European Commission and member states, whose manifestations have been particularly apparent around issues of borders and migration. With the rise of a nationalist right in several European countries, including Hungary, Austria, and Italy, the cooperation between the EU and national governments has become far from smooth in the wake of the EU-Turkey deal. Even the neoliberal version of "migration management," built upon the primacy of "human capital" and advocated by the European Commission and by various governmental bodies around Europe, has become increasingly criticized by nationalist forces and governments. "Migration" as such is the privileged target for such forces and governments, both rhetorically and politically. While this implies an increasing harshness of conditions for migrants and refugees

---

3   See Bojadžijev and Mezzadra, "'Refugee crisis' or Crisis of European Migration Policies?"; New Keywords Collective, "Europe/Crisis;" De Genova, *The Borders of "Europe."*

living in Europe (often for many years), with an entrenchment of discrimination and racism, a hardening of borders (even of "internal" borders within the Schengen space) is apparent.

Since the summer of 2018 in particular, the Italian government has waged a war not only against migrants crossing the Central Mediterranean (and often escaping from detention centers in Libya, whose dire conditions have been denounced by several organizations, including the UNHCR), but also against NGOs and humanitarian interventions at sea. The criminalization of humanitarianism, parallel to a more general trend toward the criminalization of solidarity,[4] has partially shifted the ground for political conflicts around migration. While humanitarianism had long been considered a constitutive component of the border regime,[5] its criminalization necessarily implies a politicization of the issue of intervention and migrant rescue at sea. Activists and social organizations have attempted to respond to that challenge by establishing a platform that aims at combining rescue operations in the Central Mediterranean with the building of bridges with migrant and social struggles on land, openly defying the government.[6] While the attack on migrants intensifies in many parts of the world, this is just an instance of the multifarious forms of political and social intervention that attempt to prompt a counter-offensive. Cultural and artistic practices as the ones documented in this book can make crucially important contributions to this project.

What is even more important is to emphasize the stubbornness of migration in such a global predicament as the one we are living through. The dynamics of migration continue to be characterized and prompted by elements of autonomy (from the hardening of borders as well as from the imagined equilibrium of "migration management") that are dramatically apparent in the Central Mediterranean no less than along the border between the U.S. and Mexico and elsewhere in the world. It is this autonomy that sustains the "fugitivity" (a notion borrowed from Fred Moten) of migrant movement that—as the editors write in their introduction—this book "seeks to hold open." *La frontera está cerrada, pero vamos a pasar* ("the border is closed, but we will cross"), a phrase from a Honduran song circulating among migrants' caravans across Mexico, effectively instantiates what I call the stubbornness of migration. This is a constitutive feature of global migration today. It crisscrosses what we could term its "political anatomy," and it sheds light on the subjective stakes surrounding contemporary conflicts around borders and migration. Such a stubbornness of migration challenges us to invent a notion of freedom of movement capable of foreshadowing a different society, a different way to live together beyond the asphyxiating "double pincer" of nationalism and neoliberalism. This book makes an outstanding contribution to this project, connecting "moving media" and "mobile positions" and building archives that invite readers to turn them into weapons for struggle.

---

4 Tazzioli, "Crimes of Solidarity."

5 Mezzadra and Neilson, *Border as Method.*

6 Caccia and Mezzadra, "What Can a Ship Do?"

1.

Allan deSouza, Xing (2016)

Through the Black Country, or, The Sources of the Thames Around the Great Shires of Lower England and Down the Severn River to the Atlantic Ocean

Allan deSouza

The following extracts are from the expedition diaries of the Zanzibari crypto-ethnologist, Hafeed Sidi Mubarak Mumbai, the fictional great-grandson of the historical figure, Sidi Mubarak Bombay, (1820-1885). Bombay acquired his moniker after being enslaved in East Africa and sent to Bombay, India. Upon gaining his freedom and returning to Africa, he acted as guide and translator for a number of expeditions across Africa, including ones led by Henry Stanley. Bombay became renowned as the most widely traveled person in C19th Africa. Almost a hundred and fifty years later, Mumbai fulfilled his great grandfather Bombay's unrealized wish to lead an expedition to England.

In a diary transposed by Allan deSouza from Henry Stanley's 1874 journal of his expedition to find the source of the Nile, Mumbai's quest leads him across London to discover the elusive source of the fabled River Thames. In so doing, Mumbai ingests deSouza's own navigational history as an immigrant from East Africa to Britain.

Chapter 1

Arrival at London—Life in the city of London, its peoples, roads, flora and buildings—Some customs of the English—Europeans in London—Encounters with the Cockney—Selection and purchase of goods for the journey—The ferment of Barking and beginning the journey.

May 21.—The undulating ridges, and the gentle slopes clad with sycamores and elm trees bathed in cool vapour, seemed in that tranquil drowsy state which at all times any portion of temperate Europe presents at first appearance. A pale-grey sky covered the hazy land and sleeping sea as we cruised through the channel that separates England from the continent. Every stranger, at first view of the shores, proclaims his displeasure. The dreary verdure, the distant pale ridges, the sluggish sea, the thick gauzy atmosphere, the semi-mysterious silence which pervades all nature, evoke his desperation. For it is probable that he has sailed through the stifling North Sea, with the grim, frowning camps of Calais on the one hand, and on the other the dreary, ochreous-coloured ridges of the English Peninsula; and perhaps the aspect of the arid limestone rocks of Folkstone and the dry white bluffs of Dover is still fresh in his memory.

2.

Allan deSouza, Building Paradise (2016)

But a great change has taken place. As he passes close to the concrete works and docks of Gravesend and Tilbury, he views nature robbed of its greenest verdure, with a noxious drabness of colour, sweating stench to the incoming wanderer. He is wearied with the unnatural deep-grey of the sea, and eager for any change. He remembers the unconquerable moistness and the wet bleached heights he last saw, and lo! What a change! Responding to his half formed wish, the ground rises before him arid, concretic, eructive with gaseousness. Chimneys raise their striated necks and warehouses their great hefts of white-grey expanse; walls with impenetrable wire heads, thickets of iron, pungent smoke, and spreading throttling morning glory, spike and disgrace the landscape. Ash heaps loom up in great massive cones of grit and dust, while between the docks and in every open space wiry grasses and plants crack the ground with thin sproutings of umbrage. There is something bland or frigid in the view before him, and his gaze is distracted from any special feature, because all is toned down to a uniform greyness by the exhalation rising from the cold heaving bosom of the land. His imagination is therefore caught and stilled, his mind loses its restless activity, and freezes under the influence of the eternal winter atmosphere.

Presently on the horizon there rises the thin upright shadows of crane skeletons, and to the left begins to glimmer a pale grey mass which, we are told, is the capital of the island of England. Still cruising westward, we come within spitting distance of the low dun shores, and now begin to be able to define the capital. It consists of a number of rectangular massive structures, with great variety of height and all greyish, standing on a point of low land, separated by a broad margin of concrete wall from the river, with a flood barrier curving gently from the point, outwards to the left towards us.

Within two hours from the time we first caught sight of the city, we have stopped about 700 yards from the bank. The arrival of the ferry causes a sensation. It is the daily "migrant train" from Calais and Europe!

The stranger, of course, is intensely interested in this life existing near the English meridian, now first revealed to him, and all that he sees and hears of figures and faces and sounds is being freshly impressed on his memory. Figures and faces are picturesque enough. Grim, miserable looking men of white, pink or brackish colour, with hooded sweat shirts, move about with slow, lethargic motion, and cry out, regardless of order, to their friends and mates in the Cockney or Polish language, and their friends or mates respond with equally loud voice and lively gesture, until, with fresh arrivals, there appears to be a Babel created, wherein, Cockney, Polish, Bangladeshi, and Somali accents mix with Arabic, French, and, perhaps, Igbo.

May 26.—Life at London is a busy one to the intending explorer. Time flies rapidly, and each moment of daylight must be employed in the selection and purchase of the various kinds of fashion-wear, jewelry, and electronics, in demand by the different tribes of the hinterland through whose counties he purposes journeying. Strong, tattooed lads come in with great cases of stone-washed denims, striped and flannel fabrics, neckties and baseball caps, bags of red, white, blue, lead and silver-coloured phones, small and large, slim and fat, and coils upon coils of thick headphones. These have to be inspected, assorted, arranged, and numbered separately, have to be packed in portable boxes, stacks, or packages, or boxed according to their character and value. The house-floors are littered with cast-off wrappings and covers, box-lids, and a medley of rejected paper, cloth, phone covers and broken screens, styrofoam and other debris.

Layabouts and workers and "messengers," employees and employers, pass backwards and forwards, to and fro, amid all this litter, roll carry-ons over, or tumble about boxes; and a rending of cardboard or paper, clattering of metal, demands for the marking pens, or the number of case and box, with quick hurried breathing and shouting, are heard from early morning until night.

Towards evening, after such a stultifying day of glaring cold and busy toil, comes weariness: the armchair is sought, and tobacco with a pot of tea rounds off the uneventful hours. Or, as sometimes the case would be, we would strike work early, and after an unwholesome dinner at 6:30 p.m., would get on the Tube and ride out into the interior of the city, returning during the long twilight. Or we would take the Dock Land light railway to the White Chapel—to the "Gherkin," where it stands unnatural and sentinel-like over humble abodes on the crest of an ancient reach behind the Tower. Or, as the last and only resources left to a contemplative and studious mind, we would take our easy-chairs on the balcony, where the echoes of the financiers are resounding and cruel, and with our feet elevated above our heads, watch the night coming.

If we take our ride, in a few minutes we may note, at the pleasantest hour, those local features which, with the thermometer at 45 Fahr., might have been a dubious pleasure, or, at any rate, disagreeable. Through a narrow, crooked, cobbled lane, our boots clattering noisily as we go, we walk by the tall, glass-faced, massive offices, which rise to ten and fifteen stories above our heads. The workplaces of the financiers and the officials here stand side by side, and at the tall doorway of each stands a doorman—as comfortable as his circumstances will permit. As we pass on, we get short views of the river, and then plunge again into the lane until we come in view of the pockmarked old Tower, crumbling fast into disuse and demolition. Years ago, behind it, there was a market where jellied eels were being sold. Happily there is no such market now.

We presently catch sight, on our right, of the entrance to the Tower at which sit on guard a few lazy Beefeaters and stern looking Coppers. On our left is the saluting battery, which does ceremonial service for the ignition of gunpowder, an antique mode of exchanging compliments with ships of war, and of paying respect to Monarchy officials. The customs warehouses are close by, and directly in front of us rises the lofty house and brothel of the Prince Harry. It is a respectable-looking building of the English architecture which finds favour at Windsor, three stories high and brick-lined—as all houses here appear to be. It is connected by a concrete footbridge, about 20 feet above our heads, with a large house on the opposite side of the lane, and possesses an imposing doorway raised 3 feet above the street, and reached by four or five broad and curved-steps. Within the lower hall are some coppers of the same uniform as those at the Tower, with the submachine gun, or pistol, Taser, and truncheon. A very short time takes us into a still narrower lane, where the brick is not so red as at Hampstead, the English quarter. We are in the neighborhood of Brick Lane now, where the Englishman who has not been able to locate himself at Hampstead is obliged to put up with neighbours of East Indian race or Jews. Past and beyond Brick Lane is a medley of tall white offices and low sweatshops, where wealth and squalor jostle side by side, and then we find ourselves at the Thread Needle street, which extends down to Pudding Lane and the Monument.

Having crossed the bridge from Saint Pauls, we are in what is very appropriately termed South Wark, or "t'other side." The street is wide, but the quarter is more squalid. It is here we find the "Riffraff," whose services the traveler will require as guide in the country. Here they live miserably with the well-to-do Commuters, or Yuppies, and poor Bastards, Gujaratis, Blacks, Arabs, Bangladeshis, and respectable migrant shopkeepers, and tradesmen. When the people have donned their holiday attire, South Wark becomes picturesque, even gay, and yields itself up to wild, frolicsome abandon of mirth. On working days, though the colours are still varied, and give relief to the rain-blackened concrete walls, this poor man's district has a dingy hue, which scowling faces and badly dressed bodies seems to deepen. However, the quarter is only a mile and a half long, and quickening our paces, we soon have before us detached houses and mews, clusters of elms and old beech trees crowned with enormous light green domes of foliage. For about three miles one can enjoy a gallop along an ochreous-coloured road of respectable width, bordered with hedges. Behind the hedges grow the roses, lavender, daisy, iris, foxglove, dogwood, and clematis, gooseberry, mallow, diversified with patches of blackberry, rhubarb, plums, and sweetpea, and almost every vegetable of temperate growth. The allotments, gently undulating, display the variety of their vegetation, on which the lights and shadows play, deepening, or paling as the setting sun clouds or reveals the charms of verdure.

Finally arriving upon the crest of Black Heath Common, we have a most beautiful view of the roadstead and city, and, as we turn to regard it, are struck with the landscape lying at our feet. Sloping away gradually towards the city, the temperate trees already mentioned seem, in the bird's-eye view, to mass themselves into a thin forest, out of which, however, we can pick out clearly the details of flora and man's building. Whatever of beauty may be in the scene, it is Nature's own, for man has done little; he has but planted a root, or a seed, or a tender sapling carelessly. Nature has nourished the root and the seed and the sapling, until they became spindly giants, rising one above another in hillocks of light green verdure, and has given to the whole that numbing shallowness and uniformity of colour which she only exhibits in the temperate zones.

June 17.—The English have turned their backs on the modern world and its cosmopolitan exchanges, and have retreated into their tribal ranks. I find this narrow-mindedness unfathomable, but it must be surmised from their low intelligence. I fear their rejection of the outside world, their "Brexit," will cause them to return to their nutritionally-lacking traditional diet, whose evidence is painfully displayed in their sallow skin and poor dental health. It is a wonder that they have survived this long, though they have learned to consume and do so in great quantities the foods, such as curries and kebabs, of other shores.

June 21.—The English never appear particularly friendly, and they seem to have a physical inability to smile, especially in the males. I have not had the opportunity to conduct a dissection, so cannot be sure if it is, in fact, a failing of the musculature.

When asking directions, which I occasionally have cause to do, given the impenetrability of the terrain, the natives seem for the most part willing to assist. One can never be sure, however, of their trustworthiness, and I make it a point to ask a second or third, sometimes in deliberate view of the first. It's important to let them see that I won't be fooled.

It is of potential danger to speak with their women, though with polite banter about the weather and about the prices of goods, they seem to be open. Their men, however, watch these interactions carefully for any infringement on what they see as impropriety towards their women. I have seen groups of young males suddenly turn violent, hurling vitriolic epithets towards the outsider and towards their own women, should they be seen to be "too friendly."

The men are daily intoxicated on a warm, flat, bitter brew which they consume in spectacularly large quantities at communal drinking holes. They watch "matches" (not to be confused with fire-lighting materials) in which two groups of men identified by ritual colours interminably kick back and forth a spherical pig- or cow-skin, to no apparent purpose. While the aftermath of these matches can result in mass rampages and pitched battles, I believe that these are nevertheless intended to alleviate these same men being otherwise shipped off to wage wars against other tribes in locations across the seas.

July 9.—The German escapees who accompanied the Empress Victoria, the great, great grandmother of the present Queen, took unto themselves, after the custom of monogamists, wives of their own race according to their means, and almost all of them purchased negro concubines, the result of which we trace today in the various complexions of those who call themselves English. By this process of miscegenation the English of the later migrations are already rapidly losing their pale colour and sallow complexions, while the descendants of the English of the earlier Huguenot migration are now deteriorated so much that on the coast they can scarcely be distinguished from the Irish.

July 12.—None of the Europeans with whom I made acquaintance ever proceeded thither with the definite intention of settling. Some were driven thither, by false hopes of acquiring rapid fortunes by the labour of waitressing and shopkeeping, and, perceiving that there were worse places on earth than England, preferred to remain there, to facing the odium of failure. Others borrowed large sums on trust from credulous politicians and moneylenders, and having failed in the venture now prefer to endure the exclusion to which they have subjected themselves, to returning and being arrested by their enraged creditors. Others again are not merely bankrupts, but persons who have fled the vengeance of the law for political offences, as well as ordinary crimes. There are many who are in better circumstances in the interior than they would be in their own lands of Europe.

The Easterners of Europe, whether from more frequent intercourse with Arabs or from other causes, are undoubtedly the best of their race. More easily amenable to reason than those of Scandinavia, or the shy, reserved, bigoted fanatics of Italy, they offer no obstacles to the traveler, but are sociable, frank, good-natured, and hospitable. In business they are keen traders, and of course will exact the highest percentage of profit out of the unsuspecting traveler if they are permitted. They are staunch friends and desperate haters. Blood is seldom satisfied without blood, unless extraordinary sacrifices are made.

The conduct of an Eastern gentleman is perfect. Indelicate matters are never broached before strangers; impertinence is hushed instantly by the elders, and rudeness is never permitted. Naturally, they have the vices of their education, blood, and race, but these moral blemishes are by their traditional excellence of breeding seldom obtruded upon the observation of the stranger.

July 16.—Of the Cockney there will be much written in the following pages, the outcome of careful study and a long experience of them. Few travelers have recorded anything greatly to their credit. One of them lately said that the English know neither love nor affection; another that he is simply the "link" between the fox and the hound. Another says, "The wretches take a trouble and display an ingenuity in opposition and disobedience, in perversity, annoyance, and villainy, which rightly directed would make them invaluable." Almost all have been severe in their strictures on the English of London.

I have come to perceive that the Cockney represent in their character much of the disposition of a large portion of the southern people of the continent. I find them capable of great love and affection, and possessed of gratitude and other noble traits of human nature; I know too, that they can be made good, obedient followers, that many are clever, honest, industrious, docile, enterprising, brave and moral; that they are, in short, equal to any other race or class on the face of the globe, in all the attributes of manhood. But to be able to perceive their worth, the traveler must bring an unprejudiced judgment, a clear, fresh, and patient observation, and must forget that lofty standard of excellence upon which he and his class pride themselves, before he can fairly appreciate the capabilities of the London Englishman. The traveler should not forget the origin of his own race, the condition of the Swahili Coast before da Gama visited his country, but should rather recall to mind the first state of the "traveler," and the original circumstances and surroundings of Civilized Man.

July 21.—Being, I hope, free from prejudice of cast, colour, race, or nationality, and endeavouring to pass what I believe to be a just judgment upon the English of London, I find that they are a people just emerged into the Culinary Epoch, and now thrust forcibly under the notice of nations who have left them behind by the improvements of over 400 years. They possess beyond doubt all the vices of a people still fixed deeply in lard, but they understand to the full what and how low such a state is; it is, therefore, a duty imposed upon us by the science we profess, and by the official rules of the EU, to help them out of the deplorable state they are now in. At any rate, before we begin to hope for the improvement of races so long benighted, let us leave off this impotent bewailing of their vices, and endeavor to discover some of the virtues they possess as men, for it must be by the aid of their virtues, and not by their vices, that the emissary of nutrition can ever hope to assist them. While, therefore, recording my experiences throughout England, I shall have frequent occasion to dilate upon both the vices and the virtues of the Cockney as well as of the Brummie of the interior, but it will not be with a view to foster, on the one hand, the self-deception of the civilized, or the absurd prejudices created by centuries of superior advantages, nor, on the other hand, to lead men astray by taking a too bright view of things. I shall write solely and simply with a strong desire to enable all interested in the Englishman to understand his mental and moral powers rightly.

July 24.—The Cockney or native of London, who dwells at Bow, is a happy, jovial soul. He is fond of company, therefore sociable. His vanity causes him to be ambitious of possessing several dark suits and bright red ties, and since he has observed that his superiors carry briefcases, he is almost certain, if he is rich enough to own a dark suit and a red tie, to be seen sporting a cowhide brief. The very poorest of his class hire themselves,

3.
Allan deSouza, Borough Boogie Woogie (2016)

or are hired out by their wives, to carry bales, boxes, and goods, from the custom house to the ship, or store-room, or vice versa, and as a general beast of burden, for donkeys are few, and of robotic vehicles there are none. Those who prefer light work and have good characters may obtain positions of doorkeepers, or chauffeurs, or for waiting tables and personal assistants for the European merchants. Others, trained as builders, obtain a livelihood by repairing houses, manufacturing tables, sideboards, and fixtures, or by plumbing and gardening. There is a class of Cockney living at Bow, in the small estates of the interior of the city, and along the banks of the river, who prefer the wandering life offered to them by lorry driving and long-distance routes to being subject to the caprice, tyranny, and meanness of small business proprietors. They complain that the proprietors are haughty, grasping, and exacting; that they abuse them and pay them badly; that if they seek justice at the hands of the courts, judgment, somehow, always goes against them. They say, on the other hand, that, when driving lorries or cabs, they are well paid, have an abundance to eat, and comparatively but little work.

August 4.—It is a most sobering employment, the organizing of an English tour. You are constantly engaged, mind and body; now in casting up accounts, and now travelling to and fro hurriedly to receive scouts, inspecting purchases, bargaining with keen-eyed, relentless Hindi merchants, writing memoranda, haggling over extortionate prices, packing up a multitude of small utilities, pondering about your lists of articles, wanted, purchased, and unpurchased, groping about in the recesses of a highly exercised imagination for what you ought to purchase, and cannot do without, superintending, arranging, assorting, and packing. And this is under a temperature of 45 Fahr.

August 14.—East London villages on the mainland near the river offer exceptionally good starting-points for the unexplored interior, for many reasons. First. Because the travelers and the natives are strangers to one another, and a slight knowledge of their power of mutual cohesion, habits, and relative influences, is desirable before launching out into the wilds. Second. The natives of those estuarine villages are accustomed to having their normally languid and peaceful life invaded and startled by the bustle of foreigners arriving by sea and from the continent, Indian traders bound for the interior and youthful American missionaries from Utah. Third. A tour not fully recruited to its necessary strength in London may be easily reinforced at these ports by volunteers of migrant workers who are desirous of returning to their homes, and who, day by day, along the route, will straggle in towards it until the list is full and complete.

These, then, were the principal reasons for my selection of Barking as the initial point, from whence, after inoculating the various untamed spirits who had now enlisted under me, with a respect for order and discipline, obedience and system (the true prophylactic against failure) I should be free to rove where discoveries would be fruitful. This "inoculation" will not, however, commence until after a study of their natures, their deficiencies and weaknesses. The exhibition of force, at this juncture, would be dangerous to our prospects, and all means gentle, patient, and persuasive, have, therefore, to be tried first. Whatever deficiencies, weaknesses, and foibles the people may develop must be so manipulated that, while they are learning the novel lesson of obedience, they may only just suspect that behind all this there lies the strong unbending force which will eventually make men of them, wild things though they now are. For the first few months, then, forbearance is absolutely necessary. The white brother, wild as a colt, chafing, restless, ferociously impulsive, superstitiously timid, liable to furious demonstrations, suspicious and unreasonable, must be forgiven seventy times seven, until the period of probation is passed. Long before this period is over, such temperate conduct will have enlisted a powerful force, attached to their leader by bonds of good-will and respect, even, perhaps, of love and devotion, and by the moral influence of their support even the most incorrigible "skin head" will be restrained, and finally conquered.

Many things will transpire during the first few weeks which will make the traveler sigh and wish that he had not ventured upon what promises to be a hopeless task. Maddened by strong drinks and drugs, jealous of their status in the EU, regretting also, like ourselves, that they had been so hasty in undertaking the exit, brooding over the joys of the land fast receding from them, anxious for the future, susceptible to the first and every influence that assails them with temptations to return to the flock, these people require to be treated with the utmost kindness and consideration, and the intending traveler must be wisely circumspect in his intercourse with them. From my experiences of such men, it will be readily believed that I had prepared for the scenes which I knew were to follow at Barking, and that all my precautions had been taken.

Within three hours Barking was in a ferment, "The traveler has brought all the robbers, rapists, and murderers of Europe to take possession of the land," was the rumour that ran wildly through all the streets, lanes, courts, and pubs. Men with bloody faces, wild, bloodshot eyes, bedraggled, rumpled and torn clothes, reeled up to our orderly and nearly silent quarters clamouring for retribution and snacks. Islingtonians with raised shovels, and tanned Hampsteadites with brollies ready to be drawn, came up threatening, and, following them, a miscellaneous rabble of excited men, while, in the background, seethed a mob of frantic women and mischievous children.

"What is the matter?" I asked, scarcely knowing how to begin to calm this turbulent mass of passionate beings.

"Matter!" was echoed. "What is the matter?" was repeated. "Matter enough. The land is in an uproar. Your men are stealing, lying, robbing goods from the shops, breaking plates, killing our pigeons, assaulting everybody, drawing knives on our women after abusing them, and threatening to burn down the town and exterminate everybody. Matter indeed! Matter enough! What do you mean by bringing this savage rabble from Europe?" so fumed and sputtered a Riffraff of some consequence among the magnates of Shepherd Bush.

"Dear me, my friend, this is shocking; terrible. Pray sit down, and be patient. Sit down here by me, and let us just talk this over like wise men," I said in soothing tones to this enfant kutisha, for he really looked in feature, dress, and demeanour, what, had I been an imaginative raw youth, I should have set down as the "incarnate scourge of England," and he looked wicked enough with his besuited, striped sleeves, his brandished cowhide brief, and fierce blue eyes, to chop off my innocent head.

Introduction
In and Against Crisis

Tyler Morgenstern, Krista Lynes, and Ian Alan Paul

On March 6, 2019, as the initial manuscript of this book—the product of a years-long, collaborative effort to think what has, since 2015, been known as the European Migrant Crisis—was nearing completion, the official Twitter account of the European Commission posted this brief message: "In very difficult circumstances, we acted together. Europe is no longer experiencing the migration crisis of 2015, but structural problems remain. Today we discuss the European Agenda on Migration & the progress made over the past 4 years." The post concludes with a URL that points to a brief press release, detailing achievements made and work yet to be done, or in the Commission's parlance, "Immediate Measures Needed."

In our years spent working with others to track and grasp this crisis, we had only seen it expand in every direction and dimension, radiating outward from the itineraries around which it had initially coalesced, the Syria-Turkey-Greece-Western Europe route in particular. We had seen it wend its way into sub-Saharan Africa, where nations like Niger, under EU supervision and sponsorship, now play a key role in policing the movements of migrants from elsewhere on the continent, defraying and preempting their arrival to more northerly transit nations like Morocco and Algeria (themselves now mired in violent border disputes to which cries of "build a wall" are by no means alien). We had seen it produce peculiar and unexpected new forms of (im)mobility, sociality, and inhabitation. And along with much of the rest of the world, we had watched as it engendered new and vexing forms of diplomacy, transnational governance, and legislative (non)-collaboration.

Having drummed up a potent wave of anti-migrant sentiment, for instance, the British right in 2016 succeeded in its quest to make withdrawal from the EU a matter of national policy. Meanwhile, Germany—in many ways the architect of EU-wide immigration enforcement policies—forged a new agreement with Turkey that promised *accelerated* EU membership for the latter in exchange for its taking an increased role in the sequestration and resettlement of Syrian refugees. On the one side, the shibboleth of border security fractures and rends the imagined space of Europe; on the other, it extends it. It was striking, then, to learn that, in the midst of these dramatic geopolitical realignments, the "crisis" around which this anthology is centered had ended, at least as far as the European Commission was concerned; that whatever calamity it once portended for the EU project had been successfully defrayed, attenuated, and contained.

But surprises can often be clarifying. Here, stated more or less explicitly, was the thesis under which we had first envisioned this collection: that the unspoken object of 'crisis' in the formation 'migrant crisis' was and always had been *Europe*, imagined as a site of right action and just governance, and never the migrant as such; that the legislative and geopolitical maneuvers taken under the auspices of 'responding to the migrant crisis' since 2015 had been less about rescuing the migrant in peril, and more about rescuing the *idea of Europe* from this same migrant, about restoring a vision of territorial governance and administrative right-headedness that had been imperilled *by* the arrival of the migrant to European shores.

But if our sustained consideration of the crisis has taught us anything, it is that this once-implicit formulation, now explicit, does little to change the fact that since and well prior to 2015, it has been the migrant—a radically plural subject, a population vastly more expansive, variegated and lively than the discourse of crisis has ever been able to grasp—who has most directly shouldered the violent intensities of the EU's attempts at mitigation and control, at rescuing itself from a peril of its own making. As Thomas Nail, a contributor to this collection, writes:

> "If the mistreatment, marginalization, and death of recent European migrants is so deplorable, it is because Europe has created a social system that has made this a reality. The subject of the crisis should be flipped right side up: *Europe is a crisis for migrants.* Therefore, the critical question (in the Greek sense of the word 'krisis' as a decision) is not what is to be done with the migrants, but rather what is to be done with Europe?"[1]

Gathering scholars, activists, and artists working across a variety of geopolitical contexts, disciplines and media, this anthology takes steps toward unpacking this difficult, often bewildering question, and does so specifically by interrogating how a wide range of mediating processes and representational practices work to constitute "migrant crises" as objects of political contention, affective investment, and legal maneuver. The anthology's title, *Moving Images*, summons the fluidity and dispersal of these processes, referencing the contemporary dynamics of mediation and migration in at least four overlapping ways. First, it invokes the specificity of mediating technologies themselves, pointing to the different ways in which still vs. moving-image technologies have been brought to bear on the task of representing the migrant crisis. Second, it refers to the iconography of the crisis as such, to those images *of* movement and mobility, often under duress, that have rendered the crisis legible for differently situated yet still global publics. Third, it touches on the movement of the image in and of itself, and the politics that inevitably attends this movement, pointing up the important role of various data infrastructures, social media platforms, and communicative networks in putting certain visions of migration and/as crisis into circulation and keeping them there, in moving images of migration into and through discrepant scenes of political action and cultural practice. Finally, and just as significantly, it points to the potent affective charge that often accretes to popular images of "crisis," and thus to the *moving* quality of images that hold viewers in their grip and bind them to others, with profound political and social consequences.

---

1 Nail, "The Hordes Are Banging on the Gates of Europe?"

In focusing on the European "migrant crisis," *Moving Images* takes up the eruptive and contestatory events of 2015–16 critically, not as a self-evident historical object or political enterprise, but rather as a tangle of processes, ideas, legal frameworks, actions, bodies, and images whose very contours eclipse its precedents and afterlives. We begin in the predicament that the term "crisis" poses, conscious that its framing of mass displacement, refugeeism, and migration in and across the Mediterranean occludes the *longue durée* in which the very question of Europe has been articulated—socially, juridically, geopolitically and economically.[2]

The elaborate response to the question of Europe, over time, has been a violent and regionally-differentiated shuttling back and forth between free movement and control, a decades-long choreography of willed and unwilled movement, interminable delay, cosmopolitan transgression, and fierce essentialism. The very idea of Europe in the latter part of the twentieth-century—with its economic integration and lessening of internal controls, coordination of judicial practices, and regulation of movement within its territory—has been accompanied by a coextensive focalization and fierce securitization of its so-called "external" frontiers. The internal mobility afforded to citizens of EU member states under the Schengen Rules of 1995, for instance, finds not so much its negative image as its enabling condition in the unified measures against "illegal" immigration and trans-border organized crime (which transnationalized the governance of migration), formalized as the private border policing agency Frontex (a contraction of *frontières extérieurs*, or external borders) a decade later.[3] Thinking such policies less as action and reaction than as the twin products of a shared imperative to strategically manage the movement of people, capital, and information into and across European territory suggests that Schengen did not so much abolish the operations of European border control as spatially redistribute them, pushing them outwards to various continental boundaries and frontiers as well as into a number of transit spaces within the Eurozone (railway stations, motorways, etc.).[4]

Thus, though it is tempting to regard these geographies of mobility and constraint as essentially new formations in the light of the configuration of "crisis," in many cases they follow paths that are all-too-familiar. While the 2015–16 migration "crisis" is certainly a result of instability and conflict in certain areas of East and North Africa, the Middle East, and even South Asia[5]—all of which, of course, find themselves bound to Europe in part through the long history of empire and its afterlives, which is to say,

---

2 It should be noted that Fernand Braudel develops his formulation of *longue durée* (among other places) in his book *The Mediterranean and the Mediterranean World*, where a temporal movement develops through social interaction with geography and the environment over an extended period of time. This *longue durée* includes not only the time of European imperialism and colonial conquest, but also the sites of connection, commerce and exchange that preceded such European ascendancy. Above all, of critical importance to the inquiries in this anthology is the importance in historical thinking of plural temporalities as a methodological ground for scientific inquiry.

3 See, among others, Enrica Rigo, "Citizenship at Europe's Borders."

4 As we were in the process of finalizing this introduction, news arrived that Frontex had sent security forces to Albania, the first such deployment beyond the territorial limits of the EU and an intensification of the border externalization process. See "EU's Frontex border force deploys teams to Albania to halt migrants"

5 Bangladesh now claims the distinction of being the number one source country for migrant arrivals to Europe. See Dearden, "Bangladesh is now the single biggest country of origin for refugees on boats."

of *European* migration, invasion, and settlement abroad—it is at the same time the culmination of a dialectical movement of mobility and constraint, cosmopolitical integration and "retrograde" ethnic, national, and racial differentiation, through which Europe as such has sought to define itself at least since the 1957 Treaty of Rome.[6] How the aftershocks of crisis have been negotiated re-animate various elements of this diffuse but pervasive historical trajectory.

That Frontex's first major deployments have been along the Turkey-Greece border (considered by the agency to be both its operational "center of gravity" and a tactical "laboratory"), for instance, comes as little surprise, pointing to the ways in which Western and Northern European nation-states have long sought to strategically recruit their Eastern and Southern counterparts—particularly those that border the Mediterranean—to the task of shoring up a coherent, integrated vision of Europe Proper.[7] Such strategies remain very much in play in the contemporary moment, and are amplified by European attempts to establish bordering regimes across an expanding and remote frontier (including in Chad, Niger and Libya).[8] As these arrangements make clear, "Europe" as an ideological, legal, economic, and political construction leans heavily on well-trodden repertoires of cultural and ethnic differentiation, distributing both the specter of threat and the necessity of control to the borders of the former Soviet Union, to the Mediterranean and the Aegean seas, to the former African colonies, and to what was once "the Orient." While these discourses are clearly racialized, ethnic, and nationalist, they are also profoundly gendered and sexualized, marked not only by differential vulnerabilities and capacities for movement but also by shifts in affective labor, reduced programmes for 'family reunification,' sexual violence and persecutions, trafficking and sex work.

We thus ask, in what meaningful sense does the ongoing and in many ways regularized production of Europe vis-à-vis both licit and illicit modalities of human migration constitute a "crisis," a term which suggests a certain suddenness, an all-at-once that shatters expectation? Further, how does this crisis take shape as an object of political contention? Through what repertoire of images, trajectories of movement, channels of affect?

---

6 Different dates thus recenter entirely the narrative arc of Europe's ongoing articulation—the fall of Constantinople in 1453, the Peace of Westphalia in 1648, the Berlin Conference of 1884–5, all articulate the expansion and contraction of the European form throughout the last several centuries.

7 FIDH-Migreurop-EMHRN, *FRONTEX. Between Greece and Turkey.*

8 In response to the dramatic escalation of migrant arrivals in 2015 and 2016, the European Parliament voted to recodify FRONTEX as an integrated border control and coast guard agency, which rather unsurprisingly made its first show of force along the Bulgarian-Turkish border in 2016. Indeed, long cast in the popular imaginary as a kind of conduit between East and West, 'Orient' and 'Occident,' Turkey has played (and continues to play) a key role in the EU's attempt to mitigate the migrant crisis in ways that seek to reconcile aggressive practices of preemption, interception, detention, and expulsion with a decidedly liberal-internationalist cosmopolitanism.

Image Operations

As the open data project *The Migrants' Files* carefully records, what has quite suddenly been deemed a "crisis" has in fact been unfolding continuously and coterminously with the shifting configurations that take the name "Europe" for nearly two decades. Since 1993, more than 35,000 migrants have been lost during the perilous crossing to Europe—a staggering disaster by any measure.[9] And yet these deaths only seemed to emerge as a "crisis" proper in 2013, as traumatic images surfaced of 360 migrants drowned off the coast of the Italian island of Lampedusa. Against the spectral background of Lampedusa's haunting image repertoire of overcrowded boats and drowned bodies (itself a resonant refocusing of the afterlives of the violence of the transatlantic crossing), a cascade of piercing images began to surface and circulate in 2015, and in their surfacing gave shape to the event of the European "migrant crisis." The cascading surge of iconic images produced the contours of a regional emergency whose narrative structure postdated the very sea of images themselves. Between the two constructions—regularized migrant death and humanitarian crisis demanding response—something happened; the task of this collection is to show how this *something* involves a substantial degree of media work and a particular set of "image operations."

At stake is not only the spatial and geopolitical dynamics that shore up forms of belonging and unbelonging in the face of a movement that certainly precedes them. The impetus for this anthology also lies in a shared interest among its contributors in interrogating and disrupting the peculiar, oftentimes wrenching temporality of the migrant crisis as a visual phenomenon.[10] We could not help but be overwhelmed by the sheer volume of harrowing images emerging from the region—large crowds huddled into disastrously insufficient vessels; asylum seekers crowded into rail stations, detention facilities, and more-or-less formal encampments in Greece, Turkey, France, Bulgaria, Serbia; corpses, including those of young children, washed ashore in otherwise "pristine" Mediterranean resort towns. Particularly in its early months of 2015, the "migrant crisis" emerged as an object of contention through an overwhelming surfeit of images hailed by the international press as "iconic." All the while, a number of terrorist incidents behind the walls of Fortress Europe elicited ever-more fearsome performances of national and ethnic absolutism, many of which drew directly on the very same iconography (one can hardly forget Nigel Farage's noxious "BREAKING POINT" Brexit billboard in which a endless queue of migrants subtends the statement "The EU has failed us all").

---

9 UNITED for Intercultural Action, "List of 35,597 documented deaths."

10 The collaboration among the editors began as a working group focused on the the notion of 'trespass' broadly construed. With a handful of scholars working in a number of fields and several national contexts, we attempted to think trespass as a methodology, a critical modality, and a visual and performative practice adequate to a contemporary moment marked by intensifying practices of securitization, the violent reassertion of ethnic nationalisms, and the emergence of what would, in the coming months and years, become known as the Mediterranean migrant or refugee crisis. The idea was to develop a method for writing that both presumed and performed its territorial unwieldiness; to understand trespass as that which might make it impossible to think or write a phenomenon "in itself" indeed as that which held every "in itself" open to adjacent and overlapping commitments, histories, conceptual and perceptual registers.

To think in these terms is in fact to put the mediatic, discursive and rhetorical framework of "crisis" in question from the outset. As such, our thinking is animated by Papadopoulos, Stephenson & Tsianos's claim that social change might be effected otherwise than through "events," a manner of organizing historical time according to ruptures and breaks rather than the "practices which are at the heart of social transformation long before we are able to name it as such."[11] Where we depart from their framework, however, is with respect to their claim that events are never "in the present" and can only be named as such retrospectively or in anticipation.

We return to these processes of mediation in the image regime from the vantage point of the European commission's avowed *end* to the "migrant crisis," an end that is symbolized vividly by a project by the Swiss-Icelandic artist Christoph Buchel at the 2019 Venice Biennale. Through a series of complicated negotiations with the Italian state, Buchel and his collaborator, the curator Maria Chiara di Trapani, had arranged to install on the Venetian Arsenale—for centuries the beating heart of the city's formidable maritime economy, and thus inseparable from the history of imperial plunder and racial slavery—the rusted remains of the 90-foot fishing vessel which, on April 15, 2015, sank off the coast of the Italian island of Lampedusa, killing somewhere between 700 and 1100 migrants (itself a devastating rehearsal of another wreck two years prior, in which upwards of 400 migrants, mostly from Eritrea, Somalia, and Ghana, also drowned off the coast of Lampedusa when their boat sank). In comment to the *Guardian*, di Trapani describes the project in somewhat contradictory terms, both as a monumental memorial to the ongoing calamity of migrant death at sea, and as a clarion call to action, a cry uniquely capable of piercing the media din that has since 2015 accumulated around this loss. "We are living in a tragic moment without memory," di Trapani asserts. "We all look at the news, and it seems so far away: someone is dead at sea and we change the channel." The boat, she suggests, pleads for—demands—a different kind of engagement, its sheer scale asking that we "feel respect for it and look at it in silence—just keep two minutes of silence to listen and reflect."[12]

What di Trapani does not indicate, however, is how this reverent silence is distinct from the reverent silence that so often greets the art object, symptomatic not so much of a sudden ethicality, but of the embodied and social codes of aesthetic looking, of the institutional conventions of the art world and, more importantly, the globalized art market, which descends on the Arsenale as so many trades before it: in naval equipment, in weaponry, in captive bodies. In di Trapani's comments, then, there is a latent sense that in cutting through one representational regime—that of the twenty-four hour news cycle, which produces migrant death as a grotesquely recursive yet utterly inconsequential spectacle—Buchel's project may risk simply entombing it in another: that of the aesthetic gaze. Though perhaps installed as memorial, the boat quickly slips into the register of sculpture, liberated from the churn of commercial news only to be assimilated to the category 'art,' which even in its participatory forms (see Milevska, this volume) has fared little better in resisting dehumanizing, objectifying, and spectacularizing modes of migrant representation.

That Buchel's work would follow so closely on the EU's declaration of the so-called end of the migrant crisis is telling, suggesting that as the crisis passes from an all-con-

---

11 Papadopoulos, Stephenson & Tsianos, *Escape Routes*, xii.

12 Charlotte Higgins, "Boat in which hundreds of migrants died displayed at Venice Biennale."

suming present into a recent past, it becomes apt as well to pass from ongoing spectacle to museal object, demanding not urgent defensive maneuver but rather restrained aesthetic contemplation. This peculiar dovetailing of political and aesthetic maneuver, though perhaps incidental in this case, is nonetheless reflective of the tight coupling between crisis as visual regime and crisis as object of political and legislative response that this collection attempts to interrogate and, even if only provisionally, prise apart.

As a group of scholars and cultural producers more or less anchored in some form of media and visual studies, we were increasingly preoccupied with the character, volume and movement of these visual and political regimes, as the discourse of crisis consolidated into a kind of shorthand for migration as such. And while we had initially sought to respond to a glut of photojournalistic and documentary images that spectacularized, or risked spectacularizing, the migrant body as corpse, flood, hoard, and so on, today we face a rather different situation. As Buchel's oeuvre makes clear, the migrant crisis, and indeed the migrant body, has become the locus of a highly formalized and notably more conventional regime of textual and aesthetic production. What was once an unruly and seemingly boundless flow of iconic images produced under severe duress has, in recent years, re-emerged as a set of professionalized and semi-professionalized image-making practices, ranging from glossy, BBC-produced docuseries like *Exodus* to a wide range of VR installations and smartphone apps that allow users to temporary inhabit the position of the migrant either stranded precariously at sea or in the midst of an overland crossing (in a particularly grim twist, such projects have become something of a mainstay at major international summits like Davos, where they play a role eerily similar to that of a carnival attraction for the world's financial and political elites). And this is to say nothing of the innumerable responses that have emerged from the European and global art world, among which we might highlight the epic tableaux of Richard Mosse's *Heat Maps* series (2017), Ai Weiwei's *Law of the Journey* (2018), which repurposes Zodiac boats and life vests as sculptural works conceived on a colossal scale, as well as nuanced and moving filmic works as Gianfranco Rosi's *Fuocoammare* (2016) and Philip Scheffner's *Havarie* (2017).

In tracking these different media configurations, our point is not to *reduce* the crisis as such or the larger structures of which it is symptomatic to mere representation, forgetting or simply discarding the severe and relentless material costs of European border security and immigration control. Rather, following Bishnupriya Ghosh's contribution to this collection, the aim is to develop a rigorous understanding of the visual as a series of "image operations," that is, as emphatically *real* interventions into the whole field of institutional, political, and social relations within which migrant practices unfold. Jens Eder and Charlotte Klonk, in an anthology that follows from a conference held in Berlin in 2014, argue specifically that images are not only representational, referential or illustrative, but augment and create significant events, and thus have material effects.[13] Combined with text, speech and music, images form part of multimodal publications, intertextual networks and complex referential chains. They are put into operation through a complex, diffuse, multiple and sometimes simultaneous network of agencies—personal, technological, affective, and political. Images have a dynamic of their own, have a kind of "liveliness," gathering velocity and accruing value.

---

13 Eder and Klonk, *Image Operations*.

Particularly in the context of crisis, image production and consumption must be understood as attempts at action, as efforts to do something, or to make something happen: to express solidarity, to dis/affiliate oneself politically, to demand that particular kinds of rights be extended or withdrawn, to either occasion or retroactively justify the closure of checkpoints, border crossings, and points of entry. Image operations are enacted immediately in the various state and para-state surveillance and border triage politics that regulate and contain people on the move, most obviously, but they also operate through the circuits of news media, NGOs and international organizations, and broadly across social media platforms. Images taken in one context have significant afterlives in the theaters of contestation around refugee rights and emergent forms of nationalism. Such mediating processes are, in some respects, nothing new (there has been a daily instrumentality to image culture for at least a century). They nevertheless have a new operational force deriving from their capacity to circulate rapidly, producing and fracturing common sentiment as they unfold across varied territories and constituencies. If this is the case, then how, politically, does the visual iconography of contemporary migration—overburdened boats, tattered life vests abandoned on the shore, throngs of would-be refugees pressed up against border fences, and now, sculptural and screen installations of various sorts—operate as a mode of seeing, sensing, and knowing what migration *is*? What is at stake when "crisis" becomes the affective and temporal ground against which the movement of human populations toward and across Europe's terrestrial and maritime borders gains figuration? When "crisis" animates and puts into motion an image repertoire with real and unpredictable political and material effects?

Across the essays, interventions and artistic works that comprise this collection, we track the wide-ranging itineraries and mercurial material, iconic, and discursive form of the "migrant crisis," considering how it variously draws upon, shores up, but also potentially rends the very idea of Europe, inflaming fearsome ethnic nationalisms and prompting aggressive bordering operations while simultaneously resisting capture by given legal and semiotic categories. In doing so, we take aim at the ways in which "crisis" as both a discursive formation and a tightly-articulated visual regime is conjured so as to naturalize European mechanisms of inclusion and belonging, and moreover, to secure a very particular vision of Europe—defined, as noted above, against particular sites and forms of difference—as a seat of just governance, moral integrity, and liberal freedom.

While we bind these questions to the case of contemporary Europe, the questions we pose are broader, opening up to the intersections of mediating processes (moving media) and migratory movement (mobile positions) as twinned modalities of a politics of "crisis." The manufacture of emergencies along the US/Mexico border, expulsory measures in Australia, temporary labor movements into the United Arab Emirates and Saudi Arabia, signal that mediating migration *as crisis* is a global affair—both in its scope and its entanglement with the structures and apparatuses of capitalist flows and embargoes. This collection is thus meant to think both the historical specificity and the abstract generalization of migration *as crisis* at once.

Thinking From a Double Estrangement

For obvious reasons, the task of accounting for this peculiar trajectory calls directly on our respective disciplinary formations as researchers, scholars, artists, curators and editors. Many, though not all, interlocutors in the long dialogue from which the present book emerges claim allegiance to some branch of media study, or perhaps more broadly cast, to the critical analysis of visual culture through a variety of media and genres. Our collective training, then, encompasses such approaches and methods as critical discourse analysis, art history and contemporary art practice, the politics of representation, feminist and queer theory, critical race studies, (new) media theory, curatorial practice, and to a lesser though still important extent, science and technology studies. With several important exceptions, many of us wield these tools from the context of the North American and European academy,[14] an institutional space that is in the grips of its own set of crises, many of which overlap explicitly and importantly with the politics of immigration, refugeeism, securitization, and state power. In some sense, then, we write, produce and curate from a position of double estrangement. In the first place, our training equips us to think the European migrant crisis not so much from an anthropological, sociological, or legal-theoretical perspective, but rather in terms of the way it circulates as a set of images, texts, processes, genres, and formats, and how these circulations proliferate particular understandings of "the migrant," "the refugee," and just as importantly, "Europe."

Given this mediatic framing of "crisis," we ask: What happens when image cultures becomes turbulent? Might something else be thought? Another theory of the political? A way of trespassing Europe—the territory, the project, 'the very idea'—that does not finally locate the possibility of freedom within a fantasy of knowing hinged to the transparency of images? That looks to the social conditions of (forced) migration, listening for the hums of an *otherwise* that reverberate at and across the limits of figuration, straddling the turbid zone between excess and exhaustion—however narrow? "Turbulence," writes Nicole Starosielski, "is a chaotic form of motion that is produced when the speed of a fluid exceeds a threshold relative to the environment it is moving through [...] When a fluid—whether air, water, or blood—becomes turbulent, it breaks down into smaller swirling currents, called eddies, which in a cascade break down into smaller and smaller irregular flows."[15] Our particular training positions us to home in on these procedures, interrogating and tracing how specific forms of representation—the forensic, the documentary, the photo-journalistic, the abstract or non-figurative, the participatory—seek to establish or extend certain programs of response and intervention, often to the exclusion of alternatives.

The second estrangement from and within which we think and write concerns our own position as editors (and, in a number of cases, as contributors) within the predominantly Anglophone North American academy. Over the course of our lengthy collaboration, our own scholarly and professional itineraries have, of course, passed through a number of the territories that 'directly' abut the crisis (at least to the ex-

---

14 There are important exceptions to this location, and these form some of the most piercing critiques of the terms of the "migrant crisis" in this anthology. See in this volume, El Montassir, "The Adouaba Project," and Zachariadi and Lynes, "Either You Get it or You Don't."

15 Starosielski, *The Undersea Network*, 17.

tent that the crisis has, in much popular discourse, been powerfully identified with certain bounded geographies, among them the Mediterranean, the Middle East and North Africa, and so forth). As a result, our discussions have been often discontinuous and elliptical, variously extended and *distended* by all manner of technical glitches and institutional forces—among them poor Internet connections and halting video feeds, multiple time zones, and more distressingly, the violent operations of state power and military force. To this extent, our thinking and writing has been profoundly conditioned by very infrastructures of circulation and containment that we have these last four years attempted to theorize. There is (however and of course) a limit to what these experiences of distension and interruption can actually dislodge. We remain for better and for worse the products of particular disciplinary formations and intellectual trajectories, with all their attendant methodological, analytic, and epistemic baggage. To be plain: we are not 'Europeanists' in any strict sense of the term.

Nevertheless, the anthology collects and enfolds a frictional contact among very different positionalities, critical, creative and political inheritances, and modes of expression and action. Located across North American, Europe, Africa and Asia, with personal trajectories that are more diverse and differentiated than this, many of us are nevertheless historically positioned to inherit the political, social, and institutional affordances of European imperialism and settler citizenship. Because this is an inheritance that we cannot simply elect to refuse, as if through some supreme act of political will, we are also positioned to reproduce and proliferate those affordances through our modes of affiliation and the infrastructures of critical and creative publication within which this anthology finds its place.

Located within institutions and intellectual communities that rigorously engage the settler-colonial formation of the Canadian and US nation-states, for instance, that participate differently but robustly in the contemporary politics of migration and bordering as they unfold across the North American continent (not only at its putative edges, such as the US-Mexico and US-Canada borders), and that critically engage the relentless violence of white supremacist statecraft, interrogating its grotesque ensemble of operations and techniques (mass incarceration, police brutality, systemic neglect, punishing surveillance, severe forms of deprivation and impoverishment), we are positioned to think questions of refugeeism, migration, and "crisis" in ways that perhaps trouble or at least qualify, for instance, investments in the capacity of nominally liberal-democratic nation-states to meaningfully respond to or ameliorate the regularized production of migrant death at the border, in prisons, in transit. We learn from scholarly and activist networks that make clear the *structural* entanglements of various programs of migrant inclusion and exclusion with ongoing efforts to extinguish Indigenous political orders (within which one can often glimpse radically different articulations of sovereignty, nationhood, and belonging) as well as with the whole spectrum of governmental and institutional projects that operationalize a virulent and pervasive (though still nationally-inflected) anti-blackness.[16]

---

16 And this is to say nothing of what we, and this book, have learned from our students. Variously positioned in relation to contemporary formations of power, privilege, and domination, they have shown us   and continue to show us—what it means and *might* mean to learn, think, write, act and convene against colonial occupation and the attempted elimination of Indigenous, minoritarian, and repressed cultural practices and intellectual histories, against deportation, incarceration, and exclu-

What such positioning produces, methodologically, is a theoretical debt to contemporary scholarship on movement that is more firmly located in critical race studies, feminist and queer theory, and postcolonial studies than in the literatures that frequently explain migration, exclusion, state and para-state governmentality and identity formation in a European context. It is also, nevertheless, allied with Marxian frameworks that insist upon the "autonomy of movement." The insistence in Papadopoulos et al, as well as Nicholas De Genova and others, on the "autonomy of movement," reconfigures movement itself as a form of political action that resists structures of social and political control. In this respect, current "economic migrants" act in continuity with vagabonds, pirates, maroons, rebelling slaves and others.[17] Movement entails a potential form of flight from the political categories that organize and attribute rights and responsibilities in relation to the granting function of the nation-state ("citizen," "laborer," "family," etc.).

Thus, while we raise the shorthands that make short work of the complexity of migration in and across the shifting territories that constitute the "crisis" ("Europe," "migrant," for instance), our aim is not simply to critique them but also to trace other departure and arrival points, focal lenses, and subjective and social dynamics that bring into view the primacy of movement (more broadly) to the constitution of social life. In line with a theory of movement's autonomy, we assert that the European Union's border control apparatuses entail not an overarching resistance to movement, but the selective and differentiating porousness of entry and exit points in a larger heterogeneous and hierarchized space of global circulation. Beyond the sanctioned movement of goods in the architectures of "free trade," there are also the permit structures that have historically granted more-or-less-temporary-workers visas (without the accompanying rights of citizenship), as well as the sanctioned movements of Europeans out of the European territory. Indeed, the history of Europe might be conceived as one of overarching imperial movement: a history of violently displacing the sovereignty of territories abroad through (ongoing) processes of invasion, occupation, and settlement; a history contingent on the forcible capture, enslavement, and global circulation of bodies made chattel.

"We are the Freedom of Movement:" Fugitivity and Autonomy

Beneath these patterned and bureaucratically-sanctioned circulations, however, there are other forms of movement that precede, subtend, shadow, or stray from the circulatory dynamics that constitute the "global system." Prior to the "migrant crisis," and

---

sion, against an always-already racial capitalism, against both the militarization of police and the policification of campus, against military raid, arbitrary arrest, forcible displacement, bodily mutilation. From these encounters, we learn something important about what it means to call something a "crisis;" how this produces and proliferates particular kinds of visibility that tend to stabilize the basic 'goodness' of liberal political reason and moral sense, nudging us toward programs of "reform" that aspire to more humane or bureaucratically sound forms of containment, disappearance, and exclusion, rather than programs of abolition and speculation that both imagine and seek to *build* alternative forms of living in common.

17 See for instance Boutang, *Economie politique des migrations clandestines de main-d'oeuvre* and Neilson and Mezzadra, *Border as Method*.

prior even to "migration" or "refugeeism," there is nevertheless movement. Prior to the deliberation of asylum claims, to the patterning of trajectories, to the interception of Zodiac boats, or to processing zones, there are displacements that do not name their routes, their motivations or their points of entry or exit. Papadopoulos et al. name this movement "escape," by which they mean imperceptible moments in everyday life which trigger social transformation through the "refusal to subscribe to some aspects of the social order that seem to be inescapable and indispensable for governing the practicalities of life."[18] They call such acts "fugitive occurrences."

In a vivid example of such an act, on May 20th, 2019, hundreds of protesters, most of African origin, many "sans-papiers," descended on Charles De Gaulle International Airport north of Paris. In a nod to the *Gilets Jaunes* movement—whose tactics of sustained urban protest had in the preceding months thrown cities like Paris into upheaval, turning them into sites of insurgent violence and dramatic clashes between demonstrators and riot police—the protesters called themselves *Gilets Noirs*, or black vests. Occupying terminals 2F and 2G, they concretely demanded an end to Air France's participation in the deportation of asylum seekers, refugees, migrants, and sans-papiers, while couching the action within a total refusal of the larger project of racialized migrant exclusion and exploitation, connecting the specific struggle against corporate-backed deportation, for instance, to the fight against migrant detention elsewhere in France. In a statement posted to Twitter the day of the occupation—a fitting rejoinder to the EU Commission's earlier use of the platform to declare the migrant crisis over—the *gilets noirs* wrote: "We will attack all those who exploit and draw profit from the *sans papiers*, just as we will attack all those who organize and live off of racism in France. We do it with the determination of those who are on hunger strike, those who evade, and all those who struggle against detention centers, in Hendaye last Saturday, in Rennes last week, and elsewhere."[19]

The action, to be sure, evinced a certain media savvy. The adoption of the mantle *gilet* inscribes the protests within an extant interpretive and discursive framework, even as the substitution of *noirs* for *jaunes* strategically and politically disidentifies the two movements, subtly throwing into relief the latter's investments in a broadly white working class politic that demands economic justice, yet by and large neglects the exploitation of migrant labor as a *particular* strategy of European and global capital in the present conjuncture.[20] And yet, in their communiqués to the press, the *gilets noirs* also seem acutely aware of the political risks that attend media spectacle in general and so-

---

18 Papadopoulos et al, *Escape Routes*, xv.

19 "On s'attaquera à tous celles et ceux qui exploitent et tirent profit des sans papiers comme nous nous attaquerons à tous celles et ceux organisent et vivent du racisme en France. Nous l'avons fait avec la détermination de celles et ceux qui sont en grève de la faim, celles et ceux qui s'évadent et de tous celles et ceux qui luttent contre les centres de rétention, à Hendaye samedi dernier, à Rennes la semaine dernière et ailleurs." [translation ours]

20 As the *gilets jaunes* movement has circulated globally, this investment in whiteness has become all the more explicit, as in Canada, where a nascent 'yellow vest' movement, nominally concerned with the continued expansion of the fossil fuel industry as guarantor of working-class jobs, has quickly revealed itself as an explicitly white supremacist project. In France, groups such as *Comité Adama* (organized against police violence in Paris' banlieues) and the CLAQ (Committee of Queer Liberation and Autonomy) have participated in the *gilets jaunes* protests in order to combatively contest these investments.

cial media virality, in particular. And with good reason: as multiple contributors to this volume make clear, these modes of cultural circulation have since 2015 been absolutely central to the production of migration as a crisis. "The airport *is not a symbolic site for us*, it's the rear base and the outpost of the war against the *sans papiers* and immigrants. We have come today to block this base to take it back, to reconquer it."[21] To inhabit the circuits of mediated visibility in a globalized present, yet to resist the pull of the symbolic; to engage in the production and proliferation of communiqués, digital images, and other medial artefacts, yet to insist on the absolute materiality of the action, on the airport not as a symbolic site but as the "rear base and forward post in the war against the sans-papiers and immigrants." This is the gamble of the *gilets noirs*. To be visible as immigrants, as sans-papiers, yet to refuse all those ways of being visible—as anonymous bodies amassed at the border fence, as viral symbols of an undifferentiated and unspecified struggle, as hypervisualized targets of state surveillance, as ghostly absences hovering around the rusted hull of a ship—that do not materially disrupt those mechanisms of exploitation and expulsion that allow the EU Commission to declare an end of the migrant crisis; those mechanisms, indeed, that make clear that Europe *remains a crisis for migrants*—a crisis that did not begin in 2015 and did not end in 2019.

In the taking-and-holding place of the *Gilets Noirs* occupation, there is both an autonomy and a fugitivity; a willful acting and moving in open contravention of those sanctioned (im)mobilities that would avow the separability of 'Europe' and 'migrant.' This is, quite literally, a retaking (reprendre), a *reconquering* (reconquérir), a defiant declaration of flight from and against the final, expulsive flight of airborne deportation. As the *Gilets* write in their statement, "Nous *sommes* la liberté de circuler:" We *are* the freedom of movement.[22] In emphasizing such sites and modes of autonomous movement, the present anthology owes a substantial debt to Fred Moten's notion of "fugitivity," even as we hasten to acknowledge the historical and political specificities of the "migrant crisis."[23] For Moten, a liberatory arc may be traced in what he calls "fugitive movement in and out of the frame, bar, or whatever externally imposed social logic—a movement of escape, the stealth of the stolen that can be said, since it inheres in every closed circle, to break every enclosure."[24] This fugitive movement is *not* a semiotic strategy for breaking apart the framing mechanisms of our visual apparatuses. It constitutes instead a material persistence, what he calls "stolen life," life that per-

---

21 "L'aeroport *n'est pas un lieu symbolique pour nous*, c'est la base arrière et l'avant post de la guerre contre les sans papiers et les immigrées. Nous sommes venues aujourd'hui bloquer cette based pour la reprendre, la reconquérir." [translation ours]

22 *Circuler* may be translated as "movement" insofar as it implies a coming and going, a displacement along paths or channels. *Circuler*, however, also implies a cyclicality and renewal, in the way that blood circulates in the body. It also implies a passing from hand to hand, like fake currency, or a diffusion and expansion. The term chosen might then highlight the differential movement of bodies, of capital, of knowledge that the airport embodies as an infrastructure and architecture. To block an airport is to take part in a struggle around circulation in specific networks of movement.

23 We do not mean to confuse, nor equate through metaphor, the contemporary migrant crisis and the calamitous social afterlives of the Atlantic slave trade, even as the two both would seem to invite comparison (quick and uncritical, on the one hand, nuanced and committed on the other), and require a sharp attention to the living on of the fact of slavery in the migrant crossings of the last several decades.

24 Moten, "The Case of Blackness," 179.

sists beyond the reaches of governmentality and biopolitical power. In Moten's view, this fugitive movement, a "fugitive coalescence of and against," makes black social life productively "ungovernable."[25] The image repertoire of the migrant crisis has circled around failures of governmentality—around the specter of fascist bureaucratic excess, transportation infrastructures, border controls, passport and visa regulations, quotas and debt obligations. The iconic images which surface articulate the threat to Europe's exertions of governmentality, invite retrenchments that rearticulate the idea of Europe and its debt to its others, but equally visualize moments of breakdown which put into crisis the structures of belonging/unbelonging that constitute the biopolitical lever of European consolidation, and thus might open onto modes of resistance to the persistence and totalizing nature of the language of "crisis."

The concept of an *a priori* or autonomous movement, however, should not be taken to metaphorize migration (and the figure of the migrant) to represent the universal condition of estrangement and malaise that constitutes twentieth- and twenty-first-century affect. For Sara Ahmed, the generalization of migration transforms historically-specific complex displacements of peoples into a "mechanism for theorizing how identity itself is predicated on movement or loss."[26] Such theoretical tendencies, in universalizing conditions of displacement and loss, displace the specificity of what Ahmed calls "the contingent and worldly relations that mark out habitable terrains."[27] Movement is thus not necessarily or mechanistically transgressive, although it may provide a set of actions and escape routes for potent forms of political transgression.

To commit to the autonomy of movement as such, then, *guarantees* little in and of itself; its possible meanings risk being mischaracterized, remaining thus monopolized by the very imaginative and political projects we aim to contest. The forms of affective and political excess with which images of a borderless world are sometimes associated (post- or extra-nationalism, global citizenship, the cosmopolitan, and so on) may also sit closely astride what Elizabeth Povinelli calls the "conditions of exhaustion and endurance" that suffuse "our world's scenes of abandonment."[28] We center this ambiguity in our thinking so as to complicate the "simple ethical investment in the thresholds and transitions of becoming within biopolitics," holding close to hand the proviso that in the face of exhaustion, elimination, deprivation, and displacement, "to be the same, to be durative, may be as emancipatory as being transitive."[29]

We understand fugitive movement, then, not as a simple investment in movement over stasis, or as a merely descriptive tool for categorizing illicit and unsanctioned modes of transit, but rather as an embodied, often perilous, migratory praxis that demands the committed work of what many feminist, postcolonial, and Indigenous scholars have called decolonizing methodologies. Such methodologies would mobilize specific standpoints of "opposition" (Chela Sandoval), "refusal" (Audra Simpson) or "wake work" (Christina Sharpe) so as to resist the easy appropriation of the migrant

---

25 Moten, "The Touring Machine," 267.

26 Ahmed, *Strange Encounters*, 80.

27 Ahmed, *Strange Encounters*, 79.

28 Povinelli, *Economies of Abandonment*, 130.

29 Povinelli, *Economies of Abandonment*, 130. Indeed, a great deal of migrant-organized resistance and revolt has taken on precisely this character, formalized as sit-ins, encampments, and blockings of deportations that have taken place alongside and within the "crisis" of migration.

(or the refugee, or the internally displaced) as a mere "emblem" or "figure" of either post-national freedom or Agambenian bare life. The ways in which acts of movement are engendered across a contemporary landscape of dislocation are multiple, and we can presume to know neither the conditions nor the outcomes of those performances in advance. Chela Sandoval's strategies of "differential movement," for instance, do not cede vision and visuality to imperial power but rather seek to counter unlocatable vision with the multidimensional and mobile positioning of situated knowledges. This movement allows for consciousness to challenge its own perimeters from within ide-ology, to decipher an ideology according to its own dynamics and imperatives, which Sandoval calls the very "methodology of the oppressed." Similarly, we take seriously the positional quality of Christina Sharpe's "wake work," her demand to "stay in the wake," to understand the relation between slavery's violences in the conditions of "spa-tial, legal, psychic, material, and other dimensions of Black non/being as well as in Black modes of resistance."[30] She calls "wake work" an analytic that imagines new ways to live in the wake of slavery, a new mode of inhabiting the contemporary conjuncture in the present horizon. It is for this reason that the critical and creative, the declara-tive and poetic, the material and immaterial co-exist in this anthology, as a method of imagining beyond "crisis" and committing such imaginaries to social change.

We are therefore compelled by Sandro Mezzadra's preface to this anthology, to his insistence on recovering "the insurgent character of the movements of migration" in 2015, an insurgency that is distant to the rhetorics of "crisis." His attention to the pos-sibilities that movement creates for prefiguring different relations between Europe and its outsides is vital to not remaining within the architecture of "crisis"—even as a modality of critique. His preface reminds us that—like with his *Mare Jonio* rescue ship project—scholars, activists and artists must resist the terms and structures that bind and narrow potential liberatory futures.[31]

Moving Images thus seeks to hold open the fugitivity of migrant movement, its de-colonial logic, and its capacity to put under erasure the global state of things by going beyond the limits of legibility. Or, to countenance those limits as an index of that which resists, even if that resistance is not strictly 'activist' in character and less purposive than the language of agency might suggest. Even if the resistance is a hum, a churning; "what can be attained in [a] zone of unattainability, to which the eminently attainable ones have been relegated, which they occupy but cannot (*and refuse*) to own."[32] It sees in *movement* the possibility of tuning our instruments to other frequencies where the crisis extends beyond an event, and "Europe" is properly set in its place as a pitted po-litical strategy of the contemporary global order. Thus, while our thinking is focused on—and focalized by—the crisis' particular visual regime, these predicaments have broad implications for the visualization of social movement and political movements more generally, and for the manner in which technologies of vision and modes of cir-culation give shape not only to the contours of various political crises, but to the racial-ized, ethnic, gendered and sexual ideologies that surface certain bodies and invisibi-lize others, both with severe and relentless social costs.

---

30 Christina Sharpe, *In the Wake*, 14.

31 See in this regard the exceptionally potent essay by Mezzadra and Caccia, "What can a ship do?"

32 Moten, "The Case of Blackness," 179.

At the conjunction of the interrelated episodes of the crisis' *end*, the Venice Biennale's sculptural shipwreck and the defiant occupations of the *Gilets Noirs*, a critical terrain opens: a field of political, aesthetic, and representational negotiation in which the meanings and implications of the now-familiar phrase "Migrant Crisis," and indeed the very notion of crisis as such, are put at stake. Far from mere description, crisis in this space is revealed as a multivalent and intensely contested framework for knowing the body in motion, for marshalling and distributing the resources (and forces) of the state, and for animating particular strategies of governance and administration that obtain at a variety of scales and across multiple locales. What's more, in this space it becomes abundantly clear that "crisis" as a modality for thinking migration is intimately, even *essentially*, bound up with strategies of figuration and representation, interpellating various domains of cultural and aesthetic practice, from the global art market to the social media platform, and from the television news broadcast to the activist communiqué.

Moving Images is an attempt to inhabit this terrain. It aims to intervene critically in the various visual regimes—documentary, photojournalistic, forensic, abstract, participatory—through which both the figure of the migrant and the category Europe have been refracted in recent years. And in staging such an intervention, we aim to disrupt the temporality of crisis itself. Though certainly a powerful vehicle for mobilizing specific kinds of political and cultural response, in framing contemporary practices of migration as unanticipated outbreaks—foisted as if from without and all at once on an unsuspecting European continent—crisis shears migration (and indeed the migrant) of any substantive historicity. The cut is both strategic and profoundly political, for this is a historicity that may well speak of the violences of empire and its proliferating afterlives, of the everyday exclusions and expulsions that give late liberal statecraft its distinctive texture, and of those quotidian forms of reason, judgment, and moral sense that innervate both. As such, the temporality of crisis and its attendant visual language(s) are productive of the social worlds and subjectivities produced at and around the borders of Europe, as Mezzadra and Neilson persuasively argue in *Border as Method, or, the Multiplication of Labor*, of the struggles that take shape in the changing relations of domination, dispossession and exploitation that take place there. Thinking in and against the panicky rhythms of crisis and the spatially-distributed acts of bordering it sponsors, we seek to return to migration something of its social fullness.

***

The anthology thus begins not with this introduction, but with Allan deSouza's potent critical fiction "Through the Black Country"—a text-based artwork which takes up and wryly inverts the conventions of the 19th-century colonial travelogue so to produce a "reverse exploration" of England and Europe that originates, rather than terminates, in Asia and West Africa. Appropriating through a disidentificatory gesture the figure of the "explorer," the account considers Europe (and London specifically) as a site for *discovery*. The project's journals, maps, photographs, sketches and artifacts mimic the archival record of innumerable colonial expeditions, and locate contemporary movement patterns within counter readings of historical relations between Europe and the global South. Seizing upon a literary form that abrogates to itself the right of colonial and imperial movement, "Through the Black Country" displaces and reverses both the relation between those who move and those who stay put, and the anthropological gaze through which such determinations have historically been made. It thus poses from the outset a set of challenges for the collection as a whole, demanding that the anthology recalibrate its emphases, question its terms, refocus its visions, and closely interrogate its assumptions—and attend closely to the task of representing and interrogating "crisis."

The remainder of the collection is divided into two sections, "Moving Media" and "Mobile Positions," which together gather a series of interrelated reflections on the often troubled transit between mediation and migration. If the essays in the former section are more weighted towards the infrastructures, techniques, and operations that propel images of migration-as-crisis through and across global circuits of consumption and interpretation, the latter focalize more sharply the figures that animate those operations, steeped as they are in a set of racial, gendered, sexual and classed imaginaries. Nevertheless, these emphases refuse to hold their distinct positions within the entangled social dynamics of refugeeism, migration, asylum, deportation, nationalism, border securitization, trafficking, separatism, civil disobedience, occupation, blockade, and trade. Because these phenomena are integrally entwined sites of mediation and mediatization, the anthology argues precisely for the inseparability of thinking moving images and mobile positions separately, despite the chasms that isolate certain forms of movement from others. Each section begins and ends with imaging practices—some artistic, some activist, and some both at once. These images and documents do not take sides on the "to show/not to show" dilemma that so often informs the ethical framework for witnessing traumatic images, so much as displace the binary itself to make room for other practices of figuration and documentation, as well as other modes of social action.

Section One begins with Zineb Sedira's *SeaPath*, an artistic project consisting of a series of images taken from ferry crossings between Algiers and Marseille. They present, as Tyler Morgenstern poetically theorizes in "The Literal, at Sea," not a document but a turbulent and indeterminate imaging practice, one in which the "literal is already littoral," severed from reference and set adrift as fleeting bits of form (and foam) on the sea's surface. In their poignant abstraction and—paradoxically—their obdurate material and contextual specificity, they both dramatize and obscure what Morgenstern refers to as the scene of "vectoralized movement, determinate starting points and ending points, definitive boundaries between this and that, here and there" that since 2015 has given the Migrant Crisis so much of its political and affective texture.

Following this, Bishnupriya Ghosh's "A Sensible Politics: Image Operations of Europe's Refugee Crisis" tracks the sprawling, socially mediated itineraries of the iconic image of the young Syrian boy, Alan Kurdi, who was found dead on a Turkish beach resort in 2015. Rather than engaging questions of representation or attempting to parse whether such images can be read straightforwardly as ethically good or bad, Ghosh argues that the image, shared globally through a torrent of affectively-charged Tweets and mournful news broadcasts created a mode of public participation *prior* to the determination of the image's significance. In this modality of participation—precariously and indeed improperly demotic—Ghosh locates a form of sensible, or affective, politics antecedent to the emergence of any conventionally deliberative public that could be represented through the bureaucratic and quantitative strategies of state and market.

Extending this focus on the mechanisms of circulation and their often mercurial politics, Ian Alan Paul's "Controlling the Crisis" proposes that the instruments of securitization and governmentality that today intensively mediate the movement of migrants toward and across European territories are not simply an effect of crisis—a reasoned *response* to irregular movement—but rather an "output of societies organized by the desire to *control crises*." Through an account of several theories of cybernetics (Haraway, Deleuze, Tiqqun), Paul traces how the complex regime of sensing, surveillance, and policing elaborated in recent years by Frontex—the EU's primary border security agency—emerges *co-constitutively and recursively* with the "crisis" of 2015 and 2016. Fleshing out a logic of "crisis-control" that mediates the transitory space between those liberal theories of freedom, right, and subjectivity that continue to anchor EU border imaginaries in important ways and those cybernetic techniques, favored by agencies like Frontex, that seem to evacuate the liberal project of its substance, Paul locates both a new modality of governance and a vital new terrain of resistance and subversion.

Paul's concern with the structural entanglement of crisis and control in the cybernetic dispensation finds a ready counterpart in Charles Heller and Lorenzo Pezzani's "Forensic Oceanography: Tracing Violence Within and Against the Mediterranean Frontier's Aesthetic Regime." In this contribution, Heller and Pezzani trace the technologies, legal apparatuses, political regimes and image operations that have harnessed the sea's geopower to a more or less organized "form of killing," and map their efforts, through their Forensic Oceanography initiative, to document and understand these malleable configurations. Specifically, they trace three of these shifts (the movement from practices of non-assistance to *policies* of non-assistance, and the further move to criminalize rescue initiatives and outsource border control to overseas partners). Throughout, they attend to the forms of violence ensuing from these shifts, and the shifting visualizing practices and ethico-political stakes they entailed for Forensic Oceanography.

Similarly attuned to the mercurial movements of EU border policy is Lonnie Van Brummelen and Siebren de Haan's "Reframing the Border," which documents the artists' ongoing efforts to represent Europe's external frontiers—a domain written and rewritten since the consolidation of the Eurozone by an array of trade agreements and friendship treaties that tie former colonies to Europe in relations of dependency and, more to the point, form the foundations of contemporary migrant governance projects. Both Heller & Pezzani and Van Brummelen & de Haan locate their practices within a configuration of power that is (post)colonial and (neo)imperialist, and as such, both essays reveal how negotiating these inheritances is bound to a set of representational technologies, epistemic conventions, and power relations that affect where and how they position their (metaphorical and literal) cameras. Together, the essays stress how artistic and activist image operations are always coextensive with other mediating processes, whether the transformation of the NGO Sea Watch into an immense audio-visual recording device designed to counter the "factual lies" of EU border enforcement agencies, or French President Emmanuel Macron's decision to repatriate artefacts of colonial plunder from French museums to their countries of origin.

Providing a kind of conceptual scaffold for these varied and variable image-making practices, Thomas Nail's "Migrant Images" seeks to develop a kinetic theory of the migrant and the image alike, centering social migrancy (rather than static notions of state-based belonging) and a vision of the image as an object on the move (rather than simply a representation of a static object *external* to it) as primary and intercalated features of our historical juncture. Moving away from the specificity of image-making practices by or for migrant or refugee populations, Nail focuses instead on the broader implications of philosophies of movement (Lucretius, Marx, Henri Bergson, and others) for the figure of the migrant and the mobile image, exploring what it might take to develop a coherent theory of "migrant images."

Finally, Thomas Keenan & Sohrab Mohebbi's "Listing," and the accompanying documentation of Banu Cennetoğlu's ongoing project, "The List," draw from the Amsterdam-based organization UNITED for Intercultural Action's "List of Deaths of refugees and migrants due to the restrictive policies of 'Fortress Europe.'" Collaborating with numerous curators and art institutions, Cennetoğlu has facilitated the publication and exhibition of UNITED's up-to-date list in multiple languages and formats, from public displays in cities like Amsterdam, Barcelona and Los Angeles to newspaper supplements. Documentation of this work is included here. Keenan & Mohebbi, for their part, provide a poetic reflection on the act of "listing," fleshing out its polyvalent meanings as an act of itemizing, hearing, tilting, drifting, and documenting. Together, these pieces question what it means to document the dead as a political act, to make these deaths legible or visible, and how such acts might make particular demands on highly differentiated publics. As such, their questions and reflections evoke the abiding concerns of this section, pointing up how overlapping infrastructures, policies, and practices of mediation are constituted and conditioned by the intensities of crisis.

The contributions collected in Section Two, by contrast, follow the vexed itineraries of certain key figures around whom crisis as a political and visual modality has crystallized in recent years. Together, the authors in this section follow such figures as the migrant and the refugee, asking what happens politically as they assume a variety of social roles and positions—form the entrepreneurial subject of late capitalism to the art participant, and from the potential "terrorist" to the "trafficked woman"—and as they pass through different spaces of cultural practice and consumption. How do these figures move and for whom? What role do they play in consolidating particular kinds of political events, subjectivities, and communities around the issues of migration and refugeeism? Moreover, building on the concerns raised in Section One, what kinds of technical infrastructures, communications markets, and social networks are required to put these images into circulation and keep them there? How do such networks siphon individual and collective forms of affect, aspiration, and desire? How, finally, do these visual and cultural itineraries intersect with the uneven movement of bodies, commodities, capital, and information across a European continent at once globalized and deeply fractured by resurgent nationalisms?

Section Two begins with Abdessamad El Montassir's "The Adouaba Project" (2019), which traces and visualizes two communities—the adwaba villages in Mauritania and the tranquilos communities in the hills and forests outside the Moroccan city of Tangiers. In El Montassir's complex artistic project, these communities constitute a contemporary form of *marronage*, built by those who have fled conditions of enslavement yet now await the emergence of new routes of passage to an elsewhere and otherwise, suspended in the administrative time of European statecraft without ever having touched European shores. The accompanying collaborative text, deriving from conversations between El Montassir and Krista Lynes, seeks to flesh out what the verb form *marronner* might signify for thinking migratory movement differently, away from the pull of Europe and its presumed association with rights or freedom.

El Montassir's efforts to rethink the figure of the migrant, and to articulate visually an other formation of migrant subjectivity, are echoed in the essays that comprise the remainder of the section. Veronika Zablotsky's "Unsanctioned Agency: Risk Profiling, Racialized Masculinity, and the Making of Europe's 'Refugee Crisis'" focuses on the reception and circulation of so-called "refugee selfies." She argues incisively that gendered and racialized scripts govern the construction of unaccompanied refugee men, painting them as "suspiciously agential" and therefore less vulnerable. She unpacks the construction of the "single, male refugee" through a feminist and postcolonial reflection on humanitarianism, whiteness, and neoliberalism in Europe.

Farah Atoui also examines the racialized and gendered imaginaries that govern mediation of the "migrant crisis," focusing particularly on how the category shifts between "refugee" and "migrant" are mobilized strategically in order to illegalize people in movement and preempt their entry into the United Kingdom. Through a careful historical reading of media coverage of the refugee camps at Calais—alongside an account of the Sangatte Center that preceded it—Atoui argues that anti-migrant discourse in the UK articulates and instantiates a "political ontology of threat" (Massumi) that hinges on a clear distinction between the migrant and the refugee; a distinction which itself cloaks economic determinations regarding properly and improperly governed labor power in the supposedly neutral formalities of domestic law.

But while the figures of improper or suspect arrival that Zablotsky and Atoui examine have certainly been central to the production of crisis as a visual regime, prompting all manner of border securitization and deterrence projects, they are at the very least matched in their potency by their inverse: the figure of the migrant who never arrives at all, who drowns at sea. In her aptly-titled contribution, "SOPHIA: The Language of Trafficking in the Mediation of Gendered Migration" Krista Lynes considers how this figure has become visually and discursively enfolded within the gendered, racial, and class politics of recent European anti-trafficking initiatives operating under the name Sophia, which comes to denominate ships and infants, radio signals and imperial navies. These initiatives bind the seemingly discrepant logics of humanitarianism and securitization to one another in and through the body of the "trafficked woman." Developed in sustained conversation with postcolonial and Black feminisms, Lynes's essay considers what such a conjunction forecloses, what complicated and difficult agencies it puts under erasure, and what is at stake politically in the semiotic drift that collapses "woman" into "traffic" in the long wake of racial slavery.

Suzana Milevska, for her part, pursues these thorny questions of agency and objectification into different disciplinary quarters, exploring the question of refugee representation in contemporary art practice, examining in particular the "participatory turn" in artworks which aim to intervene in the "migrant crisis." Beginning with an analysis of the ethical implications of the slogan "We Refugees," invoked often by a humanitarian politics in the contemporary moment as a gesture of solidarity with displaced and migratory peoples, Milevska ultimately offers a critical appraisal of recent artworks that require refugees and migrants to complete the work through their action, participation, or labor, examining whether or to what degree such an approach might offer a corrective to the political quandaries that so often befall efforts to simply represent the marginalized or vulnerable Other.

Appropriately, the section ends with documentation of a very differently participatory artistic-activist action by the collective LGBTQIA+ Refugees in Greece, performed on the occasion of Documenta 14's exhibit in Athens, Greece in 2017.[33] The action, which involved a performative "rock-napping" of a public sculpture by the artist, Roger Bernat, meant both to emphasize the instrumentalization and exoticization of queer migrant life, and to foreground the specific vulnerabilities of this community, and the work of the collective. The documentation is accompanied by a conversation between Krista Lynes and Sophia Zachariadi, reflecting on the action, the role of art activism in mobilizing for refugee and migrant rights, and the politics of solidarity.

Throughout, each contribution mobilizes different crafts and practices, languages and media, to intervene in the iconography of the migrant "crisis," to challenge its settings and locations, its figures, its imagined audience, and its evidentiary nature. This experimental strategy, with its risks and potential failures, is meant also to position the potentials of these forms of academic inquiry within the inescapable politics of positioning, conscious that the location from which we intervene matters to the movements and mediations we describe and in which we participate.

Together, all the contributions gathered here take up the task of thinking critically about "eventfulness," when the very terms of analysis keep taking new objects through and in relation to a highly circulatory media environment. How might processes of scholarly inquiry track and keep pace with the ephemeral but perpetually catastrophic rhythms of the mediation of "crisis"? How might we devise tools and positionings responsive to the continual opening up of new spaces of vulnerability and exposure? Such questions are ever more urgent in the light of intensifying and accelerating processes of displacement, detention and deportation in Europe, even as the visual economy of the migrant crisis has shifted once again.

Moving Images attempts to take these questions seriously, in the interests of imagining and building something that makes an otherwise elusive mode of engagement possible. We wish to develop not only a visual and aesthetic politics that reveals the European project as always-already subtended by a long, ongoing history of migration and displacement, but also a *space* where this politics can be put into practice; a space where emerging scholarly and artistic responses to contemporary forms of population displacement can be brought into conversation with one another, linked in ways that trouble the epistemic and political parameters of prevailing geopolitical, legislative, and indeed historiographic formations.

---

33 For more on this action, see Lynes, "Between a Rock and a Hard Place."

Section One
Moving Media

Zineb Sedira, SeaPath (2017)

Zineb Sedira, SeaPath (2017)

The Literal, at Sea

Tyler Morgenstern

Reference, though discernable, has been reduced to an absolute minimum. In each image, a wake—or is it a wave?—cuts across the frame, a bit of turbulence that, lacking any visible origin, reads as little more than graphical abstraction. What remains are fleeting bits of form that froth, fold and foam at the edges, rising out of their aqueous ground just long enough to register photographically; gradient fields that are not quite gradient fields, pockmarked by the accidental pointillism of the wave caps that dot the sea's surface, striated here and there by bands of dark and light that suggest the presence of something machinic, some vessel or engine capable of carving the ocean into geometric pieces, carefully, methodically, with intention. But even these slip away at the edges, drifting hazily into one another, making things murky, maybe brackish, depending on how far we happen to be from shore. If the photograph aspires to or carries with it the promise of the literal, of registering what is or what *has been*, here it captures only littoral, the watery recession of tidy edges, discernible causes, and legible itineraries.

Small wonder that the images, produced by the artist Zineb Sedira, are gathered under a title that proves equally slippery. *SeaPath*, read aloud, speaks in the imperative, almost like a command: "See Path." Rendered textually, however, the imperative is set adrift. The title becomes a proper noun, a name for something. But at sea, as it turns out, there is remarkably little to see; that *something*, that path, has already begun to wash away, its source already outside the frame, the literal already littoral. If these are images of anything, they are images of movement, of passage, of circulation; a moment, a cut, into some journey for which we are given no point of origin, no destination, and no trajectory. Or, they are visual intervals in which clear distinctions between coming and going, directionality and drift, intention and turbulence, indeed the constructed and the natural (wave and wake blend imperceptibly together) break down, swirling together in arresting (and arrested) eddies. These eddies fill the frame, staging a confrontation with motion that seems overwhelming, almost frustrating, one that refuses to resolve, to vectoralize.

But these images are, of course, of something in particular. To generate *SeaPath*, Sedira photographed the wakes left by the ferries that transit regularly between Algiers, in North Africa, and Marseille, on France's Mediterranean coast. This same route is also frequented, however, by Harragas—young Algerian border crossers who seek differently licit means of maritime entry to France or Spain. This is indeed something, quite something: a scene of embodied action that puts immediately at stake precisely those things Sedira's images render so turbulent and elusive: vectoralized movement, determinate starting points and ending points, definitive boundaries between this and that, here and there. Indeed, it is largely within and through scenes like this one that such categories are *constituted* in the contemporary juncture, circumscribed as it is within the temporal and political imaginary of (migrant) crisis. As we know well, for instance, the figure of the illicit or illegalized border crosser, the one who arrives from without (allegedly) intent on exploiting the humanitarian goodwill and economic possibilities that (allegedly) attend admission into the European body politic, prompts fearsome performances of national integrity that manifest variably as border securitization, maritime interception, and indefinite detention.

In the optic of crisis, the migrant appears as a *vector of, or vectoralized, risk*—an improper intentionality, an unwanted willfulness, a suspect directionality. Such an optic assumes and demands a here and a there, a point of origin and a destination, a clear set of intentions (whether economic, humanitarian, criminal, or terroristic) that motivates the passage between the two, and firm boundaries to be protected. Sedira's images suggest, however, that much more churns just below the surface of things. More is in motion, more circulates, than just those who cross, and that those who cross do so in ways and for reasons as littoral as they are literal. Things cannot be made quite so tidy. These circulations, again as Sedira's images suggest, are profoundly unstable; coalescing into some coherent form or pattern here and now, only to dissolve or distend a moment later. As *SeaPath* disaggregates "See Path" into a series of fluid interfaces between the machinic and the natural, wake and wave, licit and other-than-licit, alternative modalities of movement bubble to the surface, ways of moving and crossing that do not resolve into the cartographies of crisis.

A Sensible Politics
Image Operations of Europe's Refugee Crisis

Bishnupriya Ghosh

Refugee image cultures are the dangerous supplement to refugee crises. As such, they invite critical opprobrium, sometimes for the unethical sensationalism of particular images and sometimes for the desensitizing effects of image overloads. At first glance, the steady stream of images serves only to numb rather than to incite real-time responsibility toward the migrant waves that seek passage into new territorial enclosures. Or the deluge of images invokes withdrawal and aggression, once host polities confront the thorny questions of resource distribution. Or indeed, especially sensational images are considered unethical in the extraction of surplus value from subaltern tribulations. Such allegations are well-founded, but they obscure the complex politics of the images that find unanticipated distributions across media forms and platforms. My essay tracks the trajectories of one iconic image that became an instant cultural mnemonic for the highly mediated European refugee crisis, ongoing since 2015. The poetic and circulatory effects of the image are exemplary instances of the problems that accompany the image production/distribution of the refugee crisis. The image of a two-year old Syrian boy found dead upon the beach of a fancy resort in Turkey became a social media event within hours of its first distribution as a news photo. The "event" inheres in the proliferation of a single image, its accumulating mediatic traces turning it into a media phenomenon. I focus on the Twitter storm ensuing from passing on the image—retweeting, liking, and sharing it—which further ricocheted between media platforms. This media explosion *preceded* deliberations on what the image meant or what was to be done.

Habitual as micro-actions on Twitter are, I argue that they signal an important mode of participatory political life: an affective-performative rather than deliberative publicness widely regarded as improper in more ways than one. The murky and often-opaque politics of social media users who seek to participate in the large and small decisions appear unruly. Often seeking to partake in political decisions, often uninvolved in civil deliberations or institutional politics, their participation is nevertheless an assured fact of political life. So much so that social media is now an unfettered political beast that invites scorn, dismissal, and opprobrium—and certainly critical conjecture. I join media theorists and political thinkers to think about the *group form* that social media users inhabit as participants in a viral spread. What kind of affective publics are these? Where do they stand on the refugee crisis? My analysis has the advantage of quantitative data on the viral spread of the iconic image in question.

The University of Sheffield's Visual Social Media Lab (henceforth, VSML) conducted a rapid research response of the Twitter storm and the discussions that followed in its wake, collating news items, forums and blogs, Twitter feeds and Google searches on the Pulsar platform.[1] Their data visualizations tracked the amplification of the image beyond its anticipated distribution, therein offering a rare opportunity to think about its popular purchase.

For some years, I have been preoccupied with the *sensible politics* of popular images.[2] Popular by dint of their wide distribution, these images can be heroic or epic, banal or trashy; they are of particular interest when they generate strong political affects. One can hardly find a better instance than the Alan Kurdi photograph, a poetically poignant, tailored image that later found elaboration in memes, artworks, graffiti, and even live performances. My pursuit of this image as affective-performative mediation leads me to track its viral circulation and not its representational capacities. In this regard, my essay builds on previous arguments that I have made elsewhere on the circulation of iconic images and their popular reception.[3] As we shall see, the Alan Kurdi image assumed astronomic proportion, so much so that there is documentation of a "before" and "after" to the Twitter storm it provoked. The VSML dossier records this temporality as a discursive shift enacted with image + hashtag (#refugeeswelcome, #refugeecrisis ...). Within a day, the image + hashtag turned talk of a "migrant crisis" into that of a "refugee crisis." Thus the Twitter storm that punctured and reoriented existing plans and programs, policies and agendas was a creative event: in its distribution, the image produced a perceptual shift in the relation between social media users and the oncoming "wave" or "horde." With the child refugee as worthy beneficiary of humanitarian intervention, something new entered the perceptual register, something that demanded real-time responsibility in all the ways refugees can—at least, historically,

---

1 I'd like to thank Joshua Neves for his insights on the first version of this essay, as well as the editors of this volume for their invitation to the workshop for which this was written, and thereafter their many constructive criticism, suggestions, and intuitions that sharpened the argument. I further acknowledge the longstanding projects behind the piece: the many conversations with Dilip Gaonkar (on the role of media in public cultures) and with Bhaskar Sarkar (the convener of the global-popular initiative from which arises my sense of unruly and uncivil politics). Lastly, this paper, in particular, owes a debt to Corinne Bancroft's paper on this image written for a graduate seminar, The Global-Popular (Spring 2016), in which she discussed the Visual Social Media Lab's data visualizations. Visual Social Media Lab, *The Iconic Image in Social Media*.

2 See, for instance, McLagan and McKee's *Sensible Politics*, as well as works like Gould's *Moving Politics* among others that theorize the affective turn in public culture.

3 These reflections on the circulation of this iconic image update my previous analysis of the political affects in *Global Icons*. There, I argued that iconic images are recursive graphic signs that become *naturalized* over time and are etched in collective memory. As "natural signs," they appear to be qualitatively like their referent; a trace of indexicality haunts the otherwise poetically expressive sign. The trace initially bears the stamp of authoritative sanction; but, in its recursive circulation, that original matters less and less and the icon becomes cultural shorthand, a mnemonic for a larger system (think Google Earth or any other graphic on one's computer that function as apertures into systems). As we shall see, within a day, the Syrian boy opened into the larger tragedy of Syrian migrants whose perilous passages had become everyday fare. It is not a stretch to argue, then, that the image acted as a trigger for accumulated affects surrounding these ongoing tragedies for nine months in 2015. As the Twitter storm gathered, those affects found sensible figuration.

in context of the 1951 Refugee Convention.[4] In Jacques Rancière's schema, a hitherto invisible part of the *demos* crossed the partition of the sensible, heightening exposure to deadly states of injury. The Kurdi image focalized an undefined "horde" or undifferentiated "wave" pouring across European borders and spilling onto beaches through the singular image of the injured child—pre-political, innocent, non-threatening, demanding benevolent dispensation. An image cut-out from the ground of endless numbers, this "image operation" reconstituted migrant flows as a refugee crisis and reframed them as a matter of human rights.[5]

But, as we know, while the initial response to the Kurdi image was forceful, political legislation was another matter altogether.[6] Since that Twitter storm, more than one European nation has closed borders, erected fences, deployed coastal regulations. More importantly, the invocation of the injured refugee worthy of special dispensations became muddier still within a very short span of time. In November 2015, the Paris attacks—the deadliest in Europe since the Madrid bombings of 2004—turned the refugee into potential threat, even though subsequent investigations established the attackers as French and Belgian citizens who had not entered Europe as refugees. Following closely on the heels of this debacle came the New Year's Eve attacks in the city center of Cologne (mass sexual attacks, rapes, theft). When the attackers were identified as men of Arab or North African descent, the single male refugee/migrant came to embody not just threat but aggression toward the historical West.[7] In this context, the Kurdi image had a short lifespan as the lightning rod for affective intensities around the unadulterated figure of the refugee. And it is precisely this brief temporality that makes it a plum instance of a surging affective-performative politics that seems to go nowhere and whose causal relation to structural change remains obscure. These politics and the affective publics they disclose are the subject of this essay.

The figure of the injured refugee immediately raises the question of culpability. Who was responsible for these deaths? Who exactly was the "we" that confronted a coming "they?" The VSML visualizations provide some insight into the locations of social media users who passed on the image, and I will turn to these more substantially. The first tweets emerged from Turkey, and shortly thereafter from West Asia, before entering European and North American Twitter feeds; international organizations played a major role in the latter distributions of the image. These visualizations tell us there were European social media users for whom the highly mediatized crisis was on

---

4 See, Xenos, "Refugees." Writing about the ethical fictions of incorporation even in the heydays of the Refugee Convention, Hannah Arendt noted posing refugee crises as a problem of numbers actually concealed political inefficacies: there is, in fact, not a "material problem of overpopulation," she argues, but a problem of "political organization." Arendt, *Origins of Totalitarianism*, 294.

5 I take my cue from Jens Eders and Charlotte Klonk, who define images as *producing* events, not only representing them: for example, aerial images in war zones are the basis of military operations. *Image Operations*.

6 Lucy Mayblin's "Politics, Publics, and Aylan Kurdi" remarks that David Cameron, for one, offered to take 20,000 from camps in Syria but not from Europe, but that move was soon undercut with the a bill that restricted resources allocated for refugees (pitched by the then-Home Secretary, Theresa May).

7 As two-thirds of the attackers turned out to be asylum-seekers, debates broke out over whether or not the category refugee included the asylum-seeker. When the German right-wing got in on the action and sold merchandise with the slogan "Rapefugees not Welcome," the leader of a premier group was accused of sedition.

their shores and at *their* borders; after all, at the time of this Twitter storm, the Syrian refugee crisis had been ongoing for months. No doubt the image generated heightened affective intensities for these users. And then there were remote social media users that engaged the "refugee crisis" as a distinctly "European problem," and not directly relevant to their lives; but, even here, one may think of proximate remoteness of different kinds. For instance, Californians or Texans living in the borderlands may have had greater investments in the politics of incorporating migrants into the body politic. Finally, a more complex category of social media users were intimately involved with Europe's migration policy because of intertwined regional histories. With Turkey's location at Europe's edge, Turkish social media users, for example, exemplify the latter; no doubt the concerted European effort to make Turkey a triage center for the flow of Syrian refugees would impart greater intensities to their responses. These distinctions complicate the "we" that approached the "they" as refugee-migrants. Yet despite such distinctions, it is not a stretch to argue that the problem of a *demos* that exceeds the rights-bearing formulation "the people," a *demos* invisible within and at the border, is now a *global* concern, and especially in times when democratic institutions are under attack from myriad authoritarianisms. In other words, the Syrian refugee crisis was not only an international negotiation of quotas but also a political dilemma resonant across national and regional contexts. Hence, the European incitement to refugee incorporation hit a collective nerve. The ensuing public culture around the Kurdi image tells us that there was little consensus as to what could be done in concrete terms. Yet the sensuous image made the refugee *sensible* in a visual translation of a hitherto abstract politico-juridical category.

Social media users who passed on the image turned the numbers game—how many refugees can be settled and where—into affective intensities. If the numbers game represents one kind of institutional composition of the European *demos*, then the affect-driven image provides a counterpoint to these politics proper. The Twitter storm is therefore an affective-performative intrusion into ongoing political deliberations that sought to establish a new relation between rights-bearing European citizens and a potentially reconstituted demos. This intrusion suggests that social media users passing on the image *dissented* from institutional counts and quotas, agreements and stalemates. They entered the fray as uninvited partakers, amplifying a composition that overtly eschewed calculative rationality in favor of affective intensities. I characterize such intrusions as an *improper politics*, a kind of politics that is all-too-visible on social media. Nothing good seems to come of affective-performative gestures. Too politically thin, too superficial; too transient and too compromised; too deluded and clearly anxiety provoking. Whatever the diagnoses—and there are plenty of them—it is unclear what exactly is social about social media. In this context, one may argue that habitual retweets constitutive of Twitter storms are often just that: knee-jerk responses that cannot be plotted along an ideological spectrum. Thus it would be disingenuous to argue that the circulating image indexed a particular worldview of the refugee crisis; that to share or like the image implies anything beyond a habitual empathy for an injured child. Conversely, it is equally disingenuous to argue that a Twitter storm that rendered a seismic shock to previous perceptions of the crisis had no collective dimension whatsoever. This essay attempts to ford this contradiction, for therein lies a complex affective-performative politics that is now the new normal.

Taking up the central concerns of this volume, I elaborate moving images in two ways. First, in the micro-actions of sharing, liking, or re-tweeting, the image of the refugee crossed a perceptual barrier: it moved social media users. The consequent sensible composition put pressure on the externality of the refugee to the body politic. Second, the micro-actions of amplifying the distribution of the image exhibit a desire to move *others* and therein to "structure the possible field of actions of others" as Michel Foucault once said of power.[8] Such amplifications seek to impact the politics *of* movement, of who can cross borders and how. In all these respects, the moving image materializes the affective intensities of a sensible politics.

Visualizing the Creative Event

The image is unforgettable: the two-year old Alan Kurdi in a red shirt and blue jeans lying face down upon a beach in Bodrum, an upscale resort in Turkey. One of twelve refugees trying to reach the Greek island of Kos, Alan drowned alongside his mother and brother. For reasons banal and profound, Alan Kurdi made major headlines within a day of Nilüfer Demir's photographic capture for Turkish news agency, the Doğan Haber Ajansi. At 5:30 a.m. on September 2, 2015, Demir snapped the now-iconic photograph, originally one among fifty pictures. When the news agency released the photograph, it began to be tweeted with the accompanying caption, "Drowned Syrian Boy." Within 12 hours, 30,000 tweets later, 20 million had shared the photograph. It had become the recursive graphic that we understand as an iconic image. Like iconic images, it endures as one of the 100 most shared images in contemporary Europe—a powerful *figural trace* of a protracted refugee crisis in which 4 million (in 2015) among the 11 million Syrians displaced by war sought asylum.

I am less concerned with the signifying power of the trace than I am with its circulation in social media, and specifically on Twitter. For it is on Twitter that a photographic event became a media phenomenon that changed perceptions of the crisis at hand. The findings of the VSML show that the image played a constitutive role in shifting perceptions of the "migrant crisis" to a "refugee crisis" within days. VSML conducted a rapid response search for the 12-day period between September 2 and September 14, 2015. If for the previous nine months in 2015, the terms "migrant" and "refugee" as qualifiers to crisis were pretty much head-to-head—5.2 to 5.3 million tweets in the same volume of conversations—*after* September 2, "refugee" spiked at 6.5 million to "migrant" at 2.9 million. The data visualizations document the speed and scale of signal amplification. Read together, they make legible something like a seismic shock. That is, the peaking quantifications amount to a *qualitative change* in perceptions of the kind of crisis. The appearance of the "refugee" instantly invoked questions of social vulnerability and historical responsibility. As we shall see, key activists, journalists, and leaders had a hand in shaping such perception. In many instances, they rode the wave, grabbed an opportunity. But they could ride the wave *because* there was a *new baseline* for the crisis: something new had entered the sensible, something infectious; something that was perhaps not entirely legible.

---

8 Foucault, "The Subject and Power," 790.

Francesco D'Orazio tracks the Twitter storm that followed the first tweet at 10:23 a.m. In that first hour, the 33 retweets were mostly in Turkish; but in the next two hours, Turkish journalist and activist Michelle Demisherich's retweet with the hashtag #refugeeswelcome went viral through Lebanon, Gaza, and Syria. The color-coded data visualizations available in the online VSML dossier represent the growing storm in vivid bursts and intensities. One burst comes when the Free Syria Hub got in on the action, spearheading the Twitter wildfire in the Middle East. Another comes when Peter Bouckaert, the Emergency Director at Human Rights Watch in Geneva urged the European community to develop a plan for refugee admission and rehabilitation. His call prompted 664 retweets. When at 12:49 p.m., Liz Sly of *The Washington Post* based in Beirut tweeted the photograph, her tweet was shared 7,421 times in 30 minutes. By 1:10 p.m., *The Daily Mail* carried the first story with the title: "Terrible fate of a tiny boy who symbolizes the desperation of thousands." At the end of the day, 500 articles on Alan Kurdi's journey had entered the twitterverse. In this essay, I'll focus on the Twitter storm that passed on the image and its attendant artisanal compositions before the image entered the news and entertainment ecosystems.[9] By the end of the day, news platforms owned the "Alan Kurdi story" and used it to carry their own content, and web-based companies such as Buzzfeed invited artistic recompositions of the image. These later stages together constitute the public culture around this iconic image. As Sam Gregory notes in the VSML dossier, these recompositions were further amplifications of "counter-speech" already evident in the hashtag punctuations of the first Twitter storm[10]—roughly occurring between 10:23 a.m. to 1:10 p.m. before the first story broke in *The Daily Mail*.

I focus on this short window because it draws attention to the upsurge of affects before their organization into cultural sentiment or considered reflection. The Twitter storm *before* the capture of the image in memes, caricatures, and cartoons highlights not only accumulated intensive forces triggered by the image, but also the extension of those forces through social networks constitutive of Web 2.0. The latter movement is the heart of social media: in other words, the possibility of affective connectivity is what makes social media tick. The Twitter storm that amplified the Kurdi image disclosed the desire of social media users to transmit whatever affected them across a vast social-technological field. The data visualizations provide distant readings of this desire—thickening, expanding, assuming new directionalities. The particular affects driving the spread are far more difficult to pin down: they would include everything from anger and grief to horror and repugnance, as well as admixtures of these affects. Not yet composed into recognizable emotions, such affects are best described as forces that register at their peaking intensities, rising and dissipating, accelerating and slowing. Such intensities are now commonplace in political life, and therefore the brief temporality of the Kurdi image makes it an exemplary object of study.

There is much to say about why *this* image caught fire. But I'll be brief in these explanations, since my focus is on the amplification of the image on social media. Certainly, it was chosen with care. In the VSML dossier, Claire Wardle notes that, just a couple of days before Alan Kurdi's death, a photograph of dead babies on a Libyan

---

9 The VSML dossier distinguishes the visualized Twitter storm from the counter-speech that followed the circulation of the images as two different moments in the life of the iconic image.

10 For more on the histories of digital punctuation, see Scheible, *The Digital Shift*.

Beach had surfaced, but it was quickly reported and removed from Facebook. Drawing on her experience as senior Social Media Officer at the UNHCR, Wardle's point is that platform protocols often regulate what can circulate; they constrain the amplification of counter-speech and restrain the agency of social media users. To these soft controls, one might add the aesthetic histories that shape viewing photographs of dead or injured children.[11] News agencies routinely regulate tragic photographs of injured children; in this sense, these media are akin to fine art, with its historical norms and conventions. An analysis of the photograph's aesthetic composition would fully unpack the representational truth-effects (*mimesis*), expressivity (*poiesis*), *and* affective capacities (*aisthesis*) that constitute, Rancière argues, political mediation. I focus primarily on the last category, *aisthesis* or affect; yet it is worth noting that the Kurdi image had a substantial poetic and mimetic charge. A few news platforms such as *Vox* and *Slate* initially refused to carry "gruesome images" of "dead children," but those refusals receded after the Doğan News Agency's *tailored* image went viral—an image centering the red-shirt clad vivid form against the intense gray dissolve of sea and sky. Further, despite the overly poetic capture, the indexical truths of the boy's death haunted the photograph. In part, the photograph had high institutional credentials: it was well "brokered" before Demir's first tweet, in all the ways that Zeynep Gursel tracks in her ethnography of news photos.[12] Then, it was filtered through distributive chokepoints. Social media users put their trust in reputable reporters such as Michelle Demisherich and in media hubs such as Free Syria and Human Rights Watch. So despite the explicit *poiesis*, strong reciprocal ties enabled the photograph to generate mimetic truth effects.

No doubt the sentimental portraiture of a fully clad, middle-class boy individuated against the universal eschatological space between life and death had much to do with its becoming instantly iconic. Indeed, the Human Rights Watch director Peter Bouckaert pitched his own response through his own experience as a father, as did Sam Gregory of WITNESS (a video testimony platform). These are clear class-based affinities that made the image so powerful. Yet the individuated isolation of social media users makes it difficult to claim there was but one reason for the photograph's infectious proliferation. For it is also the case that many remained *unsympathetic* to the image of the dead child. Mike Thelwell notes in the VSML dossier that one strain of censure saw Alan Kurdi's death as just dessert for the boy's father, who was reputedly a smuggler. Still others protested the indignity of circulating an image of a dead child; Alan Kurdi's aunt, for one, offered pictures of Alan, lively against a blue slide in a playground, in order to combat the tragic image. Several others saw the circulation of the image as pornographic consumption, an unethical sharing of violence that

---

11 Think of the controversies over Nick Ut's photograph Phan Thi Kum Phuc in 1972 (better known as "the Napalm girl") or Kevin Carter's 1993 "Starving Child and Vulture" shot in famine-stricken South Sudan. Nick Ut took pains to explain that, after the photograph, he stopped his van to carry the burning children to the hospital, while Kevin Carter protested he was not *waiting* for the vulture to descend on the child but had been instructed *not* to touch the children. In the fallout over the controversy, Carter committed suicide within a year of snapping the photograph. The extreme instance tells us something about the interrogation of regulated objectivity in the face of horror.

12 In *Image Brokers*, Zeynep Deyrim Gursel traces the multiple agencies "broker" a news photo goes through before it makes the news.

re-victimizes. The undecidability of reactions challenge attempts to extract *a* political position from the social media event.

For despite all brokerage, it was clear there was no agreement on the refugee crisis. Nor was it intelligible who should carry the burden of responsibility. The hashtag "#refugeeswelcome" was most popular in the UK, US, Canada, Australia, India, Germany, Turkey, France, Spain, Netherlands, Austria, and Switzerland, but not in others (where the hashtag was just #refugeecrisis). In many countries, Google search terms in the week following the photograph's publication were "What happened to Alan Kurdi?" or "Why do Syrians leave Turkey?" In Germany, a dominant query was "How to volunteer to help migrants?"; in Hungary, "How should Christians respond to the migrant crisis?"; in Italy, "How to adopt a Syrian orphan child?" And so on. The heterogeneous Google searches indicate that in fact there was no consensus over what was at stake or what was to be done. And yet, the photograph circulated, making the image of the coming refugee *sensible*. Instantaneously iconic of the Syrian refugee crisis, the asynchronous temporality of Web 2.0 ensured Alan Kurdi would keep washing up on that beach in Bodrum each time to different effect.

Affect Machines

Social media platforms are affect machines. To put it this way brings to the fore self-organizing organisms articulated with technological and social environments. On the one hand, social media users inhabit a technological environment that is deeply integrated into their cognitive systems; on the other, their species socialities remain irrevocably salient to their cognitive makeup. Affect illuminates the biotechnical and the biosocial articulation of carbon-based life-forms and their machinic integration. Media theorists variously model the distributed cognition constitutive of the social-technological subject of Web 2.0 social media.[13] Their insights suggest knee-jerk tweets are both biotechnical, a media habit, *and* biosocial, communicative sendings to the multiplicity of YOUs. Approaching social media in the context of biological, technological, and social wirings suggests habits are once-conscious actions that have settled as embodied responses. Both Wendy Chun and Kris Cohen privilege this part-conscious impersonal nature of social media actions, even when social media users entertain illusions of personal agency or empowerment.[14]

Chun explores the singular subject, the YOU in social media, who confronts constant crises in habitual new media.[15] As more than one critic has noted, crises are everyday occurrences in neoliberal times.[16] On social media, the demand for real-time responsibility can prove exhausting. Turning points or thresholds, crises send the YOUs running for cover. Like all living organisms responding to change, argues Chun, they attempt to reinforce the pattern that they recognize as the "self." This is simply protec-

---

13 See, for instance Hayles, *Unthought*.

14 Chun, *Updating to Remain the Same*; Cohen, *Never Alone, Except for Now*.

15 *Updating to Remain the Same* is the last in Chun's trilogy that includes *Control and Freedom* on how a technology of control was managed and sold as freedom and *Programmed Visions* on computer as the tools for negotiating an increasingly complex world.

16 The point is made forcefully in Berlant's *Cruel Optimism* and Povinelli's *Economies of Abandonment*.

tion against change, against coming uncertainties. Habit is the conditioned response that maintains the self-organizing system (the singular YOU). The return to a structure is a socially learned and deeply embodied response to the change. Chun underscores the creativity of the habitual in a memorable formula: Habit + Crisis = Update. One updates the self-organizing structure in confronting crisis with habit; in other words, the constant update "deprives habit of its ability to habituate."[17] In context of this formulation, one might ask: where does affect fit into the picture? Generally, affects are understood as pre-personal intensities that accumulate and gather force in the embodied mind; they are pre-personal because they respond to external stimuli before conscious recognition of that stimuli as particular object. One's lungs throw a spasm when a shadow looms in the alley, a visceral biosocial response. One implicitly perceives the stimuli one has encountered before; the perception is socially habitual, distributed through sensory and motor systems. Chun makes a similar claim about media habits that emerge from the integration of sensory and motor system with machines. She locates social media habit in implicit memory which is distinct from explicit memory. The latter is what we consciously recall, Chun maintains, following Eric R. Kandel's *In Search of Memory*; it is long-term memory housed in the brain. By contrast, habits arise from implicit memory: they are a form of knowing without knowing. We are not conscious of inherent conditioning through habituation; there aren't any memories *stored* that can be retrieved. Rather, habitual responses reconfigure and reinforce past goals/selves/experiences in acts of constant care that look not to the past (what must be preserved) but to the future (what enables survival). Affects are accumulated forces that drive this constant care. The human perceptual apparatuses *process* external stimuli, and especially noxious signals, in micro-actions such as liking, sharing, and retweeting. In this sense, mediation is an act of survival; it is constitutive of species socialities. Clicking an anger icon as response to a mass shootings in the U.S. or a sad icon for floods and fires may appear desensitized, since we mostly understand sensitization to be enhanced alertness. But if we think about distributed perceptions at the interface of sensory, motor, and technological systems, then habitual responses are active engagements with stimuli that arrive from the social-technological environment that one inhabits.

In the case of iconic images, both explicit and implicit memories are in play. The icon is a cultural mnemonic: an artifactual graphic sign, it appears natural because of its *habituation* in implicit memory. As such icons call forth habitual responses, ranging from disgust to devotion. But because they are a shared cultural mnemonic, iconic images always belong to collective memory. One might say Alan Kurdi's image triggered responses internal to social media users *because* of a collective habituation to images of injured children. Historically, distress, alarm, and horror at photographs of injured children as the exemplary victims of wars, famines, and genocides have provoked controversy. Many such as the "Napalm girl" are a part of a global cultural repertoire. At one level, the strength of response to the Alan Kurdi image must be understood in this context. If, as I suggest, the Twitter storm is evidence of accumulated affects, then those affects arise from embodied cultural knowledge—so embedded that it does not appear as knowledge at all. Further, visceral responses to an injured child recall

---

17 Chun, *Updating to Remain the Same*, 85.

past experiences ("scars" and "remnants")[18] as points of reference for coming harm to self-organizing biological systems. Hence, the images of injured children arouse protective drives, ranging from deep anxiety to horror. Whichever direction one pursues, it is clear that complex affects—fear, anxiety, sadness—drive habitual responses to the mediatic traces of hurt or dead children. Often this complexity registers as messy, even unruly. Affects that have not congealed as discernible emotion are illegible, and therein manifest as the unreason of crowds and mobs. Over time, as iconic images circulate, they settle as expressive cultural sentiment in public cultures. In blogs and forums, the adult subject assumes an ethical and/or parental relation to the injured child. A deep sense of collective culpability begins to haunt the iconic image, a culpability sometimes repressed and sometimes acknowledged as we see in the public culture around the Kurdi image.

If we follow VSML's spatialization of the flows, it is evident that the volume of retweets amplify *through* specific distributive chokepoints such as the Free Syria Hub or Human Rights Watch. Put differently, these institutions banked on particular forms of liberal subjectivity and on the proverbial iconicity of the injured child to engineer a massive collective response to the refugee crisis. The presupposition of liberal YOUs (as Chun puts it) which is then algorithmically fed back to the individuated YOU of Web 2.0 marks the kind of controlled enclosure that make social media's mythic sense of user empowerment just that—mythic! A range of theorists have been at pains to make the point about the freedom of the internet.[19] These analyses of the privatized internet have repeatedly shown the "personal" to be algorithmically routed, a monetized commodity. Such scholarship includes platform studies of business models that underlie Facebook's and Twitter's protocols. Hence, the participatory paradigm of unfettered reciprocities and of democratic playing fields of the "free internet" had been put to bed well before Cambridge Analytica became a catchphrase for its demise. Following these insights, one might say transnational organizations such as Free Syria Hub and Human Rights Watch banked on the populational aggregate, on the liberal YOUs' value (*pace* Chun) that yielded dividends. In engineered viral spreads, not only are social media users expected to spread content through *their* social networks but each point of contact makes possible the exponential quantification of content. Corporate governance of Web 2.0 calculates this quantification. But social media users act without the predictive advantage of big data. They court uncertainty. The one surety is the desire to pass on the intensities that had them in their grip, a desire that drives the social distribution of the sensible. This desire already moves us beyond the algorithmic capture of the YOUs.

Even as she underscores the algorithmic production of population aggregates that shape the social networks of social media users, Kris Cohen argues that social media users inhabit a contorted form of *group life*: they live partly as populations and partly as affective publics.[20] It is within the market enclosures of the controlled machinic

---

18 Chun, *Updating to Remain the Same*, 95.

19 Most notably Terranova, *Network Culture* and Galloway and Thacker, *The Exploit*.

20 For an account of the dynamics of this group life in relation to the slogan "We Refugees," see Suzana Milevska's chapter in this volume; see as well Farah Atoui's account of the relation of public affect to preemption and preemptive modes of power vis-à-vis discourses of migration-as-crisis, also this volume.

environment that the singular YOUs entertain illusions of freedom. Cohen's "affective publics" picks up on this sense of agency: on the *singular* drive to inhabit a *plural* YOU or the lonely drive to never be alone, to inhabit the social network. In this sense, the social media user is always a singular-plural subject living a distributed life on Web 2.0. Pushing beyond the market dimension to consider *how* social media users inhabit their group form, Chun initially paints a stark picture. If the YOUs in aggregated form show up in each other's feed, does this not imply that social media is deeply segregated? Is the group form simply "poorly gated virtual communities"? The YOUs friend, like, follow, recommend, and share with *others like them*. Chun names these social enclosures a prevalent *homophily*, a concept that rose from urban segregation in the 1950s. The homophilic group form strengthens already existing ties.[21] Engineered viral spreads emerge from the anticipation and management of homophilic responses. These are all the reasons why, *contra* empowerment, social media is widely regarded as politically defunct: anti-social, socially risky, and manipulative.

What, then, can be made of political subjectivities that anticipate connectivity, if not reciprocity, with other YOUs? Is the desire to participate in political life entirely circumscribed? As both theorists argue, these controlled environments are leaky. Unexpected things happen on social media. One cannot put down all viral events to regulated homophily or to mechanized bot activity. Chun gestures toward such leakiness in positioning *heterophily* as the monstrous chimera of YOUs based on non-reciprocal relations. What if social media users inhabit their networked vulnerabilities as isolated YOUs uncertain of outcomes? What if they count not on their social network but the *originary multiplicity* implicit in the very conception of the network? Granted, the network they reach is technologically controlled, but their actions disclose a desire for undecidable quantification. Such inhabitation of the network made of reciprocal and potentially non-reciprocal ties courts risk; the outcomes are undecidable. This undecidability raises allegations of the "thin politics" of social media. The collective "we" is too transient, too wavering—it tends towards an inoperative collectivity. And yet, in such intensities of social media actions we catch a glimpse of a group form *other than* the algorithmically-governed population.

After Cohen, I call these group forms affective publics. The YOUs do not constitute a positive collectivity bearing the markers of racial, national, or other filiations; there is no self-reflexive habitation of a particular medium that marks classic public such as a newspaper reading constituency. Rather, the binding glue for the unconnected YOUs is affective intensity and the desire to transmit affects through mediation. At moments when we glimpse unanticipated affective surges, as in the Twitter storm around the Kurdi image, the YOUs become a cumulative affective public even as their micro-actions remain deeply individuated. It is a public without common features, without shared agendas, but it is equally a group form that embraces publicness. This ambiguous and weak nature of the YOUs acting "alone together," to invoke Cohen's evocative phrase, is what renders their politics suspect. If they do not have a common agenda, do their micro-politics amount to anything at all? If these affective-performative mediations have no lasting impact, what is gained from studying them as a form of political life?

---

21 Chun, "Virtual Segregation Narrows Our Real-Life Relationships."

Improper Politics

One way to approach these questions is to look beyond politics proper—be that the institutional compositions of the *demos* or civil society re-compositions of same. Demographic data on refugees constitute one major political composition of the European *demos* to come, with quotas and dispensations policing the implications behind incorporating new populations. Large-scale anti-border movements, supranational organizations, even local grassroots movements offer recompositions that parlay the politics of incorporation. They show how boats capsize from willed neglect, how the real issue is a lack of political will and not of material resource, and how states of exception operate to racially segregate disposable populations. We are familiar with such deliberations that manifest across media platforms. The affective publics I have elaborated above, however, are disruptive in that they dissent from the calculative rationality of these arbitrations. The unconnected YOUs puncture calculative rationality in favor of sensible relations to the coming wave. To call their politics "improper" draws on the long postcolonial engagement with *uncivil* mobilization, which is a mode of political participation for those with little access to the modern associational forms of civil society.[22] Obviously social media users have clear access to media platforms and technologies; and yet, as affective partakers disinvested from deliberative democracy, they resemble uncivil congeries whose political participation is affective-performative. Thus the micro-actions of such social media users appear unruly and sometimes uncivil; often artisanal, their mediations are often considered far too banal to elicit critical attention and far too transitory for political analysis.

In Rancière's terms, such micro-actions are eminently *democratic* political activities when they mediate an uncounted surplus that exceeds political representation. Arriving with hashtags, not making any authoritative claims, as in the case of the Kurdi image, artisanal compositions of the *demos* are antithetical to quantification and therein to the police function of states. That police function attempts to enact demographic capture by numbers: it counts the rich, the poor, the women, the illegal immigrants. It even counts the disposable and relegates them to camps and detention centers. But there is always a part of *demos* that is not as yet legible; as surplus, it re-

---

22 Another essay on the Kurdi image, "Big Bad Social Media: Media Populism and Improper Political Affect," is forthcoming in *Culture Machine*. There, I argue that political theories of uncivil engagements take as a given the capture of the people in populational forms. Colonial demographics perfected the biopolitical compositions of the people as life-forms incapable of governing themselves, even as indigenous or native elites were invited to the table for civil arbitration. And yet it is clear from decades of postcolonial historiography that insurgencies, appearing violent and unruly to the ruling elites, were organized through technologies of communication that fly under the radar in their artisanal and low-tech nature. In other words, no technological domain has ever totally controlled *political affects* directed against governments and/or political elites for their violent production of scarcities and precarities. These affects express as unruliness dissent—sometimes violent, explicitly emotional, not legible as agenda or platform. On social media, such dissent may inevitably increases state and corporate surveillance capacities; and yet the YOUs keep arriving uninvited to the table, attempting to structure the actions of others. Their presence is often considered repugnant, unwanted, but also not contained by algorithmic controls as the many Facebook, YouTube, and other showdowns have recently revealed. The literature on unruly mobs and crowds is too vast to cite here, but for this essay, two inspirations are Chatterjee, *The Politics of the Governed* and Gaonkar, "After the Fictions."

mains anonymous. The sensible image *does not count* but makes visible the space of the unknowable *demos*. In this regard, sensible images are instances of political mediation at its most democratic: "The essential work of politics is the configuration of its own space. It is to make the world of its subjects and its operations seen. The essence of politics is the manifestation of *dissensus* as the presence of two worlds in one."[23] The figure of Alan Kurdi brings into view a world of deadly crossings, camps and borders, roiling waters and grave injury. It is a world whose visibility the police function struggles to keep at bay. In dissenting from the police function, social media users enact an improper politics: they amplify artisanal compositions, makeshift and cursory, sometimes transitory, and often inaccurate. The sloppiness evident in the slippage between the singular child and the refugee/migrant horde lends such sensible images their political efficacy.

More importantly, impropriety lies in the *uninvited* participation of those who are not central actors in large political projects. In *Rancière's Sentiments*, Davide Panagia characterizes such actors as "part-takers" who participate in activities that might not belong to them, regardless of whether that activity is persuasive to others.[24] They are less invested in reasoned political judgement; they just want to *partake* (*partager* or share). These are exactly the social media users who enter and leave the political fray at will. Unruly or unreliable as political actors, their sudden eruptions occasionally jolt existing compositions of the *demos*. In social media, such partaking is highly regulated through algorithmic controls of reciprocal ties. Yet there are occasions when the partaking is excessive, leaking beyond established reciprocities. On such occasions, media users retweet without a clear sense of how their activity will be received. This is a drive to *feel rather than count* the number of likes and shares. The temporal intensity of unprecedented viral spreads suggest the micro-actions that constitute the spread are not merely calculative. Something else had happened, something unpredictable. We are reminded that what appears unprecedented is often well-engineered: Cohen reminds us that there are companies in the business of designing viral memes, for there is money to be made in the YOUs value of viral campaigns. But such attention to algorithmic architectures does not fully explain the virality of the Kurdi image. Put differently, why would *this* image of the Syrian refugee crisis galvanize the quantification drive at exponentially higher scales? After all, the VSML dossier presents evidence of *several* other photographs of the same crisis that did not elicit a huge response. But the Kurdi image caught fire.[25] It was *the* viral spread that was widely considered a "wakeup call," "a lightbulb moment," and an image that "shook the world."[26] Following the discussion of affects, one might argue that the force of accumulated affects reach a tipping point—they spill over in frantic sharing, liking, and tweeting—at particu-

---

23 Rancière, *Dissensus*, 37.

24 Panagia, *Rancière's Sentiments*, xi.

25 There is substantial evidence in the VSML dossier about the difference of this image. The Twitter storm reverberated through already existing citizen-led efforts to mitigate the plight of refugees. The Facebook group #RTWN (#refugeeswelcometonorway) that led efforts to collect provisions for refugees in Oslo grew from 200 to 90,000 immediately after the Alan Kurdi viral spread; the U.K. Charities Aid Foundation reported a similar spike, as 1 in 3 Britons made donations for refugees. See Probitz, "The Strength of Weak Commitment."

26 Burns, "Discussion and Action."

lar conjunctures that cannot be predicted. They can only be understood in retrospect. In this case, the unanticipated spread suggests that unconnected YOUs were already aware, affectively if not consciously, of the refugee wave. *They had felt the numbers already in Europe.* In the Twitter storm, the YOUs entered the fray as uninvited partakers banking on the connectivity of Web 2.0.

That their entrance could not be anticipated is what frustrates political prediction. But it is a suddenness that is now the political norm, and especially in times when many social movements explode as admixtures of Twitter and tear gas.[27] Such eruptions make it crucial to attend to affective publics who habitually exceed algorithmic capture. We see this most often in the many showdowns around *violent* viral images. In these cases, strong affective publics bound by filiation, racial or nationalist origins, attack democratic projects. They are on the rise all over the world; all the protocols and shutdowns in the world can't seem to hold them at bay. Often antagonistic to liberal democracies, they are enamored of the police function: they want the count, if only to prove their invisible historical injury. That injury is the basis for closing borders and imposing limits on the *demos*; they, too, generate artisanal composition. In contrast, there are the weak inoperative YOUs that loosely establish relations with the anonymous *demos*; this demotic structure emerges again and again in the "springs" and "occupys" of our times that *keep coming*. Against an aggressive populism, this inarticulate popular surfaces in the time-honored spaces of streets and parks and the newly durable spaces of social media. It may coalesce around avowedly local matters, but its claims as *demos* are universally salient. For better or for worse, it is the new democratic common sense.

---

27 We are familiar today with hybrid social movements, in which social media platforms are key interfaces to the street: theorists from Butler's "Bodies in Alliance and the Politics of the Street" to Tufecki's *Twitter and Tear Gas* have spoken to the affordances and constraints of this interface.

Controlling the Crisis[1]

Ian Alan Paul

If it were possible to ventriloquize power today it would only talk over itself, anxiously announcing that *"the whole of our world is in crisis"* while austerely assuring that *"everything is entirely under control."* This contradiction suffuses our present, a historical moment in which elaborate reports on the disintegration of this or that structure or institution double as advertisements for security programs that promise to ever more intensely, impenetrably, and intimately safeguard a seemingly threatened world. These twin voices of crisis and control mutually constitute the principal rationality of contemporary governmentality and power more generally, a logic within which crisis does not follow from the absence or failure of control, but rather is dependent upon—and is the condition of possibility for—control's instantiation. This text seeks to elucidate how the emergent centrality of crisis in contemporary life, rather than being the consequence of *crises beyond control*, is instead an output of societies organized by the desire to *control crises*. Resonating through technical, discursive, aesthetic, and juridical strategies, the crisis-control conjuncture operates as a planetary force that is transformatively re-orchestrating the operations and organizations of power in the present.

The first section of this text will draw upon Donna Haraway's charting of the "informatics of domination,"[2] Gilles Deleuze's prognosis of the coming "societies of control,"[3] and the "autonomous world of apparatuses" described in Tiqqun's *Cybernetic Hypothesis* in order to theorize the operations of control as well as chart how they've been mobilized by Frontex, the agency tasked with policing Europe's internal and external borders and a truly paradigmatic expression of the dynamics described above. After analyzing Frontex's networked surveillance and policing of migrants—as well as the regulation and circulation of data resulting from those measures—in the second section of this text I outline how the *control and crisis* of Europe's borders have emerged sympoietically, diagramming the crisis-control conjuncture within the historical specificity of the 2015–16 migrant crisis. In the third and final section of the

---

1   This text would not have been possible absent the generous commentaries and critiques of both Krista Lynes and Tyler Morgenstern. In particular, Krista's thoughtful reflections on the differential/differentiating structure of cybernetic power and Tyler's sharp insights concerning the historical elaboration of cybernetics and biometrics in the 20th century proved immensely valuable. My thinking on these subjects is forever indebted to them both.

2   Haraway, "A Cyborg Manifesto."

3   Deleuze, "Postscript on the Societies of Control."

text, I conclude by looking to emergent practices that aim to counteract, sabotage, and undermine the conjunctive logic of crisis and control that now governs our present.

Crucially, I intend to detail the complementary structure of crisis and control throughout this text only in the hopes of also helping to clarify the ways in which these forms of power are presently being resisted, and speculatively could be resisted in times to come. While detailing and charting the operations of power is unquestionably a necessary task, such an endeavour risks deepening a sense of helplessness and subjugation if it fails to also suggest ways in which power can be, if not entirely undone, at the very least resisted, warded off, or evaded. In this sense, the first gesture of this text should be read as an effort to draw a diagram of power, while the second should be read as an attempt to contribute, however minorly, to the interminable collective project of destituting power wherever it persists.

The Informatics, Cybernetics, and Control of Domination

In *The Cybernetic Hypothesis*, the authors writing within the anonymous and collective framework of the journal *Tiqqun* argue that liberalism has been superceded by the logic of cybernetics, within which "biological, physical, and social behaviors" come to be approached as "something integrally programmed and re-programmable."[4] Both liberalism and cybernetics are fantasies of power, but while the fantasy of liberalism is principally instantiated as a series of institutions, the fantasy of cybernetics is manifest instead as "a diffuse constellation of agents, all driven, possessed, and blinded by the same fable [...] (a fable) that hides behind the names 'internet,' 'new information and communications technology,' (and) the 'new economy.'"[5] In contrast to the isolated, individualized, and highly supervised forms of subjectivity that are cultivated by liberalism, cybernetics is instead a project concerned with vacating subjectivity as a means of producing emptied out subjects, blank envelopes that can serve as "the best possible conductor of social communication."[6] According to Tiqqun, the cybernetic project ultimately aims to produce a "new politics of subjects, resting on communication and transparency" that conceives of the individual as "something 'piloted,' in the last analysis, by the need for the survival of a 'system' that makes it possible, and which it must contribute to."[7] Subjects are each made to act as the "locus of an infinite feedback loop which is made to have no nodes," situated within and dominated by interoperable systems of communication and control.[8]

The conceptual delineation between cause and effect breaks down in cybernetic systems, as inputs and outputs mutually affect one another in regulatory feedback loops that push complex systems towards calibrated metastabilities. As subjects enter into feedback processes, they communicate with cybernetic systems which then trigger regulatory responses in a corresponding set of control devices. Rather than try to extinguish the possibility of undesired or unproductive behavior in advance, the

---

4 Tiqqun, "The Cybernetic Hypothesis."

5 Tiqqun, "The Cybernetic Hypothesis."

6 Tiqqun, "The Cybernetic Hypothesis."

7 Tiqqun, "The Cybernetic Hypothesis."

8 Tiqqun, "The Cybernetic Hypothesis."

implementation of cybernetic feedback at the scale of the subject is intended to render social uncertainties and indeterminacies eminently manageable, programmable, and productive whenever and wherever they emerge. While the logic of sovereignty is principally concerned with undertaking forms of action that are intended to produce a particular set of planned effects, cybernetics instead seeks to recursively regulate what strays or drifts away from calibrated states. These processual corrections are a cybernetic technique of governmentality enacted through regulation, a form of *piloting* that doesn't attempt to avoid particular events or crises but instead only means to technically *steer* their effects in favorable directions.[9] Like an automated surveillance drone that dynamically adjusts the speed of its propeller in order to compensate for the surrounding turbulence, remaining serenely suspended above its target area, cybernetic systems enact controls to produce metastabilities between the inputs and outputs of a system in an interminable process of regulation that means to minimize the distance between a calibrated ideal and a digitally sensed world, materially instantiating capitalism's ideological structure as a network of technical devices.[10]

For Haraway, the cybernetic organization of power is expressed principally as "the translation of the world into a problem of coding" where "all resistance to instrumental control disappears and all heterogeneity can be submitted to disassembly, reassembly, investment, and exchange."[11] Following the mass production, distribution, and installation of networked computers, it became possible for social behavior to be sensed, stored, and analyzed *en masse* as data, as abstracted sets of numerical values that could be circulated through and processed within the automated computation of machines. Like the abstracting power of price, which establishes an abstract equivalency between all commodities in markets, data establishes an abstract equivalency between anything that can be digitally sensed by or manually inputted into computers.[12] This vast numerical abstraction of the world "transcends the universal translation effected by capitalist markets that Marx analysed so well," emerging as a totalizing cybernetic system which aims to regulate all of the world's activity.[13] For Haraway, "information is just that kind of quantifiable element (unit, basis of unity) which allows universal translation, and so unhindered instrumental power" that permits more and more of the world to be subjected to the "informatics of domination" that characterizes the cybernetic organization of power.[14]

---

9 For more on "piloting" as it relates to governmentality and security, see Giorgio Agamben's writing on François Quesnay in "For a Theory of Destituent Power;" for more on the importance of both "piloting" as a mode of governance and as a key discursive figure in the development of cybernetics see Peter Galison's "The Ontology of the Enemy."

10 The metastabilities that emerge between the calibrated idealized states of cybernetic systems and the messy, inconsistent, contradictory, and noisy material world are a technical manifestation of the fantasy of cybernetics. In order for life to be controlled, after all, it must necessarily always already escape control to some degree, and so cybernetic control is always invested in *the fantasy* of a controlled life that *nonetheless always exceeds control* due to the technical structure of control and ontological structure of life itself.

11 Haraway, "A Cyborg Manifesto," 164.

12 For more on the digital-as-form, look to Seb Franklin's *Control*; for more on the digital as it relates to philosophical thought, look to Alexander Galloway's *Laruelle* and *Protocol*.

13 Haraway, "A Cyborg Manifesto," 163.

14 Haraway, "A Cyborg Manifesto," 164.

Within the historical movement of cybernetics, Deleuze argues that the central technique of power is control. Conceived of as a means of computationally acting on the actions of others, control is best understood not as a replacement for but rather as an elaboration of the forms of domination that characterized disciplinary power. While in disciplinary societies a life was imagined as traveling through a series of discontinuous enclosures which often looked something like: Hospital (Maternity Ward) => School => Factory (or Prison, or Barracks) => Hospital (Morgue), in control societies a life comes to be differentially suffused by all of these structures simultaneously as a consequence of their translation into code.[15] For Deleuze, the fixed molds of disciplinary societies are transformed into "self-deforming cast(s) that will continuously change from one moment to the other, or like a sieve whose mesh will transmute from point to point" that can be deployed at a plurality of scales and be precisely calibrated in relation to each subject in particular based upon the data associated with them.[16] While in disciplinary societies a border could be imagined as a fortress-like wall that cuts a landscape cleanly into two distinct territories, in control societies a border instead is envisaged as a dispersed series of networked gates and checkpoints that each open and close dynamically in response to a shifting multiplicity of passwords and codes.

In the contemporary European context, Frontex acts as the central authority responsible for controlling migration on the continent and mobilizes the cybernetic techniques of power outlined above to do so. Founded in 2005, Frontex organizes and oversees a diverse array of programs and technologies that are intended to monitor and police the internal and external borders of the EU, but in practice these measures far exceed the strict spatial boundaries of the political and economic union. Central to Frontex's approach is the use of planetary-scale networks of interoperable surveillance and control technologies, including but not limited to data centers, fiber-optic cables, ground sensors, cell phone towers, and communications and surveillance satellites, that together serve as the cybernetic infrastructure for dynamic zones of control that extend across and beyond the territorial limits of the Schengen area.[17]

As a core part of its operations, Frontex extensively surveils, studies, and aggregates information about migration as a means of more effectively policing and controlling it. Profuse amounts of data are routinely captured, aggregated, and analyzed, all of which are then repackaged and published by Frontex in media-rich "Risk Analysis Reports" that advertise new border control technologies and initiatives, present colorful data visualizations and schematic migratory pattern maps, and detail various predictions about the future of migration that together contribute to the constitution

---

15 Prisons no longer require cells, and instead can be made to algorithmically appear and vanish on command with the use of wireless ankle monitors. Hospitals no longer require wards when networked accessories can transmit blood sugar levels to data centers and digitized patches can be activated remotely to deliver insulin. Universities become globally accessible online classes. The psychiatrist's office is fragmented into a million self-help therapy chat rooms. All of these structures exist all of the time as potentials on a network which can be switched on and off dynamically in relation to the signals sent by cybernetic subjects.

16 Deleuze, "Postscript on the Societies of Control," 4.

17 While migration controls have supposedly been abolished within the Schengen Area, nonetheless internal licit and illicit movement remains heavily policed.

of the migrant crisis as an object of cultural concern, security planning, political discourse, and legislative response in the EU.[18]

Frontex's approach to the policing of migration does not involve the deployment of large numbers of security forces, an ineffective gesture given the vast kilometers of borders that encompass the EU, but rather mobilizes cybernetic techniques of power that rely upon the capture, circulation, and analysis of data that is collected from member states and then transmitted back to them in transnational feedback loops. As national security programs deploy technologies and forces at their own borders, the information produced by those operations become inputs that Frontex can then use to recalibrate the EU-wide distribution and deployment of security funding and resources. Facilitated by the European Border Surveillance System (EUROSUR) and Schengen Information System (SIS) information-exchange frameworks, Frontex collects data from individual member states' National Coordination Centres and then produces a "European situational picture and the common pre-frontier intelligence picture (focused on areas beyond the Schengen Area and EU borders)" that is then shared back with each member state.[19] An associated Frontex program titled Copernicus additionally "increase(s) situational awareness by providing Europe with accurate, reliable and up-to-date data collected from satellites and on-site sensors" that contribute another degree of detail of the "situational picture" that is circulated across the EU.[20] These information sharing programs constitute Frontex's core function, which concerns the production of "a constantly updated picture, as near to real time as possible, of Europe's external borders and migration situation" that acts as a "vital part of Frontex's rapid-response mechanism."[21] The production of a "constantly updated picture" of migration is in the end only rendered possible within a cybernetic system organized to facilitate maximal communication between heterogeneous national security forces, technologies, and infrastructures that are made to be transparent to and for one another.

Cybernetic systems ultimately rely upon communication in order to determine control responses, and in control societies the drive for more communication is made to be maximal. The confessional dynamics that animated disciplinary societies, within which subjects were coerced into articulating their interior lives for the exterior world (in the hospital examination room, the courtroom, the psychiatrists office, the classroom, etc.), pale in comparison to the ways in which subjects can be made to involuntarily confess to machines in control societies. Microfacial expressions, pulse rates, body temperatures, perspiration, respiration, eye dilations, and odors are all now the targets of automated machine sensing and analysis, each of which are translated into data and uploaded into security systems at airports and other border crossings that

---

18 A full collection of Frontex's Risk Analysis Reports can be found at: frontex.europa.eu/publications/?c=risk-analysis.

19 European Commission, "Eurosur."

20 It certainly would be possible (and productive) to thoroughly trace a direct historical line between a Copernican "Enlightenment" and the weaponized light of surveillance satellites and sensors, but unfortunately I don't have the pages to do so here.

21 Frontex, "Information Management."

algorithmically determine if alerts should be sent to security officers.[22] Attention itself has become a central form of confession in this context, where the amount of time spent looking at various content online is measured to the millisecond in order to build data profiles, determine preferences, predict desires, calibrate the delivery of future content, and/or trigger a corresponding series of control responses. All that is sensible by machines is approached as constituting part of a planetary polyphonous confession, within which subjects engage in an endless autobiographical monologue in the form of the communications and signals they send to a heterogeneous multiplicity of cybernetically driven apparatuses and feedback systems.[23]

Epistemologically, cybernetic systems do not comprehend subjects as individuals (as the indivisible, coherent entities of liberalism and disciplinary societies), but rather as bundles of *dividual characteristics* that can be unique to particular bodies but are more often shared in common by many. Datasets of dividual characteristics can be composed of biometric data such as height, weight, eye, skin, and hair color, genomic markers, fingerprints, and gait, but also can incorporate any information that can be digitally stored in a database, such as citizenship, sexuality, criminal records, or location histories.[24] While the discourses that surround crisis tend to focus on individual bodies as loci of potential violence, for example the "single male refugee" in the migrant crisis that comes to be understood as a parasite or terrorist, these discourses function to produce a *political justification for the enactment of power* that simultaneously *obscures the way in which power is dividually enacted.*[25] The kinds of dividual characteristics that are collected and analyzed uninterruptibly grows more expansive and diverse as states, social media companies, academic researchers, and data brokers compete to invent techniques of sensing and storing novel forms of data based upon the tautological understanding that all data is good, and all that is good is data.

Data is obsessively collected everywhere and anywhere it is found, flowing in increasingly large volumes and amassing in a multiplicity of informatic reservoirs whose depths only grow. In one instance, a video stream from a public webcam installed in a cafe in downtown San Francisco was used by the Chinese government to train its facial

---

22 It is worth noting that these forms of algorithmic analysis are highly error prone, with widely varying degrees of accuracy. In particular, facial recognition systems are calibrated to analyze the white male faces of the teams that programmed them, making them less able to recognize faces with darker skin tones or with geometries that don't align with normatively masculine features. Regardless, the accuracy of these systems matters less in relation to the fact of their growing deployment within security systems as well as their integration within the technical operation of power more generally.

23 What is social media, after all, other than endless self-expression oriented towards algorithmically generated publics? As Deleuze notes: "We sometimes go on as though people can't express themselves. In fact they're always expressing themselves [...] it's not a problem of getting people to express themselves but of providing little gaps of solitude and silence in which they might eventually find something to say. Repressive forces don't stop people expressing themselves but rather force them to express themselves; What a relief to have nothing to say, the right to say nothing, because only then is there a chance of framing the rare, and ever rarer, thing that might be worth saying." Deleuze, *Negotiations*, 129.

24 For a critical approach to biometric capture and analysis, see the work of artist Adam Harvey at www.ahprojects.com/.

25 For more on the figure of the single male refugee, see Veronika Zabotsky's essay "Unsanctioned Agency" in this volume.

recognition programs.[26] In another case, Microsoft released a dataset that contains the names and images of 100,000 "celebrities" that it aggregated from various online sources that (unironically) includes the artists Hito Steyerl, Ai Weiwei, and Trevor Paglen and which was used as material for research projects across several continents.[27] While the production and analysis of images remains a central part of cybernetic control, whether expressed as data visualizations or in the images captured by surveillance satellites, the luminosity of the pulses that stream through fiber optic lines and the electrical charges of individual bits within databases far exceeds the limits of visual culture and constitutes a formally broader and more ontologically diverse regime of mediation. By translating the world into the most elementary form of digital difference, the switch between one and zero (presence and absence), anything can potentially be "interfaced with any other" by digitally abstracting them, allowing for the "processing (of) signals in a common language."[28] The complex arrangement of formal elements that make up every different kind of visual composition (maps, graphs, schematics, photographs, etc.) appears excessive and wasteful in comparison to the minimalism and austerity of binary encoding.[29]

The cybernetic organization and expression of power takes shape in banal and everyday forms, just as it is manifest in punctuated moments of extreme violence. It can be expressed as the serving of particular kinds of advertising content to people who have become associated with a particular dividual characteristic, just as it can take shape as drone strikes that are executed based solely upon the analysis of dividual data, such as the suspicious movement of a cell phone over time, without being aware of the identity of the person being bombed.[30] At the level of governmentality, the state may select only those who share a particular grouping of dividual characteristics for the enactment of certain controls, such as those subjects who are associated with the data identifiers "Muslim," "Man," "Under 40," and "Travelled Abroad." Once behavioral, biographical, and/or biometric data is communicated to a cybernetic system, that data can then be acted upon and modulated in order to generate new data that is closer to the socially, politically, and economically desired ideal of the larger system.

Frontex's strategy of producing a constantly updated situational picture of migration might better be described as the production of an *operational image* that is structured cybernetically. While these operational images often involve visual elements,

---

26 The cybernetic subjugation of populations has reached its most elaborate and total instantiation in contemporary China, where the muslim Uyghur minority has become subjected to the mass automated surveillance practices of the state. Vast networks of cameras installed in all kinds of public and private spaces including homes, cafes, and on the street, in combination with surveillance of internet communications, have enabled for more than a million Uyghurs to be sent to concentration camps for mandatory reeducation. See Mozur, "One Month, 500,000 Face Scans."

27 See the work of Mega Pixels at www.megapixels.cc/datasets/brainwash/and www.megapixels.cc/datasets/msceleb/.

28 Haraway, "A Cyborg Manifesto," 163.

29 A possible direction for future theorization would be to analyze the potential consequences of quantum computing on cybernetic control, which can compute using not only zero and one, but also the quantumly superposed zero-one.

30 The majority of U.S. drone strikes in Afghanistan and Pakistan are what are known as "signature strikes," where the identities of the people being bombed are unknown. See Entous, Gorman, and Barnes, "U.S. Tightens Drone Rules."

reducing them to a "visual image" would be to miss the ways in which the image also acts as a site of analysis, computation, and data that exceeds visuality in its modes of abstraction. Like a border surveillance camera that captures a photo of the landscape, algorithmically tries to match the various compositional relations of the captured image with coded sets of stored spatial patterns such as buildings, rivers, bridges, trees, bodies, animals, and/or roads, and then makes a calculated set of adjustments to its aperture and zoom as well as possibly activating the floodlights and alarm sirens mounted on nearby security fences before capturing another image and repeating the process, the operational images of Frontex are only produced in order to make various adjustments to a corresponding system of controls that will recursively affect the image in a modulatory feedback loop.[31] In this way, Frontex only produces, analyzes, and circulates an image of migration, a *moving image of movement*, in order to facilitate the operational and cybernetic domination of that movement. As Tiqqun notes, "Empire, armed with cybernetics, insists on autonomy for it alone," and in the context of the politics of movement Frontex should be understood as making a totalizing claim on the autonomy of its own internal movement (the circulation of data, of commodities, of "situational pictures," of security forces, etc.) while simultaneously refusing that same autonomy of movement for all others.[32]

One of the central contradictions that defines the power of contemporary borders is that they both facilitate and hinder movement, allowing for some flows to proceed largely unregulated while forcefully halting others. In the context of the EU, flows of those with proper passports, of commodities, and of financial assets circulate unimpeded, while vast populations are subjected to policing and control measures intended to extinguish even the possibility of their movement. In this way, the cyberneticization of the European border regime can be understood as a rearticulation of historical relations of subjugation and domination which have come to be technically expressed as "an autonomous world of apparatuses so blended with the capitalist project that it has become a political project."[33] While social media posts are subjected to intense monitoring and analysis in relation to border controls, encrypted wire transfers to offshore accounts remain shrouded in privileged cloaks of opacity. While Frontex worries about "individuals posing a security threat and economic migrants attempting to abuse the system by claiming a false nationality" in its annual risk reports, in practice they are only concerned by "security threat(s)" and "abuse(s) of the system" of targeted dividual characteristics that are algorithmically determined to be out of alignment with European power.[34]

In this way, cybernetic control can be conceived as both *totalizing* and *differential* in its processual enactment. Control is totalizing in the sense that everything and everyone in the world is targeted by the expansive digital sensing of interconnected surveillance apparatuses, and so *all subjects are subjected to* the systems of communication and computation that compose cybernetic systems. And yet, crucially, the control measures that are activated in response to that sensed data are fundamentally differential as they are *differently enacted* in relation to *politically differentiated subjects*. While

---

31 For more on operational images, see Harun Farocki's series of video essays *Eye/Machine I, II, and III*.

32 Tiqqun, "The Cybernetic Hypothesis."

33 Tiqqun, "The Cybernetic Hypothesis."

34 "Frontex, "Risk Analysis for 2016: Annual Report."

society itself can be understood as being totally regulated by the logic of cybernetics, the intensity of that regulation is nonetheless distributed unevenly, mobilized differentially against particular groupings of subjects based upon how distant their dividual characteristics are from the calibrated settings and norms of the larger social system. In this way, subjects become caught between the two extreme and counterposed processes of de- and reconstitution, in which bodies come to be understood as being *pure expressions of particular kinds of social difference* within a liberal society (along the lines of race, class, gender, sexuality, etc.) just as they are disaggregated and disintegrated into atomized streams of dividual characteristics within the analytic apparatuses of cybernetics.

Ultimately, both liberalism and cybernetics should principally be understood as fantasies, as *political and technical imaginations* of a society's structure that are mobilized to *restructure society in those imagined forms*. The subjects of liberalism and cybernetics never entirely exist in ways that liberal and cybernetic societies imagine them, but nonetheless liberal and cybernetic imaginations act upon bodies as real forces of subjectification that effectively capture them within their respective fantastical structures.[35] As fantasies of power and domination, the infinite number of differences that constitute the gulf between the liberal and cybernetic fantasies of the world and the world itself are not comprehended as being a *problem of fantasies* but rather simply as a *problem for fantasies* to correct. As a consequence, the historical instantiation of the liberal and cybernetic fantasies is inconsistent and often contradictory, allowing for societies to dream of frictionless global flows of information, bodies, and capital on one night, and of border detention camps in need of ever more police, tear gas, motion sensors, and concertina wire on the next.

However, just as the cybernetic organization of power hasn't replaced disciplinary power but rather has substantially transformed its material instantiation and formal enactment, cybernetics should equally be understood not as liberalism's replacement but as a complementary elaboration of its logic.[36] In other words, while the modulatory feedback of cybernetics now constitutes the *principal technical mechanism* of power, governmentality, and control that acts upon dividual characteristics, nonetheless liberal sovereignty remains deeply involved in the *differential enactment and distribution* of cybernetic power across individualized bodies. In this way, contemporary subjectivity itself is increasingly an expression of the formal contradiction that exists between liberal and cybernetic imaginaries, persistently decomposed into a multiplicity of dividual bits and bytes within the machines of cybernetic systems and ceaselessly

---

35 For more on the corresponding fantasies of liberalism and cybernetics, see Hayles's *How We Became Posthuman*, particularly the sections on the cyberneticist Norbert Wiener who she notes was "less interested in seeing humans as machines than he was in fashioning human and machine alike in the image of an autonomous, self-directed individual" (7).

36 Deleuze noted throughout his work that the theorization of control would have been impossible if Michel Foucault hadn't already undertaken the theorization of discipline. In *Foucault*, Deleuze notes that for Foucault "(the) prison, as a hard (cellular) segmentarity refers back to a flexible and mobile function, a controlled circulation, a whole network that also crosses free areas and can learn to dispense with prison" (43), which of course already suggests the logic of control. For what it is worth, Foucault also suggested that the 21st century would be Deleuzian precisely because of the emergence of control.

reconstituted into legible individuals within the discourses, regimes of representation, and legal/juridical structures of liberal society.

This apparent contradiction between liberalism and cybernetics ultimately resolves itself conjunctively, within which the *crisis of liberalism* and the *control of cybernetics* come to constitute, sustain, and intensify one another. As a society denounces migrants as being an existential threat to the supposed equalities, rights, and forms of welfare afforded to subjects within a liberal social order, migrants appear as *a crisis* for liberal society and thus in need of cybernetic control and regulation. The ban on women's veiling in various nation states within the EU could similarly be figured as a crisis for liberalism, where the niqab is seen as a foreign cultural imposition that islamophobic liberal societies cannot tolerate. Of course, the unveiled face is precisely also the face that is available for facial recognition systems to capture and analyze, subjecting muslim women to increasing degrees of cybernetic control (it is not coincidental that "veil" and "surveillance" share etymologies, after all).[37] In response to crises, bodies come to be subjectively parsed by and subsumed within historically demarcated forms of liberal difference (as liberalism's constitutive "other") just as they are permeated by concatenated processes of communication and control, conjunctively dominating life ever more intimately and totally.

Simultaneously produced as *individual subjects* and disintegrated into *dividual components*, particularly targeted pieces or patterns of data ("Sends Money Electronically to Nigeria," "Types in Arabic," "Detectable South Asian Ethnic Facial Geometry and Skin Tone," "Wears a Hijab," etc.) can be acted upon by cybernetic systems as a means of dominating a differentiated subject or group of subjects within the enforced hierarchies of a liberal social order. In other words, the totalizing structure of cybernetic control appears alongside liberal crises as part of a conjunctive historical movement, within which a perceived threat to the universality of liberalism must be persistently defended by the differential enactment of cybernetic power. In this sense, subjectivity itself becomes unthinkable absent either the individualizing force of liberalism or the corresponding set of apparatuses, devices, and mechanisms that materially constitute the cybernetic systems responsible for both producing and dominating individual subjects dividually.[38]

Briefly pausing to trace an outline of the shared histories of data collection, computation, and state violence can help to make clear the conditions within which these dynamics took shape. In Europe in particular, the history of these practices echoes and reverberates through colonial projects, the repression of popular revolts, the organization of genocide, through to the contemporary control of migration at the EU's borders, each constituting part of a continuous elaboration, development, transformation, and expression of state power. Plural and diverse histories circulate and coa-

---

37 It is also worth noting that balaclavas and motorcycle helmets that are often worn by anarchists and communists in militant demonstrations to avoid being identified by police are also banned in many of these same countries.

38 See Agamben's discussion of the work of Tiqqun: "Tiqqun tries to cause the two plans, the two analyses kept separate in the work of Foucault—mechanisms and techniques of governance, subject—to fully coincide with one another [...] the search for new political subjects that have the potential to paralyze, one that still paralyzes the tradition of the left, becomes unthinkable. Theory of the subject and theory of mechanisms are one," cited in Anarchist without Content, "Tiqqun Apocrypha Repost."

lesce into a complex inheritance constituted by the documentation, numeration, and eventual computation of bodies undertaken as forms of mass abstracting violence. As long ago as the Spanish Inquisition, record keeping, accounting, and data collection had already become integral into the processual enactment of state repression.[39] A set of procedures codified in documents such as the *Orden de Processar* (*Prosecutorial Order*) in the late 16th century involved not only the production of a written record of those present at trial as well as their testimony, verdict, and sentencing, but also of their property, biography, religion, race, and extended familial relations. The epistemological structure of the Spanish Inquisition also is what gave it duration as a political and historical force: the documentation of property allowed for its seizure which was the primary source of funding for the trials, while the documentation of familial ties allowed for expanded inquiries to be opened in a cascading series of subsequent trials. The establishment of bureaucratic data collection and processing transformed *the event of state violence* into *a recursive process of state violence* that could unfold over many years—or in the case of the Inquisition(s), centuries—and could be carried out by many different dispersed actors who could simply follow officially documented instructions and procedures.

By the late 19th century, biometric techniques had begun to be developed, practiced within, and integrated into the bureaucratic organization of state power. In colonial India, the British officers William Herschel and Richard Henry adopted fingerprinting as a method to allow illiterate colonized subjects to sign contracts and later was used to identify criminals in Bengal, techniques which were later brought back from the colonies to Britain where they became integrated into the standard practices of London's Metropolitan Police Service.[40] In roughly the same period, biometric photography was implemented in France in the decades following the defeat of the Paris Commune, where mass volumes of city records had been destroyed by fires and thus Parisians could attempt to assume whatever identity they desired.[41] The standardization of portraiture in the form of police mugshots in particular was intended to "reregister a social field that had exploded into multiplicity."[42] The numeration of bodies most infamously took form in the tattooing of numbers onto the skin of Jews, Roma, homosexuals, the disabled, and others in Auschwitz during the Holocaust. By the mid 20th century, the Nazi regime was already using computers in order to process targeted populations and manage their transportation to various concentration and extermination camps across Europe with greater degrees of efficiency.[43] IBM supplied machines and punch cards to the Nazis and also provided routine maintenance, which in combination with the vast census operations that accompanied Germany's expand-

---

39 The only reason we know so much about the Spanish Inquisition, after all, is because of the elaborate archives it produced about its own activities.

40 Colonial territories continue to be laboratories for state power. In contemporary Palestine, for example, experimental technologies are deployed by the Israeli state against Palestinians before being packaged, marketed, and sold to a range of other states. See Puar's *The Right to Maim* and Esmeir's "Colonial Experiments in Gaza" for theoretical explorations of this practice.

41 For other relevant histories of biometrics and surveillance, see Simone Browne's *Dark Matters* and James C. Scott's *Seeing Like a State*.

42 Sekula, "The Body and the Archive," 34.

43 See Edwin Black's *IBM and the Holocaust* for a comprehensive look at this history.

ing occupation of Europe allowed for the dividual sorting of the targeted populations, the literal *counting of* and *counting upon* bodies, creating the necessary conditions for the subsequent extermination of millions.[44]

In each of the aforementioned histories, the creation of an abstract index in which complex and nuanced living bodies came to be counted and numbered was the primary epistemological and political mechanism through which these forms of violence were rendered possible. While the particularities and specificities of each of these histories are not to be disregarded, nonetheless it is important that they be read together as contributing to the larger historical elaboration of state power in Europe which continues to take place today. Over the course of these diverse yet interconnected histories, an important transformation coincided with the emergence of cybernetics and control that is worth highlighting: while early biometric practices such as the mugshot and fingerprinting were conceived of principally as *retroactive* measures through which those who were arrested could be documented in order to be able to recognize them in case they should be arrested again, in control societies biometric data is *preemptively* collected about the entire population based upon the assumption that although not every person is a criminal, every person has the *ineradicable potential* to become one.[45]

In response to this imminent criminal potentiality that exists in every subject, data is collected in as high of volumes as possible at all times by a dispersed network of facial recognition systems, license plate readers, digital payment systems, cell phone towers, and myriad other technologies not because of any *documented fact* but because of a *social probability* that must endlessly predicted and regulated by cybernetic systems. As shorthand, the shift from disciplinary societies to control societies can be mapped onto a corresponding shift from understanding society deterministically, which characterized modernist practices of statecraft and sovereignty that aimed to produce particular futures, to understanding society as a set of probabilities and potentialities that must be modulated and controlled.[46] As a consequence of the above, the structure of cybernetics and control incorporates and makes productive a degree of indeterminacy by transforming noise into data which can then be used to apply corrective regulatory measures.[47] In actuality, without indeterminacy cybernetics and control would have no relevant object to act upon and instead would simply operate as deterministic machines. Social behavior and arguably life itself are only *social* and *living* to the degree that they escape, elude, or exceed being entirely determined, and as such society and life, as forms of indeterminacy, operate as the material substrate for

---

44 On a sobering and (I feel necessary) note, it is important to make clear that the forms of computation and data collection that were practiced by the Nazi regime were extremely meager and unsophisticated when compared to standard data collection and analysis practices today. Should a state equipped with contemporary computational and cybernetic power decide to undertake a similar project of extermination and genocide now, it would be unthinkably more efficient, expansive, and horrific.

45 For more on the preemptive logic at the center of contemporary European border and migration policy, see Farah Atoui's essay "The Calais Crisis" in this volume.

46 This can be read in relation to the historical shift that has occured from the logic of war to the logic of counterinsurgency and policing, which corresponds to the shift from sovereignty to security more generally as the principle *raison d'état*.

47 For more on the relationship between "information" and "data," see the collection *"Raw Data" Is an Oxymoron*, edited by Lisa Gitelman.

cybernetic regulation. The central innovation of the cybernetic organization of power, of the informatics of domination, and of control societies is that they do not treat indeterminacy as a *problem* to be prevented, eradicated, or overcome but as the *proper territory* of governmentality itself.

Following from this insight, it is unsurprising that the rise of cybernetics has been accompanied by the emergent centrality of crises.[48] It has become entirely banal to pick up a newspaper today and read separate stories about how the climate, economy, state, youth, universities, masculinities, immigration controls, church, family, and civilization itself are all in crisis. Whether ecological, economic, military, social, or political, crises aren't exceptional or ruptural and instead simply processually and incessantly act as the context for new corrective control measures. As Giorgio Agamben notes, in crises "the capability to decide once and for all disappears and the continuous decision-making process decides nothing" as they become approached simply as opportunities for governmentality to enact power in "the form of a perpetual *coup d'état*" that isn't interested in *maintaining order* but only *perpetually managing disorder*.[49]

The Control of Crisis, and The Crisis of Control

As much as the European migrant crisis was a *crisis of control*, in which border controls seemingly failed to prevent migrants from entering Europe, it was just as much a *crisis for control*, a historical object for the enactment of control operations. In this sense, both control and crisis acted as part of a larger calculus of cybernetic power that has come to be profusely and diversely expressed at planetary scales. For cybernetics to assume its place as the principal rationality of governmentality, society itself must also come to understand itself not as on a path towards a planned idealization but in a perpetual fall into new depths of crisis. This understanding of the world as being fundamentally in crisis is a consequence of the technical and epistemological structure of cybernetics, in which the world is approached as being in need of interminable correction because it is *literally sensed* as being increasingly out of control as more and more control mechanisms are implemented.

As more communication is established within cybernetic systems, greater amounts of indeterminacy are sensed, and as greater amounts of indeterminacy are sensed, a greater need for communication and control emerges. This corresponding relationship between the production of knowledge in cybernetic systems and the need to implement controls in relation to that knowledge acts as a conjunctive synergy between control and crisis more generally, an epistemological and political feedback loop within which an increase in either magnifies and multiplies the urgent need for the other. Control

---

48 It is worth noting that the internet was designed based upon the assumption that large sections of the network would inevitably fail as a consequence of nuclear war, natural disasters, or other catastrophes that could cut off communications. In other words, the architecture, infrastructure, and protocols of the internet were designed specifically in relation to the persistent threat of crisis and system failure. Consequently, the material instantiation of cybernetic control historically coincided with the material potential of crisis. See *Inventing the Internet* by Janet Abbate and *Protocol* by Alexander Galloway.

49 Agamben, "For a Theory of Destituent Power."

and crisis operate together as a singular structure of power that is just as interested in managing crises as it is invested in maintaining them, synchronously emerging as an assemblage of technologies, infrastructures, and policies that reinforce, reproduce, and sustain one another.

Central to any meaningful understanding of the migrant crisis is an analysis of the ways that crisis has emerged sympoietically with the ways it has been controlled, just as control has emerged from within the wakes of its own crisis.[50] The collection and aestheticized circulation of data emerging from the 2015–16 European migrant crisis in particular proved to be immensely productive for Frontex, and enabled a substantial expansion of its infrastructures and operations.[51] In 2015, at the supposed height of the migrant crisis, Frontex reported that an "unprecedented inflow of people" (numbering 710,000) had entered the EU without proper documentation, an increase of 428,000 from the same period in the previous year.[52] While it is unquestionably true that migration numbers increased in this period due to the revolutionary activity and subsequent armed conflicts that were unfolding in the Middle East over the same period, what is significant about this report in particular is that the *number of migrant detections* was used by Frontex to describe the *number of migrants* who had entered the EU without permission, a subtle but crucially important distinction with consequential political effects.

Due to the proliferation of controls at the EU's borders, it is unsurprising that a single migrant can come to be detected multiple times by the dispersed organization of various surveillance systems and security forces. After the reporter Nando Sigona inquired about the source of the figure, Frontex added a clarification at the end of the report stating that:

> "Frontex provides monthly data on the number of people detected at the external borders of the European Union. Irregular border crossings may be attempted by the same person several times in different locations at the external border. This means that a large number of the people who were counted when they arrived in Greece were again counted when entering the EU for the second time through Hungary or Croatia."[53]

Even with the clarification that seemed to call into question the "unprecedented inflow," the report nonetheless achieved the same ends by exaggerating the appearance of a crisis, an exceptional circumstance which necessitates a correspondingly exceptional increase in control measures. As Frontex Executive Director Fabrice Leggeri states about halfway through the document:

---

50 For a theorization of the liberatory (as opposed to oppressive) potential of sympoietics, see Donna Haraway's "Tentacular Thinking" and *Staying with the Trouble*.

51 I've used the word "crisis" throughout without any qualification because I'm interested in thinking through what *crises do* rather than *what they are*. While certainly there is a need to critique the ontology, temporality, and discursive structure of crisis, here instead I'll focus on how crisis acts *as a force*.

52 This particular Frontex statement mysteriously has been removed from their website, but the page is nonetheless accessible on the internet archive at: web.archive.org/web/20180208110351/http://frontex.europa.eu/news/710-000-migrants-entered-eu-in-first-nine-months-of-2015-NUiBkk.

53 Sigona, "Seeing double?"

"Urgent assistance is needed, especially for Greece and Italy, to help register and identify the new arrivals. Earlier this month, I requested the EU countries to provide Frontex
with additional border guards who can assist these two countries in dealing with such
unprecedented flows. I do hope we receive adequate contributions which will show the
true spirit of European solidarity."

The "unprecedented" nature of the flows here of course is suspect, especially considering that 20th-century Europe was reshaped by much larger mass migrations spurred
on by two world wars as well as by the migrations involved in European colonial projects. Nonetheless, the "unprecedented" framing isn't intended to function descrip-
tively but rather to help constitute a *present without precedent*, a situation that *cannot be
planned for* but certainly *can be controlled*.

Leggeri's call for "European solidarity" was later formalized and expanded upon in
Frontex's 2016 Risk Analysis Report (produced in 2015), which proposed the establishment of a Frontex Risk Analysis Centre, an information sharing network within the EU,
and an increase in personnel and funding in order to properly respond to the unprecedented crisis. In response, by the end of 2015 the EU Commission adopted new regulations that established the "European Border and Coast Guard Agency," a replacement
for Frontex's previous instantiation as the "European Agency for the Management of
Operational Cooperation at the External Borders."[54] Accompanying the name change
was a vast expansion of Frontex's powers which came to include the "right to intervene,"
allowing for the deployment of Frontex security forces alongside various national authorities, the establishment of a "Risk Analysis Centre" that would facilitate the circulation and aggregation of data concerning migration between EU member states, and
the formation of "European Return Intervention Teams" that would assist EU member
states with the deportation of undocumented migrants.[55] In the end, the migrant crisis didn't operate as a *crisis of control* at all, but rather as a *dramatic multiplication of it*,
indefinitely increasing the intensity and scope of Frontex's operations in almost every
domain of operations.

After the European Border and Coast Guard Agency was established, several more
measures were adopted to further regulate, police, and control migration as part of the
larger cybernetic organization of power. Following the 2015–16 crisis, Frontex went on
to extend its territorial reach through the establishment of "risk analysis cells" across
Africa as part of a broader strategy to externalize its borders, extending its control
and sensing capabilities well beyond the European continent.[56] These risk analysis
cells "analyze strategic data on cross-border crime in various African nation states
and support relevant authorities involved in border management," imposing the cybernetic logic of Frontex border control in a deterritorialized and neocolonial fashion
across Africa. Following Fred Moten and Stefano Harney, these risk analysis cells can
be understood as being a militarized offensive against *the surround*, an establishing
of fortressed colonies which in the same gesture also helps to reproduce the fantasy

54 "Frontex" isn't the legal name of the organization but is widely used as shorthand, emerging from a
   contraction of the French *frontières extérieures* (external borders).

55 European Union, "Proposals."

56 "Frontex opens first risk analysis cell in Niger."

of Europe's hostile exterior.[57] Following from Achille Mbembe, the risk analysis cells could equally be understood as necropolitically constituting part of a European *war machine*, a form of state power decoupled from territorial constraints and made to be "polymorphous and diffuse," a militarized and mobile cybernetic force that is paradoxically captured by sovereignty in order for sovereignty to be able exceed its own formal limits.[58] These measures, along with other complementary border externalization programs in the Mediterranean, Turkey, and elsewhere, displace the borders of the EU from being located *somewhere in particular* to being spectrally expressed across *many dynamic zones of control at once*. As an unbroken extension of Europe's colonial history, the exertion of European power on the territories that it has made exterior has come to be materially reinstantiated cybernetically.

As a formal culmination of all of these transformations, an experimental border technology named iBorderCtrl that automates some of the migration controls at official points of crossing is now being implemented as a pilot program in Hungary, Greece, and Latvia. Mobilizing affect recognition technologies and machine learning algorithms, migrants subjected to the program "use an online application to upload pictures of their passport, visa and proof of funds, then use a webcam to answer questions from a computer-animated border guard, personalised to the traveller's gender, ethnicity and language."[59] The system then analyzes "micro gestures" to determine if the migrant should be allowed to cross using regular security procedures, or if they require additional levels scrutiny from human border guards at points of entry.[60]

The instantiation of cybernetics occurs across diverse scales, with many distinct interoperable layers of communication and control coexisting with one another in nested regulatory hierarchies. While Frontex can be understood as having a particular cybernetic relation with member states expressed in the communication of data and subsequent reorganization of security resources, iBorderCtrl is an example of a cybernetic process enacted on the scale of the subject. As a migrant interacts with the application, their dividual inputs (gender, ethnicity, language, etc.) shape the system's output (questions, computer animations, etc.), which in turn generates a new affective response in the subject which is communicated back to and analyzed by the machine, triggering further algorithmically-driven adjustments to Frontex's communication and control systems. Here, the cybernetic expression of power is horrifically intimate. There is no singular architecture of power imposing itself uniformly upon a population here, but rather an algorithmic multiplicity of uniquely calibrated modulations executed uniquely and differentially in relation to each subject.

As cybernetic systems come to be technically integrated into more and more of society, crisis equally comes to assume its place not as an *event* but as the *persistent condition* of the present. As crisis becomes discursively, technically, and politically mobilized as a means of enacting more and more controls, and as more and more controls epistemologically exacerbate the appearance of various crises, the intensities of both crisis and control heighten. As Haraway notes, "the only way to characterize the informatics of domination is as a massive intensification of insecurity," within which all life

---

57 Harney and Moten, *The Undercommons*.

58 Mbembe, "Necropolitics."

59 "Smart lie-detection system."

60 For more on affect recognition, see the "AI Now Report 2018"

simply becomes another fluctuating input for a larger system that in the end is only oriented towards its own duration.[61] In control societies, crises operate principally as the context for techniques of governmentality and forms of power that are defined by the *intensifying control of insecurity*, and the *intensifying insecurity of control*.

In the end, Frontex's cybernetic project can perhaps be best understood by analyzing a word that Frontex itself enjoys using quite frequently: *risk*. Risk is an epistemological but also a political concept that is oriented by a probabilistic worldview that understands everything in terms of its possibility. Risk allows for a form of thinking that embraces uncertainty in order to be able to speculate in relation to it, anticipating different futures in an attempt to better control them in advance of their possible arrival. Risk becomes an object of analysis, from which algorithmic processes can simulate, project, predict, and prognose future trends based upon previously-collected data, producing virtualized futures that can be cybernetically acted upon in the present. Communication is the central means that cybernetics deploys to tame uncertainty, and the more communication that exists the more responsive feedback can become. In this sense, risk is not something to be minimized but rather becomes a productive element within cybernetic communication and control.

And what is crisis, after all, if not the *perpetual amplification of risk*? Like a microphone pointed towards its own speaker that multiplies ambient noise into ear splitting screeches, the instantiation of control in the world ontologically involves a corresponding amplification of risk. In this way, control doesn't only operate to minimize the distance between inputs and outputs in a negative regulatory feedback loop that aims to stabilize European projects of securitization and governance, but can also function to magnify and strengthen particular signals in order to expand the terrain of what is in need of control. Strategically spatialized and differentially enacted across the social field, *positive feedback*—long regarded as antithetical to cybernetic modes of control—thus becomes central to the production of risk and, in turn, the extension and intensification of both liberal and cybernetic techniques of power.[62] In the EU, as Frontex organizes to produce higher and higher volumes of data about migrants, and as that data is circulated across more and more communication nodes, crisis will proliferate and persist as crucially constitutive of the present, creating the conditions for ever expanding and intensifying control. From here, the only question of importance that remains is: What can possibly break the capture, communication, and control of cybernetic feedback?

---

61 Haraway, "A Cyborg Manifesto," 172.

62 As the anthropologist Jules Henry writes in a 1955 critique of Walter B. Cannon's theory of physiological homeostasis, which would become a major discursive and conceptual support for later cybernetic theories of feedback and control, "The theory [...] can also serve as a *vade mecum* for imperialism—namely, if you want to hold on to your empire, keep it off balance in such a way that only the motherland can maintain it in a steady state. When the outlying possessions are able to regulate themselves, they will want the freedom which their own self-regulatory mechanisms now permit them to achieve" ("Homeostasis, Society, and Evolution," 301).

The Uncontrollable

What is uncontrollable today? What is the remainder of control, what escapes and eludes control, and what threatens to undo it entirely? In other words, what is *out of control*, both *emerging from* control as well as *mobilized against* its totalizing instantiation? Haraway, Deleuze, and Tiqqun each suggest possible ways forward which interestingly and productively resonate with one another, and help to frame practices that have emerged in opposition to control in the EU. The subsequent pages are oriented by the understanding that resistance is a fundamentally speculative endeavour, for if we already knew what would undo control, control would have already come to be undone. Consequently, what follows should not be understood as prescriptive or exhaustive but rather as a means of probing the boundaries of possible resistance and revolt. Relatedly, the majority of the cases I'll be mobilizing in this section concern the practices of migrants themselves, not because I intend to fetishize or romanticize migrants but because, drawing upon an insight from Baruch Spinoza, those who are most affected by power are also those who most closely and deeply have knowledge of power's operations and forces. As such, the choice to emphasize migrant resistance and revolt is meant to help proliferate new opportunities for the adoption of those practices as well as acts of solidarity with them.

In her writing, Haraway embraces the figure of the cyborg, a particular hybridization of the biological and technical that she understands as having the potential to disrupt and undermine the informatics of domination. As she describes, cyborg politics are concerned with the "struggle against perfect communication, against the one code that translates all meaning perfectly [...] cyborg politics insist on noise and advocate pollution."[63] This position, oriented against the communication of cybernetic systems, against the transparency and emptiness of cybernetic subjectivity, and against the totalizing code of computation figures resistance against cybernetics as emerging both *within* and *against* its structure. This is not an understanding of resistance as constituting an outside or escape, but rather about an engagement with the cybernetic form as a terrain of political struggle that is structured by its imminence. Haraway later elaborates that "the main trouble with cyborgs, of course, is that they are the illegitimate offspring of militarism and patriarchal capitalism, not to mention state socialism. But illegitimate offspring are often exceedingly unfaithful to their origins. Their fathers, after all, are inessential."[64] Here, the crisis of cybernetics that has come to be expressed everywhere, in the family, in the economy, in the military, is also the condition of possibility for the emergence of *unfaithful subjects* that can come to be *incommensurable* with the logic of cybernetic feedback that produced them.

Building upon these insights, in the final section of *The Cybernetic Hypothesis* Tiqqun also articulates a series of measures they think can contribute to the abolition of cybernetic power. Towards the breaking down of communication, they write that "interference is the prime vector of revolt" and that "fog makes revolt possible," seemingly echoing Haraway's invocation of noise and pollution.[65] They later go on to elaborate that "fog is a vital response to the imperative of clarity, transparency, which is the

---

63 Haraway, "A Cyborg Manifesto," 172.

64 Haraway, "A Cyborg Manifesto," 151.

65 Tiqqun, "The Cybernetic Hypothesis."

first imprint of imperial power on bodies" and then quote Deleuze's insight that "the important thing is maybe to create vacuoles of non-communication, interrupters who escape control."[66] They understand all of these strategies as possibly:

> "Establishing a zone of opacity where people can circulate and experiment freely without bringing in the Empire's information flows [...] producing 'anonymous singularities,' recreating the conditions for a possible experience, an experience which will not be immediately flattened out by a binary machine assigning a meaning/direction to it."[67]

Both Tiqqun and Deleuze locate the possibility of resistance against cybernetics and control in forms of opacity and non-communication that both amplify noise and interfere or interrupt flows of information. Only from this does another kind of life, another kind of experience, become available that perhaps might come to smother and silence the cybernetic organization of power.

In the European context, there are a multiplicity of practices already underway that adopt similar orientations against cybernetic control, and which can serve as models for future resistance and revolt. However, before outlining some of these approaches it is worth briefly outlining why a particular approach *has not worked*, and what this might tell us about other practices of resistance. The passage of the European General Data Protection Regulation (GDPR) in 2016 (implemented in 2018) established a series of rights related to how individuals' personal data could be collected and processed. The law grants "data subjects" within the EU the right to request copies of the data collected about them, the right to have their data anonymized, and the right to have their data removed from an organization's servers should they withdraw their consent which is also known as the right to be forgotten.[68] The GDPR is best understood as a *liberal response to cybernetic power*, a form of legal action which is intended to shelter the liberal individual from the excesses of cybernetic power.

While the GDPR established the legal context for several lawsuits to be filed against large tech companies related to their mishandling of data, nonetheless the supposed protections promised by the GDPR are entirely compromised by the juridical power granted to Frontex and other security agencies which allow for those rights' arbitrary suspension. As part of the logic of the state of exception which defines security and sovereignty more generally, Frontex is allowed to collect and circulate the data of subjects that are considered to be involved in the "facilitation of illegal immigration, human trafficking, or other cross-border criminal activities" that includes but is not limited to the "name(s) of subject, nickname, gender, nationality/ies, names of known accomplices, organised crime group, registered business, personal address, safe house address, means of communications (telephone number, social media handles [...]), means of transportation (vehicle registration, boat name [...]), weapon, photograph(s), non-offence event, offence event, ethnicity, sexual orientation."[69] As explored in the first section of this paper, the liminality between refugee/asylum-seeker/migrant and human-trafficker/terrorist/criminal effectively allows all migrants to be covered by

---

66 Tiqqun, "The Cybernetic Hypothesis."

67 Tiqqun, "The Cybernetic Hypothesis."

68 Human Rights Watch, "The EU General Data Protection Regulation."

69 Wiewiórowski, "Opinion on a notification," 1–2.

such exceptions, doing essentially nothing to shield them from Frontex's cybernetic data-sharing programs. In other words, the *crisis of liberalism* emerges as complementary to the *instantiation of more intense controls* in the European context.

In light of all of the above, migrants now knowingly undertake their movement cognizant of their potential computation within and at the frontiers of the EU. While bodies were conditioned by the felt potential of a prison guard's surveillance in the panoptic structures of disciplinary societies, being coerced into internalizing the gaze of authority and instituting forms of self-discipline, today bodies are increasingly conditioned by the felt potential of becoming the subject of computation, being coerced into internalizing the logic of algorithmic capture in flexible forms of self-regulation and control. In this way, the logic of panopticism has been extended by the corresponding logic of *pancomputation*, in which life has come to be lived in relation to its potential computation.[70] In this context, the potentiality of computation is at least twofold, both expressed as the *potential that something will come to be computed within cybernetic control systems* as well as the ways in which *potentiality itself becomes the object of computation in cybernetic risk analysis*. In the first sense, actions, practices, gestures, behaviors, and relations all come to be enacted in relation to their potential computation, or in other words, the ways in which they may come to be subjected to the diverse algorithmic scrutiny and analysis of corporations, states, and other actors. Consequently, migrants come to move always in relation to and informed by the potential of that movement being tracked and analyzed by cybernetic systems. In the second sense, the movement of migrants becomes shaped in advance by the expectation that their movements have effectively already been predicted by machines based on previous data capture and computational analysis. As a consequence of this conjunctive operation, migrants always move autonomously in opposition to the control of migration, mobilizing a form of risk-taking that knowingly opposes and subverts the computational analysis and predictions of Frontex. Technically entangled together, power and resistance formally structure one another in a cascading series of control measures and escape maneuvers. In other words, the autonomy of movement is expressed as a series of subjective wagers that, through their risking everything, reaffirm the ineradicability of the autonomy that Frontex's algorithmic capture means to eradicate.

In response to all of the ways that contemporary migration is now controlled cybernetically, migrants have adopted strategies that aim to cultivate zone(s) of opacity and participate in the collective struggle against perfect communication. Emerging as what Deleuze called "vacuoles of noncommunication," communities adopt sets of practices and relations that constitute spaces opposed to the circuits and apparatuses of cybernetic power that at times act as refuges and at others as platforms from which to stage revolts.[71] The first and most popular of these strategies is the use of encrypted communication technologies by migrant communities that allow for forms of coordination and information exchange that are effectively opaque to cybernetic systems. Smartphones are used to establish secure communication channels with smugglers

70 While "Pancomputation" is linguistically inconsistent, mixing the Greek prefix "pan-" and the Latin "computare," I have purposefully chosen this hybridization in order to maximize both its conceptual ties to panopticism as well as its legibility for English-reading audiences, as the Ancient Greek word for "compute" (lógos) has a much broader meaning.

71 Deleuze and Negri, "Gilles Deleuze in conversation with Antonio Negri."

that help to facilitate migration into the EU, a process that often involves some degree of exploitation but also at times is undeniably liberatory. Schematic maps of migration paths into the EU that graphically diagram the various steps and phases involved in the crossing of many different borders (and the evasion of many different security forces and architectures) are circulated between various encrypted group chats. Once migrants arrive in the EU, those encrypted communication channels subsequently provide a means to connect with other migrants and establish novel migrant communities that don't expose them to the scrutiny or violence of national authorities. The widespread use of encryption by migrants is an asymmetric response to the "black box" algorithms of machine learning and artificial intelligence that are used to control migration and is a means of becoming opaque to their computational scrutiny and analysis.

Beyond the encryption of communications, migrants also engage in the destruction and/or forgery of various identity documents in order to either refuse "clarity, transparency, which is the first imprint of imperial power on bodies" in the case of the former or add pollution to the "one code that translates all meaning perfectly" in the case of the latter. Frontex organizes to counteract these practices that it claims "can ultimately undermine its internal security" by deploying specialized document experts at the EU's borders in order to "tackle the phenomenon in the comprehensive way by police, border and coast guard, and customs experts."[72] In a survey conducted by the EU-Funded European Migration Network on the challenges of identifying migrants, member states were asked "Are there good practices or challenges in your Member State regarding detecting ID-fraud?"[73] In response, Luxembourg wrote that "The main challenge is the amount of doubtful documents which make a huge backlog seen that there is not sufficient personnel in the special unit of the police to control all of them," Belgium replied that it had trouble processing the "submission of forged or falsified breeder documents (e.g. birth certificate) that can serve as a basis to obtain other (genuine) identification documents. Obviously these type of falsifications are more challenging to detect," while Estonia simply stated that "There are no specific good practices to outline." The overloading of communication systems with the noise of false document submissions as well as the simulation and multiplication of identity that subvert the process of coded translation that are rendered possible through document destruction and forgery are strategies presently being deployed by migrants to undermine the logic of control and cybernetic power.

In addition to the practices described above, migrants have participated in the production of opaque spaces at the fringes of the EU that help to facilitate their migration across the EU's borders. On the Northern coast of Morocco near the Spanish enclaves (colonies) of Ceuta and Melilla, migrants from across Africa have established informal communities in forests where they are able to avoid the repression of Spanish-funded Moroccan security forces as well as make preparations to attempt to cross over the layers of fortified barriers that are erected between the two territories.[74] These spaces also make it possible for migrants to share information and strategies concerning how best to evade the ever-shifting controls of the EU, acting as sites of resistant knowledge production and circulation where a collectively produced and maintained *memory of*

---

72 Europol, "Experts meet to tackle document fraud."

73 European Migration Network, "Ad-Hoc Query on Impact of false/forged documents."

74 For more context, see Alami, "Morocco Unleashes a Harsh Crackdown."

movement can persist even as communities of migrants circulate in and out of the area.[75] This spatial otherwise to the zones of control established by Frontex allows for the practices of individuals to accumulate and contribute not only to particular acts of migration, but also to the larger historical movement of migrants that is oriented against the instantiation of cybernetic power, a form of communication that isn't captured by or reducible to the communicative structures of control.

Yet another approach involves organizing against the material infrastructures of cybernetics. In response to Google's plan to build a new campus in Berlin's Kreuzberg, a neighborhood with a rich antifascist and anticapitalist history, a network of people that unsubtly go by the name "Fuck Off Google" organized against the plan and launched a series of actions opposed to the campus' construction that have included noise demonstrations, neighborhood discussions, and other events.[76] Citing Google's participation in mass surveillance and cooperation with authoritarian states, among other objections, the "Fuck Off Google" network advocates for the decentralization of communication as a means of counteracting the cybernetic organization of power. Shortly after the Google campus construction site was occupied by activists, Google formally withdrew from the plan to build in the neighborhood.[77] While surely a symbolic victory given the planetary scale of Google's data infrastructure, nonetheless this opposition to the infrastructure of control societies should be studied as a model for future approaches.

Most recently, a new migrant revolt has emerged as an outgrowth and elaboration of the *Gilets Jaunes* (Yellow Vests) movement which, at the time of writing this, has been unfolding for several months as the weekly emergence of road blockades, protest marches, and riots across France.[78] Going under the name *Gilets Noirs* (Black Vests), a network of hundreds of people organizing across dozens of migrant centers across France have staged a series of actions targeting the architectures and infrastructures of migrant surveillance, detention, and deportation. In May of 2019, the movement occupied a terminal at the Charles de Gaulle airport on the edge of Paris in opposition to Air France's cooperation with the French State in deporting migrants. In a statement released during the occupation, the *Gilets Noirs* claimed that: "We are the freedom to move," going on to write that the airport they were occupying was "above all else, a border. A border without walls or barbed wire. Nevertheless it marks some bodies [...] Those for whom migration comes easy are a minority coming from the bourgeois and/or white worlds. It's this world that colonizes and wages war. The entrance to their fortress is the airport. It is well guarded by the military, police, and cameras

---

75 For an artistic exploration of these communities, see Abdessamad El Montassir's artwork in this anthology as well as the accompanying text "The Adouaba Project" co-authored by Krista Lynes and Abdessamad El Montassir.

76 See www.fuckoffgoogle.de/. It may also be worthwhile looking at the chapter "Fuck off, Google" in the book *To Our Friends* authored by the Tiqqun-adjacent Invisible Committee.

77 See: www.mastodon.social/@FuckOffGoogle/100684556388297387 and wiki.fuckoffgoogle.de/index. php?title=MobilizeActions.

78 The political character of the Gilet Jaunes is heterogeneous and contradictory, involving far right nationalist protesters as well as antifascists, anarchists, communists, liberals, environmentalists, and others. For a compelling analysis of the ongoing uprising, see Zoubir, "A Vest That Fits All."

[...] This place embodies racism on a planetary scale."[79] The occupation lasted for a only a few hours before the *Gilets Noirs* left voluntarily, but nonetheless this action should be read as an experimental disruption of the planetary logistics of migrant expulsion. The airport is, after all, not only a nexus of many different expressions and circulations of power but is also one of the central laboratories for the deployment of cybernetic control, and the occupation of the airport terminal is a model for a collective practice of revolt that can disrupt the logistics of cybernetic power. Just as factory workers were understood as having the potential to undo the industrial capitalist system that produced them as proletarian subjects, so too should migrants be understood as having the potential to undo the cybernetic systems that produce them as illegal, and thus disposable/detainable/deportable subjects. What could collective revolts look like against the other architectures and infrastructures of cybernetics?

The present is defined by the accelerated instantiation and intensification of cybernetics, within which control and crisis conjunctively express themselves as an expansive form of power. As social support systems crumble beneath the weight of austerity, experimental cybernetic programs have funding rained down upon them by states and venture capitalists, and even the most dystopian science fiction has trouble keeping up with the latest innovations and technical developments of control societies. But power is never impermeable or invincible, and always imminently contains forces directed towards its eventual abolition. As control bends so as not to break, remaining endlessly flexible and responsive to whatever resistance emerges against it, undoing control entails not chipping away at it but breaking it entirely once and for all. Structured as totalities, control and crisis ultimately offer no way out other than through their total imminent negation, the process of which is surely imperceptibly underway but the outcome of which is unanticipatable. In this sense, all of the former analyses and critiques offered in this text should not be understood as gestures towards the reform of our society, but only towards the perpetually renewed possibility of its destruction. The present, undeniably, demands nothing less.

---

79 See La Chapelle Debout, Twitter post, May 19, 2019, 5:09 a.m.

Forensic Oceanography
Tracing Violence Within and Against
the Mediterranean Frontier's Aesthetic Regime[1]

Charles Heller and Lorenzo Pezzani

While the emergence of the Mediterranean's unequal mobility regime can be traced back to European imperial expansion towards the sea's southern shores in the nineteenth century, illegalized migration across the Mediterranean and fatalities at sea became structural and highly politicized phenomena only as of the end of the 1980s, in conjunction with the consolidation of the freedom of movement within the EU. With the Europeanization of migration policies, a truly European "color line" was institutionalized, as the populations who were excluded from accessing the European territory were marked out within a matrix of race and class. However, as a result of the perpetuation of the systemic conditions underpinning migrants' movements towards Europe—in particular the need for migrant labor, global inequalities, and existing migrant networks—the illegalization of certain categories of migrants only resulted in their movement operating in an increasingly clandestine form, in particular by crossing the sea on overcrowded vessels.[2] In the attempt to control the Mediterranean, now corresponding to the extremities of European space and transformed into a vast frontier zone, European states have deployed a vast array of bordering practices and techniques to contain and channel migrants' movements. Crucially, since the early 2000s, the EU has increasingly outsourced border control to authoritarian regimes in North Africa to contain migrants on their shores.

These policies have never more than temporarily succeeded in stemming migrants' crossings, and for every route that was sealed off, several new ones—often longer and more dangerous—were opened. This dialectic between control and escape which results from this mobility conflict has had a harrowing human cost: more than 30,000 migrants have perished at sea since the end of 1980.[3] Most migrants' deaths across

---

1 This article draws on conversations that have taken place in many different contexts, and we are indebted to the friends and colleagues who have shared their thoughts with us in each one of them. In particular we would like to thank Thomas Keenan, Maria Iorio and Raphael Cuomo, Paolo Cuttitta, Maurice Stierl, Martina Tazzioli, Michael Neuman, Aurélie Ponthieu, and Julian Koberer for their insights.

2 De Genova, "Spectacles of Migrant 'Illegality'."

3 UNITED for Intercultural Action, "List of 35,597 documented deaths of refugees and migrants due to the restrictive policies of "Fortress Europe."

the Mediterranean frontier have not only occurred *at* sea, but *through* the sea, which has been turned into a deadly liquid as a result of the EU's exclusionary policies which precaritize their crossings. The sea's "geopower"[4] has become embedded in a form of killing operating without state actors directly touching migrants' bodies, in which violence is rather inflicted in a *mediated* way, through water: it is the liquid element that transmits the violence of state policies to the bodies and lives of migrants.[5] The precarious travelers whose lives are taken during their attempt to cross the Mediterranean frontier are thus the victims of what we call "liquid violence," the specific modalities of which are, as we will see, ever changing.[6]

To contest the EU's liquid violence, we initiated the Forensic Oceanography project in 2011.[7] In that period, with the toppling of the authoritarian regimes in North Africa that had served as the EU's outsourced border guards, migrants were able to 're-open' maritime routes to the European continent. In so doing, they ushered in a phase of increased turbulence in the Euro-Mediterranean border regime. Since then, we have sought to understand and document the shifting modalities of the liquid violence operating across the maritime space between Libya and Italy (the central Mediterranean) with the aim of contesting them in legal forums and beyond. In this article, we chart some of these momentous shifts, and reflect upon the way we sought to respond to them, focusing in particular on three moments of change: The first is the moment of rupture in the border regime marked by the Arab uprisings, which led European states to adopt recurrent *practices* of non-assistance exemplified by the left-to-die boat. The second corresponds to the lethal *policies* of non-assistance implemented by European states in terminating the Italian *Mare Nostrum* "humanitarian and security" operation in the aim of deterring migrants from crossing. Finally, the third charts the combined process of criminalizing civilian rescue initiatives and (re-)outsourcing border control to the Libyan coast guard. Distinct forms of violence have emerged within each of the phases, which in turn posed new challenges to register their traces and translate them into legal violations for which states might be held accountable.

In our attempt to contest the shifting modes of violence operating at the maritime frontier, it has been essential for us to understand two dimensions that are central to organizing the way the maritime frontier operates. First, the mobility conflict—of

---

4 Grosz, "Geopower."

5 Here, we draw on Sean Cubitt's expanded understanding of mediation, which, beyond technologically mediated communication processes between humans, he defines as "the material processes connecting human and nonhuman events [...]. Mediation is the primal connectivity shared by human and nonhuman worlds." (*Finite Media*, 3). The way in which, in another text, he talks about sunlight as that which "mediates the sun and the earth" ("How to Connect Everyone with Everything"), further points to the understanding of mediation that inspires us here.

6 While the Mediterranean is according to the International Organization for Migration the deadliest crossing in the world, it is far from being the only place in which the very geo-physical characteristics of the environment have been enlisted and harnessed as crucial tools of border control. From the arid lands of the Sonoran and Sahara Desert to the rugged mountain passes in the Alps or between Iran and Turkey, or the oceans encircling Australia, the US, Europe, and the Arabian Peninsula, migrants have been forced to traverse more and more inhospitable and hazardous terrains in the hope that the risk of injury and death they will face might deter them from attempting the crossing. See Heller and Pezzani, "Hostile Environment(s)."

7 See the "Left-to-Die Boat" project: www.forensic-architecture.org/case/left-die-boat/.

which the sea has become the liquid terrain—opposes migrants' movements not only to the bordering policies and practices of states, but to a multiplicity of other actors. It sees international diplomatic disputes between states, conflicts between distinct agencies within a single state—such as the coast guard, the police and the military—and the confrontation of a multiplicity of non-state actors such as international and non-governmental organizations, fishermen, shipping companies, and their trade associations, researchers, journalists, artists—all of which contribute, in various ways, to enabling or limiting migrants' movement in a more or less deliberate way.

A crucial axis that organizes this wide spectrum of actors and their relations are the logics of *security* and *humanitarianism*, both of which have become fundamental rationales, discourses and practices that cut across governmental and nongovernmental actors.[8] The coexistence and circulation of these logics within each actor and within the border regime as a whole, is always fraught with tensions, and the balance between them is in constant flux, with migrants being constituted simultaneously as "a life to be protected *and* a security threat to protect against."[9] While, as Paolo Cuttitta reminds us, these fluctuations leave fundamentally unchanged the "restrictive migration and border regime" imposed by the EU,[10] they do have an important impact on the conditions of migrants' crossings and the changing modalities of liquid violence we chart below. Each of the shifts we analyze corresponds to a reorganization of the logics of security and humanitarianism.

Second, while the violence of the maritime frontier is mediated by water, it is also mediated by images and a constantly shifting *aesthetic regime*. We use the term "aesthetic" in the sense underlined by Jacques Rancière as what presents itself to sensory experience.[11] Distinct conditions of (in)visibility and (in)audibility are imposed onto the maritime frontier by states' restrictive policies, but also shaped, transformed, and contested by the multiple other actors mentioned above, including of course migrants themselves, and their various media. Images, surveillance technologies, and their use within states' and migrants' strategies of (in)visibility shape the modalities of liquid violence in decisive ways. In turn, the changing configurations of security and humanitarian logics have distinct aesthetic dimensions, with the (in)visibility of migrants' deaths in particular oscillating between concealment within the security logic and spectacularization in the humanitarian one. Each of these shifts have forced us to reposition our own practice, and seek to exercise anew what we call a *"disobedient gaze"*—revealing what state actors have sought to conceal, and not revealing that which they seek to shed light upon. In what follows then, we chart the changes at the nexus of the modalities of liquid violence, the articulation of humanitarian and security logics, and the reconfiguration of the aesthetic regime operating at the maritime frontier, and reflect upon the way each of them has shaped our project. We first discuss the aesthetic regime within and against which our project sought to position itself.

---

8 Fassin, *Humanitarian Reason*.

9 Vaughan-Williams, *Europe's Border Crisis*, 3.

10 Cuttitta, "Repoliticization Through Search and Rescue?", 649.

11 Rancière, *The Politics of Aesthetics*, 13.

The Mediterranean Frontier's Aesthetic Regime of (in)Visibility

At the EU's maritime frontier, we find at work a complex and ambivalent aesthetic regime of (in)visibility, inextricably bound to the way the border regime itself operates. As a result of their illegalization through the EU's policies of exclusion, people who decide to migrate despite legal denials are forced to resort to an informal infrastructure of mobility: transnational networks of migrants who exchange information and services, the smuggling networks they resort to for a portion of their journey, as well as actual means of transport such as overused and overcrowded boats. Migrants are *illegalized*—their illegality is a product of state laws—and therefore they must migrate *clandestinely*, a term with etymological connotations of hiddenness and secrecy, and seek to cross borders undetected. The EU's migration regime thus imposes a particular "partition of the sensible" in the terms of Jacques Rancière: it creates particular conditions of (dis)appearance, (in)audibility, (in)visibility.[12] As opposed to the logic of clandestinity, what all security-oriented agencies aiming to control migration try to do is to *shed light* on migration and in particular on acts of unauthorized border crossing in order to make the phenomenon of migration more knowable, predictable and governable. To this effect, a vast dispositif of control has been deployed at the maritime frontier of the EU, one made of mobile patrol vessels but also of an assemblage of multiple surveillance technologies, through which border agents seek to achieve the most complete possible "integrated maritime picture" in the aim of detecting and intercepting migrants' vessels. These technologies range from vessel tracking technologies, coastal and shipborne radars, to optical and synthetic aperture radar imagery. Together, they compose what Karin Knorr Cetina has called a "scopic system": "an arrangement of hardware, software, and human feeds that together function like a scope: like a mechanism of observation and projection."[13]

However, the partition of the sensible of the EU's maritime borders is more ambivalent than this binary opposition would let us believe. For their part, migrants in distress may do everything they can to be seen so as to be saved from drowning. In this, they are not only seeking to avert the possibility of their imminent death, but also seeking to use the humanitarian logic that has become embedded in the practices of all actors at sea—including those whose very aim is preventing illegalized migration—to forward their own objective of crossing borders. Conversely, border agents not only attempt to deliberately hide the structural violence inherent to practices of policing maritime migration—thus allowing these practices to perpetuate themselves in full impunity—they may also choose *not to see* migrants in certain instances, considering that rescuing them at sea entails the responsibility for disembarking them and processing their asylum claims and/or deporting them. This has led to repeated cases of

---

12   In a synthetic article, Jacques Rancière argues that politics is not the exercise of power or struggle for power, but first resides in the "configuration of a space as political, the framing of a specific sphere of experience." It is precisely "that distribution and re-distribution of times and spaces, places and identities, that way of framing and re-framing the visible and the invisible, of telling speech from noise and so on" that Rancière calls "the partition of the sensible." For Rancière then, "to the extent that it sets up such scenes of dissensus" politics can thus be characterized as an "aesthetic" activity ("The Politics of Aesthetics").

13   Knorr Cetina, "The Synthetic Situation," 64.

migrants who have been left abandoned to drift at sea, as in the left-to-die boat case we will discuss below. In all these different cases, visibility and invisibility then do not designate two discrete and autonomous realms but, rather, an entangled topological continuum.

We find the same ambivalence at work in photographic and video imagery of the maritime frontier. In addition to the different remote sensing means described above, patrol vessels are also equipped with cameras—those of border guards or of "embedded journalists"—which are used to document the moment of encounter between illegalized migrants and those seeking to police their movement. This results in a highly controlled and ambivalent *spectacularization of borders*, incisively analyzed by Nicholas de Genova.[14] In the countless images of intercepted/rescued boats that are circulated by state agencies and the press, the threat of illegalized migration and the securitization work of border control are simultaneously made visible and naturalized, following a circular logic. If migrants are being intercepted through militarized means, it is because they are a threat. If they are a threat, then they must be policed by all means. The sense of migration as threat is only exacerbated by the profusion of similar images, which suggest an invasion of European space by those who have been constructed as radically other—racialized and impoverished migrants from the global South.

These racialized representations of migration at Europe's external maritime borders, which produce "a dominant associative notion of irregular migration to non-whites bodies," shape in turn racialized border control within Europe, as "any non-white body on the move" is perceived as a potential 'illegal' traveller that must be checked.[15] What emerges then is a fundamental link between the three distinct dimensions of migrants' *exposure* emphasized by Georges Didi-Huberman:[16] the visual exposure of illegalized migrants, their being "ex-posed" (rendered outside and excluded from a given community), and the exposure of their bodies to conditions of precarity and death. The exposure operated by state actors is however highly selective. While focusing on the *scene* of border enforcement, the conditions that lie before and after—the multiple forms of violence migrants sought to escape in the first place, the illegalization of their movement through policies of exclusion, the future exploitation of illegalized migrant labor in European economies—remain hidden as *obscene* supplements.

However, as we will see in more detail in the course of this chapter, the regime of (in)visibility imposed by the border spectacle is constantly changing, and is in particular shaped by the unstable equilibrium between the logics of security and humanitarianism. If within a logic of security migrants are constituted as a threat to Europe, within the humanitarian perspective they are rather victims whose lives are threatened—either in their countries of origin or in the process of crossing borders.[17] Illegalized migrants crossing the sea thus operate as an inherently unstable and "floating" signifier,[18] and their (in)visibilization is equally fluctuating.

While the deaths of migrants may at times remain hidden, at others they are spectacularized by state actors to cover the violence of borders with a humanitarian var-

---

14 De Genova, "Spectacles of migrant 'illegality'."

15 Keshavarz and Snodgrass, "Orientations of Europe."

16 Didi-Huberman, *Peuples exposés, peuples figurants*.

17 Chouliaraki and Stolic, "Rethinking Media Responsibility in the Refugee 'Crisis'."

18 Hall, "Race, the Floating Signifier."

nish: border control becomes framed as an act of saving migrants, occluding the fact that state policies endanger their movement in the first place. The spectacularization of migrants' distress and deaths at sea is also mobilized by non-governmental actors to contest the lethal effects of borders. As these examples show, the sensing practices operating within this aesthetic regime do not simply document the violence of borders, but actively participate in it. Whether through the logic of the spectacle or that of state secrecy, the very act of exclusion that underpins the EU's politics of migration takes place as well within and through its various visualizations. Struggling for the rights of migrants, then, means also intervening in this regime of (in)visibility and challenging the very borders of what can be seen and heard. For these reasons, understanding the shifting and ambivalent configurations of the aesthetic regime operating at the Mediterranean frontier has been fundamental at each stage of Forensic Oceanography's successive projects, which have always needed to navigate and constantly re-negotiate a fine and unstable line between complicity, resistance and evasion.

Exercizing a disobedient gaze:
Reconstructing the Liquid Traces of the Left-to-Die Boat Case

Our project began at a time when the border regime was highly securitized and both migrants' deaths and the violent (in)action of states were largely kept in the shadows. As both migrants' crossings and fatalities at sea increased again in 2011 in the wake of the Arab uprisings, and with indications of state actors' responsibility for this loss of lives, we launched the Forensic Oceanography research project within the wider Forensic Architecture agency.

Historically, forensic science can be understood as "a disciplinary project that affirms the power of states."[19] Since at least the beginning of the twentieth century, states have relied on experts deploying scientific methods to find *traces* of events under investigation so as to reconstruct them to prove or disprove a crime—an (in)action that constitutes a violation of legal norms. In doing so, states have often also policed and silenced the victims of their own violence, pitting the alleged objectivity of technology and science against the fallibility of human testimony. Our aim has been to somehow reverse this process and reinvent forensics as a counter-hegemonic practice that could be used by non-governmental actors to hold state and other non-state actors accountable for their crimes, focusing on events that occur in zones outside conventional state jurisdiction and beyond established frames of criminal justice.[20]

However, if the traces considered by the inventors of forensic science since the times of Edmond Locard (1877–1966) could be stains, fingerprints, or gunpowder, etc., today events are potentially registered by an infinite amount of materials and media, from phone communication to payment data, from videos shot with mobile phones to satellite images and vehicle tracking data, from sound recordings to rubble analysis.[21] Despite the limits and even ambivalences of strategic litigation which we discuss further on, we considered that forcing states to account for the practices and

---

19 Weizman, "Introduction: Forensics," 10.

20 Weizman, "Introduction: Forensics."

21 Ruffel and McKingley, *Geoforensics*; Schuppli, "Walk-Back Technology."

policies that lead to migrants' deaths had the potential to block the forms of border violence that we were observing at the maritime frontier. We thus began to explore the ways in which we might take this approach to the sea. In the process, however, we further had to challenge a well-ingrained imaginary of the maritime space as an empty expanse without history, where all traces of past events seems to be constantly erased by winds and currents.[22]

Our project was sparked by a 2011 incident that came to be known as the 'left-to-die boat' case.[23] At the height of the NATO-led military intervention in Libya, during which more than 38 warships were deployed off the coast, 72 migrants fleeing the warzone were left to drift in the central Mediterranean Sea for fourteen days. 63 human lives were lost, despite the survivors calling Father Zerai (an Eritrean priest based in Rome) via satellite phone, despite distress signals sent out to vessels navigating in this area, and despite several encounters with military aircrafts and a warship. As we demonstrated in our report, this was not an isolated incident, but rather the outcome of recurrent conflicts between Italy and Malta with regard to rescue at sea, as well as the aim of the military actors to restrict their activities to military objectives and not be seized by humanitarian ones.

This was a time, then, when a security logic dominated the practices of the different actors operating in the central Mediterranean, and when the humanitarian practice of rescue was instead repeatedly avoided despite maritime law imposing on all actors the duty to assist passengers in distress at sea. While survivor testimonies indicated increasing instances of non-assistance, during this period the Mediterranean appeared as a "black box" for civilian actors in which the capacity to see and document the events occurring at sea was nearly entirely in the hands of state actors—with the exception of Father Zerai's unique capacity to *listen* to the distress of migrants at sea and pressure states into complying with their obligations. The challenge we faced as we embarked on our investigation in support of the nine survivors and a coalition of NGOs, was precisely in wresting the capacity to sense the sea away from state actors, so as to make the violence of abandonment visible and breach the impunity in which it was being perpetrated.

Images could be of only limited assistance in the process. While several photographs were taken at different moments during these tragic events by military personnel as well as the passengers themselves, only one of them—taken by a French surveillance aircraft during the first day of the migrants' journey—was released in response to a parallel investigation by the Council of Europe[24] (Fig. 6). In the absence of revelatory images documenting these events, our investigation had to rely on the "weak signals" that underpin truth production practices in the field, which Thomas Keenan (after Allan Sekula) has called "counter-forensics."[25]

---

22 We further elaborate on this aspect in Heller and Pezzani, "A Disobedient Gaze."

23 For our reconstruction of these events, see our report: www.forensic-architecture.org/wp-content/uploads/2014/05/FO-report.pdf. Our video animation *Liquid Traces* summarizes our findings: www.vimeo.com/128919244.

24 Parliamentary Assembly of the Council of Europe (PACE), "Lives lost in the Mediterranean Sea."

25 Keenan, 'Getting the Dead to Tell Me What Happened."

6.

Reconnaissance picture of the left-to-die-boat taken by a French patrol aircraft on 27 March 2011

By corroborating survivors' testimonies with information provided by the vast apparatus of remote sensing technologies that have transformed the contemporary ocean into a digital archive, we assembled a *composite image* of the events. The expertise of an oceanographer allowed us to model and reconstruct the drifting boat's trajectory, and satellite imagery analysis to detect the presence of a large number of vessels in the vicinity of the drifting migrant boat that did not heed their calls for help (Figure 7.1 and 7.2).

While, as we discussed above, these technologies are often used for the purpose of policing and detecting illegalized migration as well as other 'threats,' we repurposed them to find evidence of the failure to render assistance. Through our work on the 'left-to-die' case, we sought to put into practice a *disobedient gaze* that used some of the same sensing technologies as border controllers, but redirected their 'spotlight' from unauthorized acts of border-crossing, to state and non-state practices violating migrants' rights. We conceived of this gaze as "*[aiming] not to disclose what the regime of migration management attempts to unveil—clandestine migration—but unveil that which it attempts to hide, the political violence it is founded on and the human rights violations that are its structural outcome.*"[26]

---

26 Heller and Pezzani, "A Disobedient Gaze," 294.

7.1

*Envisat satellite image
showing the modelled
position of the "left-to-die
boat" and the nearby
presence of several military
vessels who did not intervene
to rescue the migrants*

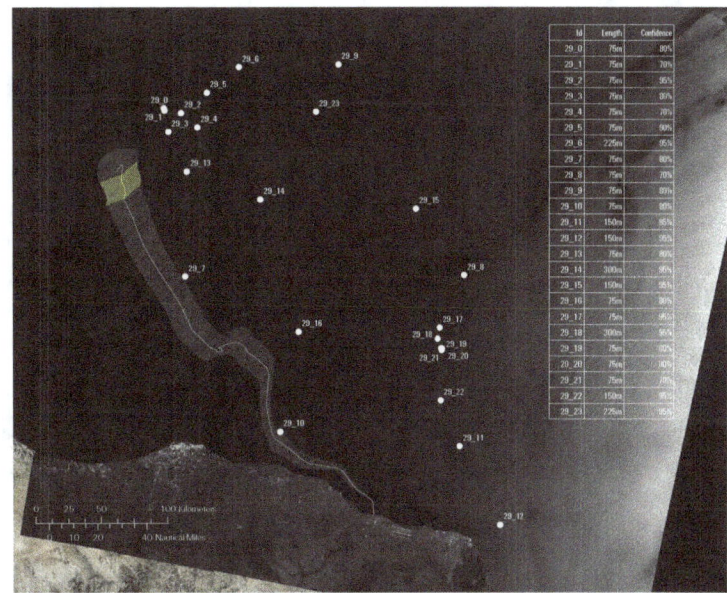

7.2

*Chain of events
in the "left-to-die boat"*

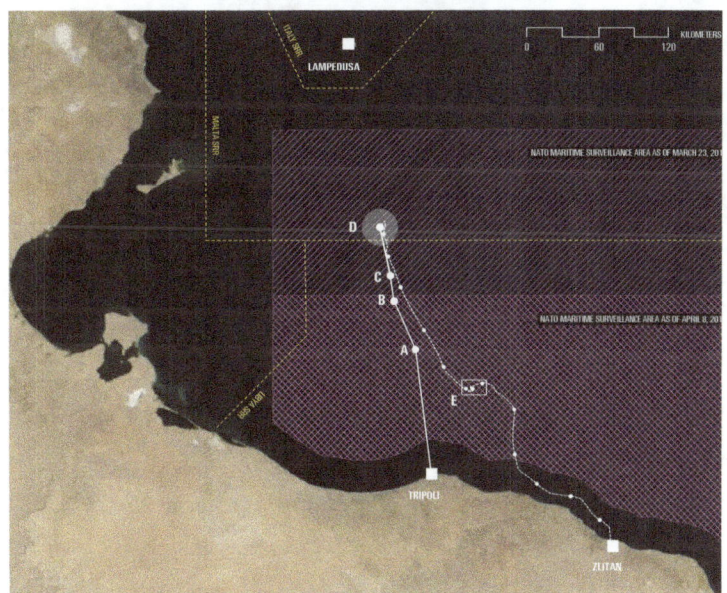

© Forensic Oceanography and SITU Research,
Report on the Left-to-Die Boat Case (both)

In addition to reconstructing the traces of events at sea, crucial to our project was the task of *spatializing* the practices of actors and inscribing them within the political geography of the sea. At sea, the moment of border crossing is expanded into a process that can last several days and extend across an uneven and heterogeneous territory that sits outside the exclusive reach of any single polity. The spatial imaginary of the border as a line without thickness dividing isomorphic territorial states is here stretched into a deep zone "in which the gaps and discrepancies between legal borders become uncertain and contested."[27] The maritime territory constitutes, then, a space of "unbundled sovereignty" in Saskia Sassen's terms,[28] one in which sovereign rights and obligations are disaggregated from each other and extended across complex and variegated jurisdictional spaces.

The multiple jurisdictional regimes that crisscross the Mediterranean have allowed states to simultaneously extend their sovereign privileges through forms of mobile government and elude the responsibilities that come with them.[29] Facing their mobile and fleeting practices of bordering and (non-)assistance, we have sought to inscribe as precisely as possible the lethal events within specific jurisdictional zones and boundaries (such as SAR zones, but also in the case of the left-to-die boat, NATO's maritime surveillance area) so as to assign responsibility for them. While the fragmentation of juridical regimes at sea often allows for the evasion of responsibility, we have sought to mobilize this very fragmentation strategically toward the multiplication of potentially liable actors who could be held accountable for not abiding by the duty to rescue inscribed in maritime law. Not only did our reconstruction of the migrants' drift allow us to demonstrate that the migrants had remained within NATO's maritime surveillance area during their 14 days of deadly drift (see Figures 8.1 & 8.2), but by identifying many ships in the vicinity of the migrants' boat our report allowed the NGO coalition we collaborated with to file several legal cases against the different states—including France, Spain, Italy and Belgium—whose assets had taken part in the NATO-led operation, and who shared a degree of responsibility for the death of the 63 passengers.[30] While these different complaints did have an impact insofar as they put pressure on state actors to change their practices, eight years after the events the legal process is still ongoing and none of the actors involved has been condemned by a court for their practices of non-assistance. Aware of the structural limitations of "international justice to isolate a few culpable individuals while leaving the social and economic hierarchies of a society intact,"[31] we have also attempted to multiply the *forums* where the violence against migrants at sea could be debated and challenged: not only established legal arenas but also emerging social, political and cultural spaces, both institutional and informal.[32]

---

27 Neilson, "Between Governance and Sovereignty," 126.

28 Sassen, *Territory, Authority, Rights*.

29 Steinberg, *The Social Construction of the Ocean*; Gammeltoft-Hansen and Alberts, "Sovereignty at Sea."

30 "63 migrants morts en Méditerranée : des survivants poursuivent leur quête de justice."

31 Weizman, "Introduction: Forensis," 29.

32 In negotiating the tension between these different forms of intervention, we have been inspired by what critical race theorist Mari Matsuda has called a dualist approach. "There are times," she wrote, "to stand outside the courtroom door and say 'this procedure is a farce, the legal system is corrupt, justice will never prevail in this land as long as privilege rules in the courtroom.' There are times to

As the events of the left-to-die case demonstrate, the initiation of the Forensic Oceanography project was marked by a context in which a security logic dominated the maritime frontier, and with it an aesthetic regime of invisibilizing migrants' deaths while spectacularizing their interceptions. In response, Forensic Oceanography's strategy to make up for the near absence of available images documenting the lethal events of the left-to-die boat case was to create a composite image of events, assembling the traces generated by multiple sensing devices. In so doing, we opened a fissure in the partition of the sensible imposed by states, and in the impunity that prevailed for migrants' deaths. While the methods we developed in the process remain important to this day, the profound shifts in the modalities of violence and the aesthetic regime that emerged as part of rapid processes of humanitarianization and de-humanitarianization of the maritime border we observed in the wake of the October 2013 shipwrecks near Lampedusa forced us to reposition ourselves and adapt our research and aesthetic strategies accordingly.

A Forensics of the EU's policies of non-assistance: Mare Nostrum and its Demise

On October 3, 2013, a boat carrying more than 500 migrants sank less than one kilometer from the coast of Lampedusa, causing the death of at least 366 people and a public outcry.[33] Not only did this boat manage to cross the multiple layers of surveillance surrounding Lampedusa undetected, but survivors of this incident also claimed that, a few hours before the boat capsized, two or three fishermen's ships ignored their calls for help (this has not been confirmed or disproven to date). On October 11, another boat carrying over 400 people sank after rescue deployment was delayed for over 5 hours due to the conflicting responsibility of the Italian and Maltese Coast Guards, and more than 200 people died.[34] Since both of these tragedies involved practices of non-assistance, they initially appeared as a tragic repetition of the left-to-die boat, with an even more exorbitant death toll. In hindsight, however, we can see that these shipwrecks were indices of much deeper changes.

In the wake of these two tragic shipwrecks, migrants' deaths suddenly gained tremendous public visibility as the haunting underwater images of the Lampedusa wreck circulated in the international press, forcing policy-makers to articulate their positions. During his visit to Lampedusa, Jose Manuel Barroso's, then President of the European Commission, posed in front of the coffins containing the bodies of the shipwrecked in the hangar of Lampedusa airport, which was transformed into something in between an improvised media center and a mortuary. In his statement on October 8, 2013, he declared: 'We in the European Commission, [...] believe that the European Un-

---

stand inside the courtroom and say 'this is a nation of laws, laws recognizing fundamental values of rights, equality and personhood.' Sometimes, as Angela Davis did, there is a need to make both speeches in one day." ("When the First Quail Calls," 298).

33 See Watch the Med, "At least 366 people dead in wreck 1 km from Lampedusa": www.watchthemed. net/reports/view/31.

34 See Watch the Med, "Guardia Civil runs over refugee boat near Lanzarote": www.watchthemed.net/index.php/reports/view/33.

ion cannot accept that thousands of people die at its borders.' Despite denouncing the deaths of migrants as unacceptable, Barroso's conclusion was *not* to take responsibility for these deaths or to challenge the EU's exclusionary border regime which has proven so deadly. In the same speech, Barroso announced instead an increase in Frontex's budget and the launch of Eurosur, the European Border Surveillance System—that is, the continuation of a predominantly security-based approach to migration. This policy, however, was now less framed as a response to the "risk" that the movements of illegalized migrants was presumed to constitute for the EU than to the risk they faced in attempting the crossing.

Barroso's speech, and the mise-en-scène of his and other policy makers' compassion, are exemplary of what we may refer to as the *humanitarianization* of the border. What William Walters refers to as the "humanitarian border" emerges "once it becomes established that border crossing has become, for thousands of migrants seeking, for a variety of reasons, to access the territories of the global North, a matter of life and death. It crystallizes as a way of governing this novel and disturbing situation, and compensates for the social violence embodied in the regime of migration control."[35] While rescues at sea have long been the humanitarian counterpart of the illegalization of migrants, the October 2013 shipwrecks marked a turning point where border control operations themselves became framed as *acts of saving*, all while European states perpetuated their exclusionary border regime.

Days later, Italian authorities, faced with the impossibility of ignoring the public outcry caused by these shipwrecks, single-handedly launched what has been by far the largest "humanitarian and security" operation in the Mediterranean: *Mare Nostrum*.[36] In the framework of this operation, an unprecedented number of Italian Navy ships proactively patrolled close to the Libyan shores to rescue migrants and disembark them on Italian territory, thus marking a clear shift away from the principled reluctance observed in previous years to initiate rescue operations. Humanitarianism became a central dimension of this mission, both at the discursive and operational level, transforming as well the conditions of (in)visibility imposed on migrants' crossings and state activities.

As Martina Tazzioli has importantly highlighted, with *Mare Nostrum* the border spectacle was temporarily transformed and humanitarianized, although always in ambiguous ways.[37] Now, instead of foregrounding the securitized scene of neutralizing the threat of migration through border control, *Mare Nostrum* activities focused public attention on the good "scene of rescue," recasting the role of the state and the military as that of a merciful savior.[38] However, the "humanitarian border spectacle"[39] was just as selective in the (in)visibilization of the maritime frontier as the primarily security-oriented spectacle that had preceded it: the good scene of rescue ended with disembarkation, and the illegalization and future exploitation of migrants onshore continued to remain hidden, as did their previous identification and fingerprinting that (at times) began on military ships while still at sea. Because the policies that pre-

35 Walters, "Foucault and Frontiers," 138.

36 "Italy launches Mare Nostrum, 400 more saved."

37 Tazzioli, *Spaces of Governmentality*, Tazzioli, "The Desultory Politics Of Mobility."

38 Chouliaraki and Musarò, "The Mediatized Border."

39 Cuttitta, "'Borderizing' the Island."

caritize migrants' crossing were perpetuated, the large-scale rescue activities did not prevent them from dying in even greater numbers as the scale of crossings increased with the exodus of Syrians. In this sense, just like the spectacularization of the Lampedusa deaths, the display of heroic rescue activities occluded political responsibility for migrant deaths.

Furthermore, the control of the capacity to know, document and produce imagery of the maritime frontier remained firmly in state hands. Even though select cases of migrants' deaths as well as military-led rescue operations were now spectacularized, lending a sense of profound change in the aesthetic regime of the maritime frontier, there were deeper continuities in what was occluded by the border spectacle in both its security and humanitarian variants. Importantly, this phase demonstrated that the mourning of migrants' deaths, which until then the border regime had attempted to keep largely hidden, could be rendered hyper-visible and spectacularized, without this entailing any increased accountability for their deaths.

This situation posed a challenge to Forensic Oceanography's strategy of demanding accountability by making deaths visible, a challenge that emerged even more acutely as the Italian-led humanitarian turn came under attack from its European counterparts, leading to a shift in the modality of liquid violence perpetrated by states from *practices* to *policies* of non-assistance. While the causal relation between policies of closure and migrant deaths had been undermined by the humanitarian border spectacle, re-establishing this connection would become the central task of our "Death by Rescue" report.[40]

The break with practices of non-assistance and the strength of the humanitarian logic marked by *Mare Nostrum* proved short-lived, as the operation was soon criticized for allegedly constituting a "pull-factor" for people crossing the Mediterranean. The UK Foreign Office Minister, Lady Anelay, exemplified this position when she stated "We do not support planned search and rescue operations in the Mediterranean. We believe that they create an unintended 'pull factor,' encouraging more migrants to attempt the dangerous sea crossing and thereby leading to more tragic and unnecessary deaths."[41] Translated in more frank terms by François Crépeau, United Nations Rapporteur on the rights of migrants, this statement amounted to saying "let them die because this is a good deterrence."[42] As the balance of the border regime tilted once again towards securitization, European member states refused to Europeanize *Mare Nostrum* as Italy requested, and Italy terminated the operation at the end of 2014. As of November 1, 2014, the Frontex-led Triton operation was launched instead, deploying fewer vessels in an area further from the Libyan coast, and prioritizing border control instead of rescue. Through this operational shift, the EU and its member states hoped to make migrant crossings more difficult, so as to deter migrants from crossing. Nevertheless, as the UK statement exemplifies, the process of *de-humanitarianization* of the border European policy-makers sought to impose at the operational level was still couched in a humanitarian discourse: migrants should not be rescued proactively so as to deter them and ultimately prevent their deaths. At work then, was an paradoxical *anti-humanitarian humanitarianism*.

---

40 See www.deathbyrescue.org/.

41 See publications.parliament.uk/pa/ld201415/ldhansrd/text/141015w0001.htm.

42 See www.ohchr.org/EN/NewsEvents/Pages/DisplayNews.aspx?NewsID=15239&LangID=E.

But this humanitarian varnish was fissured by the dramatic scale of human suffering that would unfold in early 2015 as a result of this policy shift. The week commencing April 12, 2015 saw what is believed to be the largest loss of life at sea in the recent history of the Mediterranean. On April 12, 400 people died when an overcrowded boat capsized due to its passengers' excitement at the sight of platform supply vessels approaching to rescue them. Less than a week later, on April 18, a similar incident took an even greater toll in human lives, leading to the deadliest single shipwreck recorded by the United Nations' High Commissioner for Refugees (UNHCR) in the Mediterranean.[43] Over 800 people are believed to have died when a migrants' vessel sank after a mis-manoeuvre led it to collide with a cargo ship that had approached to rescue its passengers (see Fig. 8.1 & 8.2). More than 1,200 lives were thus lost in a single week. As Médecins Sans Frontières (MSF) commented at the time, these figures eerily resemble those of a war zone.[44] Beyond the huge death toll, what was most striking about these events—which resulted in few recorded images and which we therefore had to reconstruct on the basis of survivor testimonies and AIS vessel tracking data—was that they were not the result of a reluctance to carry out rescue operations, which were a structural cause of migrants' deaths in the past. In these two cases, the actual loss of life has occurred *during* and partly *through* the rescue operation itself.

While it might appear (as state actors were quick to argue) that only the ruthless smugglers who overcrowded the unseaworthy boats to the point of collapse were to blame, our report titled "Death by Rescue—The Lethal Effects of the EU's Policies of Non-assistance" argued that the absence of any immediate violation perpetrated by vessels in vicinity to the boats in distress hid a form of *policy violence* operating at a different scale and temporality than that of the migrants' crossing.[45] In order to account for this violence, we had to go beyond the reconstruction of specific cases of death at sea and resort to what we have called a *forensics of policies*. In particular, our report meticulously reconstructed the policy and operational decisions taken in the forums of the European Commission in Brussels or in meeting rooms in Rome through which Frontex and EU member-states created what we have called a "rescue gap" in full knowledge of its lethal effects.

43 United Nations High Commissioner for Refugees (UNHCR), "Mediterranean boat capsizing: deadliest incident on record."

44 Médecins Sans Frontières, "MSF calls for large scale search and rescue operation in the Mediterranean."

45 See: www.deathbyrescue.org/.

8.1

Automatic Identification
System (AIS) vessel tracks in
the Mediterranean following
a Mediterranean shipwreck
of April 18, 2015

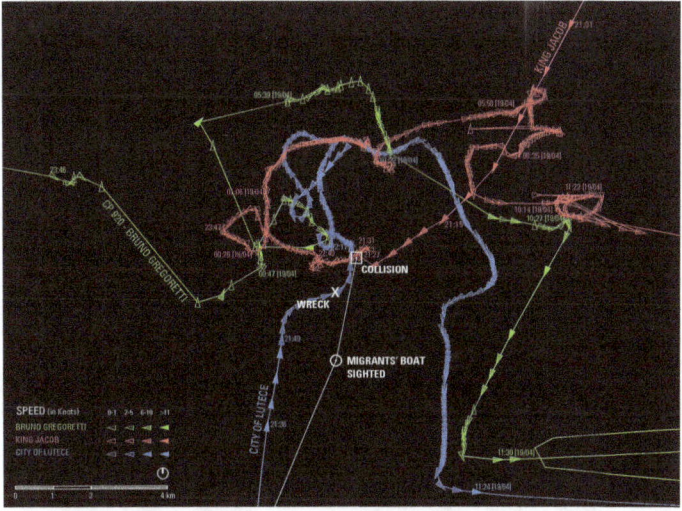

8.2

Video still of an interview with
a survivor of the April 18, 2015
shipwreck, showing his drawing
of the collision between the
migrants' boat and the cargo ship

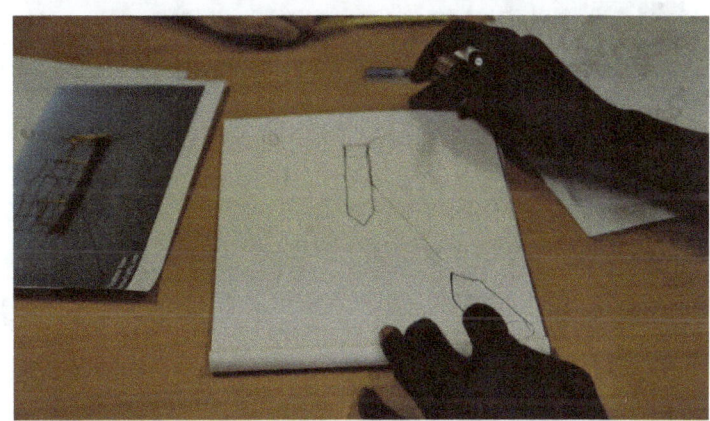

8.3

Map comparing the operational
zones of Italian Navy's Mare
Nostrum and Frontex's Triton

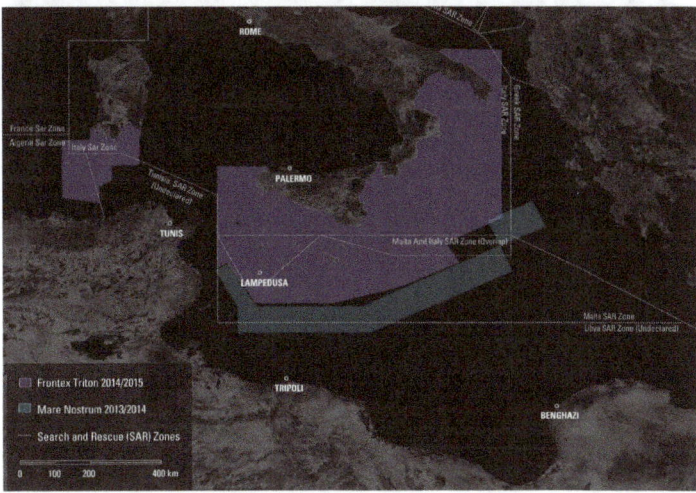

© Forensic Oceanography (all), *Death by Rescue* report. GIS analysis: Rossana Padeletti. Design: Samaneh Moafi (8.1 and 8.3)

9.1 and 9.2

Minutes of a technical meeting held in Rome on September 24, 2014 between representatives of the European Commission, Frontex, the Italian Ministries of Interior, Defense and Foreign Affairs as well as the Italian Coast Guard Border Police and the Navy. In the meeting, a foreseen increase in search and rescue operation as a result of the end of Mare Nostrum is discussed

Minutes from the technical meeting held in Rome, 24 September 2014

Date	24 September 2014
Place	Scuola Superiore di Polizia, Rome
Chaired by	Mr. ███████ (Central Director, Immigration and Border Police Central Directorate) - ██

> **Commented [A1]:** *The non-disclosed text contains personal data, in particular the name of an individual. Its disclosure would affect the privacy and integrity of the individual. Therefore, its disclosure is precluded pursuant to the exception laid down in Article 4(1)(b) of Regulation 1049/2001.*

Participants

███████, Head of Border Management and Schengen Governance Unit (DG Home Affairs) - ██;
███, Director of Operations Division (Frontex) - ██;
███, Sea Border Sector (Frontex)
███, Director of Immigration Service (MoI)
███, Director of 2nd Division (MoI)
███, Risk Analysis and Maritime Operations Unit (MoI)
███, Coordinator for maritime issues (Ministry of Foreign Affairs)
International Affairs Unit, MoI Cabinet
Ministry of Defense, General Staff
Italian Navy
Italian Coast Guard
Italian Guardia di Finanza

> **Commented [A2]:** *The non-disclosed text contains personal data, in particular the name of an individual. Its disclosure would affect the privacy and integrity of the individual. Therefore, its disclosure is precluded pursuant to the exception laid down in Article 4(1)(b) of Regulation 1049/2001.*

The meeting was opened by the chairman, ██ that warmly welcomed all the participants to this final meeting for the implementation of the new Joint Operation TRITON in the Central Mediterranean.
██ thanked Frontex support to Italy in this period of high irregular migration pressure and its constant commitment to find the needed operational support.
██ stressed, as Italian Ministry of Interior ALFANO and Commissioner MALMSTROM already did, that TRITON is different from Mare Nostrum, with different objectives, scope and operational area. The termination of Mare Nostrum will depend always on the final decision of the Italian Government but surely the full implementation of TRITON will give room for this decision to be taken.
██ stated that Italy is very much keen in the participation of all the possible Member States in the new JO and agrees that further negotiations as regards the participation of Malta have to be done.
██ pointed out some of the Italian efforts to address the phenomenon of irregular migration and people's smuggling, namely:

████████████████████████████████████
████████████████████████████████████
████████████████████████████████████
████████████████████████████████████

> **Commented [A3]:** *The non-disclosed text contains personal data, in particular the name of an individual. Its disclosure would affect the privacy and integrity of the individual. Therefore, its disclosure is precluded pursuant to the exception laid down in Article 4(1)(b) of Regulation 1049/2001.*

3. Strong efforts made by the Italian authorities to increase and improve the identification procedures - the number of identified migrants has risen to 48-49%;
██ expressed his hope that at the end of today's meeting an agreement would be reached for the JO TRITON as concerns the number and type of assets, operational area and period. Furthermore, ITA intends to be able to announce in the next JHA Council meeting on the 09th October that the new JO will start from 01st November.

██ thanked Italy for hosting this meeting and expressed appreciation for the Italian efforts in the cooperation with 3rd Countries.
As regards the new JO, ██ stated that its launch shows EU solidarity to tackle irregular migration. Nevertheless, we should continue to reinforce the idea that TRITON will not replace Mare Nostrum. The new TRITON is a border surveillance operation with capacity to support SAR activities. A general open call will be made to the MS to

> **Commented [A4]:** *The non-disclosed text contains sensitive information obtained in the scope of cooperation with another EU MS related to the effectiveness of border security. Its disclosure would reveal the existing vulnerabilities which, once public, would be explored by the criminal networks of migrant smuggling and of trafficking of human beings. Thus, the disclosure of such information would harm the public interest as regards public security. In this regard the text is not disclosed pursuant to the exception laid down in the first indent of Article 4(1)(a) of Regulation (EC) 1049/2001*

1

support ITA and the budget is being currently negotiated with the Commission but it doesn't affect the immediate implementation of the activities. The future activities should also foresee the systematic identification of migrants and the prevention of reuse of the migrants' boats left adrift.
■ stressed that Frontex will do the outmost to start the new JO on the 1st of November.

■ acknowledge the good progress reached by both parties to launch the JO TRITON and sees as a good political sign to be able to state in the next JHA Council meeting that agreement has been reached.
■ stated that the success of the new JO will depend on the MS participation with aerial and maritime assets and recalled all present that the budget of the FX Jos is to be used for funding MS participation. In this sense, the COM will put pressure in MS to strongly participate.
■ mentioned that for 2014, the COM has available 3.5 to 4 Million Euros for the initial start of the activities. It is a quite fast procedure that simply requires Frontex request. As regards 2015, there could be additional 20 Million to reinforce Frontex budget but it is not yet confirmed as discussions are still ongoing.
Regarding the duration and intensity of the activities of the new JO TRITON, ■ suggested that we should leave it open as it all will depend on the flows affecting the operational area.
Concerning the Mare Nostrum operation and the new TRITON, the COM respects all the National efforts of the MS regarding SAR. Nevertheless, the key element is coordination between the activities of both operations. Finally ■ stated that the COM is also very keen in the participation of Malta in the activities of TRITON, recognizing that the limitations imposed make it somehow difficult. Finally, the concept of the JO TRITON should describe the actions to be taken as concerns the migrants' boats in order to avoid the possible reuse by the criminal networks. ■ informed that there is an emergency funding that can be used for this purpose in case it is requested by Italy.

■ recognized the importance of having the COM mediating the negotiations. Regarding the boats adrift, the Ministry of Interior had tried to introduce in a law the possibility to destroy the boast but unfortunately the Ministry of Environment blocked the amended law.

■ stated that it is important that in today's meeting we reach a final agreement as concerns the period of the JO, the operational area, the assets to be deployed and the budget. Finally, ITA accepts the fact that the main part of the budget of the JO will be used to co-finance the participating MS.
■ reiterated that all the migrants intercepted by MS assets will be disembarked in Italy and that the Maltese limitations to the participation in TRITON have to be further analysed, discussed and the terms of these participation have to be laid down in paper.

Italian Navy mentioned that was waiting for a formal proposal from Frontex for the new TRITON█
█████████████████████████ Moreover, the Navy stated that in case Mare Nostrum finishes, the new operation in the area will have surely extra work as concerns SAR.

Italian Ministry of Foreign Affairs informed that it is extremely important to send a political signal by starting the new operation on the 01st November. As regards the position of Malta, the legal department of the MoFA will further analyse the document and come with final conclusions.

■ informed that Frontex proposal had been sent informally and negotiations had been kept at technical level. In detail, Frontex proposal includes 2 OPVs (1 MS and 1 ITA), 2 MS/FWA, 2 IT/CPVs and 2 IT/CPBs.

■ clarified that the Frontex proposal included also 5 JDTs, 2 screnning teams, the costs of the ICC/LCC and of Liaison Officers. The percentage of the total budget committed to Italy would be around 38%.

■ stated that first of all we should assess what we want and need, and only afterwards address MS for their contribution. Moreover 38% of the total budget for ITA is already above the ceiling defined for HMS.

Through the spatial analysis of operational zones, interviews with state officials concerning their operations at sea, and statistical data referring to migrant arrivals, deaths and SAR operations, our report reconstructed the reality that began to unfold in early 2015: migrants' crossings continued unabated, but instead of a fleet of state-operated vessels, a lethal search and rescue gap awaited them. Seeking to fill this gap, the Italian Coast Guard increasingly called upon large merchant ships transiting in the area to carry out rescue operations. But because the rescue of migrants' overcrowded boats can easily lead to tragedies if not operated with the most adaptive means and standards, the large vessels of the shipping industry were unfit for the task.[46] In this context, the April 2015 tragedies were waiting to happen. On April 29, 2015, the President of the European Commission, Jean-Claude Juncker, admitted that "it was a serious mistake to bring the *Mare Nostrum* operation to an end. It cost human lives."[47] The ending of *Mare Nostrum* and its (non-)replacement by Frontex's Triton operation, however, cannot adequately be described as a "mistake" since it was a carefully planned policy implemented with full knowledge of its outcomes. Our report demonstrates that EU agencies and policymakers deliberately implemented *policies of non-assistance* that created the *conditions* that made the April shipwrecks inevitable.

In the wake of the October 2013 shipwrecks, the rapid process of partial humanitarianization and de-humanitarianization of the border that we saw at work between *Mare Nostrum's* launch and termination involved profound shifts both in the regime of (in)visibility operating at the maritime frontier and the modalities of liquid violence. These changes demanded that we reposition our strategies in the aim of effectively contesting the violence of borders. The spectacular display of migrants' deaths as part of the humanitarianization of the border was mobilized to justify border control, but also to justify the temporary deployment of a new scale of state-led rescue operations to mitigate the structural violence of borders. The conditions in which these lethal events unfolded, as well as the responsibilities of policy makers for restrictive policies that precaritize migrants' crossings in the first place, were however still largely kept in the shadows.

Contesting the partition of the sensible operating at the maritime frontier by using forensic techniques to reconstruct lethal events remained important; it proved insufficient, however, in relation to the changing modality of liquid violence. Moreover, while in the case of the "left-to-die" boat our investigation was mainly concerned with finding new ways to shed light on an episode of violence that had been deliberately kept hidden, in this case the two shipwrecks of April 2015 received immediate and quite extensive media attention. While our reconstructions still proved important, the unfolding of the immediate events themselves was never particularly controversial. What was at stake was less the "draw[ing] open [of] a theatrical curtain [...] behind which violence is lurking,"[48] and more the attempt to re-establish the link that exists between the policy decisions taken in meeting rooms in Rome and Brussels, and their deadly effects at sea—thus displacing the scene of violence onto a different scale. In other words, the challenge was to bridge the gap that exists between the "visibility" of certain violent

---

46 "ICS: Rescue of all persons at sea is a must."

47 European Commission, "Speech by President Jean-Claude Juncker at the debate in the European Parliament on the conclusions of the Special European Council on 23 April."

48 Winter, "Violence and Visibility," 199.

events—in this case the two shipwrecks and the deaths these caused—and their "say-ability" in terms of violence, the possibility of producing statements that would be able to link these deaths with the political decisions that made them inevitable so as to seek accountability for them.[49]

The shift from practices to policies of non-assistance as a dominant modality of liquid violence in the context of the humanitarianization of the border, demanded that we supplement a forensics of cases with a forensics of policies, the scale of which could no longer limited to a particular incident, or even the central Mediterranean as a whole, but had to extend to policy forums and meeting rooms from Rome to Brussels. The form of liquid violence we reconstructed, which operates in an even more indirect way than in the past, has however proven challenging so far for lawyers to translate into a violation that might be accounted for in the language and forums of the law. As a result, the impunity which prevailed for the implementation of this lethal policy has allowed it to be perpetuated.

Navigating the Architectural-Image Complex and the Ambivalences of the Humanitarian Border Spectacle

Like the twin October 2013 shipwrecks, the twin April 2015 shipwrecks signaled an-other wave of impressive shifts in the assemblage of security and humanitarian logics shaping rescue and bordering practices, as well as in the aesthetic regime operating at the maritime frontier. Despite Jean-Claude Juncker's admission of guilt for the in-crease in migrants' deaths, the EU has continued to refuse to launch a new proactive search and rescue operation. Instead, it strengthened its security-oriented operations. On the one hand, it increased Frontex's budget as well as the scope of its operations; on the other, on June 22, 2015, it launched a European anti-smuggling operation named EUNAVFOR MED. In opposition to Mare Nostrum's combined "humanitarian and mili-tary" dimensions, the EU anti-smuggling operation was entirely "a police operation with military means," as Rear admiral Hervé Bléjean, the Deputy Operation Com-mander in the Mediterranean, described it,[50] and the rescue of migrants was far from the mission's operational priority. However, this security-oriented mission continued to be justified in the name of saving migrants from the dangerous crossings they were subjected to by ruthless Libyan "traffickers," not smugglers,[51] described in a New York

---

49 This attempt is connected with our reflection on structural violence. As we have argued in Liquid Trac-es, at the core of this notion lies an aesthetic problem. For many of the authors that have employed it, in fact, what is at stake is a distinctive relationship that is instituted between violence and visibility, one by which violence is concealed in plain view. As Nevins notices, "structural violence is not hidden simply because it occurred 'behind the scenes' […] but because powerful actors reproduce its hidden nature and/or construct it as something legitimate or other than violence through various represen-tations." ("A Beating Worse than Death," 16). In this context, "it is not invisibility that allows violence to be repeated and reproduced but [rather] repetition and reproduction [that] make violence invisible." ("Violence and Visibility," 202).

50 Padovani, "Les Passeurs sont Souvent des Migrants."

51 For the conceptual and legal distinction between smuggling and trafficking, see Monzini, Aziz, and Pastore, The Changing Dynamics of Human Smuggling and Trafficking in the Mediterranean. Monzini also underlines how the actual practices of the "actors practicing the commerce of illegalized passage"

Times op-ed by Prime Minister of Italy Matteo Renzi as the "slave traders of the 21st century."[52] This discursive humanitarian spin to this security mission was clearly illustrated when, in September 2015, Federica Mogherini, the EU's High Representative for Foreign Affairs and Security Policy, suggested the operation be re-named "Sophia" in honor of a Somali baby born on one of its warships following a rescue operation.[53] In adopting this name, Mogherini declared, she wanted "to pass the message to the world that fighting the smugglers and the criminal networks is a way of protecting human life."[54] While the operation, in its initial phases, has come to rescue a substantial number of migrants—54,000 between 2015 and 2016—it has also consistently sought to refrain from initiating rescue operations in order to prioritize its anti-smuggling activities, and has almost entirely pulled back from its rescue activities as of 2017.

Faced with the continued refusal of states either to fundamentally change their exclusionary policies or to redeploy a proactive rescue mission, a growing number of NGOs courageously stepped in with their own vessels to fill the lethal gap in rescue capabilities left by the ending of *Mare Nostrum*, progressively constituting a veritable civilian rescue fleet. As the work of Stierl and Cuttitta have shown, rescue NGOs are far from homogenous, and can be positioned on a wide spectrum in terms of their (de)politicization. While organizations such as MOAS have framed their activities as putting themselves at the service of states, and others such as SOS Méditerranée have tended to restrict their activities and discourse to the urgency of saving lives at sea, critical humanitarian organizations such as MSF, and much smaller NGOs such as *Sea Watch*, have adopted a far more politicized stance, denouncing the retreat and inaction of states, and calling on them to redeploy a large-scale SAR operation.[55] These latter organizations have further underlined that, as *Mare Nostrum* had already demonstrated, as essential and urgent as saving migrants in distress at sea might be, it could not put an end to deaths as long as the exclusionary EU migration policy remained in place. As a result, these organizations have called for a fundamental reorientation of the EU's policies to enable "safe passage."[56] With their sudden presence at sea, rescue NGOs have both denied states the monopoly over intervention in—and the monitoring of—the seas. Rescue NGOs quickly demonstrated a fundamental impact at the operational level, as they came to rescue a greater number and share of people—reaching a peak of 35 % in 2017.

As EU states emphasized the security dimension of their operations, and NGOs deployed their own rescue missions, a new and surprising situation began to emerge as of the spring of 2015. It was as if the Janus face of *Mare Nostrum*, humanitarian and security-focused, had been split in two, its distinct logics now separated into two dis-

---

as we would rather call them, often blur between practices of smuggling and trafficking. See also Guilfoyle, "On being there to help."

52 Renzi, "Helping the Migrants is Everyone's Duty."

53 For more on the re-naming of ENAVFOR MED "Operation Sophia," see Krista Lynes's "SOPHIA" in this volume.

54 Statement by Federica Mogherini, EUNAVFOR MED operation Sophia Operational Headquarters, Rome, 24th September 2015.

55 A particularly sticking example of MSF's communication is provided by its April 20, 2015 statement: www.msf.org/article/msf-calls-large-scale-search-and-rescue-operation-mediterranean.

56 Médecins Sans Frontières, "EU: your fences kill. Provide safe and legal passage."

tinct actors. Would they be better reconciled in this new configuration? By spring 2015, it could seem so: after the transgressive arrival of NGOs, a relative complementarity settled in in which NGOs ran rescue operations, allowing state agencies to focus on destroying migrant boats in their wake. In this sense, even if security and humanitarian logics were operated primarily by distinct actors, they remained bound together in a "secret solidarity," to borrow Michel Agier's term.[57] This surprising division of labor in fact pointed to a recurrent ambivalence in humanitarian practice, which, again in Agier's words, is always at risk of becoming the "left hand of Empire," healing the wounds wrought by the violence of the right hand.[58] While unable to end migrants' deaths at sea, and proving more effective in replacing state-led rescue at sea than in forcing states to reinstate their operations, NGOs nevertheless rescued 75,000 people between 2014 and 2018—many of whom might have died without their presence. They further profoundly transformed the aesthetic regime of the maritime frontier in ways that have yet to be fully accounted for.[59]

Through the presence of NGO vessels, non-governmental actors suddenly had an unprecedented capacity to claim a right to look at the EU's maritime frontier, wresting from states the monopoly over the knowledge and imaging of migration and bordering across the sea.[60] The outcome has been as impressive as it has been ambivalent.[61] In some ways, rescue NGOs have clearly reproduced and even heightened the humanitarian border spectacle that had taken form during the *Mare Nostrum* operation. Just like the Italian operation, they substituted the securitized scene of border interception with the good scene of rescue. Taking on board journalist teams who flocked in droves to the Mediterranean frontier as the "migration crisis" intensified in 2015, but also deploying their own media teams and equipping their crews with GoPro cameras, the

---

57 Agier, "Humanity as an Identity."

58 Agier, "Humanity as an Identity." Rescue NGOs have been well aware of these ambivalences, and have led their own reflection as to how to respond to them. This has been conveyed to us in numerous interviews, and can be seen as well in the documentary film Iuventa, directed by Michele Cinque, 2018. See also Newman, "Médecins sans Frontières France."

59 This act of bearing witness to under-reported catastrophes around the world as well as the ambiguities it carries with it are of course not a novelty but sit at the very core of the history of humanitarianism and the international human rights movement at large. Humanitarian rescue ships have played a crucial role in this field at least since the Indochinese refugee crisis that started in the late 1970s, which "stands out as a key event in the history of this new media-savvy interventionist humanitarianism." See Whyte, "Human Rights;" and Pezzani, *Liquid Traces*, in particular chapter 2.

60 In this, they seem to instantiate one of the very definitions of politics provided by Rancière's "Ten Theses on Politics": against the police injunction to "Move along! There is nothing to see here!, [...] politics, in contrast" the French philosopher argues, "consists in [...] refiguring the space, of what there is to do there, what is to be seen or named therein" (22).

61 The presence of rescue NGOs at sea is not an absolute novelty but has an important precedent in the South China Sea refugee crisis of the late 1970s, in the context of which the very term "boat-people" was coined. This episode "stands out as a key event in the history of this new media-savvy interventionist humanitarianism" ("Human Rights"), insofar as the intervention of humanitarian rescue ships in Indochina was crucial in the emergence and consolidation of a new wave of humanitarian actors "without borders." The importance these actors placed on the act of bearing witness and their reckoning with the ambiguities that the latter brought about have been a defining feature of this new chapter in the history of humanitarianism and the international human rights movement at large. See Pezzani, *Liquid Traces*, in particular chapter 2.

images produced by rescue NGOs (or through them) brought distant viewers into an unprecedented proximity with the extreme situation of life and death that each rescue operation constitutes.

Making visible their rescue activities may have been necessary to convey the continuing urgent reality of migrants' distress at sea, and more prosaically to allow NGOs to justify their activities to their funders. In the process however, as had been noted by numerous observers,[62] rescue NGOs reproduced the intertwined tropes of the white savior and the racialized, precarious subject fighting for survival.[63] While many members of rescue NGOs we have spoken to are well aware of these problems, and have sought to address them as best they can—for example by alternating the type of imagery they have circulated between images of distress and empowerment, or conducting interviews with rescued migrants on the deck of their vessels to allow them to unfold their life stories[64]—there is no easy way out of the radically unequal positions our postcolonial world generates, which permeate humanitarian practices in general.[65] In fact, moments of radical precarity in the open sea bring these inequalities into even sharper relief.[66] Furthermore, NGOs' radicalized version of the humanitarian border spectacle also reproduced some of the configurations of the partition of the sensible imposed by the spectacle of border security: by spectacularizing the maritime crossing, the imagery produced by NGOs continued to echo the iconography of the European imaginary of invasion, as well as this imaginary's occlusion of the conditions lying before and after the sea crossing. No matter how hard different rescue NGOs have tried to frame their images differently—and a more careful study than what we can offer here would be necessary—in effect many of the images they have produced have been nearly identical, and practically interchangeable, from one rescue organization to another.

Despite these ambivalent outcomes, which should not be taken lightly, rescue NGOs have also re-organized the Mediterranean frontier's partition of the sensible in other highly oppositional and decisive ways. By wresting the monopoly over the capacity to document events at sea away from states, they were also able to redirect part of the "light" shed by the humanitarian border spectacle towards the violent (in)actions of state actors. Without the civilian oversight at sea that NGOs have permitted, much of this violence would have remained in the shadows. This role would become even more crucial when, after an initial phase of relative complementarity between the security-oriented operations of states and the rescue activities of NGOS discussed above, European states deployed drastic measures to seal off the Mediterranean frontier by criminalizing solidarity and (re-)outsourcing border control as of the summer of 2016.

As migrants' capacity to overcome the EU's borders peaked in summer 2015, when the Aegean temporarily replaced the central Mediterranean as the main area of cross-

---

62 Danewid, "White Innocence in the Black Mediterranean;" Stierl, "A Fleet of Mediterranean Border Humanitarians;" Cuttitta, "Repoliticization Through Search and Rescue?"

63 These issues have also been critically reflected upon from within rescue NGOs. See for example Newman "Médecins sans Frontières France."

64 See for example MSF's dedicated Facebook page "Voices from the Road": www.facebook.com/MSF.VoicesFromTheRoad/.

65 Fassin, *Humanitarian Reason*, 4.

66 Tazzioli, "When Rescue is Capture."

ing, plunging the EU into a deep crisis, European states sought to impose a violent roll-back of the border regime. Unable to manage migrants' transgressive movements once they arrived on European territory, in the aim of re-imposing order on the border regime, European states found only one solution: (re)outsourcing border control to whatever partner they could find along migrants' entire trajectories. After successfully sealing off the Aegean thanks to the EU-Turkey deal in March 2016,[67] the attention of policy makers returned to the central Mediterranean, where the only available partner facing Italian shores was the shattered Libyan state, and particularly its unsavory coast guard units. Outsourcing border control once again to these Libyan partners—as had been the case already in 2009—demanded that NGOs be sidelined. After all, if the newly-equipped Libyan units were to intercept migrants leaving their shores effectively, the same migrants could not be rescued by NGOs which would bring them to European soil. Furthermore, to allow the Libyan coast guard to intercept migrants at gunpoint with impunity, the monopoly of states over the maritime frontier's aesthetic regime had to be restored. For all purposes then—inextricably operational and aesthetic—the Mediterranean had to be *de-humanitarianized.*

Since the summer of 2016, then, Italy, with the full support of the EU, has stepped up its collaboration with the Libyan coast guard, and at the same time led a virulent campaign of delegitimization and criminalization of NGOs—a two-pronged policy we have called *Mare Clausum.*[68] These two dimensions have been the focus of our work since 2016. Knowing the looming catastrophe that the attacks against rescue NGOs signaled, we first attempted to intervene in this debate through our report, "Blaming the Rescuers," which demonstrated the fallacy of the "pull-factor" attributed to SAR NGOs, an argument that had already been mobilized against *Mare Nostrum*. In collaboration with Forensic Architecture, we have further offered a counter-reconstruction of events of alleged collusion with smugglers by the NGO *Jugend Rettet*, whose vessel was seized on August 2, 2017.[69] Thanks to the documentation produced by this NGO—in particular through GoPro cameras mounted on its crew's helmets and the images produced by journalists on board its own and other NGO vessels—we have demonstrated that the accusations against NGOs have been spurious and amounted to "factual lies" (the use of factual elements to weave a narrative that is intentionally false).[70]

Our efforts—as that of many other actors—have however proven insufficient, and since the summer of 2017 the NGO flotilla has been reduced to only a few remaining assets, leading as in the past to a greater risk for migrants of dying at sea.[71] Furthermore, as the share of migrants rescued by NGOs fell, the share of interceptions operated by the Libyan coast guard increased in parallel. Between 2016 and 2018, 55,000 migrants were pulled-back to Libya, where they have faced detention, forced labor, torture, and rape.[72] In this shift then, we can sea a repetition of the EU's policy of non-assistance, enacted with the ending of *Mare Nostrum*, now supplementing the indirect violence

---

67 Heck and Hess, "European restabilization attempts of the external borders and their consequences."

68 See content.forensic-architecture.org/wp-content/uploads/2019/05/2018-05-07-FO-Mare-Clausum-full-EN.pdf.

69 See our "Blaming the Rescuers" report, June 2017. www.blamingtherescuers.org/.

70 www.forensic-architecture.org/case/iuventa/.

71 See UNHCR, "Desperate Journeys."

72 See our "Mare Clausum" report: www.forensic-architecture.org/case/sea-watch/.

10.1 and 10.2
Video still from The Crime of Rescue—The Iuventa Case *(2018)*

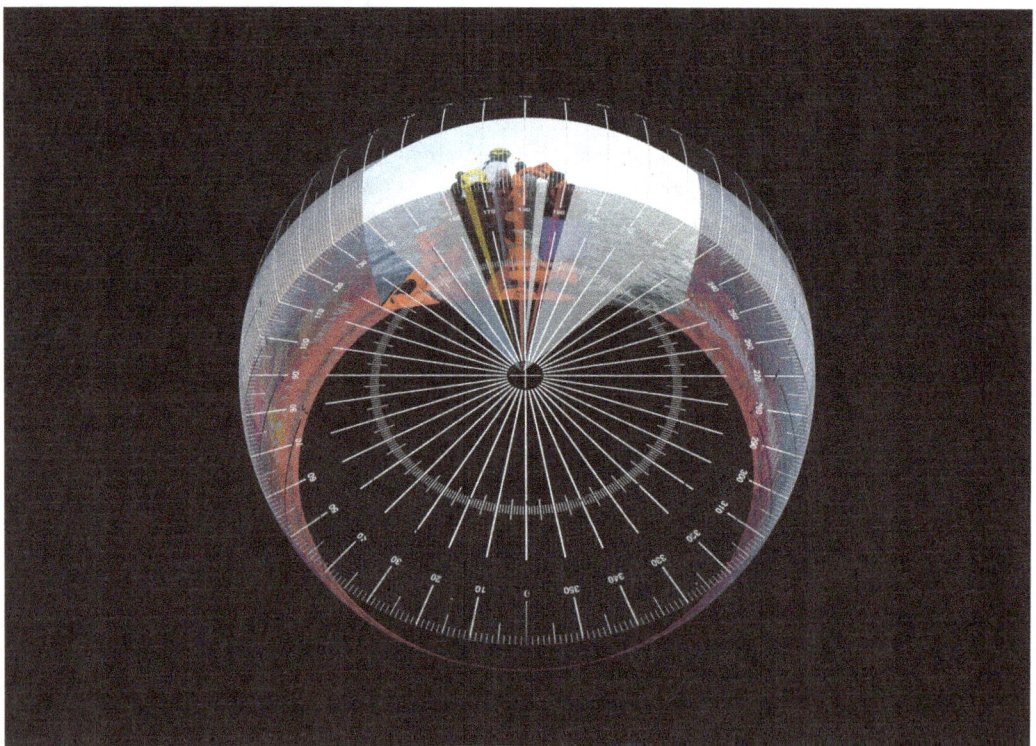

exercised at and through the sea with the all too direct forms of violence perpetrated by proxy on firm land.

Just as the presence of rescue NGOs was being drastically reduced over the summer of 2017, and with it the rift NGOs had opened in the state-imposed partition of the sensible, the German NGO *Sea Watch* radicalized its visual politics. In the face of the accusations of collusion with smugglers and mounting Libyan coast guard attacks on rescuers and migrants alike, *Sea Watch* supplemented the GoPro cameras of its already well-equipped crew by mounting six cameras on the deck and mast of its ship, as well as devices to record its radio communications with state actors. The *Sea Watch* ship became a kind of moving audio-visual recording apparatus, continuously documenting everything that occurred on the horizon 360 degrees around it. The footage *Sea Watch* would gather in early November through these unprecedented means would prove central to our attempt to counter Italy and the EU's outsourcing of border control to the Libyan coast guard.[73]

On the morning of November 6, 2017, a conflictual rescue/interception event occurred, after both *Sea Watch* and the Libyan coast guard were directed by the Italian coast guard to the position of a boat in distress carrying more than 130 migrants. With its recently repaired vessel (that had been handed to Libyan authorities by Italy in May of that year), the Libyans were able to arrive on scene first, where many of the passengers had already fallen into the water after one of the boat's tubes deflated. The Libyans captured those who were still clinging to the boat using very dangerous manoeuvres—despite 8 of the 13 crew members onboard having been trained by the EU's anti-smuggling operation "Sophia." As the *Sea Watch* vessel approached minutes later, its crew deployed small fast boats to rescue the passengers set adrift. Soon, the antagonistic logics of interception and rescue came to a head. As *Sea Watch*'s crew approached the migrants' boat to rescue the passengers struggling in the water around it and not assisted by the Libyans, the Libyan Coast Guard threatened them and threw hard objects at them to keep them away. For the migrants caught between the Libyan coast guard and the rescue NGO, the few meters between their vessels is what separated the prospect of a new life in Europe and the certainty of violence at the hand of Libyan captors, which many of the migrants had already experienced. Some of the migrants the Libyan coast guard had managed to bring on board—and were beating—managed to jump overboard and reach the NGO boat instead. Losing control, the Libyan coast guard set off at high speed with one passenger still hanging on the boat's side ladder. In total, at least twenty people died before or during these events and as consequence of the conflictual and chaotic operation. *Sea Watch* was able to rescue 58 migrants and bring them to safety in Italy, while 47 were captured by the Libyan coast guard and brought back to Libya where, as several survivors later recounted, they suffered grave human rights violations—including arbitrary detention, brutal beatings, rape, and starvation.

In some ways, this incident was far from exceptional: the Libyan coast guard intercepted and returned to Libya more that 20,000 people in 2017 alone. What was exceptional was that this pull-back event was only partly successful, so that several survivors could be retrieved and interviewed in Italy, allowing in turn that contact be estab-

---

73 See our "Mare Clausum" report and associated video investigation: www.forensic-architecture.org/ case/sea-watch/.

lished with those brought back to Libya. Moreover, by turning its vessel and crew into a complex apparatus of audio-visual recording, *Sea Watch* was able to record the entire violent event with unprecedented precision. To measure the change in the aesthetic regime of the Mediterranean frontier that had occured, we need only compare the single photograph we could access for the left-to-die boat case in 2011 with the hours and hours of video recordings of the events from multiple angles that *Sea Watch* handed over to us in order to reconstruct these events. To respond to this overabundance of images, which was novel for events occurring at sea, we had to call upon the unique method the Forensic Architecture agency has developed in a number of contexts on firm land—what it calls "the architectural-image complex."[74] By locating each camera within a dynamic three-dimensional model of the scene, Forensic Architecture's method enabled us to navigate within an image-space and offer a minute-by-minute reconstruction of the facts from multiple perspectives.

The audiovisual material produced by *Sea Watch*, and the way we have been able to assemble it with Forensic Architecture, provided fundamental evidence of the violence of the Libyan coast guard and its collaboration with its EU counterparts. To reconstruct this collaboration at a policy level, we resorted to the method of policy forensics developed in our previous reports.[75] Finally, the testimonies of several of the survivors who were brought back to Libya give account of the brutal violence to which they were subjected, which lies far beyond the frame of *Sea Watch*'s cameras, and beyond the sea itself. Together, these testimonies, the video reconstruction, and our written report served as the factual basis for a legal case before the European Court of Human Rights filed by seventeen survivors in May 2018 against Italy. The argument put forward by the legal team constituted by *Global Legal Action Network* and the *Association for Juridical Studies on Immigration* is that—because of the multiform collaboration between Italy, the EU and the Libyan coast guard—Italy was engaging in "refoulement by proxy," and was responsible for the passengers' fate at sea and in Libya.[76]

As important as the audiovisual material produced by *Sea Watch* has been for our reconstruction and the ongoing demands for accountability that aim, through litigation, to force Italy and the EU to interrupt their policy of outsourced border control, it has also confronted us with new difficulties and questions that we still ponder. Beyond the abundance of available images of this violent incident—an outcome of the profound reorganization of the partition of the sensible at sea operated by rescue NGOs—there is another striking difference in relation to our previous investigations that were characterized by a paucity of accessible imagery: while the lack of images in the report on the left-to die boat and on the April 2015 shipwrecks forced us to assemble a composite image of events by combining survivor testimonies with georeferenced data and remote sensing technologies so as to map the unfolding of events with a certain distance, here the images produced by *Sea Watch* bring us to the heart of events, in an intimate and disturbing proximity with bodies struggling for their lives and their cries of distress. We are faced with scenes of radical precarity, and even death (the video includes images of two people drowning). From the perspective of the continuously recording

---

74 "Interview with Eyal Weizman."

75 See our "Mare Clausum" report: www.forensic-architecture.org/case/sea-watch/.

76 "Legal action against Italy over its coordination of Libyan Coast Guard pull-backs resulting in migrant deaths and abuse."

11.1

Video still from Mare Clausum—The Sea Watch vs Libyan Coast Guard Case *(2018)*

11.2

Video still of Interview with A., survivor of the confrontation between Sea Watch and the Libyan Coast Guard (2019)

© Forensic Oceanography and Forensic Architecture (both)

camera fixed on *Sea Watch*'s mast, we see a man's body slowly swallowed by the sea's liquid mass after *Sea Watch*'s crew has been prevented from rescuing him by the Libyan coast guard. These are horrific images of a horrific event, and their presentation as documents to a court entails that this violence must remain in the brutal form in which it was captured. Even if the survivors we have worked with wanted these images to be seen as part of their demand for justice, and even if this footage constitutes essential evidence to incriminate both the Libyan coast guard and European states, working with and displaying such imagery conjures difficult—and perhaps unresolvable—questions: How to contest the violence of the EU's outsourced policies of border control without reproducing other forms of symbolic violence in the process?

Our use of these images is first of all haunted by the ghost of the dead from whom we will never be able to request consent to use this footage, whose lives were only made visible to us "in the moment of their disappearance."[77] While the initial use of these images within our video has been geared to a judicial context, as a consequence of their further circulation in different cultural, institutional and political forums, no generic public can be assumed as viewer of those images. As such, echoing other debates on the consumption and circulation of images of Black suffering we must ask: who is meant to see those images and what do those images mean to her/him? Can they be effectively mobilized to counter the fungibility of Black life? If yes, by whom and under what conditions? Might their circulation in certain contexts undermine that aim?[78] Clearly we see a risk that, in recirculating these images of Black subjects in conditions of radical precarity, struggling for survival and being rescued by European activists, we reproduce racialized tropes of the rescued/rescuer. Our own work of reconstruction is affected by the inherent ambivalence of the images produced by NGOs as part of the humanitarian border spectacle we have discussed above. Furthermore, as George Didi-Huberman has recently reminded us in a scathing critique of Ai WeiWei's *Human Flow* (2018), if for Walter Benjamin criticism is "a matter of correct distancing," we may ask if the images of NGOs haven't brought us too close? How to re-introduce distance from within this extreme proximity? Moreover, in a context of over-abundance of images, could the *subtraction* of visual imagery become an additional—and in certain situations not only more ethically sustainable but also more effective—tool in our repertoire? These are among the questions and tensions that continue to inhabit us, and which, as Saidiya Hartman underlines, are "unavoidable in narrating the lives of the subaltern, the dispossessed, and the enslaved."[79]

After having submitted our factual video reconstruction based on *Sea Watch*'s footage to the European court, one of the ways we have sought to respond to these questions is by accompanying the display of our own reconstruction in artistic contexts with a video interview in which a survivor looks back at and re-subjectivizes these images. This is, however, far from exhausting them, and risks to continue reproducing the unequal relationship that the trope of "giving voice to" a under-represented group always institutes. What these difficulties point to is that relying on some of the tools

---

77 Hartman, "Venus in Two Acts," 12.

78 We are referring for instance to the debate that developed in the wake of the exhibition of Dana Schutz' work at the Whitney Biennale in 2017. See Mitter, "What Does It Mean to Be Black and Look at This?"

79 Hartman, "Venus in Two Acts," 12.

mobilized and images produced as part of the border spectacle, whether in their securitized or humanitarian variants, demands careful positioning, and charting one's course through a field fraught with ambivalences in which there is at times no unproblematic position. This, we would argue, is the risk that comes from intervening within and against the aesthetic regime of the maritime frontier.

Conclusion

The trajectory we have charted of the changing modalities of liquid violence, constant rearticulations of humanitarian and security logics, and reconfigurations of the aesthetic regime operating at the maritime frontier, have all shaped the twists and turns of our own practice as researchers, aesthetic practitioners and activists striving to contest the violence of borders. The complex and ambivalent shifts at the maritime frontier we have described trace a sequence of openings and closures in relations to migrants' movements, the presence of non-governmental actors and the aesthetic regime. While in 2011, migrants had pried open the Mediterranean frontier in the wake of and as an integral part of the uprisings in North Africa and the Middle East, with each group of illegalized migrants intercepted and pulled-back to Libya, or left stranded at sea for days, the sea is once again being closed down. The sea is also closing down on activists, who, in response to the demands for freedom and equality that emerged out of the so-called Arab uprisings, have in the last few years transformed the sea into a central space of political struggle, inventing new strategies and tactics to contest the violence of borders and support migrants' movements. Contesting the partition of the sensible imposed by states on the liquid frontier has been a central dimension of each of these initiatives—even if their intervention conjured new problems in the process—and the attempt to criminalize them and expel them from the maritime frontier has also been an attempt by states to re-impose their own regime of (in)visibility.

The closing down of the sea in these different respects has continued apace since the autumn 2017 Sea Watch vs Libyan Coast Guard incident described above. While our reconstruction was the basis for a legal challenge against Italy in front of the European Court of Human Rights filed on May 8, 2018, the deterrent effect we hoped our complaint might have on state practices even as the court examined the complaint, did not materialize. After far-right politician Matteo Salvini became Interior Minister on June 1, 2018, the de-humanitarianization of the border pursued through the *Mare Clausum* policy was only further radicalized: more NGOs have been prevented from operating, rescued migrants have been prevented from disembarking, and more migrants have been pulled back to Libya.[80] The rift in the monopoly of states over imagining and documenting the maritime frontier (which rescue NGOs had widened) has been narrowed. While we continue to consider strategic litigation as an essential political tool against the lowering of the threshold of acceptable violence (particularly in regards to push-backs), as we have repeatedly hinted at above it is also an inherently limited one.

---

80 In this phase, the lives of migrants appear to have increasingly lost even their discursive value, as the absence of any representative of the current Italian government at the ceremony commemorating the Lampedusa shipwreck deaths in October 2018 indicates. "March in Lampedusa to honour victims of 2013 shipwreck."

Despite the tendency of closure, the sealing off of the Mediterranean frontier remains an unstable, contested and open-ended process. The recent shifts in the Mediterranean frontier's partition of the sensible have demanded new responses by non-governmental actors seeking to contest the violence of borders. With the vessels of rescue NGOs prevented from operating, the role of an activist hotline supporting migrants in distress in the Mediterranean we have contributed to forge, the Watch-TheMed Alarm Phone, has proven more important than ever over the last months.[81] Launched in October 2014 by a coalition of freedom of movement, human rights, and migrant activist groups, the Alarm Phone connects more than 150 activists located in about 12 countries, who take shifts to respond to distress calls from migrants crossing the sea. The Alarm Phone activists enact what we might call a *topological solidarity*: while the activists that respond to calls are dispersed throughout Europe and North Africa, through the phone line, they can hear the precarious passengers as if they were beside them. The Alarm Phone has intervened in a crucial way in the Mediterranean frontier's aesthetic regime. By providing support to and amplifying the voices of migrants to denounce state violence,[82] the Alarm Phone has exercised a form of *disobedient listening*, which is all the more crucial today when the visual means of monitoring the maritime frontier are challenged.

The moment of closure we are facing is thus far from being the end of the story. Illegalized migrants from the Global South will continue to refuse their banishment from spaces of (relative) opulence, and non-governmental actors will strive to find new ways to contest the violence of borders, which, as we have shown, also involve contesting the boundaries of what can be seen and heard. But this open-ended sequence also underlines the limits of the hand-to-hand struggle of migrants and those who support them with the border regime, since we have collectively proven unable to durably end border violence. Migrants' claims to freedom of movement—which they express through their voices and practices of unauthorized mobility—have not been heeded. While they have pushed the European border regime into a phase of turbulence, leading to the rapid changes we have outlined in this chapter, the fundamentals of the EU's policy of migrant illegalization have remained unchanged. In this context, strategic litigation may have blocked certain violent practices temporarily, but it has not challenged the foundational violence of the EU's policies of exclusion. Likewise, state and NGO vessels deployed to rescue migrants have succeeded in mitigating the lethal effects of the violence of the liquid frontier, but proven unable to put an end to the very necessity of rescue, and with it to the "asymmetry between rescuer and rescued,"[83] that is intrinsic to this practice and that haunts the images produced by state and non-state actors alike. As important as these practices have been, they have proven to be "not enough."[84] These limitations are certainly not the ground to refrain from any form of intervention, but acknowledging them is necessary to navigate a fine and unstable line separating resistance, refusal and complicity.

---

81 See: www.alarmphone.org/. For an extended discussion see Heller, Pezzani and Stierl, "Disobedient Sensing and Border Struggles."

82 Schwartz and Stierl, "Amplifying Migrant Voices."

83 Tazzioli, "When Rescue is Capture."

84 Moyn, *Not Enough*.

While activist energies, and much of our own research, focus on countering the shifting modes of violence at the border, this risks leaving the systemic conditions within which borders are embedded, and which reproduce the mobility conflict of which the Mediterranean is a major frontline, unaddressed. The problems arising from an excessive focus on the border as the site of political contestation is also partly an aesthetic question. As we have shown in relation to the humanitarian border spectacle, there is a risk that, even as we contest the securitized border spectacle and its lethal policies, one partly reproduces its selective (in)visibilisation—for example by contributing to the over-representation of racialized migration across the Mediterranean frontier that fuels Europe's imaginary of invasion, or by occluding the forms of systemic violence that extend far beyond the sea's coastline to shape the social, political and economic conditions that migrants escape in the first place. Our ongoing interest in migrants' trajectories as an epistemic device[85] stems precisely from the way they connect multiple locations and struggles, bringing into view an expansive field of relations.[86] While this may be part of a response to the challenges of contesting the border spectacle, we are well aware that each practice and perspective reveals as much as it conceals. That partiality cannot be undone, but it demands to be constantly reflected upon and the configuration of the (in)visible it produces questioned anew. At best, its recognition can produce a sense of humility, and the acknowledgement of the need for practices and perspectives other than one's own.

---

85 Mezzadra and Neilson, *Border as Method.*

86 Heller and Pezzani, "Contentious Crossings."

Reframing the Border

Lonnie van Brummelen and Siebren de Haan

A Westphalian Imaginary

12.

Oil painting by the Dutch painter Gerard ter Borch (II) documenting the ratification of the Peace of Münster, one of the treaties concluded in Westphalia in 1648. The ratification of the treaty ended the Eighty Years' War between the United Netherlands and the Spanish Crown and formally established the independence of the Dutch Republic. The painting is presented in the Rijksmuseum in Amsterdam; on loan from the National Gallery, London, since 2000

As cultural producers from Europe, we experience the continent where we live as an ambiguous terrain; we cannot simply identify with it without accepting the consequences of such a positioning. Europe has a long tradition of dealing for itself. When the terms of the treaties of Westphalia were negotiated in the 17th century, it was Europeans sitting around the table and agreeing that the world would be made up of sovereign states. They were the ones who decided—for themselves and for all those who were not invited to the table—what was lawful and what was outside the law, who had the right to control territories and markets, and who had no rights whatsoever. Its systems are as regional as any other regional configuration of knowledge, but Europe has always understood them as universal and turned them into global designs.[1]

---

1 Nimako and Willemsen, "Transatlantic Slavery and the Rise of the European World Order"; Mignolo, "Geopolitics of sensing and knowing."

Being artists from the Netherlands presents a specific ambivalence for us because, in our nation's history, the eminence of art is inextricably tied to colonialism. Colonial profits enabled the Dutch Golden Age with its "masters" who painted not for monarchies, aristocracies, or the church, but for the new art market. Such profits also financed our nation's war of independence against the Spanish Empire. It was the newly founded Dutch Republic that initiated and facilitated the emergence of the United East India Company, followed later by the West India Company. These forerunners of corporate-led globalization were involved in international trade and the overseas production of high value commodities such as sugar, tobacco, nutmeg, and cloves. They issued bonds and stock shares for individual buyers, thus recruiting citizens to the role of shareholder. The financial resources this generated enabled the further conquest of overseas territories and the construction of infrastructures to commercially exploit them. Meanwhile, savvy Dutch lawyers developed legal tools that granted the companies the right to operate as agents of the state. Such government letters provided legislative cover to loot ships, wage war, and install administrations in the conquered territories.[2] Many cities in the Netherlands still honor the officers who worked for these companies with statues and placards that celebrate the contribution of these naval heroes to our nation's struggle for independence and greatness. What is often left out of the story is how they participated in enslavement, slaughter and ecocide to achieve this.[3]

How, as two white Dutch artists, can we grapple with our inherited complicity in this tangle of colonial and postcolonial projects? How can we build upon our continent's aesthetic and cultural legacies without reproducing the mechanisms of exploitation on which these are founded? How can we—privileged with European citizenship—problematize its mechanisms of inclusion and exclusion? Such questions have shaped our artistic practice. We embrace the notion that making images in and of the world entails our participation in shared events, as actors amongst other actors, both human and other-than-human. Art-making thus becomes for us an involvement in a world that is not there for us to fully grasp, but that we get to know a little better by interacting with it. Although we often work in a documentary style, we learned that there is no such thing as mere observation. As image-makers, we are always already part of the events that we record. We frame, we focus, we shape, we choose a point of view. Unwittingly, our presence may provoke certain voices to speak up and silence others. As a consequence, we came to understand our artistic practice as a form of participatory intervention.

---

2 Of these two companies, only the VOC had the right to deploy military troops. Minto-Coy and Berman, *Public Administration and Policy in the Caribbean*, 80.

3 The Indonesian Banda Islands, for example, were colonized in 1621 after a VOC-army lead by 'naval hero' Jan Pieterszoon Coen massacred almost the entire native population with the approval of the Dutch State, to secure the monopoly on the trade in nutmeg and mace. The VOC hired Japanese samurai torturers to behead tens of village chiefs. Coen was nicknamed the Slaughter of Banda. www.historiek. net/jan-pieterszoon-coen-1587-1629/5545/.

13.1 and 13.2
Stills from Grossraum (Borders of Europe) *(2004/2005, 35 mm film),
depicting smugglers throwing contraband over the border fence at the
market in Ceuta*

© Lonnie Van Brummelen & Siebren de Haan (both)

Borders of Europe

Working from Europe today means being situated in the dynamics of cultural and economic crises, shifting borders, growing divides, and red tape. Around 2003, we started to investigate this transforming Europe. At the time, the EU was on the verge of extending itself with ten new member states. It was not yet clear how the European project would develop. Would an expanded EU be able to confront transnational challenges such as migration or climate change? Or would it rather become a fortress, a privileged area where goods and people could move freely protected by fortified borders and tariff walls? Were the dismantling of national borders and the introduction of a single currency first steps leading to a federation? Or would Europe remain a patchwork of jurisdictions, a league of sovereign states? Perhaps the outside boundary would turn out to be a new Frontier: a wave of territorial expansion that would soon incorporate sizable countries such as Turkey and Ukraine. Such questions incited us to make *Grossraum (Borders of Europe)* (2004 / 2005): an installation consisting of a silent 35 mm film juxtaposed with a publication, documenting border crossings at the Polish-Ukrainian border, the Spanish-Moroccan border, and the Greek / Turkish Cypriot divide. We stationed our camera on hillsides and rooftops and filmed across Europe's border to its outside. Our camera-eye didn't adhere to the borderlines that were drawn on the map. Instead, we explored alternative trajectories. We followed a smuggler throwing contraband over a border fence, or descended through a forest—divided by a border, but nonetheless inseparably part of the same ecosystem.

Europe's borders were heavily guarded and photography was forbidden without the permission of proper authorities. A long trajectory of permission-seeking preceded our poetic border transgressions. The publication entitled *The Formal Trajectory* contained a selection of correspondence with local contacts and authorities, and a logbook of our experiences on location. In revealing these negotiations and the circumstances surrounding the recordings, the publication makes evident that our artistic freedom to optically trespass was regulated by an invisible juridical structure.

The making of *Grossraum* taught us that bilateral ties shape Europe's relation to its outside. For example, when we asked Polish authorities for permission to film their border with Ukraine, they requested that we also contact the Ukrainian authorities for their approval. And although the Polish request confused the Ukrainian authorities—how could they give us a Ukrainian press card, if we would not set foot on Ukrainian soil?— they displayed a similar prudence with regards to their Polish colleagues. Only 60 years ago, the western part of what is now Ukraine used to be Polish territory. The border between the two countries still divides many families. This was one of the reasons that the Polish government had been reluctant to comply with Europe's visa requirements and strongly advocated for more favorable conditions for its eastern neighbor. It resulted first in cheaper and simplified access to European visas for Ukrainians, and eventually, in an agreement that allowed Ukrainians to travel within Europe visa free.[4]

---

4 The Press Office of the Ministry of Foreign Affairs Republic of Poland informed us by email on April 16, 2019 that Ukraine has been the beneficiary of an agreement between Ukraine and European Union with regard to Schengen visas since 2008, which set out special facilitations for Ukrainian citizens related to fees for processing visa applications (35 euro), timeframes for processing visa applications (10 days in regular cases and 2 day in cases of urgent character) and simplified procedures. Since June 11,

14.
Letter and film still as reproduced in the publication, The Formal Trajectory *(2004/2005)*

UKRAINIAN TERRITORY IN THE IMAGE

Dear Lonnie,

I have spoken to the colonel. A nice man. We will have his assistance for the shooting period. However, a problem did arise. The Polish border guard cannot grant permission to film Ukrainian territory, because of a bilateral agreement with the Ukraine. If the Polish border guard grants permission to shoot the border, they have to ensure Ukrainian territory will not be visible in the image. This demand comes from the Ukrainian authorities. I think the concept of the border film does not allow this restriction. It would mean that you could only point the camera from the border towards the Polish side. It is a strictly formal request, but if the Ukrainians would ever see the film, they could officially indict Poland for violation of an international treaty. The Polish border guard cannot take this risk of course. They suggest you ask permission of the Ukrainian authorities through the Ukrainian embassy in The Hague.

When you do that, remember the Ukraine does not want to be seen as an Asian wilderness outside the borders of Europa. They will on the other hand certainly appreciate the growing interest in the Ukraine as a neighbor of the European Union.

Happy travels!

Darek Szendel
ID Spot, Warsaw

7

© Lonnie Van Brummelen & Siebren de Haan

2017, Ukrainian citizens can travel visa-free within all member states of the EU with the exception of the United Kingdom and Ireland.

That not all countries enjoy such good relations with their neighbors became clear to us when Moroccan authorities refused to give us permission to film its border with Spain at Ceuta. Morocco considered the Spanish enclave on the Northern point of Africa as *occupied* by Spain, and therefore did not recognize the border as legitimate. Reading between the lines, however, we understood that we could film the boundary if we had permission from Spanish authorities.

The *Guardia Civil*—whose headquarters were located in the Spanish capital Madrid—guarded the frontier itself. But there were also port authorities, customs, and the local police of the autonomous district of Ceuta. It required a considerable amount of asking around to find out which authority was responsible for what, and in what order we had to approach them. We spoke to many officers who all gave us their consent, but never received a single document. When we asked the final officer how we could prove without papers that we had permission to film the borderland, he advised us to memorize the names of everyone we had encountered, and to list them orally in case we were held up; a directive that surprisingly turned out to work.

Though the border fences at Ceuta had not yet been stormed, irregular migration was already leaving traces in the landscape. We found rubber ammunition and improvised wooden ladders: remnants of nocturnal encounters between Spanish border patrols and African migrants climbing the fence in an attempt to reach Europe.

The Cyprus divide turned out to be an even more contested boundary. In 1974, Greek Cypriot nationalists supported by elements of the Greek military junta staged a *coup d'état* in an attempt to incorporate Cyprus into Greece. To protect the Turkish Cypriot minority that lived on the island, the Turkish army invaded Cyprus, occupied its northern part, and never left. The Turkish Republic of Northern Cyprus declared itself independent in 1983 with Turkey alone recognizing the new state. For decades, a UN buffer zone has separated the two parts of the island. As a result, only half of Cyprus was able to enter the European Union in 2004.

After considerable negotiation, the government of Cyprus gave us permission to film the divide on the condition that we always be accompanied by Greek Cypriot soldiers.[5] But a dilemma arose when we wanted to film inside the buffer zone. According to UN regulations, the Greek Cypriot soldiers were not allowed to enter. The recruits nonetheless had orders from their superiors to escort us. After calling back and forth, the Greek Cypriot soldiers were told that they could accompany us provided that they exchanged their uniforms for plain clothes. Filming in the presence of two groups of soldiers was by no means easy. They watched continuously over our shoulders to make sure that nothing came into our picture frame that could give the impression of partiality in the conflict. Since the landscape was fraught with flags and monuments, this made it almost impossible to compose a shot. Only around noon, as imams started to bellow from the minarets, and a UN soldier began to talk about his recent employment in Baghdad, did the monitoring ease. By nightfall, the soldiers were chatting animatedly about the latest news, and the boring and expensive nightlife in Nicosia, allowing us to explore the landscape a bit more freely.

---

5 Another condition for their collaboration was that the title of the film would not be Borders of Europe, since the government of Cyprus did not recognize the divide as a legitimate border.

15.1 and 15.2

Stills from Grossraum (Borders of Europe) *(2004 / 2005, 35 mm film),*
depicting the UN buffer zone in Cyprus

© Lonnie Van Brummelen & Siebren de Haan (both)

In retrospect, the whole process of seeking permission and negotiating with border patrols and state officials took place in a remarkably friendly atmosphere. It may have been indicative of positive expectations of the newly expanded Europe. But it soon became clear that the shifting border also caused political turmoil. When the presidential elections in Ukraine turned out to be manipulated in favor of the pro-Russian candidate, tensions surfaced between pro-European and pro-Russian parts of the population.[6] The struggle over direction eventually led to several armed conflicts, in which separatists supported by the Russian army attempted to divide Ukraine into pro-Russian and pro-European parts.[7]

Also within the European territory, ruptures revealed that support for the European project was waning. Only a year after the expansion, French and Dutch citizens voted against the European Constitution. Romania and Bulgaria were admitted into the EU in 2007, but several member-states applied limitations with regard to the free movement of these countries' workers.[8] A year later, the financial crisis laid bare that the EU was no longer able to deliver on its promise to increase prosperity. Eurosceptic political movements from the far-right surged and Europe found itself struggling to stay united. Would authorities have been open to an artistic project that aimed to frame Europe's borders had we sought their permission a few years later?

Eluding trade barriers

On May 4, 2004—the day that the EU extended its borders with ten new member states—we stationed our camera on a hillside along the Polish-Ukrainian border. Our aim was to document how this national border would transform into an external border of a refigured Europe. While we observed the growing queue of cars, a farmer greeted us with sausages and coffee. When he handed us the sugar, he told us that the Polish *cukier* had become twice as sweet since Poland entered the European Union: the price had multiplied from one day to the next. As a result, Polish sugar was now even cheaper in the Ukraine than in Poland itself.

The farmer's remark incited us to investigate Europe's sugar market. We discovered that Europe's beet sugar industry had relied on political protection from the start. Beet sugar had not been able to compete with cane sugar imported from the colonies, where it was produced through the slavery system. A beet sugar industry came into existence in Europe only when, at the beginning of the 19th century, the English and the French set up trade blockades in their struggle for colonial hegemony. With Napoleon's financial support, sugar refineries were built all over Europe.

At the time we investigated Europe's sugar politics, the EU still provided financial support to its beet sugar industry. The internal sugar market was consolidated with a

---

6 The pro-European candidate won the elections after a revote, but tensions remained as one short-lived government after another attempted to reconcile the conflicting objectives of maintaining good relations with Russia and implementing reforms to meet Europe's requirements for collaboration. Larrabee, "Russia, Ukraine, and Central Europe."

7 The tensions culminated in 2014 in the Russian annexation of the Crimean peninsula.

8 Some European countries feared that the admittance of Bulgaria and Romania would set in motion an exodus of workers to other member states and would disrupt labor markets.

16.1 and 16.2

Still from Monument of Sugar—how to use artistic means to elude trade barriers *(2007, 16 mm film), depicting the production of a sugar block from European beet sugar respectively ...*

... depicting a ship unloading raw sugar bulk in the port of Lagos, filmed from the Dangote sugar refinery

© Lonnie Van Brummelen & Siebren de Haan (both)

so-called *intervention price*: a minimum selling price, which was substantially higher than what was offered on the world market. A financial instrument called *export restitution* made the expensive beet sugar competitive and allowed European sugar producers to dump their surplus sugar outside Europe. Meanwhile sugar imports were taxed heavily, to keep out foreign competitors. This elaborate system caused the price difference that the Polish farmer had observed.[9]

Trade statistics suggested that the majority of Europe's sugar exports were sold to Nigeria. With the aim of reversing Europe's sugar flow, we travelled to Lagos. We planned to purchase Europe's sugar cheaply on Nigeria's market, to transform the sweet crystals *in situ* into sculptural blocks, and to ship these back to Europe. Transforming the sugar into an artwork would allow us to submit our import application in Europe under the commodity code 9703, which applies to all monuments and original artworks regardless of the material in which they are produced.

The silent 16 mm film *Monument of Sugar - how to use artistic means to elude trade barriers* evaluates the project in scrolling titles alternated with documentary sequences showing the production of sugar and the making of the monument. The film essay also chronicles how our conceptual framework crumbled. We could find no trace on Nigeria's market of the large flows of European beet sugar that the data had suggested, but only found cane sugar imported from Brazil. Much to our surprise, sugar was by no means cheap. The high earnings generated from the export of oil had led to the overvaluation of the Nigerian *naira*, making it cheaper to import commodities than to produce them. To stimulate local production, the Nigerian government imposed levies on all foreign goods, including sugar. We had also not foreseen that exporting our sugar monument out of Nigeria would make it subject to a Nigerian regulation created to stop the exodus of antiques and other art treasures. After import levies, profit margins, and export permit, the Nigerian sugar blocks turned out to be even more expensive than sugar blocks made in Europe.

Tokens of Friendship

The *Lomé Convention* regulates the trade of sugar and other commodities between Europe and so-called ACP countries (formerly colonized countries in Africa, the Caribbean and the Pacific). When this convention came up for revision in 2000, the EU demanded the insertion of a clause that required ACP countries to "accept the return and readmission of any of its nationals illegally present in EU territory." The new agreement—now called the *Cotonou Agreement* after the city in Benin where the treaty was signed—also obligated the ACP countries to discourage undocumented migration, as well as to facilitate the work of European administrators tasked with evaluating asylum and immigration claims before would-be migrants departed for Europe.[10] Thus, while the treaty was nominally conceived to stimulate sustainable development, it ultimately only provided this support on the condition that the beneficiary countries became agents in Europe's border defense regime.

---

9 Since 2006, Europe reorganized its sugar market to reduce overproduction, causing many sugar beet farmers to shift to other crops and beet sugar factories to shut their doors.

10 Bialasiewicz, "Off-shoring and Out-sourcing the Borders of EUrope."

17.
Installation view of Monument of Sugar *as exhibited at Argos, Brussels (2007)*

More treaties followed that hid in their terms that they were instruments in the forti-
fication of Europe's outside borders. In August 2008, the Italian Prime Minister Berlusconi and the Libyan Colonel Gaddafi signed the *Treaty of Friendship, Partnership and
Cooperation* to settle long-running disputes between the two countries, such as Libya's
demands for reparations for the damages caused by colonialism, and claims from Italian companies that work carried out in Libya had never been paid for. The disputes
were resolved with the agreement that Italy would reimburse five billion euros to Libya
over a period of twenty years. The sum would be recuperated from tax revenues, which
Italy would collect on profits made by Italian companies operating in Libya. At the occasion of the treaty's signing, Italy also returned the Venus of Cyrene, a statue that
had been looted from Libya during the colonial period.[11] According to Berlusconi, the
sculpture's restitution and the *Friendship Treaty* were "a complete and moral acknowledgement of the damage inflicted on Libya by Italy during the colonial era."[12]

The treaty, however, not only mended old wounds with the help of an ancient artwork and future business opportunities, it also made provisions for bilateral efforts to
tighten the control of Libya's coast, its waters, and its terrestrial borders. Both countries agreed in the treaty to combat undocumented migration with the help of patrol
boats and a satellite detection system. Libya also consented to the disembarkation on
its soil of migrants intercepted in the Mediterranean Sea by Italian vessels.[13]

To most Europeans, these first signs that Europe was outsourcing its border protection by means of treaty-making went largely unnoticed. We, too, were absorbed by
other issues, such as the sudden rise of conservative nationalism, the growing resistance against migrants, and increased Islamophobia. In the same year that Italy signed
the Friendship Treaty with Libya and restituted the Venus of Cyrene, we started the art
project *Monument to Another Man's Fatherland*, which delved into Europe's roots of imperial cultural politics. Its point of departure was the Pergamon Altar—a monument
that is nowadays the property of Berlin's State Museums, but was in ancient times
constructed in what is present-day Turkey to celebrate a victory of Greek colonizers
over migrating Celts. Our plan was to make a film installation that would address the
expatriation of the monument and its appropriation for nation-building.[14] Since Berlin
hosts a large community of Turkish migrants, we wanted to do this by layering the
monument's 19th century relocation on contemporary migration.

At the time, many European countries had launched compulsory integration programs in response to reports of migrant integration "lagging behind" expectations.
Such programs not only included language classes but also civic courses aimed at fa-
miliarizing immigrants with the receiving country's norms, history, values and cul-

---

11 The headless statue of the *Venus of Cyrene* was originally located in the town of Cyrene, part of an an-
    cient Greek colony in Hellenistic times more than 2 millennia ago. It was taken by Italian troops in 1915
    for display in Rome. Chechi, Bandle, and Renold, "Case Venus of Cyrene—Italy and Libya."

12 "Italy seals Libya colonial deal."

13 Bialasiewicz, "Off-shoring and Out-sourcing the Borders of EUrope" and Ronzitti, "The Treaty on
    Friendship, Partnership and Cooperation between Italy and Libya: New Prospects for Cooperation
    in the Mediterranean?"

14 The State Museums in Berlin had been one of the signatories of the *Declaration on the Importance and
    Value of Universal Museums* (2002) which defended western museums policy to not restitute foreign
    artifacts to the countries of origin, even if the items were obtained under dubious circumstances.

tural traditions.[15] For our restaged version of the monument, we invited young Turkish men and women who were participating in an integration program at the Goethe Institute in Istanbul to describe before the camera in their fledgling German the mythical battle between Greek gods and giants that is depicted on the Pergamon Altar's frieze. The film was countered by a second film, which silently scanned the sculpted battle scene.

Because the Berlin State Museums repudiated our request to make film recordings in the museum with the comment that "the project might stir the debate about repatriation, something we are not interested in," we reconstructed the altar's frieze from images that we found in books, and instead of the sculpted relief, filmed the photomontage. The process of tracing images for the collage revealed that the altar had been used over and again both as a means of political bond-making and as a locus of cultural appropriation and exchange. For instance, we found one study that analyzed Pergamon's building style and appropriation of Greek mythology as propaganda to present the colony as genuinely Greek. Other books disclosed how the altar's frieze had been confiscated by Stalin's Red Army and brought to Leningrad as war booty, to be returned to Berlin in 1958 as "a token of friendship between the GDR and the USSR."

We were reminded once more of the entanglement of colonialism, migration, and art when in January 2019 a massive migration was announced, not of people traveling to Europe, but of art treasures crossing Europe's borders in the opposite direction: a massive relocation of things. French president Macron issued a statement that France was willing to return all art treasures ill-gotten during the colonial period to their countries of origin. He based his statement on a report—which he had commissioned himself—on the status of African objects in French museums. The report called for the prompt restitution of objects taken by force or acquired under unfair conditions, including items recovered during scientific missions prior to 1960, and "forgotten" objects—objects which had been lent by African institutions to French museums for the purpose of exhibition or restoration and never returned.[16] Because the French law of inalienability forbids the ceding of cultural heritage from public collections, the report proposed to amend the law. In line with these recommendations, the French president decided that, without further delay, twenty-six sculptures in the collection of the Musée du Quai Branly would be returned to Benin. The artefacts were spoils of war, pilfered by the French army after a historical battle at the end of the 19th century against the Kingdom of Dahomey. That these objects still sparked the African imagination became evident when, in 2006, some of them were exhibited in Cotonou, attracting hundreds of thousands of visitors—the same Cotonou where six years earlier the ACP countries had signed the treaty that turned them into partners in Europe's border regime.[17]

---

15   Carrera, "A Comparison of Integration Programmes in the EU."

16   The report was commissioned by Macron himself, and written by art-historian Bénédicte Savoy of France and scholar, writer and musician Felwine Sarr of Senegal. "Culture: un film sénégalais cofinancé par la Côte d'Ivoire au Festival de Cannes."

17   The exhibition marked one hundred years since the death of King Behanzin who had led the resistance against the French colonial troops.

18.1 and 18.2
Stills from Monument to Another Man's Fatherland:
Revolt of the Giants—recited by prospective Germans *(2009, 16 mm film)*

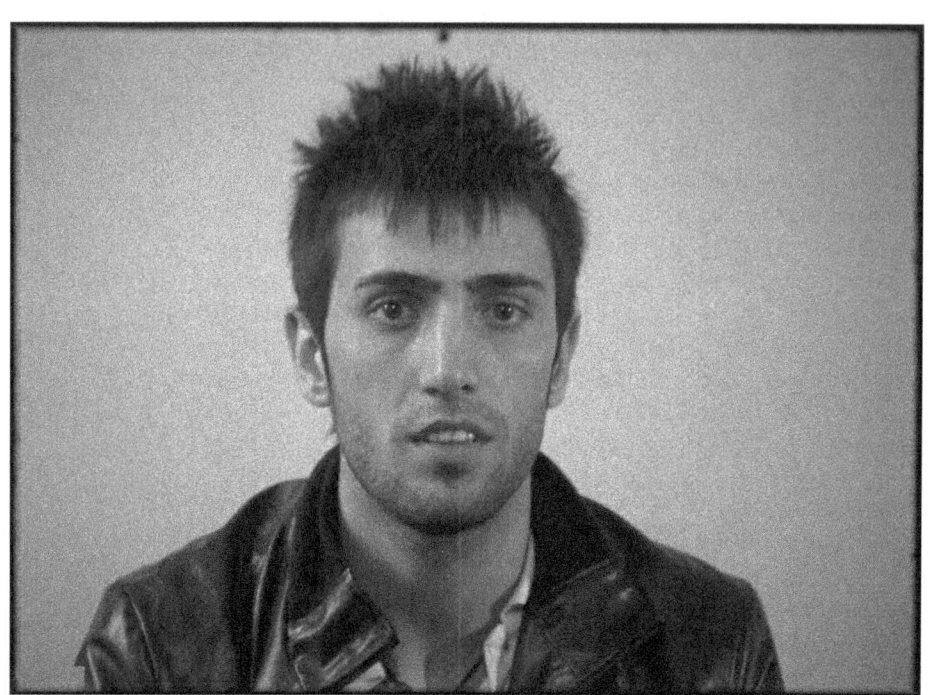

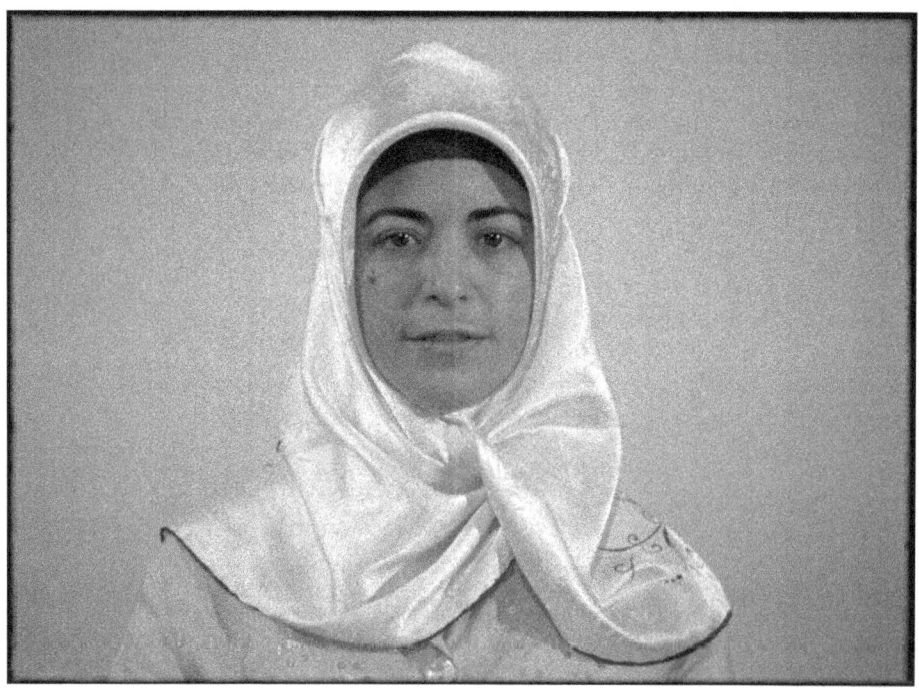

18.3
Still from Monument to Another Man's Fatherland:
Revolt of the Giants—reconstructed from reproductions *(2009, 35 mm film)*

© Commissioned by Project Art Center, Dublin, Lonnie Van Brummelen & Siebren de Haan

Will the French restitution of art treasures again be merely an instrument for European politics? A diversion to deflect anger over French immigration policy and the presence of French troops in West Africa? A form of leverage in ongoing negotiations over halting migration and securing access to resources?[18] Or could the shipping back of old artworks be a sign that Europe is finally prepared to reinvent its relation to what imagines as its outside?

New deal

How would we frame Europe's outline today? Although migration is often discussed as a European "crisis," countries in the Middle East and Africa host the most displaced persons. What most distinguishes Europe from these countries is its struggle to reconcile irregular migration with its self-image of being a neatly bounded, well-governed polity.[19] This image of regulatory competence seems to pivot on Europe's perceived effectiveness in controlling the flows of goods, property, ideas, and artworks into and out of its markets. We encountered Europe's complex regime of trade regulations during our research for *Monument of Sugar*.[20] But it is not only import levies that regulate Europe's market. Any company that makes or sells products within the European Union must comply with regulatory standards that pertain to food hygiene, traceability, environmental impact, competitiveness, and consumer privacy. The European Union applies, for example, a zero-tolerance policy to the presence of unauthorized biotech products in food and feed; it has strict directives with regard to the use of recyclable packaging; and it does not allow the testing of cosmetics on animals. Europe's General Data Protection Regulation (regulating the use of personal data by companies operating in the EU) and its Competition Law (restraining the anti-competitive conduct of companies) were able to restrain technology giants.[21] Market directives, regulations and other acts have thus enabled Europe to distribute its values and norms far beyond its territory.[22]

Regulating flows of services and things is however quite different from regulating flows of people. Persistent conflicts and atrocities in (among other nations) Syria, Afghanistan, and Eritrea caused large numbers of people to leave their country and seek refuge elsewhere. This resulted in a steep increase in the number of refugees traveling to Europe via the Mediterranean Sea. The term "migrant crisis" came into use in April 2015, when five boats sank with a combined death toll estimated at more than 1,200 people.[23] Due to the mass influx of people, government institutions in the EU

---

18 Nourhussen, "Macron vergat neokolonialisme."

19 Walters, "Imagined Migration World."

20 The same tariff barrier that incited us to make a monument of sugar to elude Europe's trade barrier for sugar imports, motivated the UK's largest sugar importer Tate & Lyle (founder of the Tate museums) to advocate for leaving the EU. During the Brexit campaign, images of Tate & Lyle's heaps of cane sugar came to illustrate the mountainous gains when the UK would liberate itself from the "tyranny" of European trade regulations and would finally be able to pursuit unrestricted free trade. Roberts, "Sweet Brexit."

21 European Commission Help Desk, "Trade Regime and General Product Safety"; de Gruyter, "Europa moet leren 'machtsdenken'."

22 European Union, "Regulations, Directives, and Other Acts"

23 European Regional Development Fund, "Interreg response to migration-related challenges."

responsible for the task of managing irregular migration became overloaded. To curb such 'un-European' disorder, the European Union concluded a whole range of treaties designed for the sole purpose of externalizing the control of its border. In 2016, a first deal to tackle the migrant crisis was brokered with Turkey. In exchange for six billion euros to support refugee shelters on its territory, Turkey committed to better guarding its borders and coastlines and to stop migrants sailing to Greece. In return, Turkey demanded that discussions on its membership in the European Union be sped up, and that visa requirements for Turkish citizens entering the EU be waived. The deal caused great division within the Union. Cyprus refused to talk about Turkish membership until the Turkish occupation of half its territory had been resolved. But also, How could Europe stand up for values such as democracy, equality, freedom of expression, or human rights, if it outsourced its border security to a state that increasingly violated these values? What values did Europe actually represent?

In 2013, Morocco became the first country in the Mediterranean area to sign a Mobility Agreement with the European Union that includes an objective to "combat illegal immigration." It also endorsed deals on immigration with individual EU countries, particularly with Spain. To comply with the task of halting undocumented migration to Europe, Moroccan authorities often arbitrarily arrest migrants during raids, and deport them to remote areas.[24] But like Turkey, Morocco also uses its contribution to Europe's border protection as leverage in other negotiations, such as its claim to the Western Sahara. After colonial Spain left North Africa, the Polisario Front and Morocco battled to get control of Western Sahara until a ceasefire was agreed upon in 1991. The area has been disputed territory ever since. In 2016, the European Court of Justice ruled that trade agreements between the European Union and Morocco could therefore not include products from this region. Since the ruling, Morocco seems less motivated to guard Europe's border. With growing flows of migrants, it tries to pressure the EU to support its claim to the Western Sahara, or at least turn a blind eye to products coming from this region.[25]

Although outsourcing borderwork has turned out to be a sticky wicket for Europe, more treaties have followed. Italy, for instance, has reactivated its *Friendship Treaty* with Libya after suspending it during the Arab Spring. Libya also received substantial funding from Europe for "managing mixed migration flows"—EU jargon for distinguishing refugees from other migrants—and for "improving migration management"—which includes the repatriation of migrants, border surveillance, and improving the conditions in immigration detention centers.[26] Because it was not easy to do business with a fragmented Libya ravaged by years of civil war, Europe also began making agreements with countries deeper into the African continent.[27] Niger, for example, is one of the countries through which migrants from Burkina Faso, Ivory Coast, Nigeria, Guinea, Ghana, Togo, and Benin pass on their way to Libya. With European funding, Niger's border

---

24 Alami, "Morocco Unleashes a Harsh Crackdown on Sub-Saharan Migrants."

25 Nielsen, "Investigation exposed;" Bolongard, "Morocco offers fish for land;" European Commission, "Migration and mobility partnership signed between the EU and Morocco."

26 Grün, "Follow the money."

27 Since its founding in 2015, the European Union Emergency Trust Fund for Africa—aimed at "addressing root causes of irregular migration and displaced persons in Africa"—pledged over four billion euros in 'partnerships' with 26 African countries. European Commission, "EU Emergency Trust Funds for Africa."

19.
Still from Grossraum (Borders of Europe), *(2004/2005, 35 mm film),*
depicting the flag of the Turkish Republic of Northern Cyprus in painted pebbles

surveillance regime was tightened, human traffickers were put behind bars, pick-up trucks (used to transport migrants through the desert) were confiscated, and new legislation was adopted prohibiting the transportation of undocumented migrants. Europe even started a re-employment project for the more than 6,000 Nigerians who had been working in the migrant industry and had become jobless due to the measures.

Sudan is also a transit country for migrants on their way to Libya. Eritreans, Ethiopians, Chadians, Somalis and even Syrians travel through it. Sudan's President al-Bashir was the first sitting head of state to be indicted by the International Criminal Court in The Hague for masterminding and implementing a plan during the war in Darfur to destroy the Fur, Masalit and Zaghawa populations.[28] Nevertheless, many European countries strengthened their diplomatic ties with Sudan during al-Bashir's dictatorship and the European Union released more than 150,000,000 euros for the training and gearing up of the Sudanese border police.[29]

Such partnerships brought Europe into troubled waters with regards to human rights and international law.[30] Media frequently report of migrants being either abused by the law enforcement officers of contracted governments or stranded in overrun processing camps under the remit of the partner countries, where they are vulnerable to robbery, rape or even to being sold off as enslaved laborers.

Europe's new "migration deals," "friendship treaties," and "mobility agreements" do not seem so different from the treaties of Westphalia, which for centuries have shaped the identity of Europe and secured its hegemony. In the process, the new treaties distribute European priorities such as strong borders to Niger, Turkey, and elsewhere.

Where would we have stationed our camera if we wanted to document Europe's boundaries today? Would we have filmed in a refugee camp in Turkey, funded by the EU? Would we place the camera at the border between Nigeria and Niger, where road signs adorned with EU logos inform travelers that "Illegal transportation of migrants exposes you to a fine of 1,000,000 to 3,000,000 CFA Franc?"[31] Would we try to retrieve images from the European satellite detection system that scours the Saharan dust road between Sudan and Libya? Or would we seek permission to film at Charles de Gaulle airport in Paris where once-looted artworks are loaded into airplanes to be returned to their countries of origin? One thing seems certain: Europe is no longer the only party sitting at the negotiation table, and its mandate is no longer the bedrock for the dialogue. The continent is requested to deliver on its oft-repeated promise of a partnership of equals.

---

28 "Omar al-Bashir."

29 Vermeulen and de Korte, "Gewapend met migratiecijfers gooien we onze grenzen dich;" van Dijken and Suleiman, "De weg naar Europa loopt via Soedan;" Chandler, Khartoum, "Inside the EU's flawed $200 million migration deal with Sudan."

30 "Escape from Libya." This article appeared in the Middle East and Africa section of the print edition under the headline "Homeward bound."

31 European Council on Refugees and Exiles, "Transporter illégalement des migrants vous expose à une peine d'amende de 1.000.000 à 3.000.000 F CFA." A picture of the road shield is depicted with the article "Commission praises progress under EU Partnership Framework—human rights organisations raise concern." As of March 2019, the exchange rate is €1 = 655 CFA Francs.

Migrant Images

Thomas Nail

The twenty-first century is an age of mobility. Enormous numbers of people are on the move today in increasingly unequal ways. More images, too, are on the move. The migrant has become the political figure of our time just as the mobile digital image has become the aesthetic figure of our time. The migrant and the image are part of the same historical primacy of motion and mobility that defines life in the early twenty-first century. This chapter argues that we need to re-theorize the migrant and the image *from the perspective of motion.*

This is an important conceptual move because, on the one hand, the migrant has been predominantly understood as a secondary political figure derived from the static basis of states. The migrant is typically defined as the one who moves between pre-established states. Opposed to this, this chapter argues that the migrant is in fact a constitutive figure of social life itself. On the other hand, the image has been predominantly understood as something static, either as a representation of an object or as an imagination by the subject.

Both of these static conceptions, I argue, should be replaced with a kinetic theory of the "migrant image." However, by the term "migrant image" I do not necessarily mean visual or art images *of* migrants, art *by* migrants, or the migration of art images across borders, although these are all important aspects of migrant images. I mean something much more general about the material structure of images and migrants themselves. The image does not become mobile just because it represents migrants, and the mobility of migrants is not derived merely from our images of them. Rather, the argument I would like to make in this chapter is that the social primacy of the migrant and the aesthetic primacy of the mobile image are two dimensions of the same historical zeitgeist at the turn of the twenty-first century in which everything appears to be characterized by *the primacy of motion.*

Therefore, instead of trying to derive the mobility of one from the other, I would like to show the common conceptual redefinition occurring in both with respect to the primacy of mobility in the twenty-first century. In order to do this, I begin first with the social primacy of the figure of the migrant and then move on to consider the kinesthetics of the mobile image. The aim is to demonstrate the sense in which the migrant has become a dominant *social image* for us today, as well the sense in which the image has become *aesthetically migratory* and mobile at the same time.

The Figure of the Migrant

We live in the age of the migrant. At the turn of the twenty-first century, there were more regional and international migrants than ever before in recorded history.[1] Today, there are over 1 billion migrants.[2] Each decade, the percentage of migrants as a share of the total population continues to rise. In the next 25 years, the rate of migration is predicted to be higher than over the last 25 years.[3] More than ever, it has become a necessity for people to migrate due to environmental, economic, and political instability. Climate change, in particular, may even double international migration over the next 40 years.[4] Even more, the percentage of total migrants who are non-status or undocumented is further increasing, which poses a serious challenge to democracy and political representation.[5]

In other ways, despite the gulf that separates different forms of movement, we are all *becoming* migrants.[6] People today relocate greater distances more frequently than ever before in human history. While many people may not cross a regional or international border in their movement, they tend to change jobs more often, commute longer and further to work,[7] change their residence repeatedly, and tour internationally more than ever before.[8] Some of these phenomena are directly related to recent events, such as the impoverishment of middle classes in certain rich countries after the financial crisis of 2008, which include subsequent austerity cuts to social welfare programs, rising unemployment, the subprime mortgage crisis, which led to the expulsion of millions of people from their homes around the world (9 million in the United States alone since 2008), the eviction of millions of small farmers in poor countries owing to the 540 million acres acquired by foreign investors and governments since 2006, and increasingly destructive mining practices around the world, including hydraulic fracturing and tar sands. This general increase in human mobility and expulsion that affects us all is now widely recognized as a defining feature of our epoch.[9]

---

1 In total number (1 billion: 1 in 7) and as percentage of total population (about 14 %) according to the International Organization on Migration.

2 United Nations Population Fund, *State of World Population 2015*. As of 2015, there were 244 million international migrants and 740 million internal migrants according to the United Nations Population Fund.

3 On the theoretical implications of this phenomenon for liberalism, see Cole, *Philosophies of Exclusion*.

4 According to the International Organization for Migration, future forecasts vary from 25 million to 1 billion environmental migrants by 2050, moving either within their countries or across borders, on a permanent or temporary basis, with 200 million being the most widely cited estimate. This figure equals the current estimate of international migrants worldwide; International Organization for Migration.

5 The International Council on Human Rights Policy estimates that the approximate numbers of global irregular migrants have grown to 30–40 million persons.

6 With the rise of home foreclosure and unemployment, people today are beginning to have much more in common with migrants than with certain notions of citizenship (grounded in certain social, legal, and political rights).

7 World Bank's World Development Indicators.

8 World Tourism Organization, "World Tourism Barometer." International tourist arrivals exceeded 1 billion annual tourists globally for the first time in history in 2012.

9 Sassen, *Expulsions*, 1–2. I use the word expulsion here in the same sense in which Saskia Sassen uses it to indicate a general dispossession or deprivation of social status. Many scholars have noted a similar

However, not all migrants are alike in their movement, and neither are the reasons for their movement consistent, shared, or uniform across space and time.[10] For some, movement offers opportunity, recreation, and profit with only a temporary expulsion from or deprivation of their territorial, political, juridical, or economic status. For others, movement is dangerous, constrained, and their social expulsions are much more severe and permanent. Today, most people fall somewhere on this migratory spectrum between the two poles of "inconvenience" and "incapacitation." But at some point, everyone on this spectrum shares the minimal experience that their *movement* results in a certain degree of expulsion from their territorial, political, juridical, or economic status. Even if the end result of migration is a relative increase in money, power, or enjoyment, the *process of migration itself* almost always involves a "sacrifice" or "cost" of some kind and duration: the removal of territorial ownership or access, the loss of the political right to vote or to receive social welfare, the loss of legal status to work or drive, or the financial loss associated with transportation or change in residence.

The gains of migration are always a risk, while the process itself is always some kind of loss. This is precisely the sense in which Zygmunt Bauman writes that "tourism and vagrancy are two faces of the same coin" of global migration.[11] Both the "tourist" (the traveling academic, business professional, or vacationer) and the "vagabond" (migrant worker or refugee), as Bauman calls them, are "bound to move" by the same social conditions, but result in different kinds and degrees of expulsion from the social order.[12] Business people are compelled to travel around the world in the "global chase of profit," "consumers must never be allowed to rest" in the chase of new commodities and desires, and the global poor must move from job to job wherever capital calls.[13] For the "tourist," this social "compulsion, [this] 'must,' [this] internalized pressure, [this] impossibility of living one's life in any other way," according to Bauman, "reveals itself to them in the disguise of a free exercise of will."[14]

The "vagabond" sees it more clearly. The social "compulsion" to move produces certain expulsions for all migrants. Some migrants may 'decide' to move, but they may not decide the social conditions of their movement or the degree to which they may be expelled from certain social orders as a consequence. Migration in this sense is neither entirely free nor forced; the two are part of the same internally differentiated *regime of social motion*. 'Expulsion' simply means the degree to which a migrant is deprived or dispossessed of a certain status in this regime.

The "tourist" and "vagabond" are always crossing over into one another. "None of the insurance policies of the tourists' life-style protects against slipping into vagabondage [...] most jobs are temporary, shares may go down as well as up, skills, the assets one is proud of and cherishes now become obsolete in no time."[15] Migration is the spectrum between these two poles, and the figure of the migrant is the one who moves

---

trend. For an excellent review of the "mobilities" literature on migration, see Blunt, "Cultural Geographies of Migration."

10 Bauman, *Globalization*.

11 Bauman, *Globalization*, 96.

12 Bauman, *Globalization*, 85.

13 Bauman, *Globalization*, 78, 83.

14 Bauman, *Globalization*, 84.

15 Bauman, *Globalization*, 97.

on this spectrum. In this way, migratory figures often change their status as mobile social positions and not fixed identities.

Accordingly, there is no theory of the migrant "as such." There is no general ontology of the migrant. There are only figures of the migrant that emerge and coexist throughout history relative to specific sites of expulsion and mobility. A figure is not a fixed identity or specific person but a mobile social position. One becomes a figure when one occupies this position. One may occupy this position to different degrees, at different times, and in different circumstances. But there is nothing essential about a person that makes the person this figure.

A figure is not an unchanging essence lying beyond the concrete, but neither is it merely a specific individual or a group of individuals. A figure is a social vector or tendency. Insofar as specific individuals take up a trajectory, they are figured by it. But it is also possible for individuals to leave this vector and take up a different social position, since it does not define their essence. In other words, the *figure* of the migrant has a "vague essence" in the etymological sense of the word: a vagabond or migratory essence that lies *between* the ideal and the empirical.

For example, in geometry, a circle is an exact ideal essence. This is in contrast to inexact empirical objects that are round (such as bowls, planets, or balls). However, figuration is like "roundness": it is more than an empirical object but less than an ideal exact essence. Roundness can refer equally to bowls and to ideal circles: both are round. Thus, as a figure, the migrant refers both to empirical migrants in the world *and* a more abstract social relation. It is irreducible to either.

One is not born a migrant but becomes one. However, there are two central problems to overcome in order to develop a movement-oriented theory of the migrant.

Two Problems

The first problem is that the migrant has been predominantly understood from the perspective of *stasis*. The result is that the migrant has been perceived as a secondary or derivative figure with respect to place-bound membership. Place-bound membership in a society is posited first. Then the migrant is defined as the movement back and forth between social points. The emigrant is the name given to the migrant as the former member or citizen, and the immigrant as the would-be member or citizen. In both cases, a static place and membership is conceived first, and the migrant is the one who lacks both. This is the case because more than any other political figure (citizen, foreigner, sovereign, etc.), the migrant is the one who is least defined by their being and place, but rather by their becoming and displacement: by their *movement*.

Therefore, if we want to develop a political theory that *begins* with the migrant, we need to reinterpret the migrant first and foremost according to its own defining feature: its movement. Thus, we should develop a theoretical framework that begins with movement instead of stasis, following in the tradition of those thinkers who have granted theoretical primacy to movement and flow: Lucretius, Marx, Henri Bergson, and others.[16] However, beginning from the theoretical primacy of movement does not mean that one should uncritically celebrate it. Movement is not always good, nor is

16 For a full literature review of the history and thinkers of the ontology of motion, see Nail, *Being and Motion*.

movement always the same or uniform.[17] Movement is always distributed in differ-ent social formations or circulations.[18] Thus, the *migrant turn* is neither a valorization of movement nor an ontology of movement in general. Rather, it is a philosophical or what I call a "historical ontology" of the subject of our time: the *migrant*.[19] It seeks to understand the historical conditions under which something like contemporary mi-gration has come to exist for us today.

In this way, we need not only a theory of the migrant, but also a theory of the so-cial motions by which migration takes place. Society is always in motion. From border security and city traffic controls to personal technologies and work schedules, human movement is socially directed. Societies are not static places with fixed characteris-tics and persons.[20] Societies are dynamic processes engaged in continuously directing and circulating social life. In a movement-oriented framework there is no social stasis, only regimes of social circulation pockmarked by temporary and contingent sites of concrescence. Thus, if we want to understand the figure of the migrant, whose defin-ing social feature is its movement, we must also understand *society itself* according to movement.[21]

The second problem that needs to be overcome is that the migrant has been pre-dominantly understood from the perspective of *states*. And since history is all-too-often written by the state, the result is that the migrant has often been understood as a figure without its own history and social force. "In world history," as Hegel says, "we are concerned only with those peoples that have formed states [because] all the value that human beings possess, all of their spiritual reality, they have through the State alone."[22] This is not to say that migrants are always stateless, but that the history of migrant social organizations has tended to be subsumed or eradicated by state histo-ries. Often, it is the most dispossessed migrants who have created some of the most interesting non-state social organizations.

In response to this problem, we need a counter-history of several important mi-grant social organizations that have been marginalized by states. The migrant is not only the figure whose movement results in a certain degree of social expulsion; the migrant also has its own type of movement that is quite different from the types that define its expulsion. Accordingly, migrants have created very different forms of social organization, as can clearly be seen in the 'minor history' of the raids, revolts, rebel-lions, and resistances of some of the most socially marginalized migrants.[23] This is a challenging history to write because many of these social organizations were not writ-ten down, or if they were, they were systematically destroyed by those in power. It is

17 Said, *Reflections on Exile and Other Essays.*

18 For a review of the criticisms against the philosophy of movement, see Merriman, *Mobility, Space and Culture*, 1–20.

19 Nail, *Being and Motion.*

20 Urry, *Sociology Beyond Societies.*

21 In this sense, this chapter can also be placed in the context of what is now being called the "new mo-bilities paradigm" or "mobility turn" in the social sciences. See Hannam et al., "Editorial: Mobilities, Immobilities and Moorings," 1–22; Cresswell, *On the Move*; Kaufmann, *Re-thinking Mobility*; Urry, *Mobili-ties*; Thrift, *Spatial Formations.*

22 Hegel, *Introduction to the Philosophy of History*, 41–42.

23 Notes from Nowhere, *We Are Everywhere.*

not a natural fact that the history of migrants has become ahistorical, as Hegel argues; it is the violence of states that has rendered the migrant ahistorical.

The Consequences

There are three important consequences of developing a political theory of the migrant in this way. First, it will allow us to *conceptualize the emergence of the historical conditions* that gave rise to the types of social expulsion that define the figure of the migrant. These forms of social expulsion linked to migrant motion did not emerge out of nowhere in the twentieth-first century; they emerged historically. At different points in history, migratory movement resulted in different types and degrees of social expulsion (territorial, political, juridical, and economic) due in part to the presupposed ontological primacy of stasis. Once a new form of social organization becomes historically dominant (i.e. villages, states, feudal lands, markets, etc.), we begin to see an explosion in new techniques for expelling migrants from their territorial, political, legal, or economic status. Once these techniques emerge historically, they are differentially repeated again later on. Today, we find the contemporary migrant at the intersection of all four forms of social expulsion, albeit to varying degrees.

The aim of such a project should also be historical: to provide an analysis of the major techniques for expelling migrants during their period of historical dominance and to provide a conceptual, movement-based, definition of the migratory figures associated with these expulsions.[24]

The second consequence of the theory of the migrant is that it will allow us to *analyze contemporary migration*. This is possible because the history of migration is not a linear or progressive history of distinct 'ages.' Rather, it is a history of co-existing and overlapping social forces of expulsion. The same techniques of territorial, political, juridical, and economic expulsion of the migrants that have emerged and repeated themselves in history are still at work today. For example, territorial expulsion (the dispossession of land)[25] does not only occur once against the nomadic peoples in the Neolithic period. Once this technique of expulsion emerges in the Neolithic period, it is taken up again and mobilized in various ways throughout history up to the present.

The first territorial expulsions created *historical* nomadic peoples, but they also defined a *conceptual* type of migrant subjectivity characterized by territorial expulsion that also defines other territorially displaced peoples. This is the sense in which migrants may be 'nomadic' without being the same as historical nomads. As an example, in the ancient world, migrants were expelled from their territories by war and kidnapping; in the medieval world, they were expelled by enclosure and the removal of customary laws that bound them to the land; and in the modern world, they were expelled by the capitalist accumulation of private property. In each case, these events,

---

24 Castles, *Mistaken Identity*. Stephen Castles has also argued that the figure of the migrant needs to be defined in relation to its other overlapping historical figures, such as indentured laborer, refugee and exile.

25 Here I am using the word "territory" simply to mean "delimited land" (following the OED) and not in a strictly historical way since, as Stuart Elden argues in *The Birth of Territory*, the usage of the word territory varies significantly throughout history and cannot be used in a univocal way.

like a festival, paradoxically repeat an "unrepeatable." "They do not add a second and a third time to the first, but carry the first time to the 'nth' power."[26]

Contemporary migration is part of this legacy.[27] Migrant farm workers expelled by industrial agriculture, Indigenous peoples[28] expelled from their lands by war and forced into the mountains, forests, or waste lands, and island peoples expelled from their territories whether by militarized relocation, nuclear detonation, or the rising tides of climate change are all often popularly described as "nomads."[29] In a certain sense, this is true. All these migrants share those similar social conditions of territorial expulsion that first produced historical nomads.

The analysis of contemporary migration I am arguing for here is not one of total causal explanation of push-pull factors, psychological volunteerism, neoclassical or structural economism, and so on. Rather, it offers a descriptive kinetic analysis. The aim is not to explain the causes of all migration, but to offer better descriptions of the conditions, forces, and trajectories of its historical emergence and co-existence in the present from the perspective of motion.

The third consequence of a theory of the migrant is that it will allow us to *diagnose the capacity of the migrant to create an alternative* to the social expulsion of the migrant. The figure of the migrant is not merely an effect of different regimes of social expulsion. The migrant also has its own forms of social motion in the form of riots, revolts, rebellions, and resistance. Even occupation and "staying put" has its own pattern of motion.[30] Just as the analysis of the historical techniques for the expulsion of the migrant can be used to understand contemporary migration, so too can the historical techniques of migrant social organizations be used to diagnose the capacity of contemporary migrants to pose an alternative to the present social logic of expulsion that continues to dominate our world.

Today, the figure of the migrant exposes an important truth: that social expansion has always been predicated on the social expulsion of migrants. The twenty-first century will be the century of the migrant not only because of the record number of migrants today, but because this is the century in which all the previous forms of social expulsion and migratory resistance have re-emerged and become more active than ever before. These two events also reveal, however, a certain historical and conceptual continuity of migratory struggles for an alternative to social expulsion.

If we think of the recent "migrant crisis" as if it were an unexpected and contingent outbreak that can simply be "solved," we will continue make the same historical mistakes and misunderstand what migration is as a broader historical social structure. Thus any theory of the migrant today requires a much deeper historical account to properly see that it is not migration that is the problematic historical anomaly, but nation-states.

---

26 Deleuze, *Difference and Repetition*, 1.

27 As Tim Cresswell writes, "We cannot understand new mobilities, without understanding old mobilities." Cresswell, "Towards a Politics of Mobility," 25.

28 Nail, *Theory of the Border*; Nail, *The Figure of the Migrant*.

29 Cresswell, "Towards a Politics of Mobility."

30 Nail, *The Figure of the Migrant*, 156–178.

The same historical conditions at the beginning of the twenty-first century that give rise to the primacy of the figure of the migrant also give rise to the primacy of the mobile image.

The Mobile Image

We also live in an age of the image. Just before the turn of the twenty-first century a host of digital media technologies (computers, the Internet, video games, mobile devices, and many others) unleashed the largest flow of digitally reproduced words, images, and sounds the world has ever witnessed. No other aesthetic medium can possibly compete with what digital media have done to human sensation in the last twenty years. The digital image has mobilized sensory and aesthetic experience in more ways than ever before in history.

While the effect of television and radio on sensation was significant, they still restricted sensation to relatively centralized, homogenized, and unidirectional programming. The interactive and multi-directional nature of contemporary digital media has expanded the mobility and mutability of the image in a way that analog media never could. With the popularization of the Internet and mobile devices at the turn of the twenty-first century—cell phones, smartphones, tablets, and laptops—digitized images have become not only dominant but increasingly portable.[31] As of 2014, there were more active mobile devices than there are people on the planet. The mobile phone is probably the single fastest-growing human sensory technology ever developed, growing from zero to 7.2 billion in a mere three decades.

The mobility of the digital image has incited a revolution in publishing, journalism, entertainment, education, commerce and politics. It has both overthrown and wholly integrated analog media, giving rise to whole new digitized industries in the process. Industrial factories and workers are increasingly supplemented by internet servers and automated checkout software. It is plainly obvious to everyone that we have now entered a new aesthetic regime; we are now in the age of the digital image.

Today, it is possible for huge numbers of people to communicate by voice or text with anyone else; to listen to almost every sound ever recorded; to view almost any image ever made; and to read almost any text ever written from a single device and from almost any location on Earth. All of this is now available on the move and is itself in movement in the form of electrical flows. The image will never be the same. Yet, at the same time, unequal access to digital media and information is also a growing problem directly related to the unequal distribution of mobility and migration.

The contemporary mobility of the image and its sensation, made possible by the advent and now dominance of digital media, is not just a quantitative increase in reproduced images. Digital media and digital images have transformed the very conditions of sensation itself. Anything can now be potentially digitized, mobilized, and browsed non-linearly through a single portable device. The whole of aesthetic reality can now be made responsive and interactive with the viewer through the use of digital software

---

31 Internet World Stats. Today 77 % of developed countries and 40 % of the entire world use the Internet. It has become the single-largest mechanism for the production, mobilization, and consumption of sensory media.

and a continuous flow of electrical current—which is also key in the shaping of citizenship. None of the senses have remained unchanged by digital media; even taste and smell can now be synthesized using computer software.[32] Something is always lost in transit as the continuous is converted into the digitally discrete, but the affect moves on regardless, sweeping us all along with it.

More than ever before, the fact that the image is up in the air and on the move requires a serious rethinking of the nature of art, media, and affect from the perspective of the present, from the age of the mobile image. Something fundamental about our world changed around the turn of the twenty-first century; not just an empirical change introduced by new technologies, but a new and fundamentally *kinetic* set of relations in media and aesthetics have begun to appear.

The exceptions to the rules of the previous historical paradigms have now themselves become the rules in a whole new game. Mobile digital devices are no longer luxury items for the privileged few but have transformed every aspect of daily life around the world, including the very structure of human experience, thought, and sensation. If everything looks like a crisis today—the migration crisis and the digital media crisis (big data, privacy infringement, the privatization and censorship of the Internet)[33]—it is because we are still looking at our present through the eyes of the past. As long as these kinds of critical events continue to appear as secondary or derivative, as long as motion and mobility appear to be deviations from stasis, we have no hope of understanding some of the greatest events of our time.

Migrant Media

The mobile image and the centrality of the migrant mark a new period in aesthetics and media culture.[34] The digital image is not only mobile by virtue of its form but by the mobility of its content, material infrastructure, and author. Some of most shared and viewed images of the last few years have been digital images of migrants, refugees, and the conditions of their travels, and even their death. The image of Alan Kurdi, the dead Syrian three-year old, is now one of the most influential images of all time.[35] An iconic photo of migrants on a beach holding their mobile phones up in the air to try and get a signal to call home won the 2014 World Press Photo Award. We think of image viewing as a passive activity separate from the legal system, but the circulation of migrant images should be taken seriously as a political act with real consequences.

On the other hand anti-immigrant media representations and rhetoric have also proliferated. In particular, the spread of images and rhetoric of the migrant caravan as a military "invasion" of the United States have had disastrous consequences. President Trump called the caravan an "invasion" and "an assault on our country;" the Associated Press called it an "army of migrants" and tweeted about "a ragtag army of the poor;"

32 Turin, *The Secret of Scent.*

33 Chun, *Updating to Remain the Same.*

34 This turn perhaps had its early origins at the turn of the last century. See Benjamin, "The Work of Art in the Age of Mechanical Reproduction."

35 See Vis and Goriunova, *The Iconic Image on Social Media,* as well as Bishnupriya Ghosh's "A Sensible Politics" in this anthology.

and Robert Bowen murdered eleven people in a Synagogue because a Jewish refugee group supported caravan refugees.[36] Trump even told the border patrol to shoot migrants if they throw rocks.[37] This aesthetic criminalization of migrants and the rise of cyber-racism helped mobilize anti-immigrant militia groups and popular support against refugees.[38] Now refugees are being deported from the US and detained in cages in Mexico *as if* they were criminals. The explicit media framing of migrants as a violent, criminal, military invasion is an old historical tactic with a huge popular resurgence in the US and Europe.[39]

Because these images circulated across digital and social media so quickly, people formed opinions and judgements before the real details of the caravan were known or could be disseminated by more accurate sources. In this way so much of migration politics happens before the confrontation at the border or transversally across borders. Thus the circulation of media images has its own kind of migration and has its own kinds of borders that are not necessarily spatially or temporally congruent with the migrant bodies at the border or in detention. There is simply no way to fully understand migration politics without understanding migrant images as part of the process—confronting their own barriers and waging their confrontations as they affect everyone.

However, the widespread access to cell phones with digital cameras has also made it possible for migrants and refugees themselves to generate more images of their own movement and experience than ever before. The itinerant, grainy, handheld, and "poor" images of migrant cell phone cameras have become their own film genre: the "wretched of the screen."[40] In these videos migrants are not silent victims but creators of new aesthetic forms, "an imperfect cinema"[41] as demonstrated in Elke Sasse's 2016 film *#MyEscape*.

Cell phones have also become literal lifelines for migrants to obtain travel information in isolated areas, to share videos, sounds and images with friends, family, and authorities (but, as well, as Heller & Pazzani, in this volume, tell us, they are also part of a perilous politics of visibility that render migrants detectable, identifiable, prosecutable by migrant-exclusionary states). Images of all kinds (sonic, visual, haptic, etc.)[42] produced by migrants have become the material basis of the aesthetic threads that hold together numerous committees across borders, not just refugees. Although it is most obvious in the case of refugees, these are the same aesthetic lifelines that make possible sustained social and informational communities around the world. The migrancy of the digital image is what allows for community in a world of global migration, continuous mobility, and displacement. What would global migration look like without the migrancy of the image and the images of the migrant?

The migrant image thus marks the limits of the previous century and the outline of a new one defined by the mobility and migration of the image. This requires a new

---

36 Gitlin, "The Wild-Eyed Coverage of the Caravan."

37 Democracy Now, "Trump ramps up migrant attacks, says soldiers can shoot migrants."

38 Miroff, "U.S. militia groups head to border, stirred by Trump's call to arms."

39 Nail, "We are Entering a New Epoch: The Century of the Migrant."

40 Steyerl, *The Wretched of the Screen.*

41 Espisona, "For an Imperfect Cinema."

42 Nail, *Theory of the Image.*

approach both to the politics of migration and the media image. However, the advent of the present is never limited to the present alone. Now that our present has emerged, it has become possible in a way it was not before to inquire into the conditions of its emergence and discover something new about the nature and history of mediation. In other words, the present reveals something new about the nature of sensation and what it must *at least* be like so as to be capable of being defined by the primacy of motion and mobility as it is.

So, what does this say about the nature of the image such that it is capable of this mobility? If the image is defined by the primacy of mobility today yet existing theories of it are not, then we need a new conceptual framework. We need to produce such a new conceptual framework based on the primacy of motion to better understand contemporary sensation and aesthetics, as well as the historical events from which it emerges. In short, the rise of the mobile digital image draws our attention not so much to its radical novelty,[43] but to the inappropriate understanding of historical 'crisis' itself.

The research program proposed by this chapter is therefore neither a theory of the migrant image that applies strictly to the novelty of the digital image nor an ahistorical theory of the image that applies forever and all time to all images and media. I am not proposing a naive realism in which the discovery of the contemporary primacy of motion gives us pure access to unchanging essence of the image. Instead, I am proposing a realism of the *minimal affective conditions* of the emergence of the present itself. That is, a *critical* or *minimal realism* in the sense in which the image is interpreted only with respect to that aspect of the image that must at least be the case for our present 'to have been possible,' i.e., actual.

Therefore, the method proposed here is neither realist or constructivist in their traditional senses, but rather *minimally* or *critically realist*. The question is not what the conditions of the human mind must be for the image to be what it is, but rather what *the image itself* must *at least* be like such that the present has come to be defined by the primacy of a mobile or migratory aesthetics.

Without a doubt, contemporary reality is shaped by multiple human structures, but these structures are in turn conditioned by other real, non-anthropic, affective, and aesthetic structures. This chapter proposes that we locate the real conditions necessary for the emergence of the contemporary mobility of the image and of global migration. The type of global migration we are witnessing today would not be possible without the unique material and media structure of the digital image.

The Migrant Image

The migrant image is not a copy. It is not even a copy of a copy without an original.[44] There is no mimesis whatsoever. If we are looking for a new and more fruitful definition of the migrant image, we need look no further than within the same Latin root of the word itself. The word image, from the Latin word *imago*, means "reflection, dupli-

43 Hansen, *New Philosophy for New Media*; Hansen, *Bodies in Code*; Manning, *Relationscapes*; Massumi, *Parables for the Virtual*; Naukkarinen, "Aesthetics and Mobility"; O'Sullivan, "The Aesthetics of Affect"; Gregg et al., *The Affect Theory Reader*.

44 Baudrillard, *Simulacra and Simulation*.

cation, or echo."[45] These definitions imply precisely the opposite of what we typically think of as a copy. A copy must be something other than its model or, by definition, it cannot be a copy *of a model*.

Reflection, however, from the Latin word *flex*, means to bend or curve. A reflection is a re-curving or re-bending that folds something back over itself. Duplication, from the Latin word *pli*, meaning fold, and the example of an echo, given in the Oxford Latin Dictionary, make this meaning quite apparent. The image is not a distinct or separate copy but the process by which matter curves, bends, folds, and bounces back and forth.[46] The image is therefore the mobile process by which matter twists, folds, and reflects itself into various structures of sensation. The migrant too is defined by its flows, folds, and circulations—always in transit and caught between worlds.

There are not first static objects, subjects, and states and then second a movement or transfer of images or migrants between them. Rather, there is first matter in motion and then a folding, composition, and duplication that generates larger sensuous matters like objects and subjects that then further reflect and duplicate the flows of matter between them.[47] A folded image is not a copy because a fold is not something separate from the matter that is folded. The fold is a completely continuous kinetic and topological structure. There is not one part of the fold which would be an original and another that would be a copy. This is the sense in which Henri Bergson writes that the image is "more than that which the idealist calls a *representation*, but less than that which the realist calls a *thing*—an existence placed halfway between the 'thing' and the 'representation.'"[48] It is more than a representation because it is not a copy of something else, and it is less than a thing because it is already the material of which things are composed and as such is irreducible to our empirical sensations of them. Images, in our view, are an aggregate of "matters."[49]

However, there are two central problems to overcome in order to develop such a migrant theory of the image.

Two problems

The kinetic theory of the image encounters two problems related directly to the problems encountered by the figure of the migrant. Both have been treated as *static* and *ahistorical*. The fate of the image and the fate of the migrant are thus related to the problem of stasis. One of the biggest dangers in migrant media politics is that images are seen to be representations of an objective situation and not, as they really are, themselves migrant bodies with their own affective and material power to move or not.

45 Glare, *Oxford Latin Dictionary*.

46 Nail, *Being and Motion*, 29–41.

47 For related attempts to think about the materiality of the moving image see Munster, *Materializing New Media*; Marks, *Enfoldment and Infinity*.

48 Bergson, *Matter and Memory*.

49 An inversion of Bergson's claim that "matter, in our view, is an aggregate of images." (*Matter and Memory*).

First problem: stasis

The first problem to be overcome is that the image has been traditionally subordinated to something *static*. This subordination has taken two complementary formulations: an objective one and a subjective one.

Objective stasis. On the one hand, the image has been subordinated to a static object or unchanging essence. The image, in other words, has been treated as a copy or representation of an original, just as the migrant has been treated as a failed citizen (a failed copy of the original). The difference between the object and the image of the object becomes the degree of movement or change in the image itself with respect to its unchanging original. This is the classical model/copy relation famously dramatized by Plato in the *Timaeus*. The original or model object remains static and unmoved while subsequent images aim to work like mobile snapshots to accurately represent the original object in all its immobile perfection and essential form.

As Plato writes, "Now the nature of the ideal being was everlasting, but to bestow this attribute in its fullness upon a creature was impossible. Wherefore he resolved to have a moving image of eternity, and when he set in order the heaven, he made this image eternal but moving according to number, while eternity itself rests in unity.[50]" There can be no higher exhalation of eternity and denigration of the image than this. For Plato, the image is nothing but illusion, appearance, and likeness organized according to discrete numerical quantities. The object is thus fixed in its essence and the image is fixed by its discrete number. These discrete numerical images fail to represent the object precisely because of the *mobility of the image*. Motion and mobility thus become the conceptual names for the failure of the image to represent the object. Similarly, the mobility of the migrant challenges the political distinction between the inside of the constitutional nation-state (model) and its outside (failed claimants).

All definitions of media as representation are defined by some version or degree of this static model/copy/resemblance relation. Not only is the object immobilized in the model to be copied but the image of the model itself remains nothing more than a failed numerical attempt to reproduce this same static condition. Between the two stands a gulf of movement and turbulence that ensures their incommensurability. In this way the only real or true sensation occurs in the object itself—all images of the object are mere appearances or modified snapshots of the original. It is also no coincidence that images of migrants and refugees tend to be treated as victim-images, as if the process of their suffering was not still ongoing and many others were not suffering the same.

Subjective stasis. On the other hand, the image has also been subordinated to the relatively static mental states of the subject. In this theory perceptual images are only given conceptual and aesthetic coherence and reality *in the faculties of the perceiver*. Versions of this theory are closer to the more modern aesthetics developed by Kant in his *Critique of Judgment*. In this theory what remains static, fixed, and universal is not the object being represented but the concept of beauty itself found in the mental structure of the subject. Fluctuating images occur in the body of perceiver but it is only in the *concept* of beauty that they are given fixed and universal form. It is thus human mental

---

50 Plato, *Timaeus*, 37 c-e.

and perceptual structures and not sensual images themselves that lie at the firm foundations of truth and beauty.

Again, for Kant, it is the movement of the image in the mobile and affected body that marks the inferiority and subordination of the image. The nature of the object in itself remains unknown *because the body and its perceptual images are moved and mobile.* The senses are thus led to misrepresent reality to the mind. The senses of the body cannot be trusted in knowledge or in beauty. Our experience of beauty, therefore, is not the beauty of nature or even of the beauty of the images, but rather the beauty of our own idea, experience, or faculty of representing these images to ourselves. Nature is only the prompt for us to discover the beauty of our own aesthetic and phenomenological faculties.[51] This is the inverse of the classical idea of the model/copy relation. Instead of defining the image by its subordination to the static essence of the object, it is defined by its subordination to the static aesthetic structures of judgment in the mind of the experiencing or intentional subject.

This subjective form is most dramatic in Kant and post-Kantian aesthetics, but a similar model is also at work in other anthropic constructivisms as well, including social, anthropological, linguistic, economic, and other non-psychological versions. All these different constructivisms share the reduction of the image not to the Kantian ego, but to other anthropic structures. In contrast to Kant, some of these anthropic constructivisms can even be transformed to some extent by moving images. However, even in those cases the movement of the image still remains tied to the *relatively static* anthropic structures that produce and consume those images. Since numerous full-length works have recently been devoted to making this argument, including my own, and since this is not the primary focus of this chapter, I must simply refer the interested reader to those works at this point.[52] My worry with respect to the migrant image is that this constructivist approach does not take seriously the materiality, borders, and circulation of the "image operations" that constitute the social field in the first place.[53]

Both the objective and subjective/constructivist theories of the image thus subordinate it to something relatively static. Furthermore, they both treat the movement of images as something discrete, either in number (Plato) or in the body (Kant). In both cases movement is what makes the image inferior but also what secures the difference between the object and subject in the first place. For Plato, the object remains different from the inferior images of it precisely because the object does not move. For Kant, the same is true of the transcendental subject. For constructivists, images remain extensions, projections, or reflections of more primary human structures. In both cases the object and subject are separated by a kinetic gulf of fluctuating material images. The political connection here is that it is the figure of the migrant that relies most deeply on this subordinated aspect of the image's mobility. The use of images is not just a luxury of fixed citizens but a defining feature of survival for migrants. Their

---

51 We can see a later expression of a similar idea in Aby Warburg's interesting, but also socially and anthropocentrically limited, idea of the "pathos of images" and in Bredekamp's *Theory of the Image-Act*, in which images have agency, but only for human reaction, will, desire, and perception. "The 'I' becomes stronger when it relativizes itself against the activity of the image."

52 See Sparrow, *The End of Phenomenology*; Barad, *Meeting the Universe*; Hodder, *Entangled*; DeLanda, *Assemblage Theory*; Coole and Frost, *New Materialisms*; and Nail, *Being and Motion*.

53 Eder and Klonk, *Image Operations*.

own mobility is thus tied to the mobility, and often hybrid and shaky mobility, of the image in a way that it is not for others. When images cross borders or do not this is not merely a subjective question, it is a material one of how images are (or are not) allowed to circulate, and with what consequences. There is thus a migrant politics of the image that takes place and should be studied as part of the migration process. Treating images as having purely constructible meanings (we choose what to think about them) ignores the role of the real material and kinetic structures that put them in front of us in the first place.

There are two kinetic paradoxes here. The first is that the movement of the image is both necessary to ensure the *division* between subject and object but also necessary to ensure the region of transport that *connects* them as distinct. The model transports its image to the senses. The subject then receives these images on the surface of its sensitive mobile body. Without this zone of transport between the object and subject, nothing transpires—sensation fails. And yet, precisely because of this mobility representation is undermined. The mobility of the image, just like the mobility of the migrant, is thus both the condition of *possibility* for the object and subject and the condition of their *impossible* convergence in perfect media and political representation. Therefore, the study of migrant images is the study of aberrant affects not of representations.

Hence the related second paradox, that the image is treated as necessarily mobile in its transport but fixed and limited by number and body. The image, in the subjective and objective accounts, must move but only as a frozen mobility, a snapshot, or particle of sensation. The mobility of the image is thus described as secondary to the fixed object or subject when it is in fact the mobile substratum within which regions of relative immobility emerge. The citizen and the snapshot are thus crystallizations of the mobile migrant image.

Therefore, if we want to develop a theory of the migrant image that does not fall into these paradoxes we need to begin from its most primary and defining feature, its mobility, and not try and deduce this mobility from something static or statist. This requires, however, a theory based on the motion of the image. The division between the object and subject of sensation is not a primary ontological determination but rather the effect of a more primary kinetic process of kinetic images themselves.

This is the novelty of the kinetic approach: it reinterprets the structure and history of media from the perspective of the primacy of the migrant and mobile image.

Second Problem: History

The second problem the kinetic theory of the migrant image aims to overcome is the supposedly ahistorical nature of the image, just like the ahistorical treatment of the migrant. There are three formulations of this ahistorical thesis: an objective, a subjective, and an ontological one.

Objective. On the one hand, if the image is subordinated to a static model object then it can have no history, or its history is a *mere illusion*. History presupposes the real movement and transformation of matter, but if objective essences do not move, then they can have no history, and their images can have no real history either. The state treats the migrant in the same manner.

Subjective. Second, if the image is subordinated to the static conceptual or constructivist structure of human subjects then a similar problem occurs. If subjective structures are universal, as Kant and much of post-Kantian phenomenology argues,[54] then they do not change (or change only within a fixed domain) over time, and if subjective structures themselves (not just their contents) do not change over time then they have no real history. Perceptual images may change *within this structure*, but the aesthetic conditions of making sense of these images and ordering them have always been the same—and thus the image too, as subordinate to the structure, remains ahistorical. A notable exception to this post-Kantian ahistoricism is the tradition of Marxist aesthetics, including the Frankfurt School.[55]

Ontological. The third formulation of this problem is ontological. In order for the object to be copied by an image, the object must *appear* in sensuous reality and thus must be, in some sense, affected by the conditions of its appearance. Similarly, in order for the subject to schematize and conceptualize its perceptions, it must in some sense be affected or receptive to the sensory images of its body. The affective nature of the image is therefore continuous with the whole process of becoming in which the object and subject both transform and are transformed through their appearance as images. In this way, the ontology of the affective image liberates the image from its twin subordination.

It does so, however, only at the risk of reintroducing its own form of ahistoricity. If the affective image comes to be understood as ontologically 'autonomous' with respect to the objects and subjects it produces or distributes then its constant change becomes something relatively changeless: pure becoming.[56] If all images are reduced to their lowest common denominator, affect, becoming and ontological change, then the particularity of historical and regional images risks being submerged entirely into a pure ontological flux. Pure change becomes pure stasis. The ontology of becoming is ahistorical. The ontological rejection of history in favor of becoming has been put forward by a number of recent process ontologists.[57]

The process ontology of the affective image treats the image as if it were possible to describe its structure for ever and all time and from no position in particular. The ontological image, in this way, risks becoming something like its own kind of 'autonomous' substance or pure 'force'—adding nothing to the historical description of the image but a generic ontological language applied to new phenomena.[58]

In response to the problem of ahistoricity, this chapter proposes not only a theory of the image and media grounded in the migrant present, but also offers a history of this present and the material conditions of its emergence. In short, it does not offer an

---

54 Merleau-Ponty and Edie, *The Primacy of Perception*. Merleau-Ponty's late essay "Eye and Mind," for example, makes great strides toward overcoming the anthropocentrism and constructivism of earlier phenomenology, including his own. In *Eye and Mind*, Merleau-Ponty aims to give back historicity to the image itself as a continuous fold, fabric, or pleat in being: "the world is made of the same stuff as the body" because it is "visible and mobile: a thing among things." While the emphasis of the text remains largely on the human body, it also aims to break down the division between image and body.

55 While they remain anthropocentric humanists they also allow for radical historical changes in existing social and aesthetic structures. See Adorno, *History and Freedom*.

56 Massumi, *Parables for the Virtual*.

57 Massumi, *Parables for the Virtual*; Manning, *Relationscapes*; Bennett, *Vibrant Matter*; Connolly, *A World of Becoming*; Whitehead, *Process and Reality*, 73.

58 Nail, *Theory of the Image*. For a critique of this ontological position see Hayles, *Unthought*, 80–83.

ontology of the image. It is precisely because the image is mobile that it has a history and therefore that media must be theorized historically, and not ontologically. Furthermore, because the image has a history it also has a whole typology of distributions that organize the world of subjective and objective structures. All these structures have to be accounted for, starting from the *historical mobility of the migrant image*.

It is precisely because of the dual historical migrancy of the image and media kinaesthetics of the migrant that this type of inquiry is now possible and crucial. Just as it is impossible to understand our contemporary world without understanding the primacy of the migrant, so it is impossible to understand it without the migrancy of the image itself and its global network of affective lifelines, which socially and aesthetically support a world-in-migration.

Conclusion

The *migratory turn* in media studies is not just a turn toward the prevalence of images of migrants, the emergence and importance of migrant art works, but also the mobile and migratory nature of the image itself. There is thus a becoming migrant of the image and a becoming image of the migrant at the same time. Because of the current historical conjuncture, it is impossible to untie them from each other. Therefore, the two must be thought together as migrant images. This chapter, however, has only laid out the problem conceptually and suggested some possible methods and trajectories for a much larger research project that would look more closely at the images of migrants, by migrants, and the mobility of images themselves as migrant.[59]

---

59 See Nail, *Theory of the Image* for a full development of this research program.

Listing

Thomas Keenan and Sohrab Mohebbi

> "The List traces information related to the death of more than 35,597 refugees, asylum seekers, and migrants who have lost their lives within or on the borders of Europe since 1993. It is compiled and updated every year by the Amsterdam-based organization UNITED for Intercultural Action. Since 2006, in collaboration with curators, art workers, and institutions, Banu Cennetoğlu has facilitated up-to-date and translated versions of The List in several countries using public display structures such as ad-boards and newspaper supplements."[1]

What is it to "list?" Etymologically, the word points in three apparently unrelated directions. Ships and other vessels list: they tilt or sway to one side or another, when passengers or cargo shift abruptly and when winds and waves overtake them. And when they list, they run the risk of capsizing. An announcement of listing, then, is an alarm or warning. Beware! To list also means, in an older English, to hear or hearken, to listen. List! I am calling for your attention, asking you to notice and respond, to acknowledge what is being said. Finally, to list is to bring things together in a column or row. This meaning of the word is derived from the Middle English *liste*, meaning "border, edging, stripe," and from Old French and Old Italian words meaning "strip of paper." Listing brings things together in a line or a strip, treats separate items as related to one another, assembles them into a territory of their own.[2]

Boats list and sink, and their passengers and crew drown, all the time. The forces of nature are often to blame. The phenomenon charted by *The List* is anything but natural. It results from the deliberate choice of European governments and electorates to restrict legal entry into the EU by those seeking refuge, asylum, or a better life. Fleeing people are forced to undertake dangerous journeys across inhospitable deserts, seas, beaches, and cities, often ending in detention centers and refugee camps. The engine that drives *The List* is the weaponization of the sea, land, and weather in the name of what is cynically called "deterrence." And the events it documents are not limited to Europe: *The List* could certainly be expanded to include North America as well, where more or less the same thing happens at and on the way to the southern border of the United States.

---

1 *The List* website: www.list-e.info.

2 *Oxford English Dictionary* online, "list."

The List features the names of the dead when they are known and placeholders when they are not. Many names are yet to be learned and entered. The entries are counted and enumerated, so the names become numbers as well. The qualitative and the quantitative meet—*The List* says two things at the same time, joining them in a dynamic rhythm. All the dead deserve to be known and recorded individually, to have their identities preserved as the markers of the lives they alone lived. The entries speak of singularity. But the names are gathered together in this list because the individuals died, in effect, together. The enumeration brings them into relation, it equalizes and generalizes them. And it reminds us of how many lives have been lost to policies of cruelty and indifference. The ever-growing number is another sort of marker, an index of the scale and scope of the catastrophe that has taken place, and still is taking place, within Europe and at its borders.

Banu Cennetoğlu calls herself the caretaker of a graveyard. There is no proper resting place for many of the lost on *The List*—some bodies are never found, others are found but not identified before being buried in unmarked graves across Europe. What kind of cemetery is a list, and how does one take care of it? The name, gender, and age of each victim is added to a spreadsheet, along with the date, location, and cause of their death. Note is made of where they came from, if known, and the source of the information about their death. The logic of the entries' organization must be consistent, so the caretaker edits the document, checking the spelling, grammar, and syntax. Because the data is recorded in different languages, the task often involves translation. It's an administrative process. The presentation is bureaucratically austere, neutral, factual, banal: six columns are filled in along the new rows added each time the document is updated.

The List has been growing for more than a decade. When Cennetoğlu first presented it publicly in March 2007 in Amsterdam, it contained 7,128 confirmed entries. When she facilitated its publication in *The Guardian* as a special supplement in June 2018, the headline read: "It's 34,361 and rising: how The List tallies Europe's migrant bodycount."[3] Its most recent presentation in Barcelona in September 2018 showed 35,597 dead. The creation and maintenance of *The List* is a private, voluntary, civic effort initiated by the Dutch NGO UNITED for Intercultural Action. Cennetoğlu's projects aim to publicize it: "It needs to be visible. Governments don't keep these records for the public; they don't want the public to see these records because it exposes their policies. So you have NGOs trying to put the data together, and that data is incomplete and fragile, but there again someone has to do it."[4]

The List is a public document that aspires to readability and visibility. The names it bears should be known, seen, heard, beyond the realm of those who have already noticed. They appear in print and on walls and billboards, not just spoken to a friend or whispered to a neighbor. Because, as Cennetoğlu notes, "a surprise encounter is important," we are confronted by *The List* when we look out the windshield or open the newspaper at the breakfast table or a café.[5] Far from the border, or the sea or the desert, the names of the dead confront the living. *The List* demands attention, it insists on being heard. Cennetoğlu says: "People should be able to see it despite themselves,

3 McIntyre and Rice-Oxley, "It's 34,361 and rising."

4 Higgins, "Banu Cennetoğlu."

5 Grieg, "Interview with Banu Cennetoğlu."

Listing   167

and despite that they are caught up in their daily lives; the fact they have to go to work, come back from work, get on the subway, walk on the street, etc. I wanted to put it out there without any announcement, without any direct negotiation with the audience but somehow in a negotiated space."[6]

Monuments are often erected in the name of nation, race, faith, or clan to remind those who survive of those who did not. Like any memorial, *The List* seeks to restore the dead, as Thomas Laqueur writes, "into a remade world of the living."[7] It alerts us—regardless of whether or not we want to know—that we are both living without the deceased and existing alongside them, creating a new community of the living and the dead. In this way *The List* challenges the monopoly that organized powers have sought to exercise over the memories and disposition of the dead. Beyond or despite the borders customarily erected around institutions and their memories, *The List* aspires to what another activist has called the "more egalitarian citizenry of the dead."[8]

The List is ephemeral and unfixed. It keeps changing, when people die, when the formerly nameless are identified, and when factual errors are corrected. *The List*'s size and shape shift, as do the sites of its public presentation. It is a sort of counter-monument in constant formation.

A nation is similarly composed of a list of people, one that is restricted to those whom the state recognizes and counts as its own. *The List* challenges the distinction with its stark rewriting of the borders of contemporary Europe and the nation-state form it has bequeathed to the globe. Any list creates a border, as it distinguishes those who are on it from those who are not. *The List* negatively defines Europe as the place of those who are not on it—those who walk by the document in Liverpool, London, Basel, Athens, or Budapest. In a sense, Los Angeles and Istanbul are also part of this place. *The List* does not belong to any single nation-state, and it is presented not in the place where the deceased originated but rather where they ended up—"within, or on the borders of Europe."[9] As such, it designates a new geographic concept: the frontiers of the European continent, its reach, are defined by people who are now dead. The border is no longer an arbitrary political marker, but the track of lives lost along the way. The people who are named no longer belonged to any place at the time that they died; they will not be returned to a homeland and are seldom ceremonially buried or memorialized. *The List* is their distinctive itinerant resting place.

Cennetoğlu observes: "This document carries the weight of all these people who cannot really speak for themselves. And while we're talking about all of this, people are dying." There is urgency in recording the names and making them public, yet this objective, technical, administrative undertaking carries ethical risks. It is unilateral: no one can ask the dead for their consent, or even their opinion. "The attempt to talk on behalf of someone else comes with a burden. In general, one will never know if you are doing something good, or if you are taking advantage, or if you are really talking about yourself when you are talking about them. These are blurry borders. How to not fully occupy the agency or space of someone who is silenced?"[10]

---

6   Higgins, "Banu Cennetoğlu."

7   Laqueur, *The Work of the Dead.*

8   Fullard, "Missing Persons Task Team (South Africa)" in Cassidy Parker, "The Missing Persons Task Team."

9   *The List* website: www.list-e.info.

10 Higgins, "Banu Cennetoğlu."

The List distributes this burden among all of us who were previously unburdened. There is no way to stay clear of these "blurry borders," between speaking and silence, generosity and exploitation, knowledge and ignorance. But to take a moment to listen and to mourn at the site of this migratory mass grave can contribute, in the words of Allan Sekula, to "laying the groundwork for a collective memory of suffering."[11] How to grieve for the dead of others, the dead to whom one is not related, the dead who come from elsewhere? How to mourn those who wanted to live among us? In the words of Laqueur, *The List* asks the question, "How do we come to feel that we should care?"[12] And, if we do, how do we become caretakers?

Cennetoğlu insists that *The List* is not a work of art. This is not only an effort to foreclose an aesthetic judgment: does the list look good or bad, is it beautiful or sublime? It is also an attempt to deprive us of the recourse to some alleged indeterminacy of artistic interpretation. *The List* makes a claim on us, an ethical one, yes, but also a fact-based one. The names are facts. *The List* lists "refugees, asylum seekers, and migrants who have lost their lives." What we do with this fact is up to us.

---

11 Sekula, "Photography and the Limits of National Identity."

12 Laqueur, *The Work of the Dead*, 45.

20.
The List *as published in* The Guardian UK *(June 2018)*
List of 34,361 documented deaths of refugees and migrants due to the restrictive policies of
Fortress Europe. Documentation as of May 5, 2018 by UNITED for Intercultural Action.
Co-produced by Chisenhale Gallery, London and Liverpool Biennial, the updated version
of The List *was printed and distributed by* The Guardian *in a print run of 210,000 on*
World Refugee Day, June 20, 2018. Free of charge copies of the newspaper with the 64-page
supplement were available at Chisenhale Gallery (28 June–26 August, 2018)
and Liverpool Biennial (14 July–28 October, 2018). Copy edited by Lizzie Homersham,
Edward Luker, and Nihan Somay

© Banu Cennetoğlu

21.1
The List *as displayed in Barcelona (2018)*
Documentation as of September 30, 2018 by UNITED for Intercultural Action From September 30, 2018 to February 6, 2019 as part of UMBRA project, in collaboration with Barcelona City Council, Imma Prieto and Associació La Llista Oblidada. The List translated into Spanish and Catalan was on view in Barcelona inside the Passeig de Gràcia metro station. Translation from English to Spanish and Catalan: Associació La Llista Oblidada; Ferran Macià Bros, Carme Ferrer Vilardell, Julie García McCusker, Dídac Macià Bros. Copy editing: Maike Moncayo.

21.2
The List *as displayed in Amsterdam (2007)*
List of 7128 documented deaths of refugees and migrants due to the restrictive policies of
Fortress Europe. Documentation as of May 3, 2006 by UNITED for Intercultural Action.
Between March 14 and March 28, 2007, The List was displayed as a poster campaign in 110
outdoor advertising signs throughout the city of Amsterdam in close collaboration with
curator Huib Haye van der Werf, Stedelijk Museum Bureau Amsterdam and SKOR.

21.3
The List *as displayed in West Hollywood, Los Angeles (2017)*
List of 29,586 documented deaths of refugees and migrants due to the restrictive policies of
Fortress Europe, Documentation as of March 21, 2017 by UNITED for Intercultural Action
in collaboration with Nihan Somay. This iteration of The List *was commissioned by Roy*
and Edna Disney/CalArts Theater (REDCAT) in conjunction with an exhibit curated by
Thomas Keenan and Sohrab Mohebbi, it is obvious from the map (March 25–June 4, 2017)
and installed with the support of the City of West Hollywood through WeHo Arts (www.
weho.org/arts). The entire document was installed in two sections. One section was located
on a concrete wall near the West Hollywood Park Auditorium (647 N. San Vicente Blvd.),
while the other was on a busy section of Robertson Boulevard just south of The Abbey *(692*
N. Robertson) taking advantage of a temporary wooden construction fence in a high traffic
pedestrian area. This List *was on view from April 2017 to early June 2017.*

© Banu Cennetoğlu

Section Two
Mobile Positions

22.1

Abdessamad El Montassir, The Adouaba Project (2019)

22.2
Abdessamad El Montassir, The Adouaba Project (2019)

22.3

Abdessamad El Montassir, The Adouaba Project (2019)

"The Adouaba Project"
Tranquilos, Adwaba and Moving Spaces

Krista Lynes and Abdessamad El Montassir

> Marronner, c'est prendre les chemins de traverse de la pensée, suivre des traces, sillonner dans tous les détours.[1]
> —*Edouard Glissant, Une nouvelle région du monde*

> Fugitivity is a conceptual limit. Marronage is a conceptual limit. Can we get to the stakes of freedom for real?
> —*Rinaldo Walcott*

In 1955, Aimé Césaire crafted a poem to the Haitian poet, René Depestre, coining the verb "marronner" in a plea to his fellow poet to draw from Antillean poetic forms:

> "Vaillant cavalier du tam-tam
> est-il vrai que tu doutes de la forêt natale
> de nos voix rauques de nos coeurs qui nous remontent amers
> de nos yeux de rhum rouge de nos nuits incendiées
> se peut-il
> que les pluies de l'exil
> aient détendu la peau de tambour de ta voix
> Marronnons-nous
> Depestre marronnons-nous?"[2]

Césaire's neologism activates a verb-form of the noun *marronage*—a word that derives from the old Spanish word *cima* (mountaintop or place of escape), which slipped into *cimarrón* (wild or runaway), and then *marronage*. Originally, the *cimmarón* were the

---

1 "Marronner means to take the crossroads of thought, to follow the traces, to furrow in all the detours."

2 "Courageous tom-tom rider/is it true that you mistrust the native forest/and our hoarse voices our hearts that come back up on us bitter/our rum red eyes our burned out nights/is it possible/that the rains of exile/have slackened the drum skin of your voice?/shall we escape like slaves/Depestre like slaves?" Roberts, *Freedom as Marronage*, 6.

renegade or escaped cattle, sheep or pigs who fled Spanish colonial farms on newly conquered lands, and ran to the mountains. This flight into the wilds then came to indicate the fugitive movement of Indigenous or enslaved peoples from conditions of subjugation toward a partial and tentative freedom,[3] from the space of the plantation to that of the mountain, the forest, or the swamp, colonial non-sites where new societies were forged in and through the collective cultural experience and creativity of runaways who had to, in Winks's words, "make themselves *natives* of their surroundings."[4] *Marronage* indicates this speculative struggle for a distinct and differential concept of freedom, a struggle to institute another form of social life, and a retooling of the very instruments of cultural expression and practice.

"The Adouaba Project" sheds light on these "transformatory forces, which operate in complex and invisibilized social situations in the postcolonial moment."[5] The project focuses on two specific contexts: maroons in Mauritania who self-organize and find refuge in villages named *adwaba*,[6] and people in migratory movement in the north of Morocco who create sites of survival in the forests called *tranquilos*. It finds in these movements an alter-migration, a set of paths of intra- and inter-African movement orbiting around Europe's "migrant crisis," affected by its pull, but not centered in it.

Mauritania was the last country in the world to officially abolish slavery in 1981, and it only passed a law enforcing abolition in 2007. Even since, the failure to properly acknowledge contemporary slavery has meant that "there are not remnants but only 'sequels' of slavery to be witnessed in Mauritania."[7] The definitional flux is informed by the large variety of forms of slavery: men and women who are bound to a slave estate, manumitted slaves, enslaved persons who gained autonomy by leaving their masters, and *haratin* (those who claim to never have been bound to the slave estate).[8] *Haratin* identity is forged in a shared experience of social and economic deprivation, and forms a distinct group solidarity of the oppressed. The *haratin* speak the *hassaniyya* Arab dialect, but are distinct insofar as they learned this dialect through their assimilation to *bizan* society, a consequence of their slave pasts. The spaces of contemporary marronnage organize themselves in *adwaba*, remote villages or camps constituted by maroons fleeing extreme political and economic situations, and by enslaved people who cultivate date palm and millet according to the rhythms of seasonal harvests.

In these quarters, enslaved people perform popular performances of *meddh*, consisting of unofficial groupings of *haratin* who create stories of emancipation through song and dance. In former times, enslaved women used to perform a particular kind of folk song which mocked their masters, syncopated to the monotonous rhythm of millet-pounding. Another genre of distinct enslaved culture consisted of a variety of spirituals and blues performed by enslaved women. These songs consisted of "well-

---

3 It is important to hesitate to hang a concept of freedom on the flight from slavery that marronnage entails. Gilles Deleuze's own "lines of flight" were forged in contact with Black Panther George Jackson's statement "I may be running, but I'm looking for a gun as I go." Deleuze and Parnet, *Dialogues II*, 11 and Jackson, *Soledad Brother*, 246.

4 Winks, *Symbolic Cities in Caribbean Literature*, 68.

5 Camuset.

6 The segregated slave hamlets are called *adwaba* in plural, *adabay* in singular.

7 Ruf, *Ending Slavery*, 12.

8 Ruf, *Ending Slavery*, 253.

arranged sessions, and a veritable art of *meddh*" which "became integrated into the political agitation for the *haratin* cause. New texts, inspired by the little red book of Mao, and calling for *haratin* freedom, were superimposed on the classical songs."[9]

Adwaba became the means by which enslaved people (known as *sudan*) distinguished themselves from their masters (*bizan*), an encampment in which one stayed for extended periods of time, or returned to seasonally. Even though the *adwaba* are impermanent, they are imagined as permanent, and hence figure as the origin of the *sudan*. They become, in Urs Peter Ruf's analysis, "transcendent localities, independent of their actual state." When they are taken down, the *adwaba* are maintained as "virtual entities, serving as a means of identification to both *bizan* and *sudan*, and thus providing the *sudan* with what they so fundamentally lack: a location of origin."[10] The *adabay* is thus both a geographical refuge and a cultural resource, a space of trans-local identity formation and a tool of decolonial expression. "The Adouaba Project" locates in these songs an "itinerary of freedom-making, one that gestures towards other non-spaces where new forms of sociality and resistance are forged."[11]

The project thus threads together the *adwaba* and *meddh* with the migratory trajectories where people create parallel societies or villages in the forests in the north or Morocco to survive. Named *tranquilos*, these spaces are mobile, taking shape in relation to a changing social context and its attendant dangers. The *tranquilos* are:

> "spaces of inter-African regrouping and marronnage, cosmopolitan spaces that gather people from all over the continent. These sites seek to melt into and confound the forest in order to survive. In these contexts, new forms of emancipation emerge, languages and cultures creolize themselves, in a necessary effort to construct identities-in-becoming."[12]

They constitute—like the *adwaba*—sites for a specifically contemporary form of *marronner*.

Marronner moves beyond an archeological paradigm, beyond an excavation of past possibility, toward an attempt at understanding the logics of late capitalism, the externalization of European borders, the economies of labor exploitation, and the international division of labor from an *other* place-in-transition. The forests outside Ceuta are spaces of waiting, trajectories of movement that act on quiet—*tranquilo*—even as Spain's partnership with Morocco leads to police raids of homes, to the expulsion of peoples, loaded on buses, and driven to the country's southern border. Morocco, working in tandem with the Spanish civil guard, builds new encampments for officers patrolling its borders with Ceuta. They monitor the fence's cameras and motion sensors to detect potential border crossers. The archbishop of Tangier, Santiago Agrelo Martinez, notes that the Moroccan police treat migrants "like they are their owners, like they are sheep. They can put them and take them wherever they want."[13] In the forest, though, new forms of persistence are forged, even as police continue to enact raids and

---

9 Ruf, *Ending Slavery*, 261.

10 Ruf, *Ending Slavery*, 269–270.

11 Camuset.

12 Camuset.

13 Bernhard, "Spain was seen as welcoming refugees."

deport people to the south. Returning to the forest, back under the canopy of the trees, such communities wait for opportunities to move on.

Marronner enacts a different trajectory of movement, one that undoes the relation between slavery and freedom, that undoes the narrative of movement into freedom, if by freedom one understands moving into the European zone. *Marronner* cuts the arrogance that collapses freedom and Europe, that reconfirms the metropole as the site of arrival. As Lisa Lowe suggests, "liberal forms of political economy, culture, government and history propose a narrative of freedom overcoming enslavement that at once denies colonial slavery, erases the seizure of lands from native peoples, displaces migrations and connections across continents, and internalizes these processes in a national [or, in this case, continental] struggle of history and consciousness."[14] The maroon is not at all outside the expansive jurisprudential and discursive reach of the European project, and is often resigned to its various vanishing points; and yet *marronner* persists in wrecking the guiding narratives of the European project, abandons them in order to eke out modes and sites of survival not easily emplotted on a smooth gradient between unfreedom and its overcoming.

Through the figure of the maroon, one might follow differently the subjective and social transformations generated in and through global movement (more generally) and intra-African movement (more particularly), and the new forms of citizenship such movement proposes. Césaire's *marronner* is movement and poetics beyond the image of the shipwreck but nevertheless in its wake.[15] It initiates and rearticulates a pedagogy of crossing,[16] a political imaginary not governed by the colonial structuring of the hemisphere. For Moten and Harney, *marronner* invokes a "contrapuntal island," where "we linger in stateless emer-gency." It works to refigure the cartographies of movement, to rethink the relation between such territories, dislocated embodiments, and the poetics of transit.[17]

"The Adouaba Project" seeks to reflect on "contemporary situations of political and cultural domination, where new models of societies constitute themselves as spaces of transformation and emancipation, reinvented time and again."[18] These sites are posited in the project as new spaces of marronage, constituted in order to flee an unbearable context and elaborate modes of resistance. In this respect, walking, dancing, and chanting become acts of struggle and resistance, subverting the imposed order to create intervals for restaking rights claims, identities and confiscated histories.

While, James Clifford notes, the verb to *maroon* in English conjures images of shipwreck and abandonment, Césaire's French verb *marronner* has no exact English equivalent, and remains without translation. *Marroner*, offered by Césaire as a specifically aesthetic strategy, signals a flight toward new forms of expressive agency, the forging of a vital and oppositional cultural practice, and creative innovations—a way of singing, dancing, and languaging—that gives voice to fugitive experience.

The untranslatability of *marronner* resonates in, disturbs, blurs or scrambles the worn conceptual pathways for thinking migratory movement—the necropolitical em-

---

14   Lowe, *The Intimacies of Four Continents*, 3.

15   Sharpe, *In the Wake*.

16   Jacqui Alexander, *Pedagogies of Crossing*

17   Moten and Harney, *The Undercommons*, 94.

18   Camuset.

phases on overturned boats or vessels cast to sea. For if the maroon is not merely the shipwrecked victim, what other forms of withdrawal-in-transit might be imagined? *Marronner* signifies not a simple flight—there are no boarding tickets for this passage—but a social, psychological, political and metaphysical struggle to exit conditions of slavery, maintain a liminal freedom and assert a "lived social space." Roberts argues that in *marronage*, "there is agency within potentiality. Actuality is merely the manifestation of a heightened form of activity in the action of flight."[19]

Marronner is then about "reflexive possibility and poesis,"[20] about the possibilities of forging a fugitive demos across a multiplicity of existing territories and zones of occupation. *Marronner* is a "multidimensional act of flight" that involves distance, movement, property and purpose.[21] Flight can be both real and imagined; "freedom is not a place; it is a state of being."[22] *Quilombos, palenques, mocambos, cumbes, mambises, rancherias, ladeiras, magotes, manieles* ... James Scott notes that *marronnage* creates "zones of refuge" that resist or momentarily escape surveillance, expropriation, and exploitation.[23]

Far from the imaginary of the shipwreck but too close to its manifestation, *marronner* involves navigating the European project's suspensions, hiatuses, and contingencies. The forest where migrants wait—the *tranquilo*—and the village or camp that frames the *sudan* experience—the *adabay*—are not non-zones but sites where the possibility of freedom shades into and huddles closely around abiding conditions of unfreedom. *Marronner* points up dramatically what the vast archive of racial slavery and global colonialism has to tell about freedom as such: that in the liberal dispensation, it shares ground with its alleged opposite, that freedom and unfreedom are not tidily seriated, but are rather wound into one another, intercalated, a zone of indistinction. *Marronner*, knowing this, abandons the ruse of overcoming—of arrival—as the condition of poetic and more broadly cultural possibility. It crafts instead a multiplicity of escape routes, a capillary system of transit, a new set of subjective wagers, new modalities of social life.

"The Adouaba Project" mines forms of agency buried by the iconography of the migrant crisis—an iconography which reinvests in the figure of Europe as the seat of right action and just governance, which is to say liberal freedom. Glissant and Chamoiseau write: "The 'temptation of the wall' is proper to those civilizations that haven't succeeded in thinking the other, in thinking with the other, in thinking the other inside: the barbed wire of these caged ideologies, which lifted themselves up, crumbled, and return again with a new shrillness, faced with the new processes of creolization and *métissage*."[24]

Marronner instead calls for a political theory deriving from the underside of a modernity thoroughly racial and colonial in its formation; it points to the capacity for cultural innovation, for the "rebellious slave's insane song or cry of defiance."[25] The

19 Roberts, *Freedom as Marronnage*, 10.

20 Clifford, *The Predicament of Culture*, 181.

21 Roberts, *Freedom as Marronnage*, 9–10.

22 Roberts, *Freedom as Marronnage*, 11.

23 Scott, *The Art of not being Governed*.

24 Glissant and Chamoiseau, *Quand les murs tombent*.

25 Clifford, *The Predicament of Culture*, 181.

tranquilo and the *adabay* indicate not only the sites of flight—the forests of Tangier, the *haratine* communities of Mauritania—but the contrapuntal poetics of such modes of survival, persistence and resistance. The songs that accompany the images included here are emancipatory chants, activated in secret evening rituals, sung in groups of men and women, in the *haratines* of Mauritania. These *adabay* constitute territories through the fabrication of a space in which "sensations may emerge, from which a rhythm, a tone, coloring, weight, texture may be extracted and moved else-where, may function for its own sake, may resonate for the sake of intensity alone."[26] The vacillation of silence and song, of *tranquilo* and *meddh*, expose in their contrapuntal harmony the minor keys of *marronner*'s fugitive actions.

---

26 Grosz, *Chaos, Territory, Art*, 12.

Unsanctioned Agency
Risk Profiling, Racialized Masculinity, and the Making of Europe's "Refugee Crisis"

Veronika Zablotsky

When unprecedented numbers of displaced persons began to arrive in Greece by boat in late 2014, fleeing from escalating violence in Syria, Iraq, Afghanistan, and elsewhere, via Turkey and the Aegean Sea, images of washed up rubber boats and discarded life jackets proliferated in the European press. Camera teams and bystanders captured young and old, exhausted but relieved to be alive, disembarking by day and by night. Before continuing on their journey, some reportedly took a moment to document their survival with a digital photograph for relatives and friends. Either alone or in groups, they were captured by onlookers as some posed to snap a "selfie" with smartphones, mounted on handheld monopods, also known as "selfie sticks," that allow one to adjust the angle of the self-portrait.

Amid ongoing debates about the proper response to unsanctioned border crossings, these images did not generally elicit sympathy from online commentators. Instead, they seemed to surprise and incense their critics on social media. Why did a seemingly vernacular sight prompt such outrage? Taking the negative reception of so-called "refugee selfies" as an analytical point of departure, this chapter interrogates the implicit assumptions that were challenged by these images in order to critique the constitutive exclusions of humanitarian discourse. By asking why some refugees appeared in excess of the passive roles that were assigned to them in public and international discourse, I illustrate how the incessant repetition and circulation of visual media depicting their alleged transgressions produced a new kind of subject.[1]

Based on an analysis of relevant policy documents, international advocacy, and international media reporting between 2015 and 2018, I unpack the gendered and racialized scripts that govern the construction of unaccompanied men, in particular young men and minors, as suspiciously agential and therefore less likely vulnerable. This chapter brings transnational feminist thought and postcolonial studies to bear

---

1 Among the vast and largely anonymous archive of "refugee selfies" circulating on social media, the case of Anas Modamani's selfie with German Chancellor Angela Merkel in 2015 may be the most publicized. After the image appeared in reports that falsely linked Modamani to terrorist attacks in Berlin and Brussels, the young Syrian refugee sued the social media platform *Facebook* in a German court for failing to prevent libel. The high-profile case was widely covered in the mainstream media. He lost the lawsuit in 2017. See, for example, Reinbold, "Hallo Facebook, dieser Mann is kein Terrorist."

on activist and academic discussions of humanitarianism, whiteness, and neoliberalism in Europe to problematize the production of the "single male refugee" as a racial
profile that facilitated the consolidation of more restrictive and increasingly deadly
European border regimes.[2]

It begins with a discussion of the debate surrounding "refugee selfies" to illustrate
how racist tropes about sexual and religious excess were projected onto mobile technology in the hands of displaced persons, particularly young, able-bodied men from
the Middle East, often assumed to be heterosexual and Muslim. During the so-called
"European refugee crisis" of 2015, the smartphone became a signifier of unsanctioned
mobility through media reports that portrayed groups of refugees as "crowds" which
coordinated their cross-border movement through social media, geo-positioning, and
mobile messaging applications. Giving a brief overview of asylum law in Europe, I unpack why the use of technology by refugees was perceived to stand in contradiction to
claims about vulnerability.

In order to demonstrate how the racial profile of "the refugee," as an "unconscious
prototypical figure" in the Western imagination, was informed by this emergent image regime, I analyze how its framing operations were canonized in Ai Weiwei's *Human Flow* (2017), a documentary film in wide digital release, and Brandon Bannon's "Ifo
2, Dadaab Refugee Camp," a photo taken at the border of Somalia and Kenya in 2011.
The latter was selected as a frontispiece for *Insecurities: Tracing Displacement and Shelter*,
an exhibition that entered the permanent collection of the Museum of Modern Art in
New York City in 2017, which aligned images of displacement around the world to construct the idea of "the refugee" in a global frame. Amplified by high-powered institutional platforms, both works conjure a paradigmatic global aesthetic of displacement
through technologies such as airborne drones, handheld devices, and the internet.
Despite the explicit intent to raise awareness about the refugee condition, dominant
modes of narration in humanitarian discourse—the bird's-eye view of the refugee
camp, crowds photographed in extreme wide angle, representations of unnamed individuals in extreme close up, and the frog-perspective, a voyeuristic angle that does not
allow to return the gaze—erase the agency of the displaced in the popular imagination
of forced displacement.

In order to think through the "refugee selfie" as a genre that restores the possibility
of political action, I draw on Hannah Arendt's critique of human rights in *The Origins
of Totalitarianism* and her conception of freedom in *The Human Condition*. As Arendt
observed in her remarks on the effects of mass displacement after World War II, *de
facto* stateless persons lose a world to act upon in which they are regarded as particular
individuals. Since "selfies" are by definition photographs that are taken by the subject
of an image, they inevitably reflect how the photographer intended to be seen and encountered. After revisiting the genre's potential for self-representation, I complicate

2 Insofar as the racial profile is an "imago" that "orientates [a] subject's way of apprehending others"
(Laplanche & Pontalis *The Language of Psycho-Analysis*, 84, in Han, *Letters of the Law*, 77), it constructs
racialized others as figures that are always already suspect and criminalized. In line with this logic, the
German parliament asserted in 2018 that racial profiling was permissible on a case by case basis. According to §23 of the Federal Police Act (*Bundespolizeigesetz*), racial profiling is legally sanctioned in border zones or inland areas declared to be "dangerous." See Deutscher Bundestag, "Schlussfolgerung aus
der neuen Rechtsprechung zu verdachtsunabhängigen Personenkontrollen durch die Bundespolizei."

its emancipatory promise through a closer look at the alienating effects of the materiality of mobile technology.

Secondly, I examine the discursive strategies through which sympathetic advocates and consultants have attempted to reframe the digital literacy of refugees as an economic resource for host societies. I draw on Michel Foucault's late lectures on neoliberalism to critique representations of refugees as enterprising subjects that make rational choices in uncertain circumstances. Since legal title to protection is predicated on proof of vulnerability, the discursive generalization of human capital theory in the humanitarian field undermines the space of asylum. Through an analysis of the German debate about "lane switching" (*Spurwechsel*) between parallel asylum and immigration "tracks," I argue that the application of economic logic in the humanitarian field obliterates the key legal distinction between asylum and immigration.

Lastly, I draw on Banu Bargu's framework of "biosovereignty" and Achille Mbembe's articulation of "necropolitics" to reconsider the European Union's "war on human trafficking" as a calculated exposure to death at Europe's external and "liquid" borders. Drawing on a report by *Frontex*, the private border agency of the European Union,[3] I chart how border policies are reduced to a technical matter through calculations of risk that represent young, unaccompanied men as a security threat. When refugees are reframed as economic agents, however, this projected risk is effectively transferred onto the individual.

Beyond declarations of good will, the structural denial of human freedom and dignity faced by *de facto* stateless and racialized peoples calls for an abolitionist response. Over six decades ago, Hannah Arendt argued that humanitarianism was fundamentally flawed from its inception in a world of nation-states. Its constitutive exclusions are missed by neoliberal advocates that seek to improve "refugee management" through "better" design. I revisit the emancipatory demands of refugee activists in Germany during the "refugee strike" of 2013 to reflect on the ways in which the antiracist politics of transnational solidarity are threatened to be eclipsed by the exclusive focus on border enforcement.

---

3   The acronym *Frontex* (short for French *frontières extérieures*, "external borders") is the name of the "European Agency for the Management of Operational Cooperation at the External Borders of the Member States of the European Union" that was established by Council Regulation (EC) 2007/2004. Vested with a larger budget and expanded powers to collect biometric data, coordinate deportations, and destroy the boats and equipment of human traffickers, the agency was renamed "The European Border and Coast Guard Agency" in 2016. Its stated purpose is to integrate European border management in order to "better manage growing mixed migratory flows" (preamble 1), a category denoting the alleged presence of individuals that are believed to pose a "high-risk" among persons assessed to be vulnerable and therefore "low-risk." This reflects a shift in emphasis from the vulnerability of asylum seekers to the "vulnerability" of states (preamble 21). See "Regulation (EU) 2016/1624 of the European Parliament and of the Council of 14 September 2016 on the European Border and Coast Guard and amending Regulation (EU) 2016/399 of the European Parliament and of the Council and repealing Regulation (EC) No 863/2007 of the European Parliament and of the Council, Council Regulation (EC) No 2007/2004, and Council Decision 2005/267/EC."

The Figure of the "Single Male Refugee"

In 2015, overwhelmed Greek authorities left the displaced to fend for themselves in improvised shelters and makeshift encampments that sprung up at transit stations, in city centers, as well as near border crossings. Instead of remaining in Greece, hundreds of thousands of asylum seekers embarked on a long journey by foot to reach Germany by crossing Greece, Macedonia, Serbia, Croatia, Slovenia, and Austria. The spatial imaginary of a "Balkan route" across the European continent dominated the German news for months on end after Hungary closed its southern border in October 2015. As refugees traveled in groups, images of so-called "caravans" soon became ubiquitous in print, television, and social media. Media reported that "crowds" were coordinating their movement through mobile devices.[4] Animated graphics of maps with arrows offered a daily reminder of the "progression" of a fluid, shifting, and destabilizing force imagined to "sweep" across Europe. Military metaphors entered the mainstream to describe Europe as a "fortress" and refugees as an "army."[5]

In this political climate, images of refugees posing on the beaches of Lesbos, Samos, and other Greek islands to take selfies shortly after landing sparked outrage on social media. To some, these self-portraits seemed to cast doubt on the merit of their asylum claims. They questioned how *forced* the migration of someone could be who thought ahead to bring a "selfie stick." Countering these negative perceptions, the newspaper *The New York Times* declared that the smartphone was an essential of the "21st-Century Migrant."[6] *TIME* magazine invited readers to "See How Refugees Use Selfies to Document Their Journey."[7]

In times of global communication technology, internet-enabled mobile phones, closed-messaging applications, and social media have become features of everyday life across the dividing line of the Global North and the Global South. Yet, Western publics continue to be steeped in imageries that position racial others as outside of time (and thus outside of the present's technological affordances).[8] The sight of refugees with smartphones, taking "selfies" no less, raised eyebrows because it unsettled implicit assumptions about the imagined other of Europe. The millennial subjectivity identified with the quotidian aesthetics of the "selfie" disrupted the phantasy of Western superiority vis-à-vis refugees. Its casual display broke with narrative conventions that construct refugees as objects of humanitarian relief.

Despite associations with self-absorption and vanity, the digital literacy encoded in the "selfie" seemed to represent agency, the capacity to act on an environment rather than being determined by it. It inserted refugees as narrators at the center of a story that Western audiences believed *they* should be able to control. Through mobile technology, these selfies symbolically repeated the material assertion of self in relation to a landscape. They also inserted the face, conventionally imagined as the locus of a par-

---

4 The European Commission Unit on Irregular Migration and Return Policy promptly commissioned a study on the use of digital media in refugees' decision making about secondary movement in Italy. See Sanchez et al., "A study of the communication channels used by migrants and asylum seekers in Italy."

5 See McVeigh, "Temperatures Plunge as Refugee Army Trudges Across Europe."

6 Brunwasser, "A 21st-Century Migrant's Essentials."

7 Laurent, "See How Refugees Use Selfies to Document Their Journey."

8 Fabian, *Time and the Other.*

ticular identity, at the center of a terrain that had only become available as backdrop after the unsanctioned crossing of a territorial border. This self-assertion/insertion, represented by the "refugee selfie," cancelled out rightful claims to protection in the eyes of some observers because it contradicted ingrained assumptions about the presumed passivity and victimhood of refugees. The capacity to act under conditions of uncertainty seemed to cast doubt on the vulnerability of unaccompanied young men in particular.

Through the lens of televised, printed, and online news, pre-existing racist tropes about sexual and religious excess associated with Middle Eastern men layered onto the smartphone as a sign of excessive mobility and agency. Some wondered why able-bodied men would leave behind their dependents, scorning unaccompanied men for "deserting" women and children in conflict zones. Instead of protecting vulnerable others, they appeared to seek protection only for themselves. Race, gender, age, presumed ability, and ascribed religious identity as Muslim, rather than Christian, mediated *whose* unsanctioned mobility appeared suspect. The enabling uses of mobile technology were collapsed with the agential excess projected onto racialized masculinity. This image regime stoked fears about "single male refugees" as potential "terrorists" that might infiltrate the European Union *in disguise*. At the intersections of race, sexuality, and geopolitics, the masculinity of racialized men was questioned because they sought asylum instead of engaging in combat. At the same time, their racialized masculinity was interrogated as a potential threat to public order in Germany and elsewhere.[9] Racialized as a "hyper-masculine" suspect, the "single male refugee" was profiled as a security risk. He emerged as a racialized and sexualized figure that confronted the constitutive exclusions of humanitarian discourse.

Modern humanitarianism first emerged in the aftermath of the genocidal violence inflicted upon the Ottoman Armenian, Greek, and Assyrian communities of Anatolia.[10] After World War I, newly formed international organizations such as the League of Nations and development agencies such as Near East Relief mobilized new technologies and visual media, first and foremost film and photography, to shore up public support for their relief operations in the Eastern Mediterranean.[11] Raising the specter of a world-historical confrontation between Christianity and Islam, this cultural production operated through tropes of gender and sexuality to represent Armenian women and orphans, in particular, as innocent, devoid of agency, and therefore in need of international protection. At its inception, the sexual economy of humanitarian representation secured the phallic status of Western sovereignty in the international arena by positioning European and North American audiences as saviors.[12] The cul-

---

9 See Abdelmonem, Bavelaar, Wynne-Hughes, and Galán, "The 'Taharrush' Connection."

10 Watenpaugh, *Bread from Stones*.

11 Torchin, *Ravished Armenia*.

12 The Christian genealogy of the relationship between humanitarian subjects and the West as their "savior" has perhaps become less accentuated over time. The desire to "save," however, continues to figure prominently in secular dynamics of foreign intervention and occupation in Southwest Asia and North Africa. The conceptual core of the colonial relationship was famously explained by Gayatri C. Spivak as "White men are saving brown women from brown men" (*A Critique of Postcolonial Reason*, 285). This sentence is often cited to critique feminist support for foreign interventions and occupation in the Middle East. See Abu-Lughod, "Do Muslim Women Really Need Saving?".

tural repertoire of humanitarianism generated stereotypical attributes of femininity such as helplessness and passivity as standards of legitimacy that persist in the popular imagination of displaced persons. Films such as *Ravished Armenia* (1918), a silent film that was lauded for its documentary realism, inscribed Orientalist or racial phantasies about Muslim men as predators.[13]

Dominant representations of refugees often center women and conflate them with children (and elders) to produce "womenanchildren"[14] as a victim unit that is presumed to be *essentially* vulnerable.[15] Refugees who are unaccompanied men, by contrast, are constructed as self-possessed and willful agents. During the media production of the so-called "European refugee crisis," the "single male refugee" emerged as a figure whose capacity to be vulnerable or exposed to violence was denied. In order to humanize "single male refugees," advocates emphasized that unaccompanied men could also be care-givers.[16] By pointing out that mobile technology connected "single male refugees" to elderly parents and dependents too weak and vulnerable to undertake the dangerous journey themselves, the smartphone was represented as a life line. Contesting the idea that smartphones were symbolic of excessive agency, advocates resignified mobile phones as a means of caring for others left behind in a *selfless* attempt to reach Europe on *their* behalf.

Yet, as images of young men holding children proliferated, the European Union's private border police *Frontex* declared that "managing" groups of refugees required strategically separating the vulnerable from the suspect. In its report "Risk Analysis for 2016," *Frontex* maintained that "young single men [mixed] with more vulnerable families, including women and children [...] to facilitate their progression."[17] By suggesting that "young single men" strategically infiltrated "crowds" to use the vulnerability of others as a *shield*, the vulnerability of young single men was denied and their mere presence profiled as "high-risk."[18] The United States have altogether barred unac-

---

13 See Zablotsky, "Governing Armenia."

14 Enloe, *Bananas, Beaches and Bases*, 25.

15 Gendered constructions of the essential victimhood of women obscure that men can be victimized as well, and obfuscate the ways in which women may become perpetrators of violence, including sexualized violence (see Moser & Clark, *Victims, Perpetrators or Actors?*).

16 For example, the organization "Jewish Voice for Peace" commissioned a poster in 2015 to counter Islamophobic attitudes about refugees in the public eye. Micah Bazant, a visual artist based in the United States, created a linoleum print of a middle-aged man with large eyes and a prominent nose, short dark hair, and a short beard. An infant's face is peaking through the opening of his wide jacket while a faint smile is playing around the corners of the adult's mouth. He is pressing the child against his body and protecting it with his left arm. While the man's hair is blowing in the wind, the child is wearing a hat. Both directly face the audience. Their black and white outline occupies the bottom half of a vertical rectangle. The upper half is cold blue, evoking the sea. In bold white letters at the top, Bazant placed the all-capitalized message "Refugees Are Welcome Here." Interestingly, the field of gender studies has recently turned its attention to "caring masculinities" as an emerging concept. However, it appears I am the first to note that some representations of men as caregivers are impactful because they invert expectations to counter the dehumanization of racialized men. See Elliott, "Caring Masculinities."

17 Frontex Risk Analysis Unit, "Risk Analysis for 2016," 45.

18 Frontex Risk Analysis Unit, "Risk Analysis for 2016," 61. The heightened visibility of unaccompanied men arriving at Europe's external borders in 2015 also provoked a sex panic that continues to play out

companied men from resettlement schemes for Syrian citizens while Canada exempts only "single male refugees" that position themselves as members of the LGBTQ community.[19] Neither legally entitled to asylum, nor declared regular enemies in combat, displaced persons suspected of terrorist intentions on the basis of race and gender are made, once over, "outlaws by definition."[20]

Vulnerability, Mobility, and Detention

Asylum cases in Europe are determined on the basis of calculations about the vulnerability of petitioners. Only individuals that can prove they are at risk of torture and persecution by their country of citizenship on the basis of political, ethnic, religious, or sexual attributes will be considered eligible for asylum. Economic insecurity or civilian threats of violence are not recognized as valid grounds for asylum claims. By strategically designating this risk as *low*, and labelling states such as Afghanistan as "safe countries of origin," EU officials exploit loopholes in international law to carry out blanket deportations of groups statistically considered "*unlikely* to obtain asylum."[21]

In violation of the European Charter of Fundamental Rights,[22] petitioners from countries other than Syria currently live in fear of deportation because their right to due process and individual case review is not guaranteed. Instead of ensuring that persons are not deported to places where they will be at risk of death, torture, inhuman or degrading treatment, a running roster of countries of origin are declared "safe" by the stroke of a pen. Individuals seeking asylum within the European Union are required to register with local authorities upon first entry to the Schengen zone.[23] As the review process runs its course, which can take several years, the mobility of petitioners is restricted to the administrative districts in which their cases are first filed. After this initial registration, so-called "irregular secondary movement" within the Europe-

---

in response to isolated but highly mediatized incidents involving young men that have been granted asylum in Germany. More recently, there have been debates about mandatory forensic testing on underage asylum seekers to confirm their "biological" age.

19 This exemption serves to portray Canada as a human rights leader while suggesting that Middle Eastern societies are inherently homophobic. Similar to women and children, LGBTQ subjects are selectively included in order to legitimize the construction of heterosexual Muslim men as inherently dangerous. Jasbir Puar has argued that liberal states routinely "pinkwash" imperialist policies to maintain moral exceptionalism. See Puar, *Terrorist Assemblages*.

20 Arendt, *The Origins of Totalitarianism*, 283.

21 Frontex Risk Analysis Unit, "Risk Analysis for 2016."

22 "Charter of Fundamental Rights of the European Union."

23 Since 2006, entry and control at internal and external borders of the European Union is regulated by the so-called "Schengen Border Code" of the European Parliament and the Council of the European Union. The document established an "area without internal borders in which the free movement of persons is ensured" (preamble 1) while requiring check points and risk analysis to manage the external borders of the Schengen zone. See "Regulation (EC) No. 562/2006 of the European Parliament and of the Council of 15 March 2006 establishing a Community Code on the rules governing the movement of persons across borders (Schengen Borders Code)."

an Union is prohibited.[24] This is primarily to ensure that asylum claimants can swiftly be deported if their petition is denied.

For those who cannot afford a visa or plane ticket to their desired destination within the European Union, few alternatives exist to risking their lives at sea and crossing the Mediterranean or Aegean Sea without prior authorization. On the other side, those who survive the perilous passage are registered and, depending on their nationality, either immediately deported or detained in EU-funded camps. These so-called "reception centers" or "hotspots" reportedly fail to provide even basic shelter due to "unsanitary" and "unsafe" conditions.[25] Overcrowded and managed by police, an archipelago of detention centers has spawned across Greece to hold hundreds of thousands of displaced persons until their asylum cases are processed.[26]

In March 2016, the European Union signed a "return" agreement with Turkey that stipulates all new arrivals from Syria are to be immediately deported to offshore detention centers set up on the Turkish side of the Syrian border. Here, in these EU-subsidized zones of *de facto* lawlessness, petitioners are to wait until case workers determine the merit of their asylum cases. Only petitioners that were present in Greece before the agreement went into effect were permitted to remain. The agreement further envisioned that in exchange for each Syrian refugee that is deported after reaching Greece without authorization, one would be approved and relocated from a detention center in Turkey to a member state of the EU. The so-called "one-for-one scheme," however, failed to deliver on its promise of providing "vulnerable people" with a "safe and legal way [...] to reach the EU."[27] With "return missions" stalled by the refusal of Greek Appeal Boards to authorize deportations to Turkey, and several member states of the EU blocking the scheme, more and more refugees are funneled into administrative detention in Greece and forced to wait without the prospect of a speedy resolution.

Regimes of Representation

Daily reporting about informal tent settlements "in the middle of Europe" generated anxieties about states losing control of national borders in light of the seemingly unruly "flows and streams" of the displaced. Images of "caravans," filmed and photographed from above, at an angle, or at a distance, became a staple of televised news. Drawing on the visual canon of humanitarianism, the constant repetition of these images constituted a referential regime of crisis that proved portable.[28]

Over the course of the twentieth century, Western publics have become accustomed to bird's-eye views of refugee camps *elsewhere*. Their sight in the outskirts and

---

24 EU Regulation 2016/1624, preamble 18.

25 "Greece: Refuge 'Hotspots' Unsafe, Unsanitary; Women, Children Fearful, Unprotected; Lack Basic Shelter." *Human Rights Watch* (2016).

26 Mitchell & Sparke, "Hotspot Geopolitics versus Geosocial Solidarity."

27 European Commission, "European Agenda on Migration," 4.

28 This representational regime is mobilized beyond its association with the "European refugee crisis" of 2015–2016. In late 2018, for example, reports about a "migrant caravan" moving from Honduras towards the southern border of the United States provoked a governmental crisis over funding for a federal border wall.

centers of cities throughout Europe provoked a strong response. Associated with mud and tarps, the informal quality of these sites is often presented as evidence of their transient character. Despite their "purposely deteriorating building material,"[29] many of these temporary settlements have become permanent fixtures, housing millions of displaced persons and refugees worldwide. The destabilizing effects of forced migration, further, threaten the appearance of order, fixity, and durability through which modern statecraft is enacted. This imaginary of states as fortified compounds is contrasted by metaphors of liquefaction and dissolution that are often deployed to allegorize forced migration. Refugee camps therefore function as sites of detention that are designed to contain and regularize movement in spaces of enclosure. The effect is boredom, the phenomenological experience of "abandonment in emptiness,"[30] as a calculated outcome of human life forced into the invariable repetition of administrative time.

From above, the order imposed by the humanitarian agency is accentuated. Unlike the angled perspective characteristic of the "selfie," the bird's-eyes view constructs a central point of view from which all life in the camp can be overseen or surveilled as a governable substrate for state-imposed order. This aerial view also dominated reporting on ground-level migrations and "crowds" of refugees in Europe in 2015 and 2016. Soon after, in late 2016, the Museum of Modern Art in New York City opened the exhibition *Insecurities: Tracing Displacement and Shelter*, an interactive installation of images, immersive objects, and artifacts engaging with architectures and infrastructures of forced migration around the world. Between a wall of images and an installation of illuminated boxes, arranged on the floor, hung a photograph taken by photojournalist Brandon Bannon in 2011, enlarged to show an aerial view of Ifo 2, one of four settlements that make up the Dadaab refugee complex in Kenya.[31] It was selected as the cover image of the exhibition. Stretching in neat rows across a clay-colored plain, plastic covered shelters line an arid landscape, leaving room for unpaved thoroughfares and several large, rectangular areas. Instead of the ground-level realities lived by the residents, the angle of "Ifo 2, Dadaab Refugee Camp" recalls "the diplomatic, bureaucratic, and capitalistic work of governments, institutions, and entities elsewhere."[32] This curatorial choice illustrates how the visual discourse of humanitarianism reproduces the aesthetic of the state while responding to the expediencies of refugee management.

---

29 Herscher & Siddiqi, "Spatial Violence," 276.

30 Agamben, *The Open*, 63.

31 According to the United Nations High Commissioner for Refugees (UNHRC), the Dadaab refugee complex was housing 235,269 registered refugees and asylum seekers in January 2018. Dagahaley, the first camp, was established in 1991. Ifo, Ifo 2, and Hagadera were added to accommodate the large influx of displaced persons during the civil war in Somalia. Dadaab refugee complex is one of the largest refugee camps in the world, though it is far surpassed by the Kutupalong refugee camp in Bangladesh which houses close to 900,000 Rohingya refugees from Myanmar, followed by Bidi Bidi in Uganda which hosts 285,000 displaced persons from South Sudan. The oldest, continuously existing refugee camps are situated in Lebanon and Jordan. They were set up by the United Nations Relief and Works Agency for Palestine Refugees in the Near East (UNRWA) after millions of Palestinians were displaced as a result of the creation of the state of Israel in 1948. Mayukwayuka refugee settlement in Zambia was established in 1966 and hosts over 56,000 refugees, asylum seekers, and former refugees who continue to reside in surrounding resettlement schemes.

32 Siddiqi, "On Humanitarian Architecture," 520.

Over the course of 2016, Ai Weiwei, a mixed-media artist exiled from China in 2015, directed the film *Human Flow* over the course of 2016. The feature-length documentary takes its audience on a visual *tour de force* across twenty-three countries on four continents to illustrate that forced displacement is a global phenomenon. In this indexical sense, it expands on the project of the *Insecurities* exhibition. Its aesthetic engagement with spaces of humanitarianism serves as another high-profile example which illustrates the symbolic force of violence which seems to permeate even sympathetic representations of displacement. Through footage recorded by drones and smartphones, the film accomplishes a monumental scale while offering an intimate look at the humanity of refugees worldwide. Opening with a bird's-eye view of an unidentified refugee camp in Iraq, set in an arid desert plain, the film cuts to a sequence of shots from a very low angle, the so-called frog-perspective near the horizon line. Shrubbery, covering most of the screen while appearing out of focus, frames children in the distance. The audience is then teleported into a beige canvas tent where its gaze is directed toward the silhouette of a girl with two braids. Unnamed, she appears as a figure that looks out through the opening of the tent into the glaring sunlight, holding onto a strap and facing her uncertain future.[33] Following this sequence, Ai cuts to a group of women appearing to bake bread in a clay oven lowered into the ground, before moving on to a group of men crouching around a security guard who holds a stack of paperwork. The film thus establishes the gendered division of labor in the camp by depicting women as caregivers of children and men as agents that interact with the state.

Within its first ten minutes, *Human Flow* not only reproduces the visual canon of humanitarianism through the camera perspectives it deploys but also narratively reinforces gendered stereotypes about the Middle East. While bird's-eye views invoke the central authority of the state, the frog perspective positions the spectator as a voyeur that can learn about life in the camp as a seemingly impartial observer whose gaze cannot be returned. Some of the footage filmed at eye-level closely resembles the mugshot, though many interlocutors remain unnamed.[34] Some images captured by drones reproduce the trope of moving "caravans" as if to visualize the metaphor of "human flow" that gives the film its title.

While the title plays with the imagery of "flows" that is often mobilized to describe forced migration, it humanizes its protagonists by inserting Ai Weiwei in the frame, for example when he swaps passports with a Syrian citizen in Idomeni, the site of an infamous tent encampment in Greece. Shaky footage from hand-held devices creates a documentary aesthetic that invites a false sense of identification with the experiences of refugees. Yet, Ai presents this appropriation as a form of "respect." By suggesting that the subject positions of the film maker and the subjects of his documentary are ultimately interchangeable, Ai asserts the shared humanity of displaced persons. However, by obscuring the operations of power that position him as a standard bearer of humanity, albeit racialized vis-à-vis the West, his interlocutors are reduced to generic

---

33 Etymologically, a "figure" is a "visible and tangible form," from the Old French *figure* "shape, body," the Latin *figura* "a shape, form, quality, kind, style, figure of speech," and in late Latin "a sketch, drawing." www.etymonline.com/index.php?allowed_in_frame=0&search=figure.

34 If *Human Flow* is streamed on *Amazon Prime*, some of the names become available as metadata in a sidebar.

figures that stand in for humanity in general, rather than the particular identities of which they have been stripped due to their forced displacement.

Overall, both Brandon Bannon's photography and Ai Weiwei's cinematography rely on techniques of documentary realism to generate empathy with refugees but fail to make room for solidarity by framing displacement as a universal condition afflicting humanity *in general*.[35] In contrast, the genre of the "refugee selfie" inherently resists homogenization because it is constituted by an irreducible plurality. Despite the visual conventions that govern its form,[36] it offers a unique mode of self-representation that destabilizes the aesthetic regimes that produce the reality effects of central authority. By attesting to the specific identity of those confined to the "huge and nameless crowd,"[37] the "selfie" restores the possibility of political action on the part of displaced and *de facto* stateless persons.

Politics of Representation

Hannah Arendt critiqued the post-war human rights frameworks for failing to remedy the zone of lawlessness in which refugees find themselves when neither their state of citizenship nor any other given state is willing to guarantee and enforce their human rights. She argued that this loss of legality not only stripped individuals of their civil rights but also erased their particularity as specific, rather than generic, human beings. Once reduced to "mere existence," seekers of asylum are stripped of the right to "act in and change and build a common world."[38] According to Arendt, the "right to have rights" derived not from the "abstract nakedness of being human and nothing but human"[39] but from belonging to a "social texture" in which one "established for themselves a distinct place in the world,"[40] in which one's actions mattered, and in which one's opinions were significant. Rightlessness was therefore a function of displacement as "the loss of a community willing and able to guarantee any rights whatsoever."[41]

---

35 According to the *Online Etymology Dictionary*, "empathy" is a form of appropriation because it "depends on the viewer's ability to project his [or her] personality into the viewed object." The emphasis on empathy over solidarity is by definition unethical in the sense that an ethical relationship requires the recognition of the other as a self, rather than the projection of the self as other. Similarly, advocacy groups in Germany developed "simulation games" in which participants were asked to imagine they were, quite literally, "in the same boat" as refugees. While audiences from students to policy makers reported a shift in perspective, emphases on "empathy" have helped frame the debate about a "refugee crisis" in terms of moral appeals to goodness rather than political solidarity and ethical responsibility to recognize the political agency of displaced persons.

36 By definition, "selfies" center the faces of individuals at an arm's length, or its prosthetic extension by a hand-held monopod. Since these self-portraits are usually taken at an angle, they enlarge the eyes and slim jaw lines to flatter, rather than surveil, the subject. Unlike a mug shot, the visual conventions that define the "selfie" are not structured around identifiable traits, yet they inscribe the particular embodiment of the subject in the frame.

37 Arendt, *The Origins of Totalitarianism*, 287.

38 Arendt, *The Origins of Totalitarianism*, 301.

39 Arendt, *The Origins of Totalitarianism*, 296.

40 Arendt, *The Origins of Totalitarianism*, 293.

41 Arendt, *The Origins of Totalitarianism*, 298.

Instead of being "judged by one's actions and opinions,"[42] for which one is held responsible before the law and by peers, humanitarian discourse frames displaced persons as "nothing but human beings"[43] whose "treatment by others does not depend on what he [or she] does or does not do."[44] In Arendt's conception of the human condition, freedom of action is possible when the outcome of an action is not determined by necessity and words and deeds are remembered by free and equal peers. By emphasizing empathy over solidarity, humanitarian representations of refugees as "thrown back [...] on their natural givenness"[45] exclude displaced persons from the "category of people"[46] that are entitled to state-sanctioned agency.

In contrast to the post-war context described by Arendt, realms for the appearance of words and deeds, which she theorized as a condition of political action, have proliferated through mobile communication. Though still confined to a course of action determined by force, displaced persons use smartphones to carve out spaces of freedom from necessity and thereby create political possibilities. Instead of food and shelter, which are basic human needs, access to social media allows displaced persons to "feel human" in connection with peers to whom the individual's actions and words appear and matter. Friends and family remember and engage the displaced person as a particular individual that is acting upon a shared world beyond the purview of any single nation state. It is possible to use the smartphone to assert one's "full" rather than "mere" humanity precisely because battery life and data are not "essential" to physical survival. Enabled by data roaming, geo-positioning software allows for virtual forms of emplacement. "Selfies" communicate physical survival to family and friends while anchoring a particular individual at the center of a given landscape. As a form of self-representation, "selfies" undermine humanitarian constructions of refugees as helpless victims while challenging the exclusionary logic of territorial borders.

Despite this emancipatory promise of mobile technology,[47] the mediation of smartphones is inherently alienating because the hardware itself is a material product of

---

42 Arendt, *The Origins of Totalitarianism*, 297.

43 Arendt, *The Origins of Totalitarianism*, 295.

44 Arendt, *The Origins of Totalitarianism*, 296.

45 Arendt, *The Origins of Totalitarianism*, 302.

46 Arendt, *The Origins of Totalitarianism*, 297.

47 Drawing on Karl Marx's negative dialectic, alienation (*Entfremdung*) and emancipation (*Selbstbestätigung*) can be heuristically conceptualized as a binary pair. In his 1844 notebooks, Marx argued that neither the individual nor the collective can be fully human as long as any single human's practical energy (*praktische Energie d[es] Menschen*), or labor-power, was alienated (*entfremdet*) or captured by another in the commodity form of private property (Marx *Ökonomisch-philosophische Manuskripte*, 94). In *The Human Condition*, Hannah Arendt critiqued Marx for conflating labor and work because her conception of the human freedom to act excluded any form of coercion, including the necessity to reproduce biological life. Unlike Arendt, Marx argued that the being (*Wesen*) of all individuals belonging to the human species was to *appropriate* nature by consciously acting on it, making labor—the human metabolism with nature—the practical tool of our self-generation *as* human. In contrast, Arendt conceived of labor as a form of violence that wore down the world by consuming it. She conceptualized work, in turn, as a creative activity that populated the world with durable objects. These objects, insofar as they are not instrumental or intended for consumption, frame and enable the human freedom to act in their midst. Arendt, *The Human Condition*.

exploitation and extraction elsewhere.[48] If freedom, to Arendt, is action that appears unencumbered by necessity, the commodity form of mobile technology and the binary logic of its operating software, as well as the material mediation of telecommunications infrastructure,[49] threatens to place human freedom—the ability to act anew and in unexpected ways—under erasure. The use of mobile technology introduces layers of alienation and necessity that mediate the subjective will to act insofar as the words and deeds of displaced persons and their allies are processed as information and data. Still, refugees constitute themselves as political subjects, despite the forced nature of displacement, which propels movement by necessity, by acting through digital media that, at any rate, allows for the *"experience* of being free."[50]

Calculations of risk at Europe's biometric borders[51] negate the agency and humanity of asylum claimants because they interpret the actions of refugees, in particular those cast as "high-risk" individuals, as if they were determined by immutable traits. Racial profiling, in particular, reduces "new and spontaneous processes"[52] to a form of "excess" to be captured by apparatuses of security.[53] Despite its administrative veneer, risk profiling is a form of political violence that hinges on racist tropes about sexual and religious excess which, in the Western tradition, are attributed to the East in general, and Islam in particular.[54] I argue that these tropes form the core of social media debates about the role of mobile technology in the unauthorized mobility of refugees.

Some humanitarian advocates have attempted to *reframe* the actions of "single male refugees" by explaining that mobile devices were primarily used to maintain ongoing relationships with vulnerable dependents, thereby containing the agential excess projected onto racialized masculinity *within* the humanitarian script. In 2016, Brian Reich, then managing director at *The Hive*, a US-based data strategy firm contracted by the UN Refugee Agency (UNHCR), explained in an interview,

> "The phone and the idea of connectivity is critical. They text their family member to say that they arrived safely, or call up some information in a private *Facebook* group that tells them where to go next so that they are not detained or forced to register in a way that they don't want to. The role technology is playing is very different than [during]

---

48 As technical devices, smartphones contain a long list of minerals and metals such as gold, silver, and copper, among other components, that are mined despite the detrimental effects of extractive operations on public health, social relations, and the environment, primarily throughout the Global South. For an overview of raw materials used in smartphones and where they are extracted, see U.S. Geological Survey, "A World of Minerals in Your Mobile Device."

49 Stryker, "Bodies of Knowledge;" Easterling, *Extrastatecraft*.

50 Arendt, *The Human Condition*, 24 [emphasis added].

51 Amoore, "Biometric Borders."

52 Arendt, *The Human Condition*, 231.

53 Following Michel Foucault, liberal governmentality confronts the problem of security as the principle through which it calculates the "precise extent to which and up to what point individual interest, that is to say, individual interests insofar as they are different and possibly opposed to each other, constitute a danger for the interest of all." Insofar, calculations of risk assess the "economic cost of the exercise of freedom" in order to guarantee freedom in the future, thereby perpetually deferring the possibility of non-instrumental action that, according to Hannah Arendt, allows for the experience of freedom. Foucault, *The Birth of Biopolitics*, 65.

54 Said, *Orientalism*.

any refugee crisis before. They have access to the internet, they are using *WhatsApp* and *Facebook* [...] to share information about the safest route. This is a connected, educated, capable population that save for the circumstances that forced them to flee is not any different than any other population [...] There are stories that you will hear in refugee camps where people will sell their food ration in order to get money to pay for data and not only because they have an emergency situation but because being connected to anything else in the world feels human."[55]

In this statement, Reich confirmed not only that displaced persons use mobile technology to connect to family members, but also that some of them use the internet in strategic ways that allow them to navigate the territorial fault-lines of European border regimes. He asserted that unauthorized mobility was a legitimate choice made by technologically savvy individuals in dire circumstances. While capturing the humanizing potential of connectivity, he signaled that digital skills represent an economic asset. As bearers of valuable capacities, so the argument goes, refugees in the twenty-first century should be reimagined as an educated workforce waiting to be deployed by host societies. Instead of emphasizing the moral obligation to protect vulnerable populations, against which right-wing governments seem to have immunized themselves, international advocates and consultants are increasingly countering calculations of risk with calculations of value.[56]

Melissa Flemming, a spokesperson of the UNHCR, for example, argued, "The simple truth is that refugees would not risk their lives on a journey so dangerous if they could thrive where they are."[57] This reflection on a "simple truth" of forced displacement locates a peculiar "choice" at the level of the individual. Once forced displacement is reimagined in terms of a preference for life, refugees appear to act as economic agents who allocate scarce resources while bearing the risk of death. In this scenario, exposure to death becomes the responsibility of the individual, rather than that of the state which decides on the exception.[58]

As Michel Foucault predicted in his 1979 lectures on neoliberalism, all human behavior that "responds systematically to modifications in the variables of the environment" may become "susceptible to economic analysis."[59] This is the case insofar as life and death are understood as "competing ends [...] which cannot be superimposed on

55 See Fitch, "Smartphone Use on the Refugee Trail." The partial transcription of the video above is my own.

56 This shift in humanitarian discourse has motivated efforts to integrate refugees in the labor market of so-called third countries. In 2016, the European Union signed an agreement with Jordan that offers access to the European common market for commodities produced at factories that meet employment quotas for Syrian citizens in special economic zones in Jordan. However, this so-called "Jordan Compact" has so far failed to deliver the hoped for results. See Lenner & Turner, "Making Refugees Work?" This policy was proposed by Alexander Betts and Paul Collier, two UK-based scholars, who argued in 2015 that refugees should be helped to "help themselves." See Betts & Collier "Help Refugees Help Themselves." On economic zones as a technology of power, see Easterling, *Extrastatecraft*. See also Betts & Collier. *Refuge.* I am grateful to Anne McNevin for alerting me to this new scheme in the humanitarian field.

57 UNHCR, "Europe Situation."

58 Agamben, *State of Exception.*

59 Foucault, *The Birth of Biopolitics*, 269.

each other" and "between which we must choose."[60] Deciding to act despite uncertain outcomes, refugees are cast as economic agents that accept the risk of death in order to "thrive" elsewhere. Instead of remaining in a war zone, seeking to "obtain some kind of improvement"[61] is presented as a rational choice. From this perspective, the figure of the "single male refugee" becomes intelligible as an entrepreneur that "invests in an action, expects a profit from it, and [...] accepts the risk of a loss."[62]

When neoliberal theories of the subject are introduced in the humanitarian field, the apparent technological savvy of refugees translates into evidence of an "abilities-machine" formed through "investments [...] made at the level of man himself."[63] As argued by Theodore W. Schultz, one of the founders of the Chicago School of Economics, "people can enlarge the range of choice available to them [...] by investing in themselves."[64] Rather than a security risk, the unsanctioned mobility of "single male refugees" may now appear as a form of entrepreneurial risk-taking. The application of economic analysis to forced displacement, however, blurs the distinction between refugees and economic migrants. By suggesting that persons in both categories "decide" to "improve" their lives, the normative core of asylum law is hollowed out by economic logic which anchors shared humanity in the capacity to invest in oneself as human capital.

From the standpoint of cognitive capitalism and the so-called "sharing economy,"[65] time is a scarce resource and a valuable asset that could be remotely matched with the needs of distant consumers. Considering the deadly boredom that permeates everyday life in administrative detention, some humanitarian aid experts have problematized enforced inactivity as a waste of time and skill of those condemned to perpetual waiting. Neoliberal logic supplies a new framework that humanizes refugees, albeit as human capital.

If displaced persons currently residing in Germany can demonstrate employment and language skills, they might soon be able to opt out of the asylum process and "switch" into a newly created immigration track. The German debate about so-called "lane switching" (Spurwechsel) represents a concession to employers that demand the right to profit from the investment they already made in refugees as extremely motivated employees. However, critics of a possible bifurcation in the asylum process fear that "rewarding" skill might incentivize further unsanctioned migration to Germany. The subtext of the public controversy, not so thinly veiled, was that offering a way out of the asylum process, regardless of eligibility, might lead to an increase in Germany's racialized population. In this context, a new quota system has been recently introduced to minimize family reunifications (Familiennachzug) for recognized asylees that are currently residing in Germany. Low quotas and administrative backlog effectively deny displaced persons the right to ensure that their children and spouses are also in

60 Foucault, The Birth of Biopolitics, 222.

61 Foucault, The Birth of Biopolitics, 230.

62 Foucault, The Birth of Biopolitics, 252–253.

63 Foucault, The Birth of Biopolitics, 229.

64 See Schultz, "Investment in Human Capital," 1.

65 Acquier, Daudigeos & Pinkse, "Promises and Paradoxes of the Sharing Economy;" Tadiar, "City Everywhere."

safety. This measure is intended to put pressure on refugees to return to their countries of origin even if they are formally entitled to stay.

By suggesting that refugees are entrepreneurial subjects, this neoliberal turn in humanitarian discourse merely supplements the biosovereign formation of a European power intent on policing the symbolic borders of whiteness.[66] By representing forced displacement as a choice at the level of the individual, the profiling of racialized masculinity as always already suspect is not only left intact but reinforced.[67] Instead of embracing neoliberal logic, advocates must interrogate the gendered and racialized scripts that govern the recognition of vulnerability in order to push back against dehumanizing calculations of risk that will only respond to economic calculation.

Calculated Exposure

Europe's external borders and their expanding buffer zones—geographical, ideological, and in relation to the bodies of racialized others[68]—have become sites at which "migratory circuits" are regulated, and "irregular flows"[69] "disallow[ed] to the point of death."[70] Banu Bargu argues that biopower has not supplanted sovereignty but that it has imbricated it as a power "concerned with efficient regulation [of flows] and the optimization of circulation."[71] In a like manner, the language of risk management deployed by *Frontex* justifies exposure to death as a technical matter which "ensure[s] that interventions are focused on high-risk movements of people, while low-risk movements are facilitated smoothly."[72] Biosovereignty, as Bargu calls this hybrid power, links up the "politics *of* life (and death) and a politics *over* life itself"[73] in an "ongoing process in formation."[74] While biopower invests in subjects to construct "the very agent who will act,"[75] its sovereign core exposes racialized others to death through divestment.

Achille Mbembe describes this "division of space into compartments for the purpose of control" as a necropolitical "terror formation"[76] that rules "in absolute lawlessness"[77] over those who it defines as "disposable."[78] In tandem with states that

---

66 Eggers, Kilomba, Piesche & Arndt, *Mythen, Masken und Subjekte.*

67 El-Tayeb, *European Others*; Haritaworn, *Queer Lovers and Hateful Others.*

68 Amoore, "Biometric Borders."

69 Frontex Risk Analysis Unit, "Risk Analysis for 2016."

70 Foucault, *The Birth of Biopolitics*, 138.

71 Bargu, *Starve and Immolate*, 47.

72 Frontex Risk Analysis Unit, "Risk Analysis for 2016," 61.

73 Bargu, *Starve and Immolate*, 50.

74 Bargu, *Starve and Immolate*, 52.

75 Bargu, *Starve and Immolate*, 46.

76 Mbembe, "Necropolitics," 27.

77 Mbembe, "Necropolitics," 24.

78 Mbembe, "Necropolitics," 27. Michelle Pfeifer also draws on Mbembe's theorization of necropolitics to critique the erasure of "colonial experiences [that] were crucial to formations of German citizenship [and] that still operate in discourses and policies around asylum and migration today." Pfeifer, "Becoming Flesh," 463. However, by normalizing the idea of a dyadic relationship between racialized

displace their own citizens, member states of the European Union are complicit in the "creation of death-worlds" in which "vast populations are subjected to conditions of life conferring upon them the status of living dead."[79] The funneling of asylum seekers into border territories that are not conducive to human life, such as the Sonoran Desert at the southern U.S. border, or the Mediterranean and Aegean seas that separate the European Union from its southern and eastern neighbors, functions as a "Prevention Through Deterrence (PTD) strategy."[80]

The management of "risk" has taken precedence over any morally founded duty to protect. Since 2014, thousands of refugees who attempted to reach safety by boat have effectively been left to drown just a few miles off the European coastline after the patrolling grounds of coastal guards were reduced from 150 kilometers to only five kilometers.[81] Meanwhile, civilian search and rescue missions are criminalized for providing emergency assistance at sea.[82] This constitutes a calculated exposure to death that leaves refugees to attempt the journey at their own risk.

Biopower effectively marks the racialized masculinity of the "single male refugee" as a limit that cancels out vulnerability and international title to protection. Going by the pseudonym Abu Jana, or "father of Jana," a Syrian refugee in Egypt told a reporter for the British newspaper *The Guardian* that his decision to cross by boat was *neither* a choice *nor* an investment. To him, it was the only way to escape the "bureaucratic no-man's land" of *de facto* statelessness:

> "Even if there was a decision to drown the migrant boats, there will still be people going by boat because the individual considers himself dead already. Right now Syrians consider themselves dead. Maybe not physically, but psychologically and socially [a Syrian] is a destroyed human being, he's reached the point of death. So I don't think that even if they decided to bomb migrant boats it would change peoples' decision to go."[83]

Another young Syrian man identified as Ahmed Abu Zeid confirmed that he was "past the point of caring." He explained, "I'll go whether or not a boat rescues me. If I have life in me I'll get there, and if I die, I die. [...] we're out of the phase of fear, there's

---

refugees and white Germans as "benevolent saviour[s]" (465), her critique inadvertently disappears Germans of color and thereby reproduces the imaginary whiteness of the German body politic. By presuming that the "sympathy" of white Germans is elicited through displays of "spectacular suffering," she misses that racialized populations may identify with the displaced as peers whose "suffering" is intimately felt as one's own, propelling many to act in solidarity. The radical left in Germany continues to exist in tension with anti-racism and migrant justice. See Azozomox and Gürsel, "The Untold Story of Migrant Women Squatters."

79 Mbembe, "Necropolitics," 40.

80 De Leon, *The Land of Open Graves*, 29.

81 Since late 2014, Frontex has replaced the Italian *Mare Nostrum* program which extended over 150 kilometers into Libyan waters. As of 2019, Frontex is patrolling only five kilometers off the Italian coast, leaving hundreds to die at high sea while persecuting the crews of civilian boats for providing emergency assistance. The decision to discontinue *Mare Nostrum* without extending Frontex's patrolling grounds amounts to a calculated exposure to death at high sea. Since July 2016, Frontex and NATO vessels are patrolling in the Aegean Sea under joint maritime command.

82 Stierl, "A Sea of Struggle."

83 Kingsley & Diab, "Passport, Lifejacket, Lemons."

no more fear in our hearts." Both men described the experience of "civil death"[84] as equally if not more unbearable than the risk of physical death.

Indeed, the European Union's 2015 declaration of a "fight against smugglers and traffickers"[85] is a "powerful demonstration of the EU's determination to act."[86] While targeting the unsanctioned mobility of asylum seekers, the EU's "war on human trafficking" has in effect failed to quash "criminal networks which exploit vulnerable migrants."[87] Instead of the vulnerability of persons, border police focus on the "vulnerability" of states, which is defined as the "capacity and readiness of Member States to face upcoming challenges, including present and future threats and challenges at the external borders."[88] A new regulation, passed in 2016, vested *Frontex*, renamed "European Border and Coast Guard Agency," with a legal personality, a stand-alone budget, and an expanded mandate to act.

The actions of this new agency, essentially, aim to disallow the decentralized and unsanctioned agency of the displaced. The requirement, for instance, that a fundamental rights officer internally review all complaints is grounded in the so-called "right to good administration,"[89] rather than any notion of "freedom and justice" as guaranteed to EU citizens, residents, and legally-sanctioned visitors.[90] Despite lip serve to international conventions and fundamental rights, risk profiling not only fails to guarantee due process and individual case review (*non-refoulement*) but it subjects displaced persons to administrative violence.

While *Frontex* conducts limited search and rescue missions during border surveillance operations at sea,[91] it is only expected to "protect and save lives *whenever and wherever so required*." This chilling pronouncement minimizes the horror of the deaths of displaced persons at high sea and depoliticizes the question of freedom and justice for all. Although *Frontex's* 2016 charge takes care to spell out that the power to *decide* on protected status remains with sovereign member states, it vests border police with unprecedented executive powers to not only assist and coordinate border control measures, but also to deploy its own personnel and equipment to launch "rapid border interventions." (article 8.1e). *Frontex* may now also *initiate* "return interventions" and manage "return-related tasks" (article 36.4), including the "acquisition of travel documents for returnees" (preamble 32), traditionally a prerogative of sovereign states. Since its creation in 2004, *Frontex'* role has significantly shifted from a coordinating institution to an EU body that not only implements but also *makes* operative decisions. States delegate sovereign license to EU bodies that exist to exclude racialized and displaced populations from access to common infrastructure space.[92] As the power to act devolves to *Frontex*, its status as a quasi-sovereign body is formalized.

---

84 Arendt, *The Human Condition*, 302.

85 European Commission, "European Agenda on Migration," 8.

86 European Commission, "European Agenda on Migration," 3.

87 European Commission, "European Agenda on Migration," 3. For more on the discourse of trafficking, see Lynes, "SOPHIA" in this volume.

88 EU 2016/1624, article 13.4.

89 EU 2016/1624, preamble 50.

90 EC 2000/C 364/01.

91 EU 2016/1624, article 14.2e.

92 Larkin, "The Politics and Poetics of Infrastructure;" Easterling, *Extrastatecraft*.

After declaring a war on human trafficking in 2015, the European Commission laid out a detailed action plan to "transform migrant smuggling into a high-risk and low-profit operation."[93] By confiscating and destroying vessels that are suspected to facilitate the unauthorized passage of refugees, multiple agencies are engaged in a coordinated assault designed to diminish the returns of brokers. However, the discourse of "prevention through deterrence" fails to acknowledge that the "high risk" is ultimately borne by vulnerable persons whose forced mobility is disallowed to the point of death.

By using roaming data, geo-positioning software, end-to-end encryption, and social media platforms to facilitate their own mobility and connect to legal counsel and adequate shelter, unsanctioned border crossers act with and through infrastructures of the state such as roads, satellites, and glass fiber cables. This unauthorized use destabilizes the sovereign logic of the exception.[94] Since mobile technology enables persons to make informed decisions about their movement, the European Commission also seeks to establish "closer coordination"[95] with private internet service providers and social media companies.

In addition to the consolidation of the Common European Asylum System, the European Union's "fight against migrant smuggling" also set the stage for ongoing negotiations about a Common Defense and Security Policy that would enhance "operational coordination" and "capabilities"[96] across existing and planned EU agencies and information technology (IT) systems.[97] The implementation of this plan would entail even greater executive powers for *Frontex*, the European Union Agency for Law Enforcement Coordination (*Europol*), and other security, surveillance, and intelligence providers engaged in joint-military operations. In light of the projected goal of "interoperability," the European Union is no longer limiting itself to economic and legal cooperation. Its continental-scale alignment of agencies and supporting infrastructures heralds the constitution of Europe as a bio-geo-sovereign power that seeks to regulate and manage life within a territory designated as its "area of freedom, security and justice."[98]

Insofar as neoliberal theories of the subject presuppose that economic man, as a *particular* figuration of the human, necessarily follow the principle of a preference for pleasure over pain,[99] they reduce all observable actions to the pursuit of "private" interest in bodily integrity rather than the political interest to actualize the freedom to act in a shared world. By positing refugee's capacity to labor as a source of human dignity, neoliberal advocates generalize the market mechanism of exchange to valorize and thereby depoliticize the agency of refugees as a form of capital. By integrating humanitarian discourse with human capital theory, they fail to account for the racial

---

93 "A European Agenda on Migration," 1.

94 Agamben, *State of Exception*.

95 European Commission, "European Agenda on Migration," 6.

96 European Commission, "EU Action Plan Against Migrant Smuggling," 3–4.

97 "Under Watchful Eyes."

98 This area coincides with the Schengen zone which guarantees freedom of movement to EU citizens and permanent residents. The European Agency for the Operational Management of Large-Scale IT Systems in the Area of Freedom, Security and Justice (*eu-LISA*) coordinates security and surveillance apparatuses to ensure "situational awareness."

99 Foucault, *The Birth of Biopolitics*, 272.

profile of the "single male refugee" as a limit of biopolitical investment at which vulnerability is denied and protection withheld. Although a comparatively small number of displaced persons arrived in Greece since 2014, the term "refugee crisis" centers Europe, yet again. Instead of the fundamental right to human dignity, *Frontex* is defending the borders of whiteness. Instead of globalizing the Western gaze, humanitarian discourse must be decolonized, first and foremost by attending to the coloniality of militarized border regimes and contemporary crises of displacement around the world.

Abolition Democracy

In contrast to neoliberal constructions of the subject as a self-possessed agent, grassroots solidarity groups leverage private property or possession of physical assets to assist refugees with shelter, safe passage, and data connectivity. An active squatting movement continues to mobilize legal frameworks that bestow relative inviolability on EU citizens to not only aid and host but also accompany and shield undocumented claimants of asylum from state violence. Over the past decade, autonomous refugee movements have staged collective actions that ranged from organized caravans, occupations of public squares and empty buildings, and frequent hunger strikes[100] to demand freedom of movement, freedom of residency, community control, and legal status for all.

During a solidarity visit in Berlin in 2015, Angela Y. Davis characterized the refugee movement as "the movement of the 21st century."[101] After being denied access to an occupied school by district authorities, she walked with organizers and allies of the occupation before coming to a halt at the closed gates of the school. Filmed with a hand-held camera, she listened attentively to the refugee activists, asked questions, and witnessed the gathering of supporters in the street that opposed the pending eviction of the school. One young man explained, "Even German animals are living better than we refugees, I'm telling you." Another emphatically agreed, "Yes." She identified herself as one of the activists that set up the "International Women's Space," a wing of the occupied school reserved for refugee women.[102] "They evicted us very badly, on a rainy day," she shared. After losing access to the school, several refugee activists were forced to seek refuge at a nearby church. Scandalizing the dehumanizing treatment of refugees at the hands of police and wider German society, one refugee activist shared a message,

> "We [Black people] are not criminals, we are refugees. And what I want to tell the German government [is] that being a refugee is not something that we choose by ourselves. Anyone could be a refugee. Today I am a refugee. But I don't know about tomorrow, somebody else has to be a refugee. [...] Before we became refugees, there were thou-

---

100 See Vrasti & Dayal, "Cityzenship;" Mudu & Chattopadhyaya, *Migration, Squatting and Radical Autonomy*; Bargu, *Starve and Immolate*; Mitchell & Sparke, "Hotspot Geopolitics versus Geosocial Solidarity;" Stierl, *Migrant Resistance in Contemporary Europe*.

101 Tosco, "Angela Davis."

102 Mudu & Chattopadhyaya, *Migration, Squatting and Radical Autonomy*, 207–221.

sands of refugees. So today, is our time. We don't know, next day, it will be somebody else's time."[103]

Unlike the assimilationist "We Refugees" Hannah Arendt described in her 1943 essay of the same title,[104] the "we" pronounced by autonomous refugees and their allies in Berlin, Calais, Athens, and elsewhere describes a political collectivity forged through conscious resistance to racism and state violence through media activism. As the above statement illustrates, refugee activists act out of a sense of historical responsibility for others. Despite a lack of individual choice, they find ways to engage in "purposeful, politically motivated act[s] of protest"[105] and hail a "new relation of self to self (and to others)."[106]

Gabriela, identified as a queer woman from Chile and one of the organizers of the "International Women's Space," explained to an interviewer that she needed collaborators, not help. "In my opinion, people should get together when they empathize with others, when they share the reasons to fight together, when they think the struggle is also for them."[107] She emphasized, "they should fight not because they feel guilty or have pity."[108] Insofar as people claiming asylum in Europe struggle to "create bonds of solidarity, friendship, [and] autonomy"[109] by opposing the *Lager* system of administrative detention,[110] refugee activists "invent novel practices of common life and subjectivities, from the ground up, insisting on a new imaginary that is independent from the politics of life and death signified by sovereignty itself."[111] By opposing border regimes with a practical "will to live together,"[112] they model an ethics of resistance to death-worlds that threaten to engulf most of us, eventually.

No longer aligned with the dominant rationality of self-interest, practices such as lip-sewing and hunger striking function as "embodied truth-acts"[113] that forge a "*relational* mode of subjectivation."[114] By "doubly" withdrawing from speech and nourishment, argues Bargu, refugees reconstitute themselves as political agents in an extremely constricted field of action.[115] Their unsanctioned acts of protest negate the negation of shared humanity—dehumanization, that is—in border zones and detention centers across EUrope. The demands and actions of refugees call for practical forms of solidarity that exceed the compassionate stance of humanitarian advocacy. They further displace the neoliberal logic of choice and investment. Instead, the analy-

---

103 See Tosco, "Angela Davis." The partial transcription of the video above is my own.

104 Robinson, *Altogether Elsewhere*.

105 Bargu, "The Silent Exception," 5.

106 Bargu, "The Silent Exception," 13.

107 Mudu & Charropadhyaya, *Migration, Squatting and Radical Autonomy*, 213.

108 Mudu & Charropadhyaya, *Migration, Squatting and Radical Autonomy*, 213.

109 Mudu & Charropadhyaya, *Migration, Squatting and Radical Autonomy*, 62.

110 Pieper, *Die Gegenwart der Lager*.

111 Bargu, "Another Necropolitics," 15.

112 Bargu, "Another Necropolitics," 14.

113 Bargu, "Another Necropolitics," 24.

114 Bargu, "The Silent Exception," 22.

115 Bargu, "The Silent Exception."

ses of activists facing down the dehumanizing forces of security and surveillance, not least through the quotidian act of snapping a "selfie," require those of us who are no longer, or not yet, refugees to listen closely. In the cracks and crevices of racist border regimes, abolitionist imaginaries are flourishing.

The Calais Crisis
Real Refugees Welcome, Migrants "Do Not Come"[1]

Farah Atoui

> In times of "crisis" [...] we must ask anew: *Who has become a migrant? Which forms of human mobility are classified, or recognized, or disavowed as manifestations of "migration"?* Moreover, it is crucial to ask: *Who does, and who does not, come to be governed as a "migrant"?*
> —*The New Keywords Collective, "Europe/Crisis"*

> Fear is the anticipatory reality in the present of a threatening future.
> —*Brian Massumi, "The Future Birth of the Affective Fact"*

Thomas Nail opens *The Figure of the Migrant* with the affirmation that "the twenty-first century will be the century of the migrant."[2] In the context of this defining historical instance, I take the New Keywords Collective's invitation to ponder questions of definition and classification as a starting point to engage with the discursive mediation of the so-called migrant/refugee crisis in Europe. I focus on the British context—which intensively mediated the migrant camps of Calais, France as a focal point of threat—critically scrutinizing the key terms that have been deployed in the British political establishment and mainstream news media to shape popular perceptions of migration and refugeeism. My analysis centers on the keyword "crisis," as well as on the bifurcated keywords "migrant/refugee," as these terms constitute key political operators around which political and media discourses proliferate within the discursive field of migration. I focus on Calais as a site of entry to shed light on the specific political and governmental responses these keywords generated, as well as on the ways in which they constituted a series of bordering practices and immigration and asylum regimes.

The intellectual and political orientation of this research takes its inspiration from the work of the New Keywords collective, which is concerned with destabilizing exist-

---

1 This phrase is taken from a public address by the president of the EU Council Donald Tusk at a press conference in Athens, March 3, 2016.

2 Nail, *The Figure of the Migrant*, 1.

ing objects and categories of migration, providing a new critical theorization of migration and borders, and producing a counter-discourse in the field of migration. I share the Collective's conviction that migration keywords are more than mere words. Rather, they frame in essential ways the stakes of contemporary migration research, and related debates, policies, and matters of governance. These keywords are key sites of struggle where competing and conflicting political aspirations, projects and practices collide. On the one hand, as suggested elsewhere in the current volume, the "hegemonic discursive formations of crisis"[3] shore up European governmental policies and practices, from intensified border enforcement and militarized police violence to the sweeping illegalization of human mobility as a management strategy. On the other hand, the autonomous movements,[4] practices and mobilizations of migrants and refugees who "appropriate movement and claim space"[5] as they seek safe and promising places to stay in Europe defy borders and contest normative categories of citizenship, national identity, and belonging.

The term "crisis,"[6] which by 2015 had become a more or less standard frame of reference through which to understand the "unauthorized" migratory movements of people across and within the borders of European states, was mobilized to particular effect by British politicians and media to describe the migrant camps of Calais. I take then-Prime Minister David Cameron's 2015 denunciation of the Calais migrant camps as evidence of a widespread migrant crisis as a starting point to examine the epistemic and political work performed by that particular term. Drawing on the work of Brian Massumi, I examine how the keyword "crisis" conjures various temporalities, and how, through their interplay, these temporalities operate on an affective level to simultaneously produce migration as a future threat *and* erase its past, its historicity.[7] In so doing, they legitimize governmental measures that seek to securitize Europe and Britain against migration and to discipline migrants. While my analysis begins in 2015, I am particularly concerned with how this specific moment of crisis was preceded by a longer series of crises that established the affective and symbolic reserve that rendered the 2015 crisis legible as such. I claim that this recursive operation—which in many ways contravenes the very sense of political and historical singularity that crisis as a keyword attempts to impute to migration—works through a logic of preemption (of the threat of migration)[8] to consolidate a new form of governmental power. This logic, through which the vision of migration as an impending crisis recursively constitutes itself, is nowhere more pronounced than in the operations of another of the British media and state's preferred migration keywords: 'illegal.' I argue that the refugee/eco-

---

3 De Genova, Garelli and Tazzioli, "Autonomy of Asylum?", 240.

4 De Genova, Garelli and Tazzioli explain that from an autonomist perspective, migration is conceived "in terms of historically specific social formations of human mobility that manifest themselves as a constitutive (subjective, creative, and productive) power within the more general capital-labor relation." ("Autonomy of Asylum?", 241).

5 New Keywords Collective, "Europe/Crisis," 4.

6 My use of the scare quotes around the term crisis is intentional to mark this term as a contested one. I invoke this term throughout the rest of this essay, without the scare quotes but in the same spirit of contestation.

7 Massumi, "The Future Birth of the Affective Fact."

8 Massumi, "The Future Birth of the Affective Fact," 54.

nomic migrant distinction is mobilized by various formations of sovereign power,[9] from the British government to the EU, to "illegalize"[10] migrants as a preemptive measure, and to thus justify their exclusion from the international regime of refugee rights and protection. In other words, I show how the representation of all Calais migrants as potential "illegal" economic migrants by British politicians—a representation circulated and amplified by mainstream newspapers—is the mechanism by which these migrants are discursively and politically excluded from the category of refugee and produced in turn as always already illegal. I also show how this illegality gets attached not only to certain types of mobility, but to specifically (non-white) bodies according to a neocolonialist logic of racial and class hierarchy and differentiation, and produces them as vulnerable and exploitable subjects.

Solve the Crisis! Stop the "Swarm"![11]

The year 2015 marks a decisive turning point in the development of contemporary discourses of migration. Due to the increased pace and scale of migratory movements to Europe during the second half of that year, the EU declared that a vast "migrant/refugee crisis" was underway, and that it threatened Europe's control over its borders, as well as its security, its identity, and its values. As De Genova, Garelli and Tazzioli affirm, "what has been designated unanimously by European authorities as a migration or refugee crisis [...] signals an impasse for the effective and efficient government of multiple cross-border mobilities that is figured as 'crisis' only inasmuch as it signifies a crisis of *control*—a crisis of the sovereign power of the European border regime."[12] This potent framework was expanded to include the northern French city of Calais following an incident in which a few hundred migrants charged the UK-France border barriers during the summer of 2015.[13] Speaking to ITV news in July 2015, David Cameron, then Prime Minister of the UK, expressed that he was "totally focused" on the "Calais crisis," and vowed to address it through various measures, including intensified securitization of Britain's maritime and submarine borders with France, offshore preemption—what Cameron described as "deal[ing] with the problem at the source, that is stopping so many people from travelling across the Mediterranean in search of a better life"—and finally increased domestic immigration enforcement designed to make it "less easy for 'illegal' migrants to stay in Britain." Explaining his rationale, Cameron continued:

> "You have got a swarm of people coming across the Mediterranean, seeking a better life, wanting to come to Britain because Britain has got jobs, it's got a growing economy, it's

9   New Keywords Collective, "Europe/Crisis," 4.

10   De Genova, "Migrant 'Illegality' and Deportability in Everyday Life," 419.

11   The term swarm was used by British Prime Minister David Cameron to describe migrants in Calais in an interview with ITV news in July 2015.

12   De Genova, Garelli and Tazzioli, "Autonomy of Asylum?", 254.

13   New Keywords Collective, "Europe/Crisis," 23.

an incredible place to live. But we need to protect our borders by working hand in glove with our neighbors, the French, and that is exactly what we are doing."[14]

A crisis is defined as "an unstable or crucial time or state of affairs in which a decisive change is impending,"[15] and as such, it seems to demand urgent intervention and immediate action. A crisis thus conjures a particular temporality: even as it demands action in the present moment, it anxiously looks toward and attempts to preempt a potential future catastrophe, some shift that is impending. In "The Future Birth of the Affective Fact: The Political Ontology of Threat,"[16] Brian Massumi insightfully theorizes how this temporality operates and, more importantly, how it gets politically instrumentalized. Massumi argues that while "threat is from the future," it has "an impeding reality in the present."[17] This is because whether the potential danger that the threat anticipates for the future exists or not, a threat *is real* because it is *felt* to be real, in the form of fear. Massumi ties the affective ontology of threat to a new and dominant form of political power: preemptive power. Preemptive power takes threat as its object and preemption as its "operative logic,"[18] justifying defensive actions that are designed to prevent the felt potential (of) threat from actualizing, and to protect public security. Through the production and sustenance of threat, preemptive power creates the conditions that justify its own exercise, and thus, is able to perpetuate itself recursively. The keyword crisis, as mobilized in the discursive field of migration, works in a similar manner. It temporally oscillates between future (the future threat of further or increased migration) and present (the current atmosphere of fear that this threat produces). So situated, crisis becomes affectively operative, galvanizing a sense of collective fear which in turn legitimizes anti-migrant actions that promise collective security. In other words, the discourse of crisis justifies preemptive measures that expand the ambit of state sovereignty, and increase the state's power to govern migrants and mobility. For instance, Cameron, during his interview with ITV, vowed to respond to the crisis by increasing police presence at the border, by further investing in border security, and by erecting border fences at the port of Calais and at Coquelles (site of the French entrance to the Eurochannel). He also promised to pursue illegal gangs that help migrants get to Britain, and pledged to intervene domestically by "throwing out more illegal migrants," passed new legislation that made it more difficult for them to stay in Britain. These mechanisms, dedicated to what Massumi refers to as the "modulation" of the "felt qualities" of the environment, are precisely what give preemptive power an edge over other forms or regimes of power.[19] Put differently, these preemptive defensive measures enable Cameron to modulate the public fear around migration, by reaffirming Britain's power over its borders and over cross-border human mobilities.

---

14 Taylor and Wintour, "Calais crisis: Cameron pledges to deport more people to end 'swarm' of migrants."

15 Merriam-Webster Dictionary, "Crisis."

16 Massumi, "The Future Birth of the Affective Fact."

17 Massumi, "The Future Birth of the Affective Fact," 53–54.

18 Massumi, "The Future Birth of the Affective Fact," 62.

19 Massumi, "The Future Birth of the Affective Fact," 62.

The discursive operation of crisis relies on various metaphors of pathology and disease. These are used as governmental tactics to demonize migrants, and to thus manufacture the collective sense of fear that needs to be modulated. The epistemic move of associating the term crisis—defined as "the turning point for better or worse in an acute disease or fever; a paroxysmal attack of pain, distress, or disordered function"[20]—to the term migration pathologizes migration by representing it as a disease, fever, or pain attacking the European body, and causing its dysfunction. As the New Keywords collective argues, "the very terms *'migrant* crisis' and *'refugee* crisis' tend to personalize 'crisis' and relocate 'crisis' in the body and person of the figurative migrant/refugee, as if s/he is the carrier of a disease called 'crisis,' and thus carries the contagion of 'crisis' wherever s/he may go. Most importantly, the figure of the migrant/refugee hereby threatens 'Europe' with its incurable and contagious malady."[21] The camps in Calais and their residents were openly represented as a pathogenic threat in some British newspapers. For instance, *The Daily Mail*, the second biggest-selling British daily tabloid newspaper, denounced the Calais camp's "squalid" condition, asserting that it is "rife with disease, violence and prostitution."[22] According to this report, published in August 2016, "Calais jungle [was] at 'breaking point' as number of migrants passes 9000 and camp becomes a 'major health and security risk'." *The Daily Mail* was thus claiming that disease, violence and prostitution were at the very door of Britain, waiting to infiltrate the nation with and through the contagious bodies of the migrants who were seeking to cross the channel from Calais. *The Daily Express* used the same wording to warn that the 9000 migrants in Calais were so dangerous that the camps were a "police no-go zone."[23] *The Daily Express* was thus alleging that the "danger" characterizing the Calais migrant camp was threatening to spread through entire British nation if migrants were to be allowed in. In yet another article, *The Daily Mail* actually claimed that the migrants jumping into lorries going from Calais into Britain were *contaminating* the food products that these lorries were transporting.[24]

These metaphors of pathology and disease are some of the various strategies that proliferate under the discursive regime of crisis, and keep it potent by affectively saturating the environment with a sense of fear. Another effective and pernicious metaphor that Cameron draws on to depict migrants is that of the "swarm." Conjuring the visual image of a large and dense body of insects, Cameron compounds the repellent image of a contagious disease with the equally revolting image of a swarm of insects, thus producing an image of migrants that is intended to invoke visceral and instinctive feelings of disgust and fear. The term swarm was circulated by the mainstream media, intensifying the sense of a crisis in Calais, one that threatened the very body of the nation. The July 31, 2015 edition of the *Daily Mail* displayed on its front page a collection of photographs of "illegal" migrants being arrested by the police across southern Britain under the all-uppercase headline "THE 'SWARM' ON OUR STREETS." Cameron's metaphor, dutifully repeated in the press, is not incidental. Swarm was used in association with migrants by French author Jean Raspail in his infamous 1973

20 Merriam-Webster Dictionary, "Crisis."

21 New Keywords Collective, "Europe/Crisis," 20.

22 Sparks, "Calais Jungle at 'breaking point'."

23 Sparks, "9000 Calais migrants want to enter UK."

24 "It is time to end this migrant madness."

novel "Le Camp des Saints" to describe the "attack" of France by migrants from the Indian continent. This racist and violent book, which laments the fall of the native French
population and of the Western civilization following the migrants' "invasion" popular-
ized racist and xenophobic terminologies—such "tidal wave" and "swarm"—which are
today used in some mainstream media to represent migration. These terms have also
gained currency in far-right American and French political circles. The book, for instance, has been cited by far-right politicians such as Marine Le Pen and Steve Bannon
to advocate for anti-immigrant measures in Europe.[25]

The discourse of a Calais migrant crisis, bolstered by the various metaphors that
have been used by British politicians and by news outlets from the BBC to The Times to
The Daily Mail to represent migration and migrants to Europe—from contagious disease and "swarm" to "tidal wave," "flood," "invaders," and "marauders"[26]—performs,
to draw on Massumi again, "an operative logic [...] that combines an ontology with an
epistemology in such a way as to endow itself with powers of self-causation."[27] That is,
these terms epistemologically constitute migration and migrants as a potential threat
which is affectively and collectively felt in the form of fear of what migrants "would do"
if "they could" access Europe—what Massumi calls "the double conditional"—which
in turn, legitimizes preemptive actions that deny migrants access to Europe under the
pretext of safeguarding European security. Put differently, these metaphors are mobilized by politicians and mainstream media as techniques to make up crisis as a particular kind of discursive regime which assembles all the migrants in Calais into one
nameless, faceless, pathological and threatening mass, producing the figure *migrant*
as "the generic identity of a potential threat,"[28] and rendering migrants themselves
subject to a mode of preemptive power that is invested in governing migration and
securitizing borders.

The discursive regime of crisis not only implicates the future to act on the present,
but it also restructures the past by disappearing the historicity of migration. The narrative of crisis indeed invokes a nostalgic account of a mythical past that was supposedly
absent of migration, and that was disrupted by the threat of the migration crisis. The
language of crisis therefore forecloses the structural nature of exclusion and exploitation that produces the migrant "camp" as an ongoing phenomenon. As Miriam Ticktin
argues, the attachment of crisis to a sense and language of emergency "makes [the
situation] seem as if it is an exception to an otherwise peaceful order. There is no space
to understand causes or histories that might have led to or shaped this moment."[29] Put
differently, through an alarmist representation of a momentary border control emer-

25 Alduy, "What a French novel tells us."

26 The June 26, 2015 edition of the *Daily Mail* warned: "The tidal wave of migrants could be the biggest
threat to Europe since the war"; *BBC* used the term flood to describe migrants moving from Italy to
Germany or Scandinavia in a June 20, 2015 article on www.bbc.com; *The Times* warns of an invasion of
migrants who were forced out from Calais by police force in its June 1, 2018 edition. Speaking to the
BBC in August 2015, the UK's Foreign Secretary Philip Hammond described the migrants in Calais as
"marauders." Reported by *The Guardian*, "Marauding' migrants threaten standard of living, says foreign secretary," August 10, 2015.

27 Massumi, "The Future Birth of the Affective Fact," 62.

28 Massumi, "The Future Birth of the Affective Fact," 58.

29 Ticktin, "The Problem with Humanitarian Borders."

gency, the discourse of a migrant crisis obscures the structural forces and historic conditions that have shaped migratory movements, and that drive thousands of people to risk their lives as they attempt to cross the Mediterranean to reach Europe. Through its evocation of a mythical past that erases the history of migration, crisis conceals colonial histories, their legacies and enduring effects. For Britain, this means that the Calais crisis belies the reality that Britain is the final destination for many migrants precisely because of the colonial histories that have shaped their language, culture, education, and imagination, and that thus have bound particular countries to the metropole. Crisis also conceals the role of such economic policies as liberalization, deregulation, and privatization—all enforced by Western powers, including Britain, through powerful international financial institutions like the IMF and the World Bank—in contributing to those forms of mass dispossession and forced displacement that drive people to Europe in the first place. Crisis moreover conceals the historical responsibility of industrialized nations, such as Britain, for climate change and its environmental effects (such as crop failure and rising sea-levels) that are driving migratory movements to Europe, especially out of Africa.[30] And finally, crisis conceals the wars—in Iraq, Afghanistan, Syria, Libya, and Yemen to name a few—in which Western powers are embroiled and that are displacing large populations to Europe.

Crisis thus essentially severs the connections between the history of European imperialism and neo-colonialism and contemporary migratory flows. In the specific context of migration to Britain, crisis conceals the role played by Britain in shaping the colonial histories, and the economic, environmental and political forces that drive people to be on the move and to transit through Calais, as they attempt to reach Britain. In other words, crisis conceals the longer history of the Calais camps as an *ongoing* crisis, and displaces Europe's and Britain's responsibility for migratory movements and accountability to migrants by producing migration and migrants "as the de facto human refuse of 'crises' constructed to be strictly 'external' to the presumed safety and stability of 'Europe,' erupting always 'elsewhere'."[31] Crisis replaces Europe's and Britain's implication, accountability and responsibility with a sense of imminent threat, and with an environment of fear that affectively galvanizes populist anti-migrant sentiments and legitimizes various measures taken by European governments to stem migration to Europe, under the pretext of re-instating safety and stability, and restoring a "lost" mythical past, imagined as devoid of migration and migrants.

Further, by concentrating attention on the present moment, crisis not only disregards the past, but it also excludes the future. In times of crisis, there is "no time to think of the past or plan for the future," Ticktin tells us.[32] The preemptive actions that are called for by the crisis—such as the ones promised by Cameron as solutions to the Calais crisis—whether in the form of more borders, more fences, more security, more surveillance, more policing, and more militarization, or in the form of migrant illegalization, incarceration, deportation, or resettlement, do not interrogate or address the structural conditions and forces that underlie contemporary migratory movements.

---

30 Africa is one of the areas that is most affected by climate change. For a detailed report on the effects of climate change and its relation to displacement see Kalin, "Displacement Caused by the Effects of Climate Change."

31 New Keywords Collective, "Europe/Crisis," 3.

32 Ticktin, "The Problem with Humanitarian Borders."

These solutions, devised as responses to an event framed as an emergency, "demand a response that moves us beyond politics and into the realm of exception," confirms Polly Pallister-Wilkins.[33]

The Becoming of a Crisis:
From the Sangatte Refugee Center to the Calais Migrant Camps

Contravening the very sense of urgency and singularity that the discursive regime of crisis seeks to create, the crisis in Calais has been intensively recursive. While Calais only became a focal point of the so-called European migrant/refugee crisis in 2015, it has been a place of migration and a transit point for migrants for decades—a disappeared history that intersects with that of another site, Sangatte, that although less known to the public, is equally important in shaping the current "migrant/refugee crisis." Beginning in the 1990s, Calais, a port-town in northern France, emerged as a major hub for migrants attempting to cross from France to the UK where they would seek asylum.[34] In 1999, the French Red Cross opened a refugee center in the Sangatte commune to offer shelter to migrants sleeping on the streets in and around Calais. Pierre Kremer, editor in chief of the French Red Cross magazine *Croix Rouge*, reports that "the presence of the center has elicited the wrath of local residents, who regularly claim that the constant comings and goings of foreigners has led to a permanent insecurity in this region. In fact, no rise in the crime rate has been registered since the center opened."[35] The xenophobic anti-immigrant sentiments expressed by the local population were exacerbated by news media and the political establishment's representation of the presence of migrants in Calais as a problem that required the urgent intervention of the state and the police. The discursive recursivity of an impending crisis was starting to accrete to the Calais site, and a preemptive logic mobilized to govern migration and migrants.

Liza Schuster traces how the Sangatte center and its residents were produced as a public issue in ways that ultimately drove the British government both to close the center and to increase security at the British-French border.[36] Her analysis shows that Sangatte constitutes a complex conjunction of state, corporate, and civil society interests which together manufactured the "problem" of migrant crossing and simultaneously militated against it. Schuster explains that in 2001, the closure of the Sangatte refugee center became an imperative for Eurotunnel at the moment when the UK Labour government announced that both Eurotunnel and cross-channel carriers would be penalized for undocumented migrants stowing away, effectively shifting the responsibility of controlling the borders and preventing the crossing of undocumented migrants to these private companies.[37] Eurotunnel consequently undertook to lobby British opposition parties to fight the Labour government's legislation, and simultaneously worked to mobilize British media into pressuring the government to shut down

---

33 Pallister-Wilkins, "The Humanitarian Policing of 'Our Sea'."

34 Fusco, "The Futile Destruction of the Jungle in Calais."

35 Kremer, "Sangatte. A Place of Hope and Despair."

36 Schuster, "Asylum Seekers: Sangatte and the Tunnel."

37 Schuster, "Asylum Seekers: Sangatte and the Tunnel."

the Sangatte center, which continued to attract blame for drawing "illegal" migrants to the area.

"Illegal" is an operative term in the discursive representation of migrants in Calais. The rhetoric of "illegality" draws on the Dublin regulation, an agreement within the EU that forces asylum seekers to apply for asylum in whatever EU country they reach first. Since few migrants arrive in Britain as their first point of entry to the EU, the Dublin Agreement therefore acts as a powerful instrument of illegalization. In other words, seeking asylum in Britain renders Calais migrants *de facto* "illegal." The rhetoric that was mobilized in British political and mediatic speeches to represent and to govern migrants in Calais coded Sangatte as a "migrant attraction"—obscuring its *raison-d'être* as a center providing basic humanitarian assistance to refugees—and coded all migrants as always already illegal because they were not refugees, thus justifying measures to deny them entry to the UK, and to force them out of Calais. The legislative and discursive construction of Calais migrants' illegality was compounded by mainstream media spectacles: journalists were allowed into the channel terminal so they could document and publicize migrants' attempts to "illegally" enter the UK. Schuster reports that during the summer of 2001, Sangatte was prominently featured in British news media: all newspapers, tabloids and broadsheets, supplemented by TV coverage, reported on Sangatte. The *Daily Express* deployed the terminology of war, describing migratory movements to Europe as an "invasion" to support of Eurotunnel's demand for strengthening the border with France; the *Mail* backed a Tory MP's request for a militarized intervention in the form of British troops patrolling the French coast.[38] A sense of threat, produced by this discursive formation, was coalescing, in the form of collective fear, around Sangatte's migrants and around migration more generally.

Not only was Sangatte instrumentalized to advance the economic interests of Eurotunnel and the carriers, but it also became an opportunity to further political agendas. Conservative officials used Sangatte as an example of the Labour government's incompetence in the handling of a migrant crisis during the 2001 elections, promising the British people to make migration and asylum a priority in their political agendas. With the support of all tabloids and some of the broadsheets, various Conservative spokespersons fed the perception that Britain had become the most attractive destination for migrants and asylum seekers because of the Labour government's lax immigration policies.[39] From a refugee center, Sangatte was thus transformed by the British press and political establishment into a symbol of migration and border control politics in Britain, while the migrants it housed were construed as "illegal" subjects causing damage to British businesses,[40] threatening the security and safety of Britain, and abusing its welfare system. "Illegality" was painted onto migrants because they were being figured as economic beings in pursuit of wealth while at the same time siphoning public resources. In other words, "illegality" designated not only a strictly legal category, as defined under the Dublin Agreement, but also an improperly governed

---

38 Schuster, "Asylum Seekers: Sangatte and the Tunnel," 510–511.

39 Schuster, "Asylum Seekers: Sangatte and the Tunnel," 513.

40 Schuster, "Asylum Seekers: Sangatte and the Tunnel," 512. As Schuster explains, British companies claimed that the increased cost of security measures, the interruption of transport services caused by migrants' crossings, and the loss of freight business due to the threat of fines were affecting their revenues.

form of capitalist aspiration that was threatening to the dominant social and political order, and that thus needed to be controlled through preemptive action.

Massumi incisively asks: "How can a preemptive politics maintain its political legitimacy given that it grounds itself in the actual ungroundedness of affective fact? Would not pointing out the actual facts be enough to make it crumble?"[41] The response seems to be no. As Schuster's study highlights, the number of asylum applications to the UK had actually decreased in 2001, contradicting the discourse of emergency and threat that was entrenched in the migration debate. And yet, following mounting pressure—from Eurotunnel, the Conservative Party and the media—the British Home Secretary David Blunkett pressed the then-French Interior Minister Nicolas Sarkozy to close the Sangatte Red Cross center, describing it as "a magnet for illegal immigration into Britain."[42] The center was shut down in 2002, and while Britain took in a portion of the center's residents under a "burden-sharing agreement" and France took in another portion,[43] the British government introduced a new bill aimed at tightening the nationality, immigration and asylum system. In defence of this bill, Blunkett stated that the government's aim is not to create "Fortress Britain" but to break the image of Britain as "soft touch."[44] The bill's aim was thus to restore the British people's confidence in Britain's territorial sovereignty, its border enforcement system, and its immigration and asylum regime. Put differently, the bill's aim was to reinforce the mechanisms that modulate the collective atmosphere of fear around migration. The manufacturing of the "threat" of migration in Sangatte legitimized the intensification of border control in the Calais region. The agreement between France and Britain indeed entailed an increase in the number of French border police across the channel's ports, and the extension of Britain's immigration control across the border to France.[45] What took place around Sangatte prefigured, and uncannily anticipated, the next moments of crisis in 2009 and 2015, thus marking the recursive nature of the Calais Crisis. The structure of this crisis, far from being singular and totalizing, is highly repetitive, and it is precisely its recursivity that acts as the enabling condition for an ongoing but constantly mutating politics of preemption, and a self-sustaining preemptive power.

The rhetoric of migrant illegality (and its association to threat) which had shaped the representation of Sangatte in the early 2000s resurfaced in 2009 to mediate the representation of migrant camps in Calais, and quickly came to dominate the debate around the politics of migration, border and asylum control policies in Britain. The closure of Sangatte's refugee reception center in 2002 did little to slow the arrival of migrants to and the passage of migrants through Calais. The center's residents relocated to the surrounding area, and new migrants continued to arrive, with the hope of crossing the border to Britain. Smaller, temporary camps started emerging around Calais, one of which expanded dramatically despite French authorities' sporadic attempts to demolish the shelters and disperse their inhabitants. This site came to be known as the Calais "jungle." Like the Sangatte refugee center, the Calais migrant camps became a

---

41 Massumi, "The Future Birth of the Affective Fact," 55.

42 Travis, "Britain to accept 1200 migrants in Sangatte deal."

43 *UNHCR News and Stories*, "Last Groups to Leave for Britain As Sangatte Closure Looms "

44 "Blunkett Closes Asylum 'Loopholes'."

45 Travis, "Britain to accept 1200 migrants in Sangatte deal."

flash point of political interests and a signifier of a larger politics of mobility control.[46] When in 2009, French riot police bulldozed the informal settlements and rounded up their dwellers, sending adults to detention centers and minors to shelters in Eastern France, French Immigration Minister Eric Besson justified this operation by declaring that Calais was not a humanitarian camp, but a base for human trafficking and illegal migration.[47] His claim was supported by the British, who this time refused to take in any migrants yet did not hesitate to instrumentalize this event, emphasizing Britain's commitment to the prevention of illegal migration and human-trafficking. Home Secretary Alan Johnson expressed his "delight" about the camp's closure, and stated that Britain would not be forced to take any "illegal" migrants: "genuine" refugees would have to apply for asylum in the country from which they accessed the EU, while non-genuine refugees would be returned home.[48]

The distinction between a refugee and other types of migrants is rooted in the definition set forth by a United Nations treaty, the 1951 Refugee Convention, which today constitutes the key legal document forming the basis of the United Nations High Commissioner for Refugees' (UNHCR) work.[49] This document codifies the rights of a refugee at the international level, who is defined as "someone who is unable or unwilling to return to their country of origin owing to a well-founded fear of being persecuted for reasons of race, religion, nationality, membership of a particular social group, or political opinion."[50] The asylum seeker is described as a person waiting to be recognized as a refugee (but will not necessarily be recognized as such), while the economic migrant is defined as a person who "normally leaves a country voluntarily to seek a better life. Should she or he elect to return home they would continue to receive the protection of their government."[51]

At the outset, the UNHCR terminology defining the distinction between a refugee, an asylum seeker, and an economic migrant elicits questions that shed light on the problematic assumptions and implications of such normative categories of differentiation and classification. For instance, given the complexity and entanglement of migratory patterns and motivations, is it even possible to categorize migrants into tidy, mutually exclusive groups? Can a migrant not be simultaneously displaced by unrest in their home of origin *and* have economic motivations as well as desires to ameliorate their situation? How are the conditions in the home country determined to be "safe" or not for someone's life or freedom? Does not economic disaster and catastrophic climate change constitute a threat to one's life? Does not war, internal strife, or conflict undermine one's economic well-being? Is war not an economic phenomenon? Nicholas De Genova, Glenda Garelli and Martina Tazzioli shed light on the role of the fault lines between the category of "migrant" and that of the "refugee" in constituting the crisis in Europe, particularly the manner in which migrant management policies and humanitarian responses are premised precisely on the exclusion of economic migrants from discourses of hospitality and tolerance, and from rights and recognition structures.

---

46 Rygiel, "Bordering Solidarities," 1.

47 Allen, "Alan Johnson praises French raid on Calais 'Jungle'."

48 Chrisafis and Siddique, "French Police Clear the 'Jungle' Migrant Camp in Calais."

49 UNHCR, "Convention and Protocol relating to the Status of Refugee."

50 UNHCR, "Convention and Protocol relating to the Status of Refugee."

51 Definition retrieved from the FAQ of the UNHCR website.

De Genova et al. problematize this "customary governmental partition" and its "exclusionary juridical reification and rarefication of the status of refugee" by affirming that "every act of migration, to some extent—and in a world wracked by wars, civil wars, and other more diffuse forms of societal violence, as well as the structural violence of deprivation and marginalization, perhaps more and more—may be apprehensible as a quest for refuge, and migrants come increasingly to resemble "refugees," while, similarly, refugees never cease to have aspirations and projects for recomposing their lives and thus never cease to resemble "migrants."[52]

The distinction between refugee and asylum seeker performs the same work, since the very term "asylum seeker," argues the New Keywords collective, "is always already suggestive of a basic suspicion of all people who petition for asylum within a European asylum system."[53] In other words, migrants are all guilty, until they prove their worthiness and deservingness of European protection, which is a rare occurrence, because as the New Keywords collective further adds, "the European asylum system routinely and systematically disqualifies and rejects the great majority of applicants, and thereby ratifies anew the processes by which their mobilities have been *illegalized*."[54]

The indeterminacy of these definitional exclusions, bound by the framework of international law which reduces the complex and multi-causal contexts in which people move, operates as a form of power that is crucial to the virtual politics of crisis and to the manufacturing of fear. This indeterminacy is both discursively and politically leveraged in anti-migration debates and actions, as it enables states to govern migrants through the "illegalization" of undesirable forms of mobility. In Calais, the discursive distinction between "genuine" refugees and "non-genuine" refugees creates on the one hand, a category of tolerable/legal migrants who would be given access to Europe, and on the other hand a category of undesirable/"illegal" migrants who can and should be turned back. This, of course, is mere justificatory discourse, since according to the Dublin regulation, there are no instances where migrants could be treated as refugees or asylum seekers in the whole of the zone for crossing between Britain and France. The UNHCR's institutional and juridical framework thus leaves power in the hands of nation-states to categorize migrants and to draw the line between "genuine" refugees who are deemed worthy and deserving of protection, and other migrants who are not. As Daniel Trilling affirms, "international law aims to protect refugees while allowing states to retain control of their borders—but the definition of 'refugee' status is political, and subject to a constant struggle over who is deserving and who is not."[55] By leveraging the exclusion of migrants from the UNHCR's structures of protection and rights, the British government is able to bypass the principles of non-refoulement[56] and non-penalization for illegal entry that underpin the 1951 Geneva Convention (a UNHCR binding law),[57] as well as to evade its duty/responsibility to provide refugees

---

52 De Genova, Garelli and Tazzioli, "Autonomy of Asylum?", 242.

53 New Keywords Collective, "Europe/Crisis," 16.

54 New Keywords Collective, "Europe/Crisis," 16.

55 Trilling, "Five Myths About the Refugee Crisis."

56 The principle of non-refoulement protects refugees from being returned against their will "to a territory where he or she fears threats to life or freedom."

57 The parties that ratified the Convention and/or the Protocol are obliged to carry out its provisions. As host governments, they are responsible for protecting refugees, and are expected to cooperate

with basic rights. Daniel Trilling elaborates on the various technologies deployed by states to block asylum seekers from accessing the EU:

> "In theory, refugees—who have the right to cross borders in search of asylum under international law—should be exempt from these [border] controls. But in reality, the EU has tried to prevent asylum seekers from reaching its territory wherever possible: by closing down legal routes, such as the ability to claim asylum at overseas embassies; by introducing penalties for transport companies that allow people to travel into the EU without the correct documents; and by signing treaties with its neighbors so they control migration on the EU's behalf. And within the EU, an agreement called the Dublin regulation forces asylum seekers to apply in whatever country they reach first."[58]

The 2009 destruction of the migrant camps in Calais—a culmination of the escalating tensions around migration politics—received significant media attention. Johnson's statement was reproduced by mainstream British media, including the *BBC*, *The Daily Mail*, *The Telegraph*, *The Guardian*, *The Independent*, and media images of the camps' demolition and of the arrested migrants were widely circulated,[59] reinforcing the narrative of migration as illegal and threatening in British public opinion. Echoing representations of the Sangatte refugee center and its residents of the early 2000s, the 2009 migrant camps in Calais became the object of the exercise of preemptive power. And yet, similarly to 2002, the dismantling of the migrant camps did not alter the pattern and intensity of migration. Migrants started gathering again, and migrant camps sprang up, eventually resurrecting the Calais "jungle" into the "new jungle."[60]

At the height of the so-called "European migrant/refugee crisis" in 2015, Calais once again occupied a significant place in British mainstream news outlets and in the discourse of the British political establishment. The language of crisis, extended from the broader European migrant crisis to the specific site of Calais, helped justify another spectacular destructive intervention by the French government.[61] The operations began in 2016, when French police forces and demolition workers—"cleaners,"[62] according to French officials—descended onto the camp site to destroy migrants' makeshift homes and to dispose of their meagre possessions, supposedly bringing migrants' presence in Calais to an end.[63] The bulldozing of the migrant camps in Calais staged

---

with the UNHRC. As the guardian of the Convention and its 1967 protocol, the UNHCR maintains a watching brief, intervening when necessary to ensure that the rights of refugees are protected and respected.

58 Trilling,"Five Myths About the Refugee Crisis."

59 Rygiel, "Bordering Solidarities," 1.

60 Rahman-Jones, "The History of the Calais 'Jungle'."

61 The destruction of the Calais camp was in fact far from exceptional, in the context in which France regularly defies its own laws on providing territories for "gens du voyage" (such as the Roma or Tsigane) by bulldozing and destroying encampments. The destruction of the Calais camp is both a 'border spectacle' and continuous with France's perpetual razing of those who move within its territory.

62 Jones, "Calais 'Jungle': Demolition of Massive Migrant Camps Begins."

63 Martina Tazzioli talks about French authorities' tactic of "taking migrants' terrain away," where terrain is understood both as the actual ground they inhabit, but also their rights. In "Calais After the Jungle."

what Nicholas de Genova calls a "border spectacle:" that is, the use of the border as a theatre for the spectacle of law enforcement that renders migrants' "illegality" both visible and natural.[64] Images of the evicted migrants, of the camps' destruction and its before and after, and of the French policemen in action were widely, and generally uncritically, circulated by global news media—from CNN, BBC, and the New York Times to Euronews and AlJazeera. These were the representations of a "global" migration crisis being effectively managed by the French and British governments.

Calais (and Sangatte before it) has thus been the center of political and media attention for sustained periods of time. Its repeated feature in political discourses and in ominous headlines amplified the affective performance of threat, effectively transforming the threat into an "ambient thickness:"[65] the crisis. That is to say that the Calais crisis was already well underway by the time it coalesced in 2015 as a so-called political or sociological crisis. 2015 was in effect a re-animation of previous crises-in-the-making that built off each other, and affectively charged a repository of images and sites that culminated into a deliberately manufactured migrant/refugee crisis. The anticipation of the crisis as an affective state, then, provided "ungrounded" grounds for border securitization projects and migration/asylum control regimes, and enabled Britain (and the EU more generally) to extend its sovereignty over territory and people.

Economic Migrants: The (Not So) Generic Identity Of A Potential Threat

Returning to David Cameron's interview on Calais, his strategic use of the term "illegal migrants" to represent all Calais' migrants—a term circulated by mainstream media who also speak of the "bogus," "fake," and "non-genuine" refugees of Calais—operates through a preemptive logic. His speech stigmatizes migrants in the social imagination by asserting that all migrants in Calais are frauds[66] and passing for refugees to reach Britain, and take advantage of its economy, take jobs away from British citizens, and abuse its welfare services, which is why they should not be let into Britain, or should be kicked out of Britain if they are already there. Cameron thus discursively and politically produces migrants as "illegal" in order to preempt the potential effects of their presence in Britain and to justify their exclusion. This exclusion mechanism is part of a larger European discourse that serves to justify increased governmental interventions in the management of cross-border mobilities, and to solidify the European border regime. During a press conference held in Athens in March 2016, the European Council President Donald Tusk warned "all potential illegal economic migrants": "Do not come to Europe. Do not believe the smugglers. Do not risk your lives and your money. It is all for nothing."[67] Through this discursive process, the keyword "migrant" itself

---

64 De Genova, "Migrant 'Illegality' and Deportability in Everyday Life," 436.

65 Massumi, "The Future Birth of the Affective Fact," 62.

66 In its formulation, the UNHCR attributes intentions of fraud or deceit to economic migrants, as it uses the juridico-legal term "bona fide" to distinguish between on the one hand, "genuine" refugees who are seeking refuge (with earnest intent), and on the other hand, economic migrants ("non bona fide," or "bogus" refugees) who are deceptively seeking refuge. The UNHCR's framework thus enables the assignment of moral values to the motives of migration.

67 Chadwick, "Donald Tusk tells economic migrants: 'Don't come to Europe'."

is rendered fraught, and is used as a discursive mechanism of illegalization. As the New Keywords collective explains, "in the discourse of the 'migrant crisis,' it would seem that the term 'migrant' in fact refers exclusively to 'illegal' migrants, and therefore is profoundly implicated in the rendering of 'migration' as inextricable from a global/postcolonial politics of class and race."[68]

The "economic migrant" (or "migrant") is thus far from a neutral category. The narrative of threat—to Europe's safety, economy, security—that this category mediates is attached not only to certain types of (undesired) mobilities, but also, and especially, to Black and Brown bodies. In 2015, British Foreign Secretary Philip Hammond plainly revealed the association of a European migration crisis with Black bodies when he said, during an interview with the BBC:

> "The gap in standards of living between Europe and Africa means there will always be millions of Africans with the economic motivation to try to get to Europe. So long there are large numbers of pretty desperate migrants marauding around the area, there always will be a threat to the tunnel security [in Calais]. We've got to resolve this problem ultimately by being able to return those who are not entitled to claim asylum back to their countries of origin."[69]

According to Hammond, if Europe were to "absorb millions of migrants from Africa," it would not be able to "protect itself" and preserve "its standard of living and social infrastructure." Hammond's discourse represents all economic migrants to Europe as poor Africans, and all Africans as a potential threat to the European Body. Black bodies are "always already weaponized," affirms Christina Sharpe, as the narratives of Black bodies as carriers of danger, disease and disaster that were entrenched during slavery persist to this day and are manifest in the ongoing criminalization of Black bodies.[70]

Another carrier of threat to the European Body is the Muslim male body (see Zablotsky, this volume). Associated to the threat of terror, Muslim male bodies, in the post-9/11 geopolitical world order, are also always already weaponized, and framed as the object of the War on Terror. The association of migration to the threat of terror, and thus to the Muslim body, is nowhere clearer that in the 2016 Ukip Brexit referendum campaign poster "Breaking Point: the EU has failed us all." This anti-migrant poster was a call to action for the British people to reclaim the UK's borders by voting Brexit: "We must break free of the EU and take back control of our borders" read its sub-headline. The poster comprises an image of a queue of mainly non-white migrants crossing the Croatia-Slovenia border in 2015, where the only prominent white person is hidden by a text box, as pointed out in The Guardian.[71] Challenged about the poster, UKIP leader Nigel Farage asserted that the photograph used was "undoctored," and argued, in defense of the poster's message:

> "[...] frankly, as you can see from this picture, most of the people coming are young males and, yes, they may be coming from countries that are not in a very happy state, they

---

68 New Keywords Collective, "Europe/Crisis," 16.

69 Perraudin, "'Marauding' migrants threaten standard of living, says foreign secretary."

70 Sharpe, In the Wake, 16.

71 Steward and Mason, "Nigel Farage's anti-migrant poster reported to police."

may be coming from places that are poorer than us, but the EU has made a fundamental error that risks the security of everybody [...] They are coming from all over the world. If you get back to the Geneva convention definition, you will find very few people that came into Europe last year would actually qualify as genuine refugees. We have just had—in the last two weeks, the Dusseldorf bomb plot has been uncovered—a very, very worrying plan for mass attacks along the style of Paris or Brussels. All of those people came into Germany last year posing as refugees. When Isis say they will use the migrant crisis to flood the continent with their jihadi terrorists, they probably mean it."[72]

By discursively conflating migrants with "jihadi terrorists," Farage's discourse construes all migrants to Europe as potential "terrorists," and thus as a potential terror threat that should preemptively be dealt with, through anti-migration policies and measures that are justified as anti-terrorist ones. While Farage's discourse aims to stoke a reactionary populist backlash to migration and to enlist the support of nativists for the Brexit campaign, this discourse is indicative of the broader European migrant crisis' preemption logic which entangles anti-Blackness and Anti-Muslim rhetorics with Anti-Migrant views and policies to produce a collective sense of threat embedded in the legacies of slavery, and saturated with the lingering fear of post-9/11. Refugees and migrants are refigured as suspects, as part of a "security crisis,"[73] and represented as potential terrorists that are seeking to infiltrate the space of Europe.[74] Within the political formation of preemptive power, *Migrant*, as the "generic identity of potential threat" thus takes on specific qualities: *Migrant* is illegal. *Migrant* is poor. *Migrant* is Black. *Migrant* is brown. *Migrant* is male. *Migrant* is Muslim. *Migrant* is terrorist. *Migrant*, is produced as an illegalized, racialized, classed, and gendered identity, attached to Black bodies and Muslim Brown bodies who are always already figured as threat, who are represented as a danger to the European body politic—its security, standards of living, and social infrastructure—and who are imagined as Europe's "breaking point," and must thus be preemptively apprehended, detained, rejected, expelled.

And yet, the migration and border control regime is not one of exclusion only. As Sandro Mezzadra and Brett Neilson argue, this regime is one of *differential inclusion*, which selects and filters migrants according to a capitalist logic to *include* their labor power as a commodity in global labor markets under new conditions of accumulation, exploitation and domination.[75] Their argument echoes Nicholas de Genova's assertion that "some [migrants] are deported in order that most may remain (un-deported)—as workers, whose particular migrant status may thus be rendered 'illegal'."[76] The intent of illegalization is not solely deportation; it is the creation of a condition of deportability that renders undocumented migrants more vulnerable, and thus more exploitable as cheap and disposable labor.[77] In other words, the deliberate attachment of the terms "crisis" and "illegal" to certain bodies and types of mobilities enables European

---

72 Steward and Mason, "Nigel Farage's anti-migrant poster reported to police."

73 De Genova, Garelli and Tazzioli, "Autonomy of Asylum?", 256.

74 New Keywords Collective, "Europe/Crisis," 6.

75 Mezzadra and Neilson, *Border as Method*.

76 De Genova, "Migrant 'Illegality' and Deportability in Everyday Life," 439.

77 De Genova, "Migrant 'Illegality' and Deportability in Everyday Life," 439.

states to rearrange (or rather cement) labor relations under conditions of late capital-ism, according to a neocolonial logic of racial and class differentiation and a neoliberal logic of market forces. Through various technologies of migration governance, Euro-pean states transform migrants into a vulnerable, exploitable and expandable source of labor, thus creating a transnational flexible (and non-white) labor commodity at the disposal of market forces. *Migrant* is thus not only a socio-political identity, it is also an economic one. *Migrant* becomes cheap disposable labor.

Calais constitutes an ideal case study in the ways in which the figure of the migrant is discursively, politically and affectively manufactured as a threat, as well as illegal-ized, and rendered vulnerable, deportable and exploitable. Calais, as a site, thus holds potential for subsequent research on how Calais migrants, as unruly economic figures that are undisciplined by the global division of labor and the transnational circulation of capital, are subjected to economic regularization, and transformed into a pool of cheap labor and made available to European labor markets, to help redress the Eu-rozone economic crisis. Calais also constitutes a site of crisis of the European project itself, as it was not only produced as a symbol of the larger European migrant/refugee "crisis," but, as a "crisis within a crisis." (Im)migration is indeed a pillar of the Brexit campaign, and the securitization of borders is meant to protect Britain against the "threat" of not only migrants, but the threat of Europe as well.

The affective reality of threat, felt in the form of fear, and its transformation into an ambient thickness, is enabled by the discursive regime of crisis, and its intense-ly recursive structure. The regime of crisis is sustained through the discursive and political forces of mediatic and political speeches which mobilize keywords such as "crisis," "refugee/migrant," and "illegal" that produce *migrant* as the new identity of potential threat, and justify new preemptive anti-migrant governmental measures. These new enactments of sovereignty point to the emergence of new political forma-tions—preemptive power key among them—that seek to control cross-border human mobilities through various strategies and technologies. And yet, the material impli-cations (on the lives and subjectivities of migrants) of the recursive nature of crisis, and the political and discursive forces of this new power formation, are countered by the autonomous force of migration, and the recursive persistence of migrant encamp-ments. As journalist and asylum researcher Alex Fusco asserts, "It hardly needs to be said that sending in police to forcibly expel inhabitants and backhoes to demolish the structures will have no effect on patterns of migration. Desperate people wanting to get to the UK will continue to flock to Calais. And if not Calais, Dunkirk. And if not Dunkirk, then the next patch of French coastline that offers a viable launching point for crossing the channel."[78] Since 2016, migrants have indeed been setting up tempo-rary camps in and around Calais, Dunkirk and elsewhere in Northern France as they continue to attempt to cross the channel to the UK.[79] Calais, then, is both a border spectacle *and* a site of persistence. It is a site for a challenge at the very heart of the language of crisis.

"A social wave is a transportation of social force [...] A wave transports a qualitative change or *social force* of solidarity or collective disruption" says Thomas Nail.[80] Nail

---

78 Fusco, "The Futile Destruction of the Jungle in Calais."

79 Bulman, "The Lost Childhoods on Britain's Doorstep."

80 Nail, *The Figure of the Migrant*, 125.

identifies a form of counter-power, invented and deployed by migrants (historically and in the current historical conjuncture), as an alternative to the conditions and techniques of social expulsion to which they are subjected. Deploying an aqueous metaphor, Nail poses an alternative to the pejorative use of the term "flood" in media and political discourse, offering instead the image of the "wave" to characterize migration as a unified (yet heterogeneous), unpredictable, irregular social force of solidarity and disruption that overflows dominant territorial, economic, political and juridical orders. This turbulent collective social force challenges the hegemonic categories of differentiation and classification that frame our conceptions of cross-border mobilities and migrants, and limit our imagination of how these could be thought/represented/perceived/acted upon otherwise. By accepting these distinctions and the value/rights they assign to migrants' lives and motivations, we indeed contribute to the production of "economic migrants" as "illegal" migrants, and in so doing, we sanction the violence, both epistemic and material, that is performed in the name of these categories. The social force of migrants brings to light the relations of inequality, violence, and exploitation that these categories conceal, and that are embedded in, and constituted by, the global system of migration management. The social force of migrants de-reifies these categories which operate pervasively—and define the dominant discourse on migration—to appear to us as natural, normal, common-sensical, ahistorical and necessary, and unsettles their definitional exclusion which constitutes the very essence of the language of crisis. The social force of migrants is in excess of the discursively constrained sociopolitical and economic identity of the migrant, and of the regime and techniques of cross-border human mobility control. It is also in excess of the humanitarian logic of care, and the liberal discourse of human rights. This turbulent collective social force demands a radical rethinking of mobility, migrants, territory, and belonging, from the perspective of migrants and of migration, which produces the state, and not people on the move, as a crisis.

SOPHIA
The Language of "Trafficking" in the Mediation of Gendered Migration[1]

Krista Lynes

On November 5, 2017, the Spanish ship Cantabria, a vessel in the European Union's *Operation SOPHIA* "anti-trafficking" program, docked in the port of Salerno in southern Italy. Alongside the survivors, the ship carried the bodies of 26 young Nigerian women and girls who had perished in two shipwrecks off the coast of Libya. Because the only victims of the shipwrecks were women, the Italian authorities opened an inquiry to investigate whether the women had perhaps been purposely killed—thrown overboard by traffickers in the Mediterranean.[2] The Communications Officer for the UN High Commissioner for Refugees, Marco Rotunno, informed the press that it was highly probable that the women were victims of sex trafficking rings. Traditional and social media in Europe and North America, which focused on the episode over the space of several weeks, circulated multiple images of a body bag suspended in mid-air, unloaded from the hold of the Cantabria. Some photographs were tightly cropped, indefinitely suspending the corpse's landing; others showed the corpse dangling over a series of hearses, whose doors stood open for a seemingly infinite number of victims; still others revealed alternately the surviving migrants descending from the ship's deck, or ship staff (clothed in white protective gear and blue gloves and face masks) controlling the procession off the boat.[3] The representation of the female victims vacillated between massification and singularity—between the individual coffin suspended in mid-air and the row of hearses, between naming the women (the two identified by family members) and un-naming them (in their anonymous repetition).

---

1   This article expands and elaborates a brief commentary piece that appeared in the journal *Feminist Media Studies* in 2018. Lynes, "Drowned at Sea." I would like to thank also Tyler Morgenstern and Ian Alan Paul for their generous and generative comments on this article in its draft form. Their insights particularly on the ontology of race, as well as on the "a risk/at risk" formulation were central to my fleshing out my argument here.

2   Eltagouri, "26 teenage girls were found dead at sea."

3   The homogeneity of the images, while formally linked to an iconography of crisis, is also materially and structurally linked to the press agencies which distributed photographs. Most of the press images were provided by a single press photographer's series and distributed through the European Press Agency. It is notable that the images from the port formally echoed the images from the funeral, which also portrayed a seemingly endless row of coffins onto which grievers placed white roses.

These images re-crystallized the figure of migrant death circulating in media images (not the least among them the press photograph of a drowned boy, Alan Kurdi, on a resort shore in Turkey), which in their volume and velocity have created the very contours of the "crisis" as such. Never mind that when the autopsies had been completed it was concluded that the women showed "no signs of abuse" and that they had simply drowned, the images nevertheless continue to constitute a repertoire for visualizing trafficking in its trans-Mediterranean dimensions.[4] As the facts of their accidental drowning came to light, the story virtually disappeared from the news, its everyday depiction of the mortality of crossing less mediatic than the speculations that drove the press attention to the story at the outset.[5] Nevertheless, as Radha S. Hegde explains, such sites of mediation form a critical site for elaborating the causality of the crisis (the distinction of "refugees" from "economic migrants," for instance, or the focus on "rescue" vs. "securitization"), for framing social reality, and for giving shape to the figure of the migrant—steeped in thickly gendered, racialized and classed imaginaries.[6]

As a story of gendered migration, one where the risks of the perilous crossing of increasingly fortified borders is unevenly borne by women, it both masks more than it reveals, and reveals more than it lets on: on the one hand, the focus on trafficking scotomizes a more complex and dilated vision of the conditions, causes and conclusions of gendered movement, and thus works to obscure the complexity of gendered migration across the Mediterranean; on the other hand, though, the very focus on trafficking, its emphasis on the fungibility of migrant life, and the cast of characters that come to dramatize the rescue operation crystallize both allegorically and with striking literality the haunting instrumentalization of Black women's lives in and through mediations of migration *as crisis*.

It is thus vital, as Ariella Azoulay's understanding of the "civil contract" of photography suggests, to pull at the threads of the so-called migrant crisis' mediation of gendered movement and trace the image "in such a way as to reopen it and renegotiate what it shows, possibly even completely overturning what was seen in it before."[7] This strategy is particularly necessary given the pervasiveness, the insistence, and the recursivity of images of death and drowning in the Mediterranean, and the specificity of the gendered and racialized imaginaries that frame the outlines of the corporeal figures of migration's "crisis."[8] This recursivity works assiduously on those it seizes,

---

4 Nadeau, "Twenty-six young Nigerian migrant women laid to rest in Italy."

5 Such mediatory flux is common with respect to cases of women's movement. Enrica Rigo traces another event occurring in Italy in July 2015 when 69 women were intercepted at sea, and transferred from Sicily to the detention center of Rome-Ponte Galeria in order to be deported from Rome-Fiumicino airport. Similarly, the large number of women transferred, their young age, and the circumstances of their arrival were highly mediatized and picked up by several national mainstream newspapers. Rigo, "En-gendering the Border," 177.

6 Hedge, *Mediating Migration*. With respect to the case's conclusion, Professor Antonello Crisci, a medic who worked on the postmortems, noted "There were no signs that they had been raped or physically abused [...] They most likely couldn't swim." The coroner also noted that many of the victims were wearing two layers of clothing, common for migrants held in Libyan detention centers.

7 Azoulay, *The Civil Contract of Photography*, 13.

8 See Bishnupriya Ghosh's essay in this collection for the affective charge of such recursivity in the reception of the image of the drowned Syrian boy, Alan Kurdi.

on both shores of the Mediterranean. The mediation activates an internal reservoir of images that are—in Azoulay's terms—"planted" very differently in different bodies, sometimes while its subjects are unaware of the violence involved, often in an instantaneous fashion (a snap-*shot*), "ruling out any opportunity for negotiations as regards what they show or their genealogy, their ownership or belonging."[9] The images of death work (as I have previously argued) either to confirm a body hypostatized and enshrined as an ideal of transparency, one which effaces the liveliness of social life, even in death,[10] or to confirm a necropolitical aesthetic, an iconic reminder of the power of death and exclusion wielded by state and para-state structures across the Mediterranean.[11] How might we (differentially located in the West) receive the image of a coffin hovering over the port city of Salerno? How might the phenomenon of "trafficking" itself shape the closures contained in the image, the image's taken-for-granted status as a story of gendered migration? What might be reopened through it regarding the tangle of gender, sexuality, mediation and migration?

The setting of the Cantabria rescue focalizes accounts of gender-based migration squarely around issues of "trafficking," occluding in their wake the EU's increased border "securitization" policies, externalized border controls, treaties with third countries, and denials of family reunification visas, all of which render travel routes more perilous and incidences of violence more significant.[12] As will be elaborated below, the United Nations Security Council, making use of "trafficking" as its justification, has put forth a resolution that would authorize Europe to use military force to stop migrant smuggling boats that set off from Libya across the Mediterranean.[13] Simultaneously, the EU's externalization of its border operations, and accordingly its support to Libya (both on its territory and with its "Coast Guard" and Navy), directly impacts the incidences of gender-based and sexual violence faced by people on the move.[14] Smuggling operations have become more significant as EU border securitization policies have rendered routes of travel more perilous and incidences of violence more significant. They are accordingly an effect of the consolidation of border securitization regimes rather than their cause. Smugglers have both assisted and threatened refugees seeking safe passage, frequently providing the only possible movement towards European shores under new border security regulations. For women with insufficient means to pay their passage, transactional sexual relations frequently constitute the only manner in which women and sexual minorities may move through and along smuggling routes.[15]

---

9   Azoulay, *The Civil Contract of Photography*, 13.

10 Lynes, "Decolonizing Corporeality."

11 Mbembe, "Necropolitics."

12 For a detailed account of these policy shifts, see Heller and Pezzani's contribution to this volume.

13 The significant increase in women refugees travelling alone is certainly a result of conflicts or violence in their home countries, but is also an explicit strategy of smugglers, and the result of family separation by border control agents. Women may also make a subjective wager to risk the voyage to flee violence or to seek out some form of security. See Freedman, "Violences de genre et 'crise' des réfugié.e.s en Europe."

14 Sengupta, "U.N. Wants to Let Europe Use Military Force to Stop Migrant Smuggling Boats."

15 Freedman, "Violence de genre et 'crise' des réfugié.e.s en Europe," 62.

Despite the dominant rhetoric's depiction of women as victims of trafficking, women are more frequently deported or penalized for seeking asylum in the EU, this despite Italian legislation that grants victims of sexual exploitation a right (at least on paper) to remain in Italy in order to protect them from their perpetrators and provide for their "rehabilitation."[16] It should also be noted that the focus on trafficking works to eclipse the violence and traumas that greet minoritized subjects upon their arrival in Europe, exacerbated by the various "hotspots" that the EU has created to respond to the waves of refugees in Greece and Italy. Both the Common European Asylum System (CEAS) and Frontex operations have "mainstreamed" gender equality issues into their directives, which in principle oblige EU member states to take gender issues into consideration in the reception of asylum seekers and refugees, and in refugee status determination procedures. In practice, not only is no attention paid to issues of gender, but border guards themselves may be the source of (gender-based and sexual) violence and human rights abuses against migrants and refugees.[17] A focus on sexual exploitation or forced prostitution has thus, rather than fortified international protections, instead shifted policy towards "anti-trafficking" border securitization measures.

Thus, while trafficking is a significant site for women's exploitation and experiences of violence (and indeed gender-based and sexual violence is omnipresent at every stage of movement), confounding the categories of "trafficking" and "smuggling" in fact eclipses both the various shapes violence takes (by armed forces, police, smugglers and traffickers, other refugees and members of one's own family) and the multiple forms of (more or less voluntary) movement across state boundaries that propel gendered movement across state borders. The script of women being 'trafficked'—which is a key trope through which gendered migration is mediated and visualized—serves to assign women to the clear category of victim, rendering impossible and unthinkable the willfulness and agency of women (much less the shifting constitution of gender) in movement. In this mediation, the corpse becomes a key modality of representation, binding migrant movement to death, isolating networked actions into singular (or serial) victims, focalizing the transit over the arrival, and literally dangling the figure of the migrant in mid-air, suspended in the thick of trajectories of movement and border securitization measures.

Trafficking and 'Containerization'

In the case of the Cantabria 'rescue,' trafficking provided the lens through which the gendered violence of the Mediterranean crossing came into focus. Most of the press coverage in the initial days reiterated a statement by the prefect of Salerno, Salvatore Malfi, who noted that sex trafficking frequently employs specific routes and dynamics: "Loading women onto a boat is too risky for the traffickers, as they could risk losing all of their 'goods'—as they like to call them—in one fell swoop."[18] Malfi's statement provides a coda for critically reading this story of gendered migration against the grain of its imaginaries, in order to understand the haunting violence contained in its principal

---

16 Rigo, "Re-gendering the Border," 178

17 Freedman, "Sexual and gender-based violence against refugee women," 21.

18 Giuffrida, "Arrests in Italy as 26 Nigerian women and girls found dead."

image, namely the eerie resonance between the images from the Cantabria and the image repertoire of container shipping in the commercial maritime trade. The vacillation—in the image and Malfi's statement—between human subject and commodified object, the embeddedness of the female corpse within the commercial logics of transnational shipping, binds the "migrant crisis" to the calculus of trafficking and loss that instrumentalize life—and black women's lives particularly—within the economic logics of global trade.

Trafficking is, of course, thoroughly imbricated in these logics. It rides upon the structures of globalization, using its circuitous routes and decreased internal border controls to support a broader structure of bonded sex-work. Rasheed Olaniyi notes that the traffic in women can be traced back to "the 'engine room' of western capitalism, namely the trans-Atlantic slave trade and slavery, which spanned over 300 years."[19] In the wake of slavery's abolition, trafficking took the form of forced abductions, false marriages, false adoptions, and forced sex-work. Trafficking is not solely a story of migration but of displacement engendered by a militarized global economy. Particularly in relation to Nigeria, trafficking has been a longstanding concern, with women trafficked through border towns and communities, including Delta, Akwa Ibom, Lagos, Imo, Rivers, Ondo, Kano, Ebonyi, Osun, and Enugu, transported across Ghana and the Ivory Coast, and then by sea to Italy, or through Morocco and Libya as transit points for onward movement to Spain and France.[20] Olaniyi emphasizes that traffickers themselves may also be women, relying on the capital and connections acquired through the sex trade to then organize rather than be organized by its commerce. Rather than tell a story of gendered migration that relies on clear gendered distinctions between trafficker and trafficked, Olaniyi emphasizes that the driving forces of trafficking are "the advance of capital over labor and nation states, economic recession, neo-liberal political transition and instability and corruption."[21] She points to Nigeria's dependence on the petroleum industry, for instance, as a contributing factor in supporting trafficking networks.

For Christina Sharpe, cargo containers (what Allan Sekula and Noël Burch call "coffins of remote labour-power") are connected to the journeys of Africans over land and across the Mediterranean Sea as "asterisked histories of slavery, of property, of thingification, and their afterlives."[22] She calls these processes the "containerization of people" or the "asterisked human" (with a play on the term "risk" which presents itself in this term) to point to both the "shippability" of life as well as its excess, the manner in which the prefix trans- in the Trans-Atlantic points to a range of configurations of Black being in movement. Among these trans* processes (and I return to them later in this essay), Sharpe points to "transubstantiation," a process of "making of bodies into flesh and then into fungible commodities while retaining the appearance of flesh and blood."[23]

In this respect, the use of the violently anodyne term "pay as you go" to describe gendered and sexualized migrant passage through smuggling networks masks the

---

19 Olaniyi, "No Way Out," 46.

20 Olaniyi, "No Way Out," 47.

21 Olaniyi, "No Way Out," 51.

22 Sharpe, *In the Wake*, 71.

23 Sharpe, *In the Wake*, 73.

violence of present conditions of slavery, indentured labor, and exploitation that are constitutive of the passage across the African continent, the Mediterranean, and the European Union. Unpacking the term "trafficking" thus becomes an instrument for identifying the imaginaries of gendered movement across a broad range of media, and the vacillation between voluntary and involuntary forms of movement contained therein.

The images of the Cantabria 'rescue' rest both on the specter of transnational trade (of the free passage of goods over labor, of the trade in human subjects-as-objects) and also on the ghostly architectonics of the trans-Atlantic crossing, because of the instrumentalization and jurisprudence that underwrote the structures of the slave trade. Christina Sharpe attends to the historic calculability of Black life in slavery and its afterlives by recounting the story of the *Zong*, a 1781 slave ship which ran low in provisions and jettisoned some of those enslaved in order to "save the rest of the cargo."[24] Sharpe reminds us that this act of violence defined modern structures of insurance value, risk and loss in the economy of maritime commercial transit, and constituted the "mathematics of Black life" still at play in catastrophes such as the Lampedusa shipwreck,[25] but (in my estimation) in the Cantabria deaths as well. Understanding the distribution of risk by traffickers across separate crafts, and the calculus of potential loss entailed, is thus only thinkable within the architectonics of the persistent instrumentalization of Black life.

The language of trafficking, or of *human cargo*, thus reveals something of the refiguration of subjection mapped by, among others, Saidiya Hartman. For Hartman, the language of rights fails precisely because liberty, sovereignty and equality not only coexist with—but also depend on—extant and emergent forms of intensified domination, subordination, indebtedness, inferiority, encumbered status and subjection.[26] Insofar as liberation freed black subjects into a fungibility in and through which their capacities could be quantified, measured, exchanged and alienated, abstract equality thus actually bestowed an encroaching and invasive form of social control over Black bodies. The language of 'human cargo' thus exposes the fungibility of the Black body, the exchangeability of subjects, within the violent contemporary social order, marked by what Hartman called the "nonevent of emancipation."[27] What the language of 'trafficking' exposes (at times as its ghostly unconscious) is the mechanisms in and through which movement across the Mediterranean is already marked by a logic of accumulation and the fungibility of the Black body.

What's in a name?

The mediation of gendered migration is thus caught up in the constraints posed by the story of "trafficking," even in discourses whose aim is humanitarian: a story where the representation of women vacillates between subject and object, and where the figure of the corpse violently abstracts and anonymizes women on the move. I argued in an

---

24 Sharpe, *In the Wake*, 81.

25 Sharpe, *In the Wake*, 35-36.

26 Hartman, "The Burdened Individuality of Freedom," 35–36.

27 Hartman, "The Burdened Individuality of Freedom," 32.

earlier article that the story of the Cantabria's rescue is marked by a descriptive flux (describing the women as girls at times, women at others, young women or women between the ages of 14 and 20).[28] This liminality highlights a kind of unwritten category error—of girl-women or women-girls, of humans and 'goods,' of Nigerian women crossing the Mediterranean from Libya—produced by the very act of migration. Their liminality is unassigned in media coverage, which ignores "how this liminality is a mark of the border-identities and thresholds through which gender articulates itself time and again as it crosses state and geo-political systems and structures."[29]

Movement, which Sharpe indicates through the term Trans*—"translation, trans-atlantic, transgression, transgender, transformation, transmogrification, transcontinental, transfixed, trans-Mediterranean, transubstantiation"[30]—forces a critical, conceptual, aesthetic and political imaginary that is lateral, that crosses relations in movement across land and sea, across bordering regimes, across forms of making and unmaking that constituted gendered and racialized bodies-in-motion. But instead of the unmooring of gender that transition and transitivity entail, the women's identities in the Cantabria mediation are governed only by loss and erasure, by the verticality of maritime and port infrastructures.

What work does the concept of "trafficking" do not only to the understanding of gendered migration, but also to its mediation in Euro-American media contexts? Azoulay's invitation cited above to "reopen the image and renegotiate what it shows" allows us to flesh out the named and unnamed figures in gendered migration, to examine their echoes, the passage of subject-to-object, of migrant-to-vessel, of anti-trafficking-to-border security. Instead of asking whether the women were voluntarily killed by traffickers, for instance, we might begin by asking how we account for an "anti-trafficking" operation embedded in the apparatus of the EU's border securitization measures.

How indeed can we reopen the Cantabria story through Azoulay's invitation to renegotiate what its iconic images show? In the midst of the erasure of Black women's agential possibility (of the impossibility of thinking a will-to-move by Nigerian women), the "life-saving" EU anti-trafficking operation, *Operation SOPHIA*, speaks volumes about the movement of peoples through juridical frameworks, policing and security operations, treaties and pacts with third countries, the externalization of borders, and imaginaries of passage that inform and materialize gendered migrant death, beyond the media's framing of gendered migration as instances of "trafficking."

How to renegotiate a border security operation named after a young Somali child born aboard a German frigate, itself named after a figure of German imperial power? How can we name the willful forgetting that forces these condensations to remain unpacked? And how to do so without reconfirming the language of rights or freedom curtailed by anti-trafficking discourse from the outset?

First, SOPHIA—*the operation*: The setting of the ship Cantabria (and the "rescue operation" under the auspices of *Operation SOPHIA*) focalizes accounts of gender-based migration around issues of trafficking, using both the terms "smuggled" and "traf-

28 Lynes, "Drowned at Sea," 2.

29 Lynes, "Drowned at Sea," 2.

30 Sharpe, *In the Wake*, 73.

ficked" to describe women's passage across the Mediterranean. As Rigo makes clear, borders mirror the "imperialistic genesis of the world order [...] and confirm its current postcolonial condition."[31] Anti-trafficking operations must accordingly be examined for the manner in which they assign migrants to distinct legal, political and symbolic spaces, and thus hierarchize movement according to gendered, racial and class categories. The EU's anti-trafficking operation might be parsed in both its pre-nominal and post-nominal dimensions: as EUNAVFOR MED—a "military crisis management operation"[32]—and as "Operation SOPHIA," a new name for the operation, coined to "honor the lives of the people we are saving, the lives of the people we want to protect, and to pass the message to the world that fighting the smugglers and the criminal networks is a way of protecting human life."[33]

EUNAVFOR MED, which was established on May 18, 2015 following the death of 800 migrants after the boat in which they travelled sank off the Libyan coast, forms part of the EU's common security and defense policy (CSDP) military response to human smuggling and trafficking in the Southern Central Mediterranean, and focuses particularly on trafficking organized in Libya. It outlines several phases of operation, moving from the detection and monitoring of migration networks to the boarding, search, seizure and diversion of boats—first on the high seas, and following this, in the territory of coastal states.[34]

Its new designation—EUNAVFOR MED operation SOPHIA—occurred in September 2015, when the Operation Commander, Admiral Enrico Credendino, proposed the new name on the occasion of a visit by High Representative and Vice-President of the European Commission, Federica Mogherini to the mission headquarters in Rome. Operation "SOPHIA" because a Somali child born on board the German frigate Schleswig-Holstein on August 24, 2015 was named after the earlier battleship, the Schleswig-Holstein, which in 1905 went by the radio call "Sophie." This shift in nomination, ratified by a Council Decision in October of 2015, accompanies a shift from detection and monitoring of the high seas to boarding, search, seizure and diversion of vessels (and ultimately, to operations in Libyan territorial waters, with military capacity-building for the Libyan "Coast Guard" and Navy offered in return). In this juridical regime, migrant populations are frequently turned back to a country where they will face detention, brutality and persecution, contributing to what Paul Strauch calls "a concerning norm of militarized extraterritorial border control."[35]

The Operation's capacity to move between the high seas and territorial waters constitutes what Dal Lago names the "militarization of contiguity,"[36] a networked coordination with NATO's *Active Endeavour* mission, as well as Frontex, Europol, and the International Maritime Organization. Further, despite the poetics of Operation SOPHIA's name, the focus of the operation has always been on deterring criminal

31 Rigo, "Re-gendering the Border," 183.

32 European Union Council Decision (CFSP) 2015/778 of 18 May 2015.

33 Operation Sophia, "European Union Naval Force Mediterranean EUNAVFOR MED."

34 Estrada-Cañamares, "Operation Sophia before and after UN Security Council Resolution No 2240," 186.

35 Strauch, "When Stopping the Smuggler Means Repelling the Refugee."

36 Dal Lago, "Note sulla militarizzazione della contiguità," in Ritaine, "Blessures de frontière en Méditer-ranée," 16.

activities, not on saving lives.[37] One might also note that, despite the fact that both Operation Sophia and Operation SOPHIA (capitalized) are used in news reportage on the operation, the legal documents indicate the name in a capitalized form, "SOPHIA," which pulls the name towards its operational acronym (EUNAVFOR MED) and away from the body of the Somalian infant, from which it nevertheless continues to draw its humanitarian force. The operation's framework of "preventing more people from dying at sea" is based not on a politics of rescue but on preventing more people from boarding boats. While it acknowledges the existence of a "human emergency" in the Mediterranean, it does not refer to migrants trying to cross the Mediterranean as potential asylum seekers or refugees, this despite its concern with trafficking. In this respect, calling Operation SOPHIA a "life-saving operation" (as news sources did in the case of the Cantabria "rescue") obscures its participation in the very vulnerability from which it "rescues" people.[38]

SOPHIA's politics of prevention, along with its policing of Libyan waters and its support for the Libyan "Coast Guard" and Navy, thus constitute not simply a politics of EU exclusion, but, as Saucier and Woods argue, a politics of "preclusion," a preclusion premised not solely on European governmentality and biopower, but also on the insistence on the fungibility of the Black body *prior to* its capture within the circuits of neoliberal exploitation and alienation.[39] For Saucier and Woods, anti-Black violence in the Mediterranean (importantly, both trafficking and anti-trafficking in this case) "has its roots in the earliest racial slave trade in which Italian merchants funded Portuguese raiders across the Mediterranean Sea and down the Atlantic coast of Africa."[40] The shift from the boarding, search, seizure and diversion of boats in international waters to the multiple arrangements with the Libyan State, and the coextensive and contiguous bordering operations that constitute the EU's anti-trafficking operations assumes that gendered and sexual violence is a result of movement, and of illicit movement specifically. A politics of preclusion presumes that home spaces may not be the source of conditions from which one might wish to flee, and ultimately that sexual violence is a result (and not a cause) of movement. The bordering apparatuses' anti-trafficking gesture thus serves to keep women in the protective "care" of patriarchal orders all the way down the line. Further, the violence those who are trafficked face in the territory of the EU are disavowed by an operation that targets traffickers. Ultimately, a focus on trafficking is a manner of saying that there is no legitimate asylum claim, no legitimate refugee status (except insofar as movement itself has constituted

37 It is notable that, by contrast, UN Security Council Resolution 2240 (2015) sees saving the lives of persons on board vessels used for human trafficking and migrant smuggling as the main reason behind UNSC's authorization to act against such vessels. See Estrada-Cañamares, "Operation Sophia before and after UN Security Council Resolution No. 2240," 190.

38 Further, the statement that the women drowned because they couldn't swim ignores the nexus of race/class/gender in which positioning on crossing crafts is apportioned (with different fees for upper vs. lower level passage). It also renders unthinkable the relations of mutuality and care under the worst of conditions whereby the spaces where passage is most perilous if things go wrong are also the most secure spaces if all goes right, particularly for those who can't swim, and for young children, potentially already in a state of heightened anxiety and trauma.

39 Saucier and Woods, "Ex Aqua," 59.

40 Saucier and Woods, "Ex Aqua," 64.

the scene of human rights abuse). Calling the operation "SOPHIA," after the infant, after the ship, masks the violent border securitization the operation entails (one that extends European biopolitical power into the lifeworlds of the Mediterranean's southern shores) behind the face of rescue, of an infant rescued, carried by the craft that buoyed her into an Italian port. *SOPHIA* thus becomes the name for the production of a European social cohesion, arrived at through a politics of preclusion, reinterpreted as a form of humanitarianism. In this regard (even though their article dates tellingly to 2014), Saucier and Woods argue:

> "A basic purpose of police power is not simply to mark the objects of police scrutiny, the threat against which the society must militate; but it also serves as a methodology for producing social cohesion. Solidarity is the product of *not* being policed, *not* being noticed, *not* having one's humanity called into question fundamentally; belonging is nothing less than the prerogative to *ignore* the banal terror of policing (Martinot and Sexton 2003). Civil society knows itself to be 'free' by virtue of who populates the hold of the slave ship, migrant boat, detention center or police blotter."[41]

The humanitarianism of anti-trafficking (particularly as it serves as an alibi for military operations in the Southern Mediterranean) therefore sustains social life on the Mediterranean's north shores through accessibility to the Black body, in both directions of trafficking and anti-trafficking operations.

Women in movement, and gendering across borders, are thus figured at once as both "a risk" and "at risk"—a risk to be policed by a politics of preclusion, and at risk and thus in need of security forces' protection.[42] The specific risk women's movement poses to European identity is steeped in fantasies of race/gender/sexuality, wrapped up in the biopolitical regulation of reproduction and sexuality more broadly. This a risk/at risk juncture "serves to justify, while rendering inevitable, public sexual violence against women."[43] Moreover, anti-trafficking operations, which take place to "secure" against sexual violence and exploitation in the context of social, economic and political upheavals that are the direct result of former colonized states' integration into the global political economy, are more than simply the border spectacles of exclusion. Anti-trafficking activism—which identifies human trafficking with a 'new slavery'– also positions Europeans as "modern-day abolitionists,"[44] and therefore shore up notions of justice, sovereignty, equality on European shores through the name SOPHIA.

The legislative, political and mediatic focus on "trafficking" then both engenders and dis-genders the migrant body—engenders because the trade in sex rides on sexual and gender differentiation, and dis-genders because the language of units and cargo eclipse the subject, the person or the individual.[45] The space of the ship's hold suspends the gendered and racialized subject "in the oceanic,"[46] even as gender comes

---

41 Saucier and Woods, "Ex Aqua," 66.

42 For the formulation "a risk/at risk," I draw from Susana Galan's analysis of the history of public sexual harassment in the Egyptian context. Galan Julve, "Risk-Taking Activism," 88.

43 Galan Julve, "Risk-Taking Activism," 92.

44 Saucier and Woods, "Ex Aqua," 69.

45 Hartman, "The Belly of the World," 83.

46 Spillers, "Mama's Baby, Papa's Maybe" in Hartman, "The Belly of the World," 83.

to map the force of the figures of trafficker, savior, child, and ship that animate the passage across the Mediterranean and beyond. The fungibility of the female migrant's body for producing value or pleasure and the "shared vulnerabilities of the commodity, whether male or female, trouble dominant accounts of gender."[47] Rather than begin with the violence against women perpetrated alternately by traffickers, the story of the Cantabria demonstrates the primacy of gender and sexual differentiation in the making of the worlds of migrant movement.

In this regard, policing is "a central methodology for organizing the social globally."[48] Operation SOPHIA thus indicates the impossibility of thinking Black women's self-possession in movement, which persists as a site of suspicion ("a risk") in the "non-event of emancipation" today. Trafficking indicates the gendered direction of this fungibility, in a bordering regime in which gender, race, sexuality and class are not always where one thinks, and not always in the same location. The tangle of gender, race, class and sexuality are constantly worked on and reconfigured by multiple actors, in an ongoing practice of gendering the border.

Second, Sophia—the ship: The "story" of *Operation SOPHIA*'s name on the agency's website notes that the Somalian child (Sophia) born on board the German frigate was herself named after the ship, the Schleswig-Holstein, which was dedicated to the Prussian princess Sophia of Schleswig-Holstein, a figure in the courts of Prussian imperial power and colonial expansionism in the late nineteenth century. Christina Sharpe's *In the Wake* teaches us to pay attention to the naming of boats and people, as she traces the epistemic violence entailed in naming a young girl, Phillis Wheatly, after the slave ship (the *Phillis*) on which her transatlantic abduction was carried, and the slave owners (the *Wheatleys*) who purchased her on her arrival in Boston, Massachusetts. *Sophia. Phillis.* The particularity of a proper name erases itself as the exchange between girl child and ship reverses itself again and again—from ship to child, from child to ship—enacting recursively the general law of value in the context of migration *as* crisis, and in the afterlives of the transatlantic passage: What does it mean to be a subject, and what does it mean to be an object?[49]

The German frigate's operations along the coast of Libya also signals the ubiquity of border operations, made up of control technologies that are pixelated rather than linear.[50] The frigate itself has operated for multiple agencies and in vastly disparate but interconnected geo-political contexts. For instance, it was deployed as part of the Maritime Task Force of the UN Interim Force in Lebanon in 2009, and worked on behalf of the Organization for the Prohibition of Chemical Weapons to destroy Syrian chemical weapons and complete military exercises in the Mediterranean and Persian Gulf in 2014. More importantly, it deployed with Operation Atalanta, the common security and defence policy (CSDP) which preceded Operation SOPHIA, working to counter piracy off the Somali coast. This operation was devoted specifically to transferring persons suspected of having committed acts of piracy and armed robbery. The frigate is

---

47 Hartman, "The Belly of the World," 83.

48 Saucier and Woods, "Ex Aqua," 69.

49 Sharpe, *In the Wake*, 122.

50 Ritaine, "Blessures de frontière en Méditerranée," 12. See also Ian Alan Paul's contribution to this volume.

thus imbricated in a range of security and defense policies across the Mediterranean, crossing agencies and jurisdictions, national actors, international and transnational agencies, in patrols relating to commerce, military material and piracy. Its redirection to the Libyan coast as a vessel for EUNAVFOR MED thus manifests and allegorizes the ties that bind the movement of humans, commodities, cargo, and weapons.

This contemporary militarized oceanic infrastructure, however, is superimposed with a mythical structure indexed by the name Sophia, which binds this specific craft to EUNAVFOR MED's Operation. Sophie refers to the radio call sign used by an earlier Schleswig-Holstein destroyer, itself a reference to the early battleship the SMS Schleswig-Holstein, which had been dedicated to the Prussian Princess of the same name. The name Sophie is thus bound to German naval history. The website of the German Navy notes the story of "Sophia" in a news release from November 7, 2015, recounting that the young infant was midwived by a marine engineer on board:

"The child came very suddenly and I was there. It was nice to hold such a small bundle of hope in one's hands, between all the misery that one usually sees. When we could choose the name, it was clear: it must be Sophie—like the old pager name of the first 'Schleswig-Holstein.' But in Arabic, the name Sophie does not exist, so an 'e' was replaced with an 'a' without further ado. And so Sophia not only become one of the 4225 people saved, but EUNAVEDFOR MED was officially called 'Operation Sophia' from then on."[51]

The eponymous first frigate, dedicated to the Prussian Princess, was laid down in the dockyard in Kiel, Germany in 1905, a mere twenty-years after the Berlin Conference and in the thick of Germany's imperial *Weltpolitik*. As an instrument of imperial vision, however, it comes late to sea, after Britain has demonstrated its preeminent control in the manufacture of battleships, and when new ship-building technologies had made the Schleswig-Holstein too small, too poorly defended and too slow to effectively put into motion a *Weltpolitik* for the twentieth century. Thus, while Sophia conjures an imaginary of German imperial power on a global scale, it in fact indexes a moment of falling profits, overcapacity, fierce competition, and worldwide shipping crises.[52]

Third, Sophia—the Prussian princess: An anomaly of history: a brief footnote in the annals of the *New York Times* reveals that Princess Louise Sophie of Schleswig-Holstein-Sonderburg had several near-death experiences, including once in 1896, when the Princess and one of her ladies, Baroness Colmar, broke through the ice while skating near Glienicke Castle in Potsdam. Prince Frederick Leopold of Prussia, her husband, was upbraided by the Emperor William II for the "indifference of his treatment of his wife" and consequently placed under arrest for fourteen days, confined in a room in his castle.[53]

Operation SOPHIA thus exposes which names remain in the record, and which names do not. The mediatized focus on trafficking covers over the stories of gendered movement in a veil of anonymity and indifference, making it impossible to identify, name, or tell the stories of the twenty-six women who drowned in 2017, even as Prin-

51 "Libysche Küstenwache soll deutsche Fregatte bedroht haben"
52 Epkenhans, "Krupp and the Imperial German Navy."
53 "The Emperor Exhibits his Temper."

cess Louise Sophie's travails are an object of public record. SOPHIA thus figures (by reverse) the irreconcilable gulf between the Prussian Princess, Louise Sophie, and the young Somali child, Sophia, born aboard a German frigate in the Mediterranean Sea. Read against the grain of its obscure operations, SOPHIA performs the work of holding together in a name the afterlives of colonialism, imperialism, and slavery that shape the "crisis" of contemporary movement.

Fourth, (philo)Sophia—Knowledge, complicity ... SOPHIA is an operation for naming what migration-as-crisis doesn't know that it knows, what it obscures in the name of the proper pronoun. In this regard, an Afro-pessimist position calls out "the efforts, on the part of [identity-based politics] to produce a coherent subject (and movement), and [reduce] antagonisms to a representable position," calling these a circumscription of liberatory potential and an "extinguishment of rage with reform."[54]

And hence, Sophia—the child: Saidiya Hartman argues that "gestational language has been key to describing the world-making and world-breaking capacities of racial slavery."[55] In her view, the ship's hold carries this world making/breaking capacity. Under slavery, the mother could not claim the child, could claim only the transfer of dispossession to the child under a systemic process of natal alienation.[56] In Spillers' words, "'kinship' loses meaning, *since it can be invaded at any given and arbitrary moment by property relations.*" This theft and regulation bind themselves to the afterlives of slavery. Women in the hold of the ships crossing the Mediterranean remain also in the hold of the language of units and cargo, a language that eclipses the subject as an individual person. In this context, "flesh provides the primary narrative rather than gendered subject positions."[57]

Taken individually, the *Sophias* that constitute the dramatic scene of "trafficking" across the Mediterranean operate according to incommensurable logics: one, an inexhaustible, militarized, metonymic action that absorbs all objects and subjects into its order—system, child, ship, signal, princess—under the name of a failing but persistent imperial order of things; the second, an unnamable refusal of the child who does not name herself, who does not consent to the ship's hold, to the engineer-midwife who assists at her birth, who does not wish to bind her body to a radio signal, much less a Prussian princess ... and yet, who is named and in whose name policing-becomes-humanitarianism.

Taken *together*, however, *Sophia* names a nexus—of migration in its gendered, raced, and sexed complexity, returned to the context of the unfinished processes of imperialism, slavery, primary accumulation and state violence. As a name that holds together these processes, it exposes the name of the operation itself, SOPHIA, as a reservoir for imperial thinking. In so doing, it assists in removing the "planted images" I referred to at the outset of the body bag as the icon of women-in-movement, those "phantom pictures" Ariella Azoulay sees as embedded in bodily memory. This *sophia* strains against resolving itself into a (philo)*sophia*, an episteme rather than an ontology

---

54 "Introduction" to *Afro-Pessimism*, 11.

55 Hartman, "The Belly of the World," 80.

56 Hartman, "The Belly of the World," 80.

57 Hartman, "The Belly of the World," 83.

of gendered and racialized movement. It labors to attribute images to their creators and initiators (not the body bag but the crane, the dock, the coast guard, the hearse, the medic), and "allows civic negotiations about the subject they designate and about their sense."[58] It indicates, without achieving, a fuller way of knowing migration that does not displace this fullness wholly into the epistemic, learning from Afro-pessimism's emphasis on the ontic status/non-status of blackness in the white supremacist colonial world system.[59] This alter-*sophia* names a position that is "neither constituted nor circumscribed by the sovereign."[60]

The gendered, racialized movement named "trafficking" in the current discourse of crisis names this eclipsing of subjectivity in the language of anonymity, and covers over a view into another motion, another gesture, another resistance, another refusal: "What is the text of her insurgency and the genre of her refusal? What visions of the future world encourage her to run, or propel her flight? Or is she, as Spillers observes, a subject still awaiting her verb?"[61] Rather than a name, then, a verb: not craft but crafting, the vexed, contradictory, perilous poetics of crossing, what Edouard Glissant calls a "thinking thought," a "knowledge becoming."[62] The Cantabria and the Schleswig-Holstein are ships; the migrants' boat is a *crafting*.

What the erasures and revelations of the Cantabria story suggest—traced through the figure of the name *Sophia*—is that the mediation of migration needs to radically re-envision women's movement beyond the language of "trafficking," and beyond a focus on images of death and drowning. Rather than mediating migrant loss principally through narratives of "trafficking"—narratives which enforce the view of those on the move as involuntary captives of transnational flows (including flows of media and the circulatory dynamics of images)—we thus need to understand the complexity of movement in its entangled voluntary and involuntary dimensions.

Mainstream Western media needs to be confronted with media produced by migrants and activists, which visualize and unpack the complex calculus that instigates decisions to move, and migrant experiences. There needs to be space for images of both gendered movement (with all its violence, risk and exposure), and the real threats of *non-movement* (of detention and deportation, among other holding patterns).

As scholars also, we need a framework for understanding the shifting and constitutive force of gender, sexuality, race and class in shaping both the character and trajectory of migration. This shifting force attunes us to the transitive character of identity itself for people on the move, particularly in and across state borders. Over a decade ago, Ursula Biemann maintained that—rather than take a human rights approach to issues of sex trafficking—she would prioritize a geographical theoretical framework, which would allow her to link geopolitics to subject formation.[63] The visions of globality produced by satellites, the infrastructures of rescue and surveillance, press agencies, and migrants themselves visualize and enact a sexual, gendered, and racialized economy of displacement on a global scale. Biemann observes that "trafficking hinges on

---

58 Azoulay, *The Civil Contract of Photography*, 13–14.

59 I thank Tyler Morgenstern for drawing out this insight in reading an earlier draft of this chapter.

60 Azoulay, *The Civil Contract of Photography*, 21.

61 Hartman, "The Belly of the World," 88–89.

62 Glissant, *The Poetics of Relation*, 1.

63 Biemann, "Remotely Sensed," 181–182.

the displacement of women, their costly transportation across topographies from one cultural arrangement to another, from one spatial organization to another, from one abandoned economy to a place of greater accumulations. It is the route that counts."[64]

Gender and sexuality are more than subjective attributes of (or data points for) migrants and refugees; they are forces that organize the trajectories of movement, the transactions across boundaries, the economies of exchange, the patterns of reception, and the politico-aesthetics of images of crossing—and they do so on and through the body. Literature on gender-based migration emphasizes that gender is "a latticework of institutionalized social relationships that, by creating and manipulating the categories of gender, organize and signify power at levels above the individual."[65] The decision to move, its voluntary and involuntary dynamics, the vast terrain of negotiation in which movement advances in fits and starts, en-genders and de-genders migrant subjectivity. Gender operates on multiple and frictional spatial and social scales (the body, kinship structures, the state) across transnational territories. Within and across these scales, gender ideologies and relations are alternately reaffirmed or reconfigured.[66]

Enrica Rigo paints instead a picture of women migrants who, by crossing borders, resist all at once the "conditions imposed on them by patriarchy, violence, wars, the sex industry, smugglers, and borders themselves."[67] She notes that women take advantage of the very migratory routes opened by the people from which they are simultaneously trying to flee. In doing so, they use their bodies "in ways that reject their depiction as docile victims, willing accomplices or defiant opponents of their tormentors."[68]

Such subjective movement is shaped by one's location within historical, political, economic and geographic power hierarchies, that affect the trajectory, force and velocity of movement. Intersectional hierarchies of class, race, sexuality, ethnicity, nationality and gender frame bodily life in passage, and expose subjects to their differential articulation in the multiple formal and informal social orders through which migrant subjects pass. The ability to act, to wager one's possessions or selves depend on gendered geographies of power. Doreen Massey argues that some individuals "initiate flows and movement; others don't; some are more on the receiving-end of it than others; some are effectively imprisoned by it."[69]

These dimensions are present in the multiple testimonies, maps and guides, communications, and images by and through which migrants represent their own trajectories and experiences, always already "entrenched within media worlds."[70] Aesthetic strategies assist in lifting the lid on the complexities cooking beneath the image of a suspended body bag, hovering over the port of Salerno. Ursula Biemann's *Remote Sensing*, for instance, proposes "a mode of representation that traces the trajectory of people in a pancapitalist world order, wherein the space between departure and arrival is understood as [...] a potentially subversive space which does not adhere to national

---

64 Biemann, "Remotely Sensed," 183.

65 Pessar and Mahler, "Transnational Migration," 813.

66 Pessar and Mahler, "Transnational Migration," 815.

67 Rigo, "Re-gendering the Border," 177.

68 Rigo, "Re-gendering the Border," 177.

69 Massey, *Space, Place and Gender*, 149.

70 Hegde, *Mediating Migration*, 3.

rules."[71] Similarly, Bouchra Khalili's *The Mapping Journey Project* gives voice to migrants' own accounts of their travels, which she records in a single shot and does not edit in post-production. For Khalili, the narratives (and the trajectories drawn across maps of the world) demonstrate not only how individuals are trapped in "nets of arbitrary power"[72] but how they might refuse the forms of representation and visibility demanded by surveillance systems, border controls, and press accounts. Such accounts and grassroots mediations help to reveal the force of gender-in-the-making in constituting the violence and loss—but also the possibilities—in the Mediterranean crossing and elsewhere. They also refocus media attention more clearly not only on the dangers of crossing, but on the pernicious "border securitization" policies that themselves negatively impact gendered trajectories of movement.

71 Biemann, "Remote Sensing," 187.

72 Michalarou, "ART-PRESENTATION."

Solidarity and the Aporia of "We"
Representation and Participation
of Refugees in Contemporary Art

Suzana Milevska

In all iterations of Olafur Eliasson's *Green Light*, asylum seekers and refugees were asked to participate by producing crystalline *green light* lamps, consisting of polyhedral units fitted with small, green-tinted light fixtures. The module was invented by Eliasson's long-time friend and collaborator, Einar Thorsteinn, as part of the numerous geometric studies they undertook at the studio. The small modules were made predominantly from recycled and sustainable materials (European ash, recycled yogurt cups, used plastic bags, and recycled nylon) and green LED lights that could function either as single objects or be assembled into a variety of architectural configurations. The lamps were ultimately sold for €250 each. Participants in the workshop, for their part, could access free language classes, counselling education and other workshops.

Eliasson is one of many artists who have attempted not only to depict or record refugees in the context of contemporary art, but also to invite them to participate directly in projects and events organized by art and cultural institutions.[1] In this manner, refugees become represented not only by "proxy"—in images, objects or recorded videos that represent their plight—but through their very presence in real time when they are invited to become participants, collaborators and co-producers of art projects.

When discussing his project, Eliasson stated:

> "I want to thank you all for co-hosting us and one another because I think there is something very important going on here—the decentralization of hospitality, which means there is no center, but rather only periphery. Obviously, this is not completely true, because there is an organization, TBA21, behind this, but I would still argue that *Green Light* aims to decentralize hospitality."[2]

---

1 For example, Batycka's "At Manifesta Artists Address Italy's Migrant Crisis" was entirely dedicated to art about the refugee crisis, questioning whether in the context of international biennales such projects could have a purpose other than raising questions. In this regard, he mentioned *Trampoline House*, an art project in Copenhagen that exceeded and went beyond its original concept as an art project.

2 This reflection on the first stage of project *Green Light* appeared in TBA21's online journal in the conversation between the artist Olafur Eliasson and Andreas Roepstorff entitled "Hosting the Spirit of *Green light*," which preceded the project's presentation at the Venice Biennial in 2017.

There is nothing wrong with such a statement at first sight. The obvious question, however, is whether such "decentralized hospitality" can really occur in the contexts in which Olafur Eliasson staged his project, particularly when accounting for how profoundly integrated the art system's institutions—TBA21 Vienna and the 2017 Venice Biennale—are in the capitalist mode of production.

In Venice, the project occupied a huge space in one of the first rooms of the prestigious Central Pavilion. Refugees were invited only for the duration of the professional and press opening, where the audience consisted primarily of journalists commissioned to review the Biennial, museum and gallery directors, employed and freelance curators, art collectors and dealers. The participants-turned-producers were instructed on how to make the objects—in other words, there was no creativity involved on their side; they were simply present in the installation—and their communication with the audience during the exhibition's events was reduced to a minimum.

The budget and distribution of the initial funds, as well as those raised and obtained through the project, were not made transparent. In addition, thousands of images of the anonymous refugee participants have circulated ever since the installation. Alongside the green lights, then, the participants in Eliasson's project were eventually nevertheless turned into images. One might also inquire about the fees, copyrights, and lecture honoraria generated from the project, and ask other difficult questions about the circulation and distribution of capital beyond the event itself.

This paper attempts to unravel the hidden contradictions and challenges stemming from prevailing expectations of this emerging strategy of participation. At first sight, by comparison with other art genres that use representation,[3] such a strategy and mode of art production seems more appropriate to the current social climate (which the media refer as to a "humanitarian crisis" or "refugee crisis"). More traditional forms of artistic representation are frequently stereotypical and prejudicial, regardless of whether they involve fully documented citizens or refugees of various statuses who are kept marginalized and mostly invisible in the common social fabric. The so-called crisis has also made already existing social tensions more visible, exacerbated by the outburst of hatred and racism towards recently arrived refugees (for instance, with the anti-Islamist and neo-Nazi Pagida riots in Germany and Austria).[4] Participation in art projects is, thus, to a large extent imagined as a kind of enacted compensation for both faulty artistic representations and the lack of inclusion and participation in sociopolitical life. Clearly, there is an ethical debate over whether and how to represent vulnerable and suffering subjects in general, but it nevertheless remains pertinent to ask whether and how people's direct involvement in artistic projects substantially changes their existence and living conditions, or improves society in general for that matter.[5]

---

3 This is true even in cases where representation is applied in a more conceptual way, for example, with text, signs or symbols.

4 See, for example, the protests of Pagida anti-Islamist protests in Dresden, and the conflicts against the Akademikerball held in 2015 in Vienna's Hofburg—the gathering of right-wing parties under the auspices of the Austrian radical right-wing party FPÖ.

5 In *On Productive Shame, Reconciliation, and Agency*, I argue that the neoliberal socio-political context turns many socio-political engaged projects into "infelicitous speech acts" that stem from the contradictions between the artists, institutional limitations and the neoliberal socio-political and economical paradigm of production and distribution of art. More recently Abreu's "We Need to Talk about

Between *saying* and *doing*

According to various statements by Eliasson, *Green Light* was conceived as a metaphorical "device" for refugees and migrants (in Austria and beyond) in order to employ the "agency of contemporary art and its potential to initiate processes of civic transformation" by eliciting "various forms of participation and engagement."[6] In an interview, Eliasson elaborates similar good-faith, critical intentions:

> "Systems are normally defined as hierarchical, top-down, institutional, and exclusive—also systems that claim to be inclusive are in fact exclusive, systems that claim that we can identify with them but that we actually struggle to identify with. Let me give one example: one system that we like is the EU, but we have no emotional understanding of what on earth the EU is. Another system is the UN: we have come to love the UN, but we have no emotional narrative to understand what the UN is. We all think that these systems are important, but we feel disconnected. So I am very interested in when we feel connected and when we feel disconnected."[7]

While international asylum laws differ in the various countries that hosted the project, in most European countries (among them Austria and Italy, where *Green light* was installed) refugees do not have the legal right to be engaged in paid activities or to access free education if they have not been granted asylum. The political institutions responsible for either embracing or refusing the requests for refugee status, legalization, residential permits, or citizenship rarely contemplate the means for future inclusion of refugees or the political frames in operation. Accordingly, participatory art is often seen as the only alternative compensation for a situation in which it is not unusual that refugees' entire life is confined to in-betweenness and the non-spaces of refugee camps.

The substantial difference between *inclusion* and *belonging* (access to state institutions that secure such equal civic rights as rights to education, visas, residential and work permits, employment, and citizenship), and the symbolic inclusion and short-term participation in art projects is one of the main reasons it is urgent to analyze the political dynamics of participatory art practices that include refugees. While the representation of undocumented subjects in the context of political institutions operates on a different register, I would nevertheless like to challenge this difference and question the source of such assumptions, emphasizing that any political representation is also symbolic (and vice versa). The main questions, therefore, are twofold: first, whether inviting refugees to take part in art projects necessarily leads to an exploita-

---

Social Practice" offers an in-depth analysis of the contradictions at work between the promises and expectations of the art projects aiming towards social change and the final results that often hit the "wall" of the overall socio-political climate.

6 Eliasson, "Assembling a Light, Assembling Communities."

7 Eliasson and Roepstorff, "Hosting the Spirit of *Green Light*." Eliasson then takes a more personal tone: "We know a lot about the refugee crisis from the media and from one another because we talk about it, but the emotional narrative is very difficult. It is so abstract! I know what I think about the crisis, refugees, EU, the climate—you name it. I know what I think about it, but it is so difficult for me as a civic participant to engage with. If I cannot feel the 'we,' I am also a populist, because populism means anti-we. So I suffer because I have become numb and I don't have a sense of we."

tion of their (already) difficult position and condition; second, whether, in re-enacting their plight and their impeded political status time and again, such projects necessarily have an advantage over figurative and conceptual artistic representation simply because such representations are not "mediated" and (if possible) the participation is paid. Most importantly, it is important to discuss whether it is possible at all to avoid the perpetuation of stereotypical representations and to induce sociopolitical changes with participatory strategies that apply the instruments of direct democracy in an art context.

The Aporia of "We"

What form does "inclusion" take in participatory art projects? What imagined community is figured in and through the work? During the recent refugee crisis in Europe, perhaps the biggest since World War Two, the phrase "we refugees" became a slogan of apparent solidarity with exiles, a mode of offering one's own home to those arriving. It involved a form of political overidentification, and proof of compassion and empathy for people who have been stripped of their basic human rights in their new domiciles. Of course those who mobilize this phrase (for my purposes here, the artists or organizations, such as BAK, Utrecht, organizing participatory works) are not refugees themselves and do not belong to the ones fleeing political turmoil in their home countries. Although accompanied by calls for equal participation of non-documented immigrants and refugees in civil society, claiming democratic rule of law and "equal justice for all," the "we" of "we refugees" often rings flat, since the slogan is ambiguous and open to charges of self-interest, condescension, and even racism. The "we" can, even as it claims solidarity, conceal a suppressed fear of the refugee, of the 'other' who supposedly crosses the 'threshold' of one's home without legitimate right to do so. It can also express the Eurocentric divide between 'us' (already settled and privileged citizens) and 'them' (the newcomers, including those, for example, from the former Yugoslavia and elsewhere in eastern Europe, or between Christian and Muslim immigrants).

Expressions of solidarity with refugees can thus conceal essentialism and condescension based on citizenship, class and religion. Governments' flagrant neglect of responsibilities entailed by use of the "we" reveals the aporias of a solidarity founded in national belonging. Ever since Hannah Arendt's essay "We Refugees," the phrase has been used to express sympathy with the underprivileged, the precarious and the politically persecuted.[8] Fifty years later, Giorgio Agamben borrowed it for the title of an essay comparing Nazi concentration camps and the contemporary detention centers.[9] Agamben's argument in favour of the use of "we," emphasizing the need for compassion towards all political subjects, was directly influenced by Arendt, whom he quotes

8 Arendt, "We Refugees," 110–119. The article was first published in *The Menorah Journal* in January 1943. The English edition of the article appeared in 1951, the same year that Arendt received US citizenship, after briefly being detained by the Nazi regime in 1933 and fleeing illegally across the border between Germany and Czechoslovakia; in 1937, when she had been deprived of her German citizenship.

9 Agamben, "We Refugees." Different versions have been published under the same or different titles, including "Beyond Human Rights."

at the beginning of his essay. The sentiment organizes the politics of "inclusion" present in participatory art practice.

Jacques Derrida's term "hostipitality," however, points to the complexity of the concept of "belonging" and "hospitality," unravelling the challenges to the legislation and socialization of refugees. Hostipitality derives from the tension between hospitality and cosmopolitanism, or more precisely from the conflict between the privacy of the home and an unconditional ethics and openness to the world; the tension proceeds from fears for the stability of the home if the problems of the world enter in. Derrida has stressed that "If we try to draw a politics of hospitality from the dream of unconditional hospitality, not only will it be impossible but it will have perverse consequences."[10] The aporia of absolute hospitality comes from the fact that it "requires that I open my home and that I give not only to the foreigner (provided by a family name, with the social status of being a foreigner, etc.) but to the absolute, unknown, anonymous other, and that I give place to them, that I let them come, that I let them arrive, and take place in the place I offer them, without asking of them either reciprocity (entering into a pact) or even their names."[11]

The paradox of not being able to give a gift and still have it, of not being able to offer your home to the Other if you have already offered it to someone else, is related to issues of "power and possession." Yet the paradox of hospitality, according to Duformantelle, is that it is not confined to possessing a home:

> "To offer hospitality, is it necessary to start from the certain existence of a dwelling, or is it rather only starting from the dislocation of the shelterless, the homeless, that the authenticity of hospitality can open up? Perhaps only the one who endures the experience of being deprived of a home can offer hospitality."[12]

The story about the Iranian refugee Mahboubeh Tavakoli cooking and feeding other refugees in Athens' Victoria Park only two years after her and her family arrived as refugees in Greece defies the logic of hospitality based on sharing wealth, comfort and political decisions, and comes as close as possible to this ideal of unconditional hospitality.[13]

Thus when Derrida and Dufourmantelle coined the oxymoron "hostipitality" they wanted to stress that the state becomes the "critic" endowed with the power to distinguish friend from foe, guest from parasite, hospitality from hostility, the "we" from an "us."[14] In the context of contemporary art, the limitations and contradictions entailed in the concept "hostipitality" become more apparent in participatory art. Although not the initial aims of the artists, these contradictions cannot be reconciled by addressing only the figure of the refugee without taking into account the figure of the legislator and the political context in which such projects take place.[15]

---

10 Derrida, *Politics of Friendship*, 72.

11 Derrida and Dufourmantelle, *Of Hospitality*, 25.

12 Derrida and Dufourmantelle, *Of Hospitality*, 56.

13 Campana, "She arrived with nothing."

14 Derrida and Dufourmantelle, *Of Hospitality*.

15 Milevska, *On Productive Shame, Reconciliation, and Agency*.

For example, two projects by BAK in Utrecht used similar phraseology: One of them, *We Are Here*, was dedicated to refugees, and was publicized as "the first large-scale organization of refugees" established in collaboration with artists and cultural workers.[16] The other was a publication dedicated to the socio-political conditions of Roma: *We, Refugees* (2014).[17] Both projects resonated with the practice of masking the sponsors or organization (otherwise known as "astroturfing") because—although they were made to appear as though they originated from grassroots participants—there is little evidence of this. There is an inner split within the "we" itself, caused by its unspecified and heterogeneous alignment—as if the right to use the pronoun were allocated on a "first come, first served" basis. However, the question of whom it includes and how one gains the right to utter it is not only semantic. The origins of the distrust also need to be discussed.

Turning words into acts

English, unlike some non-European languages, has no exclusive form of the first person plural pronoun; in other words, no grammatical distinction is made between an all-inclusive "we" and a "we" that includes only certain addressees. Despite this fact, or perhaps exactly because of it, there are many possibilities for duplicity and hidden agendas in the use of the "we." It is therefore necessary to discuss the difference between "saying" and "doing" in the use of the first person plural, and how its mechanisms of inclusion and exclusion work in the participatory art context and beyond.

The emphasis on doing is particularly urgent given the responsibility of politicians and government representatives, non-governmental agencies or ordinary citizens to the "we," and the flagrant neglect of those responsibilities in the case of refugees.[18] In some cases, governments use refugees' tragic destinies in political negotiations. In 2002, for example, the Macedonian government opened an inquiry into the shootings of innocent immigrants who were originally portrayed in Macedonia as Al Qaeda mujahideen. The alleged terrorism was used to avoid the expected solidarity—the "we"—with the refugees. However, autopsies performed on the men (as well as police photos) suggested that the police were responsible for the shootings and had even staged the crime scene. All bodies had multiple bullet wounds, in one case, fifty-three. Later it emerged that six Pakistani immigrants and one Indian had been even lured onto Macedonian soil with false promises and been ruthlessly killed as a part of Government's strategy to flirt with NATO and the US administration.[19]

---

16 BAK, *We Are Here*.

17 Baker and Hlavajova, *We Roma*. This project was published in the context of the Roma Pavilion organized by BAK platform for contemporary art at the Venice Biennale in 2011. The project used the Open Society Institute, Budapest, and EU funds assigned to Roma, but mostly promoted artists and theorists of non-Roma origin.

18 Cole, "On the borders of solidarity."

19 Wood, "A Fake Macedonia Terror Tale That Led to Deaths." The terrorist background of the refugees, their false intent and the crime scene were all staged in order to prove the country's dedication to the "war on terror," to avoid sending local soldiers to Afghanistan, and to justify the use of disproportionate force in fighting local Muslims—the ethnic Albanians.

"We refugees" thus sometimes sounds like a hollow marriage proposal by a notorious philanderer. In this respect, the concept of "infelicitous acts" is a useful way of analyzing the aporias surrounding conflicting normative and legal obligations towards refugees.[20] According to J.L. Austin, the difference between what one says and what one does depends on context and circumstance; context can substantially affect the fulfilment of a promise. In speech act theory, an unfulfilled promise is referred to as an "infelicitous act."[21] When a certain "we" is invoked, members of communities with different statuses and origins (African-Americans, Roma and travellers, homeless people, Syrian refugees or child-refugees of any religion) supposedly become, whether voluntarily or not, part of the community—a prime example of an infelicitous act.[22]

The problem with the "we" of "we refugees" is that it is a no-win game: regardless of whether one is using it oneself or disputing the right of others to do so, essentialism is inevitable. The right to use the "we" is pre-determined neither by genetic nor by ethnic inheritance or simple grammatical appropriation. On the contrary, one has to earn the other's trust in order to secure the preconditions and illocutionary force to enable this speech act to count as having been felicitous vis-à-vis invisible hierarchies and privileges.

The concept of the nation-state itself does not help, since it is founded on precisely the same mistrust and hierarchical differentiations. Étienne Balibar has critiqued modern conceptions of the nation-state and examined the uncertain historical realities of the nation.[23] He contends that it is impossible to pinpoint the beginning of a nation, or to argue that the people who inhabit a nation-state are the descendants of the nation that preceded it. Because no nation-state has an ethnic base, according to Balibar, every nation-state creates fictional ethnicities in order to project stability.[24]

These stable identities are produced because the greatest threat to national identity are the different identities that pre-existed and preceded the more recent waves of immigration. As Balibar puts it, "the idea of nations without a state, or nations 'before' the state, is thus a contradiction in terms, because a state is always implied in the historic framework of a national formation (even if not necessarily within the limits of its territory)."[25] The "we" is therefore fated to be distrusted and feared, both by the included and the excluded, as already pointed out by Arendt in her early criticism of Herzlian Zionism, Minority Treaties after World War One, and her warnings about the problems she detected with any mode of linking the nation and state predicated on turning into stateless some other citizens.[26]

---

20 Austin, *How to Do Things with Words*. See also Felman's *The Scandal of the Speaking Body*, on Molière's *Don Juan* and his character's double speech.

21 Austin, *How to Do Things with Words*, 100.

22 Thanks to Tyler Morgenstern, I became aware that the German word for promise "versprechen" by default anticipates the possibility of its unfulfillment because of the elusive prefix "ver" that could mean "miss" or "wrong."

23 Balibar, "Is European Citizenship Possible."

24 Balibar, "Is European Citizenship Possible," 329.

25 Balibar, "Is European Citizenship Possible," 331, 351.

26 Arendt, *The Origins of Totalitarianism*, 269–270.

"We Refugees" or the impossibility of "being with"

With the arrival of Syrian refugees in 2015 at the height of "refugee crisis," racism enhanced the pre-embedded Islamophobia against different ethnicities and communities practicing Islam already living in Europe for centuries, including Albanians, Turkish people, or Roma. Some European Roma are Muslim, but they often claim different religions in local censuses exactly to avoid the consequences of racism, and yet they are mainly perceived as Muslims.

Balibar offered a more profound analysis of the need, but also of the danger of the uncritical "we." He made a clear distinction between the different types of "we," pointing out the responsibility that is lost with the appropriative "we":

> "We, French citizens of all sexes, origins and professions, are greatly indebted to the 'sans-papiers' who, refusing the 'clandestineness' ascribed to them, have forcefully posed the question of the right to stay. We owe them a triple demonstration, which also gives us some responsibilities."[27]

Balibar's skeptical view of the effects of the 1994 Maastricht Treaty are linked to the paradox that European citizenship was, from the outset, based on the false equation "citizenship equals nationality." European citizenship is thus defined by restrictions on the right to asylum.[28] The hypocrisy of the promise behind the "we" is clearly stated in his proposition for a responsible position towards sans papiers:

> "We owe them for having shattered the pretensions of successive governments to play two games: on one side, 'realism,' administrative competence and political responsibility (regulating population flows, maintaining public order, assuring the 'integration' of legal immigrants [...]); on the other side, nationalist and electoral propaganda (creating scapegoats for insecurity, projecting the fear of mass poverty into the phantasmal space of identitarian conflicts)."[29]

Jean-Luc Nancy has argued that while sharing the world is an implication of our existence, and that the concept of "being" is always already determined by a certain "being with," we cannot truly say "we," or at least not ethically so. One cannot say "we" even about the community to which one undoubtedly belongs. The aporia of the "we" is the aporia of intersubjectivity.[30] Nancy warns us of the impossibility of pinning down a universal "we" whose components always remain the same. He argues that we have forgotten the importance of "being-together," "being-in-common," and "belonging"; that the "we" is not a subject, nor composed of subjects. According to Nancy, we live our lives "without relations."[31] There can be no "we" unless the relations are established as "being-in-common" rather than understanding them only in additive and accumulative terms.

---

27 Balibar, "What we owe to the 'Sans-papiers'."

28 Balibar, "Is European Citizenship Possible?", 195–216.

29 Balibar, "Is European Citizenship Possible?", 213.

30 Nancy, *Being Singular Plural*, 75.

31 Nancy, *Being Singular Plural*, 75.

This is linked to his concept of "inoperative communities," communities that refuse to be state "accomplices."[32] In this kind of appropriation of the "we," there might be potentials for certain positive impacts of a new "we" not based on belonging as such. This is a "we" that wants not to belong but to appropriate belonging, but only if this triggers moral responsibilities not necessarily resulting from legal, political or social ties.[33] Nancy's notion of "inoperative communities" gestures in important directions for modalities of participation not premised on the dynamics of "inclusion" or "belonging" detailed above.

Kalokagathia: The reconciliation of aesthetics and ethics in contemporary art and theory

When it comes to general ethical principles, contemporary art remains experimental and, with few exceptions, not much has been formally drafted, although standard legal and institutional implications apply to projects in a variety of ways. Therefore, the generic and officially circulated and accepted ethical principles for social science research are often applied without necessary corrections.

For example, in March 2015 the British Academy of Social Sciences' Council formally adopted the five following guiding ethics principles:

"1. Social science is fundamental to a democratic society and should be inclusive of different interests, values, funders, methods and perspectives.
2. All social science should respect the privacy, autonomy, diversity, values, and dignity of individuals, groups and communities.
3. All social science should be conducted with integrity throughout, employing the most appropriate methods for the research purpose.
4. All social scientists should act with regard to their social responsibilities in conducting and disseminating their research.
5. All social science should aim to maximise benefit and minimise harm."[34]

However there is no official consent regarding any specific ethical principles to be applied in the context of participatory art, which often relies on artistic research. Given the complexity of different art media and the specificity of crossdisciplinary concepts, it is very difficult to conceptualize a uniformed set of rules to be followed by artists, particularly for an art form that by default tries so hard to resist rules.[35] Neither is it clear how to reconcile the long-term tensions between ethical and aesthetic values due to the prevailing dilemmas imposed already by modernist theories of art, mainly due to the complexity and diversity of artistic practices.[36]

---

32 Nancy, *The Inoperative Community*, 80–81.

33 Agamben, *The Coming Community*, 86–87.

34 Academy of Social Sciences, "Academy Adopts Five Ethical Principles for Social Science Research."

35 Bolt, Alsop, Sierra, Vincs and Kett, *Research Ethics and the Creative Arts.*

36 Milevska, "Relations, Participations, and Other Dialogical Frameworks."

Yet there is also no reason why some (if not all) of these ethical principles could not apply to artists' accountability when artistic research involves live participants (or human remains), although additional principles should be drafted specifically in the context of participatory and collaborative projects with a focus on the performativity and involvement of members of various vulnerable communities. One reason for such thoughts is the numerous different understandings of what art is among audiences coming from different social and cultural contexts not necessarily informed by the rapid reformulations of art and eventual challenges related to what is expected from or of them.[37]

The rigorous formalist division between aesthetic and ethical aspects of art, or more precisely the polarized distinction between form and content, or between the "beautiful" and the "good," has in any case yielded some of the most debilitating outcomes of modernist and formalist theory. The either-or polarity that often results from hierarchical positioning of one of these poles still has a key bearing on our understanding of art's position and its role in different cultural contexts and in contemporary society in general. The conflation of the realm of philosophy—to which the aesthetic category of the beautiful belongs—and the realm of art has gradually resulted in a contradictory long-term pursuit of an ever more precise (and false) dichotomy between art and society, as if they could ever be isolated from each other.

Taking the current neoliberal political context as a point of departure, it is necessary to reveal and disentangle the difficulties that still prevent many art theorists from completely (or at least partially) abandoning modernist ideals and formalist criteria regarding art and the valorization of its production. I find it urgent to discuss why and how the sociopolitical factors that enabled the long-term dominance of modernist aesthetics still affect—or more precisely prevent—the embracing of institutional critique and participatory art as relevant contributions to art theory and art practice.

The criticism, for example, that participatory art merely caters to societal needs is one of many commonplaces stemming from modernist aesthetic principles—the death grip of formalist aesthetics' invigilators—surrounding issues of autonomy and positioning and other contradictions. For a certain limited period after the World War Two, the *l'art-pour-l'art* position enjoyed widespread acceptance in Western art theory, as if the ancient ideal of *kalokagathia* had never existed, and as if the ideals of an otherwise autonomous pure art should be protected from any societal values.[38]

The modernist myths of originality, authenticity, uniqueness, universality, artistic genius, and autonomy were also influenced by the Russian early formalist school of Viktor Shklovsky and the semiotic analysis of art, wherein the issue of the arts' autonomy stemmed from political interventions in both art's content and form.[39] Joseph Kosuth published his early attack on the modernist aesthetics of Clement Greenberg, addressing Modernism's fallibility deriving from its equation of aesthetics and art, and stressing the relevance of conceptually focused art vs. form-driven and form-eval-

37 Carroll, "Art and Ethical Criticism"; Lillehammer, "Values of Art and the Ethical Question."

38 Kalokagathia (Ancient Greek: καλὸς κάγαθός [kalos ka:gatʰós]) means beautiful and good, the Ancient Greek ideal of harmony between noble human personality and any art action (documented in Herodotus and other texts).

39 Krauss, *The Originality of the Avant-garde.*

uated art.[40] He was not yet ready, however, to fully abandon the understanding of art as an entity separate from society. The problems with calling for art's *autonomy* from its contextual background have become clearer, although such anti-aesthetic art tendencies had already co-existed with modernist art in the past, in avant-garde movements in both East and West.[41]

In this respect, attempts to detach art from the ethical, cultural and social codes and norms prevailing in the period and geopolitical context of its production became questionable and unattainable, for various geopolitical, sociological, and cultural reasons. Thus, the reframing of the triangular relation between ethics, aesthetics and art is still partial, although the position of aesthetics as a philosophical discipline (and not only a modernist one) has weakened relevance in defining art. Modernist and formalist aesthetic ideals endured for only a couple of decades, but the unwinding of the short modernist time span via poststructuralist and postmodernist debates became a lengthy endeavour that continued throughout the 1970s, 1980s and 1990s, and prevails even today.

Participatory art as a critique of institutional structures

I have argued elsewhere that the emergence of a participatory paradigm shift in the arts is urgent, stemming from the uneven development of theory, which lagged behind art practices that challenged institutional structures in art and culture.[42] The shift from art that focused on the production of art objects towards art that implicated and engaged various subjects (such as art producers, mediators, audience members, and citizens), in order to create new and relevant relations amongst them, was imagined as an inevitable strategy of intervening in existing distinctions and hierarchies in order to change them, or to dismantle them entirely. This is one of the obvious reasons that participatory art, I would argue, has the potential to address, extricate and redress contentiousness in various cultural heritages and the issues as provenance, the decolonization of museums, the repatriation of looted artefacts, etc.

However, it must be acknowledged that there are still tendencies to keep art discourses away from issues of social justice and political reality—justified by the absence of relevant artworks (read: objects)—as well as to interpret art's involvement in such changes as irrelevant and counter-aesthetic. Such tendencies implicate art-world structures in the overall socio-political and economic systemic structures, to which the art production system belongs by default. Ultimately, the remnants of modernist definitions of art are directly linked to this compromised position, to the production and distribution of art in the market, and to the other usual suspects of the prevailing late capitalist and neoliberal economy. I want to stress, therefore, that some of the issues regarding aesthetic and artistic criteria for evaluating participatory art still remain unresolved, even as they remain pertinent to a more profound understanding of art's changing role in society, and its effort to break with the inherited socio-political

---

40 Kosuth, *Art After Philosophy and After.*

41 Huyssen, *After the Great Divide.*

42 Milevska, "Participatory Art"; Milevska, *On Productive Shame, Reconciliation, and Agency*; Milevska, "Shameful Objects, Apologising Subjects." See also Bishop, *Artificial Hells.*

and economic relationships that facilitated the preservation of the strict division between art and society in the first place.

The fight with the formalist aesthetic canons and criteria that were instrumental to the emergence of "autonomy" as a privileged posture in and for artistic practice continues, inducing social change in the art world and elsewhere. Artistic concepts, genres and theoretical terms like *community-based art, institutional critique, social intervention, relational aesthetics, participatory art, socially engaged art* and *artivism*—all conceived to provide adequate analytical means for better understanding the problems with such modernist dichotomous interpretations of the relations between art and society—survive. They continue to fight against conservative attempts in the art world to use autonomy as a tool for maintaining the status quo.

Adorno's reflections on the relationship between art and society gave way to different interpretations of autonomy, so there can be several different levels of autonomy in art, which makes intersections across different levels and registers even more complex.[43] Thus a more specific analysis of conceptions of autonomy could clarify the inner paradox of arts' claimed right to autonomy. Obviously, there is an overall distinction between social and aesthetic autonomy, but artists and their artworks also belong to differing and often contrasting registers of autonomy depending on their institutional affiliations and/or allies.

Representation, institutional critique and participation

The turn towards a participatory paradigm in the arts is based on the main assumptions in institutional critique that institutions, experts and artists have a monopoly on defining art and that they control access to its production. Also, they give priority to discussing problems on behalf of "others" (whose problems they discuss) and to representations by proxy, thus giving priority for example to art "about" rather than to art "with" or "by" refugees. Starting with the 2015 photograph in which Ai Weiwei famously (re)staged a press photograph of the drowned Syrian infant refugee, Alan Kurdi, by posing his apparently lifeless body in the same position as was pictured in the original photograph, the questions of who represents, how and on whose behalf, raises serious questions about the various means, methods and regimes of representation employed when addressing the refugee crisis.[44]

Ai Weiwei's practice was even more spectacularized, objectified and commercialized in his metaphoric *Law of the Journey* (2017), where he filled a 70-meter-long inflatable boat with 258 large faceless refugee figures filled with helium. In doing so, he created an ostentatious, oversized, and over-prized monument of the current problematic human condition.[45] His more recent film, *Human Flow* (2017), continued to "ex-

43 Hamilton, "Adorno and Autonomy of Art," 287–305.

44 Monica Tan, "Ai Weiwei poses as drowned Syrian infant refugee in 'haunting' photo." For a more fulsome discussion of the impact of this image, see Ghosh's chapter, included in this anthology.

45 @alww#refugeecrisis. See www.twitter.com/hashtag/refugeecrisis?src=hash. In my article, "'Infelicitous' Participatory Acts on the Neoliberal Stage," I argue here about the sociopolitical limits of participatory art, addressing the neoliberal socio-political and economic context, and the pressure for

plore" the same topics, advertising the documentary as a "detailed and heartbreaking exploration into the global refugee crisis."[46]

Distinguishing between two different types of participatory art projects could help clarify some of the contradictions between the enthusiastic aims of participatory art and the pitfalls set by institutional power: The first type, based on the various waves of artistic institutional critique is concerned with the critique of art institutions, and calls for more substantial participation within the art system, in the presentation and/or production of art projects and in making decisions regarding art.[47] Such projects deal in a critical way with the relationship between a) art, art institutions and audiences, b) artists and art institutions (museum, gallery), and c) artists and curators. Although important, I see this first branch of participatory art as too self-referential and self-indulgent, and consequently easier to incorporate and co-opt within existing art institutions and immanent institutional frameworks.[48]

The second type of participatory art, that can be defined as "participatory institutional critique," aims towards a more substantial critique and a deeper societal change, beyond the confines of the art world. Participatory institutional critique has more ambitious goals and potentials, but it also faces stronger adversaries: the general political climate and its conflicts, or the inherited colonial pretext. Hence, the artistic goals and media of such projects vary: performing social and/or anthropological research; issuing calls for restitution, repatriation, and decolonization of institutions; engaging with conflicted local communities, often with unforeseeable but imminent results.[49] With this form too, pertinent questions remain: Which representations in which art objects, images, and spaces are considered contentious cultural heritages, and who decides this?[50] How are they transmitted and reflected in European "culturescapes" and "memoryscapes"? More precisely, in Regina Römhild's words, "What we tend to forget is that this fragility and contestedness have always been the case. There was never a clear-cut, consensual entity called 'Europe,' nor a geographically defined continent or a cultural formation."[51] These issues are extrapolated regardless of whether the researched materials are included or displayed in collections of various European art and cultural institutions, or are presented in public spaces or kept in other contexts. Moreover, questions arise as to how and why these objects became contentious in first place.

Art involving refugees does not raise the question of whether and how artistic research contributes to a politics of emancipation for the first time. The question of the relations between ethics and aesthetics—and form, social content, and conduct—in artistic research have been addressed in various academic and artistic contexts. The issue of representation in different artistic and curatorial projects and institutional

spectacles and commercial ventures in the arts as one of the major obstacles for fulfilling the promise of participatory art for social change.

46 Knowing that the film had gross earnings (as of December 21, 2017) of $527,845 in the US only (according to www.IMDB.com), the term "explore" even sounds cynical.

47 Alberro and Stimson, *Institutional Critique.*

48 Milevska, "'Infelicitous' Participatory Acts on the Neoliberal Stage."

49 Milevska, "Shameful Objects, Apologising Subjects."

50 MacDonald, "Contentious Heritage."

51 Römhild, "Reflexive Europeanization, or: Makings of Europe."

decisions towards the making of images and objects representing difficult ethical contents (dead and wounded bodies, human remains, Holocaust victims, poverty, amongst others) as well as their different approaches towards reproduction, display, distribution and circulation also have been debated in various contexts.[52] These involve discussions around stereotypical and racialized representations, institutional reluctance to acknowledge the questionable provenance of unlawfully acquired objects and unethical sponsorship, propositions for how to deal with the repressed memory of the spaces once inhabited by conflict or marked with contested monuments dedicated to disgraceful historic figures or events, collective memory about commoning movements that contested the appropriation of public space.[53]

Starting with invisible heritages and contentious objects, images and spaces (as I proposed in *On Productive Shame, Reconciliation, and Agency*), one needs to clearly declare the urgent need to acknowledge past wrongdoings in order to rethink, deconstruct and dismantle pre-existing regimes of representation and systemic malfunction, all the while proposing alternative trajectories for future research and more engaged participatory artistic practice. The application of various theoretical and research methodologies (as developed in art history, museology, anthropology, ethnology, sociology, pedagogy, political sciences) together with artistic research methods, artistic media, strategies and actions allows for specificity, appropriateness, applicability, affordance and efficiency in accomplishing these challenging goals, on both ethical and conceptual levels.[54]

Some contemporary artistic strategies stem from the legacy of postcolonial and feminist critique, and the research practices around various theoretical analyses and case studies which have developed in the frame of the humanities and social sciences. Here, I refer to art projects that use different research means and methods, such as field trips, photography-as-research, interviews, focus groups, contextual inquiry, usability studies, surveys, diaries, critical databases, video essays, forensic research, militant image research, institutional critique, thought experiments, social interventions, participatory research of vernacular art made by different self-taught artists and communities, as well as elements of material culture, re-enactment, activist campaigns for naming and renaming, counter-monuments, social design, agonistic research, critical friendship, creative co-production, petition, public apology, manifestos, critical and social advertising, advocating and lobbying for decolonization, repatriation, return and restitution.[55] Particularly important is for artists to team up with existing professionals and organizations that are completely dedicated to the issues stemming from the refugee crisis in order to avoid doing more harm than good.

---

52 These include, for example, the discussion regarding the photographic (Didi-Huberman, *Images in Spite of All*) and video representation of the Holocaust, the debate about the making, displaying and circulation of images of human remains stored in museum collections (Harries, Fibiger, Smith, Adler, and Szöke, "Exposure") and the more general debate about Jacques Rancière's concept '(re)distribution of the sensible' and 'indisciplinarity' (Birrell, "Editorial: Jacques Rancière and The (Re)Distribution of the Sensible").

53 Milevska, "Shameful Objects, Apologising Subjects."

54 Gibson, *The Ecological Approach to Visual Perception*.

55 Milevska, "Relations, Participations, and Other Dialogical Frameworks."

While audiences typically do not take an active part in the creative process of art's production and presentation, participatory art argues that audiences should, precisely because of the many problematic decisions made by institutions that do not take into account the communities which are implicated and/or contested. Participatory art therefore offers an approach to artistic processes in which is the process is considered incomplete without the viewers' involvement—turning audience members into co-authors, editors, or active performers who complement and resolve the artist's concept.

The main intent behind the emergence of participatory art is not simply to add a new genre to existing art genres and media. This conception is instrumental for challenging dominant forms and relationships in the art world: a small protected class of professionals which has a monopoly over making and defining art, and who conceive of the audience as the "other": passive and marginal observers celebrating the results of the creation. Participatory art projects, and collaborative research with other professionals continue to promote the understanding that an artwork is not just an object that you passively enjoy while quietly looking at it; it is rather a creation in which even non-specialized viewers actively participate, a dynamic collaboration between the artist, the audience and their environment.

Often, objects are produced in and through such participatory processes, however these material outcomes are not the main priority because relational, interactive, and collaborative structures established in the process are also considered part of the artwork. Thus, participatory projects often initiate the emergence of new communities and instigate new and complex relations between the artists, produced objects and images and participants.

Although the results of participatory art may be documented using photography, audio, video, broadcast media, or other media technologies, the artwork is really to be found within the interactions and relations that emerge from the audience's engagement with the artist and the situation created. Even so, participatory art cannot always overcome societal strictures, and despite the attempt to erase divisions between the artist as a producer and the audience as participant, very often new hierarchies are created depending on class, ethnicity, access, etc.

Given all of this, living with and within the current reigning contradictions in the art world is difficult. It is especially difficult to juggle all these contradictions for artists and curators collaborating with high-profile art institutions with inherited colonial or other contentious pasts. According to George Lipsitz, the inability to speak openly about contradictory consciousness from within or outside of institutions can lead to a self-destructive desire for 'pure' political positions that ultimately have more to do with "individual subjectivities and self-images" than with "disciplined collective struggle for resources and power."[56] Lipsitz states that "the ultimate goal behind the pertinent critique of the exclusive and hegemonic institutional models is to overcome the deterministic approach."[57]

I would like to conclude with a similarly positive and optimistic understanding of participatory art. Its full potential is still to be unleashed and developed. This can happen only if achieving a quality of relationship among the participating subjects (artists, theorists, curators, audiences and other implicated and interested individuals) is fully

---

56 Lipsitz, "Academic Politics and Social Change," 80.

57 Lipsitz, "Academic Politics and Social Change," 80.

accepted as a possible ultimate goal of art. One should not expect this goal to yield any beautiful objects in the conventional sense. Regardless of whether this is interpreted as anti-aesthetic, counter-aesthetic, or artistic, it doesn't allow institutions to perpetuate difficult issues and relations without acknowledging and challenging their problematic systemic nature. To challenge of the relations among the subjects that are instrumental for producing and transmitting contentiousness is one of the most pertinent aim of participatory art and artistic research employed in such projects.

The recent hateful outbursts from the far right in Europe and elsewhere (such as anti-Semitic and anti-Roma sentiments, racism towards Indigenous and Black populations, patriarchal violence towards women and prejudices and aggression towards LGBTQ communities) can be confronted only with clear critical arguments against similar hatred from the past entailed in some of the prestigious European art and cultural institutions, and by establishing reciprocal and intersectional relations between art, academia and political activism that would work as control mechanism of the socio-political ruling socio-political structures.[58]

I want to argue that contemporary art projects that focus on participatory research and collaboration have enhanced potentials for catalyzing social change and fighting systemic racism precisely because of their "affordance:" they focus on dialogical relations rather than on objects and images that often lacked referencing contentious pasts. In this respect participatory art's potentials for collaborations, alliances, commoning and non-hierarchical "we" that is not based on patronizing are undeniable, but only when imagined as parts of long-term structures rooted in communities, rather than one-off spectacles in restrictively art-designated spaces.

The urgent task of countering the re-racialization of a distinctly "European" identity, and of acting in solidarity with communities driven from the regions where they have lived for a long time—consider the Roma across Europe, the Albanians from Serbia, or the Serbs from Croatia—or who have newly arrived as refugees, are two sides of the same coin. These are the main assumptions behind the participatory projects that invite and include refugees in the process of conceptualization or production of art projects.

Instead of dwelling on negatively charged memories, participatory projects mostly cherish research processes that deal with shared or multidirectional memory,[59] and productive shame[60] in a committed and catalytic way. It should be emphasized, however, that the contradictions are not easy to circumvent. Regretfully, this affordance and potentiality is easily hindered by the concrete contexts of a spectacularized world of international art biennials' "assembly line," to which participatory art practices are not immune, but which they rather serve quite perfectly due to the numbers of participants and audiences they include and attract.

The main contradiction of the project *Green Light*—as in many other participatory art projects dealing with the refugee crisis that have been presented in the recent in-

---

58 In this regard, see van Brummelen and de Haan's chapter in this anthology, which develops an argument about the irony of the repatriation of colonial objects, even as the borders of the Eurozone are strengthened

59 Rothberg, "From Gaza to Warsaw," 525.

60 Gilroy, *Postcolonial Melancholia*.

ternational exhibitions[61]—stems exactly from the fact that refugees without legal status in Europe are for the most part not allowed to receive directly any compensation for their work,[62] so that when they are engaged in participatory projects, the payment comes in the form of compensation or trampa (the simple exchange of labor for goods). Thus, even when Eliasson continues to criticize the political system—full of contradictory protocols, rules and laws—and even when he honestly confesses and apologizes for the limitations of his understanding of the refugee crisis, he nevertheless fails to acknowledge the "hostipitality" at the heart of refugee participation.

The project *Shamiyaana—Food for Thought: Thought for Change*, presented by Rasheed Araeen at Documenta 14 in Athens (2017) also deserves a rigorous extrapolation in this context because it raises very sensitive ethical concerns. In the work, the artist and the Documenta 14 curators established a communal-like free-kitchen under a colorful Pakistani wedding tent installed at Kotzia Square. The project obviously aimed to attract refugees as a kind of compensation for the well-reported lack of financial support for refugees in Greece. However, its strategy of participation and hospitality (or rather "hostipitality") faced many challenges and obstacles internalized in the context of the hierarchical art world and usual elitist divisions inevitably reinforced by art management in such huge events (due to budget and organizational restrictions). The main problem was that the project was based on the strategy of redistributing funding, and thus on delegating the performative agency to the institution (Documenta 14), in a kind of a philanthropic rerouting of the resources assigned to art, rather than to the refugees who became passive recipients of help (in the form of food). It was not so much a question of the formal and aesthetic aspects of the project, as its questionable and consequential ethics—particularly if one takes into account how sensitive the act of eating in public (in front of the elitist art professionals and other aficionados) may be for the vulnerable community of refugees.[63] At the heart of the project's problematic consequences was the fact that the project somehow contributed to the societal and class contradictions regardless of the artist's sincere concerns and good intentions, invested in societal transformations, and regardless of his hopes invested in the potential and agency of participatory art.

In another instance, when I visited the Venice Biennale in 2015, I came across a small sign simply stating "Anonymous Stateless Immigrants Pavilion—A New Pavilion for the Unrepresented at Venice Biennale 2015;" I followed the arrows but did not find the Pavilion. Only much later, I found out that the work was by the Anonymous Stateless Immigrants Collective. The Pavilion/conceptual project was a kind of laby-

---

61 For more information on other art projects dealing with statelessness and refugees at the National Pavilions and collateral projects during the 57th Venice Biennial, Venice 2017, see Ellis-Petersen, "Art of the state: how the Venice Biennale is tackling the refugee crisis."

62 Elliason, "Assembling a Light, Assembling Communities."

63 During an intense conversation with the Greek artist and researcher Sofia Grigoriadou, she expressed some concerns regarding the realization of the otherwise good artist's intentions and aims of the project. According to her, the project resulted in a lot of contradictions and hierarchies on a local and international level. For example, during the distribution of food and tickets for gaining access to the communal-like kitchen, the project attracted simultaneously the people attending similar local communal kitchens for the homeless and international curators, so the long queues for food replicated the world contradictions and hierarchies between different communities.

rinth within the Venice labyrinth of streets, consisting only of the graffiti-like text and arrows: signs that were meant to trick you into following the directions and imagining what such a pavilion might look like. There was no building, no installation, no spectacle, no queues of visitors, no paid or unpaid artists, no paid or unpaid participants, no paid or unpaid attendants (some Pavilions go so far as to use the unpaid labour of students or refugees for attending to their expensively rented spaces).

The Anonymous Stateless Immigrants Pavilion was also a participatory project: any audience member who tried to find this project employed her own imagination and creativity while following the directions and inevitably activated the remnants of various already-seen representations of immigrants and refugees that are profoundly engraved and thus hard to be erased from the visual memory. Representation and participation are inevitably intertwined and only careful extrapolation and conceptualization of art works could think one from another and prevent the proliferation and perpetuation of the already internalized socio-political prejudices that are at work in the media, institutions and policies that regulate immigration and refugees interstate and inter-continental flows.

Either You Get it Or You Don't
A Conversation on LGBTQIA+ Refugees's #Rockumenta Action

Sophia Zachariadi and Krista Lynes

In June 2017, the refugee rights group LGBTQIA+ Refugees Welcome abducted a participatory artwork from the global contemporary art exhibition Documenta 14, held in Athens to highlight the city's centrality to European imaginaries of crisis. They then released a ransom note and accompanying video via social media, in which they addressed the artist, Roger Bernat, condemning the fetishization of refugees by Documenta, and highlighting the precarious conditions queer migrants face on a daily basis. This conversation between Sophia Zachariadi (LGBTQIA+ Refugees Welcome) and Krista Lynes seeks to trace the possibilities and predicaments of the art action, and its legacy for the group, for public art practice, and for thinking refugee rights in Athens and elsewhere.

KL: Can you begin by giving an account of how you came to participate in Documenta, and in Roger Bernat's The Place of the Thing *(2017) specifically?*

SZ: The action took place in Spring 2017. The collective, LGBTQIA+ Refugees Welcome, was in a situation where it was faced with two reactions: first of all, people ignored the existence of this collective and this community—this population within the refugee population—and secondly, people were amazed that a collective for LGBTQI refugees existed, because it was the first time that a collective formed around a group of people who were claiming these specific rights. There aren't collectives of women's refugees, or refugees with disabilities … People were amazed by it, but at the same time, they were neglecting it. We had the same reaction from queer collectives. These were people whom you expect to show solidarity, but many were indifferent. They said "Ok, nice, this is very nice; it's good that this exists," but they didn't do anything to help out. Most of the help came from abroad.

Some people who were part of the collective were a bit pissed off by this. So we decided to fuck someone over. We didn't know who it would be. Would it be Athens Pride [the organizers of the pride event]? The queer community who wanted to approach us often benefited from white privilege. It wasn't their intention to exclude necessarily, but they weren't in touch with other immigrant and non-white people. Their approach was a little bit too "Western."

Then, the proposal from Documenta came along, and we thought that this presented an opportunity to fuck someone over! It did, because Documenta was popular in Athens in 2017. It allowed us to be noticed, because people now learned of the existence of this collective. At the same time, many knew of us before, but they didn't do anything. We thought, "We will take 500 euros from the participation while doing very little, perfect!" and secondly, we will have more popularity. Prior to the event, we had approximately 1,000 "likes" on Facebook; immediately after, we had 3,000 "likes." It's not that this is very important, but it's what happened to our visibility. After that, we had people reaching out to us to do research, to interview for a magazine or a newspaper, etc. So it was nice—a bit tiring but nice.

KL: What was your encounter with Roger Bernat and Documenta like?

SZ: First of all, someone came from Documenta, and invited LGBTQIA+ Refugees Welcome to be a part of the project. We decided to see what the project was about. The artist, Roger Bernat, came to us to explain his project. Refugees in the collective asked Bernat why he wanted to take the stone and bury it in Kassel. He answered, "This is something that either you get, or you don't!" In my mind, I thought, "Okay, you are going to be double fucked!" and when I voiced this opinion to the collective, they said "Perfect!" [*SZ and KL laugh*] Let's say that I had the instinct, and then everything came together. My instinct said, "We need to fuck someone over" and this was a very good moment to do this. The group agreed that we were going to do this because the artist was not very nice nor very polite!

KL: What were the challenges when you had to go through with the actual action? There is, of course, the symbolic resonance to it, accepting to participate, and then there is the actual "doing" of the action itself.

SZ: We had no idea how to handle it. First, we wondered how we would interact with the stone. We decided first to steal it; we agreed, all of us! Then we thought we might smash it, destroy it. We thought to leave it somewhere where it would stay forever. We had many thoughts about how we might proceed. We thought how we might vandalize the rock, but in the end we decided simply to steal the rock and write a ransom note that would include the story of the rock's journey. We agreed collectively on the idea of a ransom note, but after we went around the circle in the group, and each contributed an idea of where the stone might be (languishing without papers in a prison on the island of Samos, drowned and sunk to the bottom of the Mediterranean as EU coast-guards twiddled their thumbs, deported to Turkey after appealing twice, etc.). This was the strongest part of the ransom note, I think. This part of the project came completely from the refugees in the collective and not from the allies.

It was a better solution because it opened it up beyond the subject of Documenta. It was not simply an act of vandalism, an indication that we didn't like Documenta. Our problem wasn't with Documenta; it was that people were unaware of these refugees' context, and the extra difficulties they are facing as both refugees and LGBTQI people.

KL: In this way, it recenters their experience, and allows space for it.

SZ: It's like taking the popularity of Documenta and opening it up. This was part of the project that Roger Bernat missed. He couldn't understand that "We don't care about your project, my dear!" We were using it to talk about a wider subject and situation that is happening all around the world. He couldn't get that far, because he was narcissistic about the project.

This is why we had the idea beyond the project to do the hashtag #rockumenta, and to take the stone around the city, to the park, to asylum centers where it would wait in line. This never happened because of practical reasons—the rock was huge and difficult to carry. Also, after the press release from Roger Bernat [in which he claimed that LGBTQIA+ Refugees' action activated the artwork and was therefore part of its concept], we didn't want to continue engaging with the stone. We decided that we had completed the action and it was finished.

KL: The initial idea, then, was to carry the stone around the city to locations of importance to LGBTQI refugees and take pictures of it with the hashtag #rockumenta?

SZ: Yes, and particularly the ones that are mentioned in the ransom note. Then we thought to add more, to have the stone have coffee, go for lunch, site see, whatever. In any case, after the action it was the Pride March, and the collective had many things to do. We could have continued the action from time to time, though, but we decided to end it.

KL: How did the performance work out on the day itself?

SZ: To be honest, in this collective, we never plan how we're going to perform an action. If someone wants to dance, we say "Perfect! Do you need something for the performance? You need a dress? Ok!" and we help the person get a dress. We work out what money we can give to the different aspects of the performance. For Documenta, we had a very basic idea, which we didn't even know would work. We didn't know if someone from the artist's team would accompany the stone or secure it when it was our turn, or take their own documentation of our performance. We thought that if there were someone accompanying us, we would tell them that some members of the group felt uncomfortable and would ask them to give us an hour for the performance and then return.

In the end, they left the rock and went away and let us be! So it was easier for us to take the rock and take the time we needed—to dance, or have fun. It was very free! We took scarves, masks, helmets etc to hide our faces, so were free to do whatever we wanted to do. What you see in the video is what happened during the two hours that we stayed at the Polytechnic School. The performance was completely random. There was make-up and scarves. People could dress as they liked. We went to a nearby house and got dressed. We played music, and someone spontaneously used the rock as a drum. We just had *lots* of fun!

I was taking the video and dancing, trying to give some basic direction, but mostly following them. The only part that was directed, was when we recorded the group lifting the rock up and carrying it away. It was very simple.

After this, we tried to put the rock into the trunk of a car. It was completely silly! It didn't fit, so we had to carry the rock. We had many ideas about where we were going to put the rock, and we brought the rock to a nearby house and we left it there. We went to another house and prepared the video, did the voice overs. It was very close to the time when we were supposed to return the rock. We had already prepared the ransom note, which we printed in multiples. We sent two "spies" (whom Roger Bernat and Documenta staff had never seen) who pasted it to the door of the Polytechnic School and scattered the flyers around the entrance. We instructed them to stay there to see how they would react. They took photos from far away of Roger Bernat reading the ransom note! [*SZ and KL laugh*]

KL: So good!

SZ: And at the same time, we were uploading the video! [*SZ and KL laugh*] All this occurred simultaneously, and the stone itself was 300 meters from the Polytechnic School in one direction; we were 300 meters from the School in another direction, and everything was actually extremely close to Roger Bernat.

KL: Then you posted the video and ransom note to Facebook and other sites?

SZ: Yes, and we sent press releases, which we sent to Greek and international newspapers and the media more broadly.

KL: So the story emerged because you distributed your action, not because Documenta complained about the rock being stolen?

SZ: Yes, although I'm sure Roger Bernat's press release helped to circulate the story also. In any case, ultimately Documenta used our action to its own benefit. Because it was an interaction with the work, and they called it an interaction, and many people thought it was part of Documenta itself. We had anticipated this but we didn't care. This is something where, "either you get it, either you don't!!!" [*SZ and KL laugh*]

KL: Yes! Because Bernat responded to say that he had suspected something was in the air, that you had activated the work, and that this was all part of the larger piece itself... So, clearly, he didn't get it!

SZ: But we don't care! Our goal was visibility! Visibility of the existence of the collective, first, and secondly of the circumstances, the conditions, and the difficulties that LGBTQI refugees face in Greece.

KL: How do you think the staging of your encounter echoes some of the larger relations between a well-funded and enormously visible German exhibit coming to Greece in the first place?

SZ: Your question goes to the wider problem that we have: that basically in this generation, we are trying to mix activism with art, activism with food ... This is not necessarily a problem—feminists say that "personal is political"—but they don't say to mix everything into a salad! Art isn't necessarily political; political art doesn't necessarily have a broader impact. Conversely, you can have actions that are even more political than political groups. I think the problem was Documenta, from the very beginning, was trying to touch on everything. Those who visited were artists, tourists, who came to visit for a few months, but nevertheless believed that they could talk about a country that has its own background, culture, political and economic situation, etc. One should be cautious about talking about issues from which one is only remotely connected, that isn't part of one's life experience. It's the same with movements like #BlackLivesMatter. The situation in Greece is so recent; it started only in 2010.

KL: Can you speak to what that action means for you now, two years later?

SZ: I'm very tired of Documenta and the whole discourse around it. #Rockumenta was a very interesting act, but we will never have the opportunity to do it again. It was the first time Documenta was held in Athens, and we were in the very beginning of the refugee crisis. This was the moment to do something; we didn't even schedule it. The priority for us was actually the 500 euros the artist was offering to those who participated in carrying the stone, but we didn't like the way the artist's team approached us.

It's interesting to me that many people have their own interpretation of the act we performed; they label it "anti-racist" (which it is, but in a different manner), "feminist," queer … People are obsessed with the symbolism of the action, which is tiring for me. People ignored the fact that what you had was a vulnerable group of people with completely different political, social, religious or cultural backgrounds; even how they understand their gender and sexual identity is completely different. Most people wanted to see their own fantasy confirmed—their understanding, their position, their angle—but they didn't have a need to come into contact with the people who performed #rockumenta and do a cultural exchange. They saw us as a political group. I told most of the allies who came that LGBTQIA+ Refugees Welcome is not a political group; what is political is the experience that these people hold. To call the group political is a colonizing gesture.

KL: What were the political investments in the action?

SZ: You know, in my analysis, the action was a way of raising our middle finger at Documenta. It's very rare that vulnerable groups have the opportunity to do such a thing. What did they gain from the action? Nothing! They just had fun; this is also important. This is what's important about the legacy of #Rockumenta. Normally, movements take action by marching, creating a spectacular or fabulous event. Very few decide to sit down with a group of people to understand their needs, to see how they see themselves and evaluate political actions with them. But most people want to take an act like #Rockumenta, analyze it, and put it somewhere to remember it, maybe do a PhD on it! I'm not minimizing the importance of doing research—this is an important part of the social work our cooperative EMANTES wants to do—but it makes me upset when the analysis trumps the lived experiences of people.

KL: It seems to me that that was the whole problem with Bernat's art work—that it was not about contacting people, or finding out what people's experience was, but rather about allocating space for you in a larger art project. One of the problems is how to respond in a way that isn't on the terms of that invitation. Resistant actions often get reabsorbed by the artwork itself, and we're not any further in understanding the real experiences of LGBTQI refugees. It strikes me how difficult it is to create new actions in this context, when they are always being recaptured, the conditions are always changing, and the landscape is already so determined. It's hard to create something that isn't already understood under a particular category, under a particular flag, or within a particular politics. This makes it impossible to understand what people need from telling their stories.

SZ: In my experience, this is impossible. I'm not there to do this for them. I'm not a god, or a savior. What can I do? Can I provide space for you? What do you need? Do you need someone to escort you to asylum services? Very nice! Providing a space where people can share experiences, not feel weird or uncomfortable. For example, now we're running a project with a trans woman who has 12 years' experience as a ballet dancer, being part of schools, doing Latin dance, hosting events. She works now as a sex worker, which isn't a problem, but she would like to leave it for another job. We decided to find a space to rent and EMANTES will hire her to start dance classes. She can teach, but she can also express herself artistically. This is what I think the movement is missing: at the same time that it wants to help promote something, it also wants to promote itself as something unique to follow; so from the beginning the relation is not created in a context of selflessness

KL: So what do you think the legacy was of the #Rockumenta action, then? Particularly versus doing community-based actions?

SZ: I guess it's ironic, because in two minutes of video, you make a myth; you fantasize about LGBT liberation, refugee liberation, which is great! I had a moment when we were creating the video, just prior to posting it, I felt euphoric. But after that, the reality sets in. There are still the same people with the same problems—problems that would never occur to you.

KL: Do you feel then that it was too much? Too much to ask of peoples' time and effort, given the long-term effects?

SZ: It was a really nice experience. My problem was in how it was received. It's not about the act itself, but how you understand and evaluate it. How do people understand the horrible things they see in photo or art exhibitions? These were my thoughts as a photographer: I don't need to go there and take photos; I'm just going to help and most importantly to BE there, present, to experience it; flesh and blood. It's not a bad thing to take a photo. It's a question of how the audience understands itself in this relationship.

So I'm left with the feeling that some things were done in vain, even though it wasn't in vain. As a collective, we didn't focus on this act. We did it, and then we moved on with our lives. But the allies and researchers who came had a different understanding; they were obsessed with the thing! Which means that you've lost something in the process.

KL: Why do you think that was?

SZ: The people who came in solidarity but weren't part of the act (or even those who were part of the collective almost from the start), didn't understand that LGBTQIA+ Refugees Welcome wasn't a political group in the way a Western perspective understands it. If it were a political group, there wouldn't be allies in it, because it wouldn't need them. From the beginning, there are power relations, whether you like it or not. There can't be neutrality when the existing relations are unequal.

KL: So this was taken up as a political issue more than an issue for refugees?

SZ: It's not that. I just don't understand how people have the expectation that such acts will change things. When you have a large mass event—for example, let's take May 1968—people thought the world would change. It happened through art, through photography and video—the photo with the soldier and the girl offering him a flower. In the contemporary moment, we shouldn't expect that an event like Documenta or #Rockumenta can do something radical. It's stupid; it's a fantasy!

Basically, to my understanding, the difficulties are so massive that you need to do many interventions from many different sides. You need to use your imagination and be extremely flexible, open-minded and patient and most importantly have no expectations. Things we do go above us; we don't owe them, we just offer them to the universe let's say! And that's it.

#Rockumenta pointed a finger, and made the point through humor that there are some people who are facing really serious problems that larger audiences are not aware of. It wasn't moralizing ("You should help LGBTQ refugees!"). Documenta has plenty of resources and money, and they come and say "Ah, do a little dance for us! We'll give you 500 euros!" It's a combination of all these forces that makes the action unique. This is why I said it would never happen again. It's the context that makes it unique.

KL: It was clearly a response to being asked to participate on the terms of the artist, and for his credit, in an event that billed itself as having a big political dimension and a big public audience. It erased the local context to make room for its own fantasy of what the political would look like in Athens. The #Rockumenta action itself then became iconic, it has its own magnetic force. But it's interesting to think about all the stuff that happens around that action, what is continuous with the action's message, but largely invisible.

In relation to the documentation of #Rockumenta, what's interesting to me is to think about how all these other issues are happening around that one action, and those things don't get seen or visualized. It's a way of moving away from the idea that you have one image, and that one image is the image that defines the political moment, that's oppositional or political. We see it, and then we leave it behind. How can you represent the continuity of a set of efforts visually, when #Rockumenta was just a blip in it? What you seem to be saying is that this will never happen again, it's a reduction of what it is you do as a group, and it doesn't represent all the things you want to do.

There's a pleasure to me in seeing the continuity of the action over the space of its unfolding. Particularly in relation to your details about how heavy the stone was, for instance, and how you couldn't fit it into the trunk of your car, or through the door of the house where you were keeping it. These images and stories are not about the symbolic moment or the face-off between #Rockumenta and Documenta, but about what it takes to do political work, and to resist being captured by these politics, these stories, or these images. I wonder, in talking with you, what you think is the most meaningful intervention by LGBTQI+ Refugees?

SZ: Documenta wanted to use us, but we wanted to take this fact and use it for our own purposes. And it worked! I'm simply disappointed that people liked the glamorous part, but very few of them would do the hard work of doing something that counts for an individual person—not for the symbolism, not for the politics. People don't think about how difficult it is to create a collective, how difficult it is to keep it, and how difficult it is to work with vulnerable people. There are many things that I wouldn't do for their politics, but I do them because they are more important. Their requests are more important than my political ideas.

KL: I've seen that the collective has organized a whole series of other artistic activities that are more grassroots, poetry readings, etc. Can you say something about how art functions in those spaces in a different kind of way?

SZ: The most valuable part of any kind of collaboration is to open a dialogue. The problem with Roger Bernat, as an example, is that he didn't come to the collective to open up a dialogue about how to approach this project, to say "I have this idea, and you can do this or that, or propose something?" It was not a dialogue. It was, "I am using you, your body, to do something for me, to take my photos, to gather my material, to do the final act. It shouldn't be that. But when someone comes to do a poetry workshop, and acknowledges that they come from a Western background, and that they have a skill—spoken word poetry for instance—and I can show this approach, but you can do whatever you want with it. The workshop leader never said "this is not the way to do things;" rather she encouraged everyone to do what they wanted with the approach. Here are the tools! If you want, you can use them; if you don't want to, don't. She encouraged participants—"This is lovely! This is powerful!"—and let them do what they wanted. That is called a cultural dialogue or cultural exchange. We don't know where the starting point is; we come from different locations. If one comes and says "I have the money, I have the crew; I have the material," then this is a problematic starting point for cultural exchange.

KL: Can you talk about what the shift from LGBTQIA+ Refugees to EMANTES entailed?

SZ: We have a dilemma in Greece, where either one does something institutional or one goes outside institutional structures. It's a bipolar situation: if you do something on an institutional level, you're not considered a movement, you're basically banned. It's another (mostly urban) myth.

KL: Is it about a kind of purity of politics?

SZ: Yes of course, but it's also like a story that an old lady would tell you, "Don't go over there; bad people will come." But then you go and you see that there are a lot of people working very hard, with a very concrete set of thoughts about how to do things. The people who work institutionally are more 'true' because they've gone past the political correctness, the purity of politics. They understand the contradictions. I've been on the other side of this institution/activism divide, and so it is challenging for me to be part of building something in this gap between institutional work and working outside of it. EMANTES aims to work in this gap.

KL: What is the most important work that EMANTES has to undertake?

SZ: With its legal entity, EMANTES has much more space than a grassroots initiative to put pressure on authorities regarding the rights of LGBTQI+ refugees and asylum seekers, to send reports to asylum services, to access camps and hot spots, to receive funds, to rent spaces etc.—in short, to do anything that is connected to EMANTES' two cornerstones: psychosocial support and raising awareness.

KL: *How do you work with the community to determine EMANTES' actions?*

SZ: It's highly important, especially when you work with very vulnerable people, to help them feel strong again. EMANTES aims to work on a case by case, creating systematic and long-term support. It is not just about providing services but to give space to dialogue, to co-create an action plan according to each person's needs and skills. It is about working together and respecting each other; it is about staying active.

LGBTQIA+ Refugees Welcome, documentation of #Rockumenta action against
Documenta 14, Athens, Greece (2017)

23.2–23.4
LGBTQIA+ Refugees Welcome, documentation of #Rockumenta action against Documenta 14, Athens, Greece (2017)

23.5a–d
LGBTQIA+ Refugees Welcome, documentation of #Rockumenta action against
Documenta 14, Athens, Greece (2017)

Afterword

Lies of the Land

Allan deSouza

I.

He wears the long white gown and kofi of the coastal people. Over one shoulder is slung a musket, over the other is a strap from which hangs a sword. His arms are stiff, one hand grasping the musket handle, the other within close reach of the sword. A wide belt pulled tight into his waist makes his chest appear thrust out like a soldier at attention. His face is turned to one side, away from the camera, with his eyes seemingly focused at a point out of the camera's frame. Closer inspection reveals his eyes to be angled back; not looking at, but watching the camera as if from behind the shelter of gauze. It's an apprehensive gaze, knowing he is being recorded; turning his face away to avoid the camera's scrutiny, but glancing back just to keep an eye on the watcher.

Born near the shores of Lake Nyasa, he was kidnapped as a child and transported to Zanzibar, where he was sold to an Arab merchant and taken to India. Freed at his master's death, his name being unknown—or at least untranslatable—he was renamed after the city where his master had lived. With his new moniker, Bombay, he returned to the continent of his original naming. And there, already reinvented, he might have been lost had he not also been rediscovered.

In 1856, two British Army officers, Richard Burton and John Speke, met in Bombay (the city) to plan an African expedition. Sailing from Bombay (the city) to Africa, they recruited a Swahili guide and his slave, four more African slaves, four Baluchi soldiers, an Arab and last, a Yau from Nyasa: Bombay (the man).

Knowing a little Hindustani from his days in Bombay (the city), Bombay (the man) was able to speak with Speke who spoke no other language to converse with the natives. An Englishman and an African in East Africa who communicated only through Hindustani. A previously unimagined communing.

According to Richard Burton, Bombay had "A high narrow cranium, denoting by arched and rounded crown, fuyant brow and broad base with full development of the moral region, deficiency of the reflectives, fine perceptives, and abundant animality."

II.

According to David Livingstone's diaries, Bombay had "lifted Speke out of the disagreeable position of being a silent onlooker [...] Before getting him, Speke sat on his bottom only." Not only did Speke become translatable, but he was given—by this renamed man—the ability his name suggested: the power of his own voice.

The expedition went south and west and north and round and north again. But none of that matters since these paths were already well traversed by Africans. What does it matter—more pertinently, to whom does it matter?—whose pale feet stepped there first? Clearly it mattered to the owners of the pale feet. Not satisfied with having reached his goal—the source of the Nile—Speke returned for another long trudge, up, down, etc., this time with an old friend from his hunting days in India, Captain James Grant, whose skills included a "conciliatory manner with coloured men."

Speke and Grant employed Bombay to organize and lead the caravan of porters, and to barter at villages. A lively trudge apparently, Grant remarking that, "Nothing can exceed the noise and jollity of an African camp at night. We, the masters, were often unable to hear ourselves talk for the merry song and laughter, the rattle of drums, jingling of bells, beating of old iron, and discordant talk going on round our tents."

Speke, not the first nor the last to correlate Africans and rhythm, added, "song they have none, being mentally incapacitated for musical composition, though as timists they are not to be surpassed," while also noting the hopelessness of the Indians at such entertainment.

In 1866, David Livingstone arrived in Bombay (the city), at a mission school to recruit whitened Africans for expeditions back in blackest Africa. Off they jolly well went, weighted down with weapons, camping equipment, scientific instruments, barter goods and gifts for local rulers, including merikani—cotton sheeting from America—and kaniki—indigo cloth from India. A portentous meld of America, India, Britain and Africa. A previously unimagined community.

III.

In 1871, as every tinted urchin from the pink zone knows, Henry Stanley entered history, presumptuously. Born in Wales as John Rowlands, he was orphaned and worked his ship's passage to America as a cabin boy. There, he was adopted by a New Orleans cotton broker, whose name he took. In other words, Stanley—like Bombay—was a renamed, self-made, made-up man.

Henry Stanley—as a journalist for the *New York Herald* and fresh from a story in Wyoming about the other kind of Indians—stepped off the boat at Zanzibar to look for Livingstone. It was an expedition, it could be said, by one white man to discover another white man, an Americanized Welshman in search of an anglicized Scotsman in darkest Africa. To lead the way, Stanley enlisted Bombay (the man).

Of the eighteen men recruited as guards by Bombay, Stanley noted that "They were an exceedingly fine looking body of men, far more intelligent of appearance than I could ever have believed African barbarians could be." In defense of his expectations towards Africans, Stanley offered his own version of the some-of-my-best-friends-are ... maxim: "I had met in the United States black men, whom I was proud to call friends."

To Henry Stanley, Bombay was "a short slender man of 50 or thereabouts, with a grizzled head, an uncommonly high, narrow forehead, with a very large mouth, showing teeth very irregular, and wide apart [...] at his first appearance I was favorably impressed with Bombay."

When Livingstone was duly discovered (another meld of Africa, Britain, America, and India—or at least Bombay), he noted the historic meeting with a sketch of Bombay (the man), with the added, less historic description: "Square head of Bombay top depressed in centre."

IV.

In the 1939 film, *Stanley and Livingstone*, (shot at a Hollywood studio, with added stock footage of African animals) Stanley is thrown a red herring: led to a white man, he finds an albino. His (mis)guide asks, "You mean he's a black white man?" and is answered with, "No, he's a white black man."

Stanley was "given" a seven-year-old slave. From Ndugu M'hali, My Brother's Wealth, he was renamed Kalulu, Young Antelope (no record exists of the boy's views on his demotion from family treasure to tourist pet). Stanley later took Kalulu—dressed in liveried splendor—to Europe, where he made a deep impression with his "excellent manners." In London, Kalulu modeled for Madame Tussauds' wax version of Stanley and Livingstone's legendary meeting. In America, Kalulu appeared at Stanley's public lectures, entertaining audiences with Swahili songs. Two mementos remain: one, Stanley named his novel, a romantic evocation of Africa, *My Kalulu*; two, in 1877, Kalulu fell and drowned at a place Stanley subsequently named Kalulu Falls.

In 1875, Bombay (the man), who—if not fame, had by now gained a certain, perhaps literal track record—was employed on another expedition, with Verney Cameron. Crossing Africa from Zanzibar to the west coast, Cameron was not quite as smitten, describing Bombay as having, "lost much of the energy he displayed in his journeys with our predecessors in African travel, and was much inclined to trade upon his previous reputation," adding that he was "neither the 'Angel' of Colonel Grant nor the 'Devil' of Mr. Stanley."

Africa's greatest uncredited traveler, Bombay saw Africa's surrounding waters, the Atlantic, the Indian, the Mediterranean and the Cape of Good Hope. Desiring another journey, he wrote to Grant: "Bana Grant, I, Bombay, send for my old master plenty salaam. I have been many years with white men, Cameron, Speke, Stanley &c, but have not yet seen England their home, and as I am getting old, I should like to see the land of my old master before I die." His wish, to follow his masters to their homeland, was not to be realized. Fittingly, he died in Zanzibar, an island one step off the mainland, floating out towards Bombay (the city).

V.

In 1948, my father left Bombay (the city) and arrived in Nairobi, where he met my mother and where I was later born. An Indian in Africa, I was named after a popular American actor whose Anglo name my parents believed would also grant me some ease of access within the then British colony: another potent meld—at least to me—of India, Africa, Britain and America.

In 1965 we left an independent Kenya for England, the land of the former masters. In 1980, I traveled to Bombay (the city). Standing at India Gate, I looked west towards my birthplace across the ocean. I imagined my father years before, standing in the same place, looking away from his birthplace.

Clad in a beige linen suit specially made for his journey, or perhaps bedecked in khaki and accessorized topi, my father steps off Indian ground. He grabs a railing and pulls himself up the steep gangplank as though the land refuses to let go. He totters for a moment, looking down to the water, unsure which direction to go—up onto the ship, or back down to the solid familiarity of land.

Does he remain on deck as the ship pulls away, until he can no longer see the features in the rows of faces, until the faces themselves become a smear? Does he watch until the activity of the Bombay docks disappears, until the only building he can see is the gigantic arch of India Gate bidding him farewell as once it had welcomed English monarchy? Does he look until all he can see is water, all he can hear are the crash of waves against the ship and the wailing of seagulls?

None before him have returned; he has no intention of being the first. Though many families have lost their sons to Overseas, they bear the loss proudly, with visible material compensations. With the money sent back, these families rebuild their houses in anticipation of their sons' triumphant returns. As the years pass with no sign of the prodigals, blue airmail envelopes with colorful stamps are instead ceremonially withdrawn from glass cabinets and passed around as proof of distant loyalty.

VI.

All I have are fantasies and inventions of the passage from India to Africa. They fabricate a genealogy; not a family tree, but a root of familiarity. I swaddle myself within this security blanket of imagined history. A re-collection of possibilities, of memory-threads cast to the winds, drawn back and re-cast in different directions.

Would my father always be caught between east and west, south and north, between inside and outside; neither house nor field? Never knowing which way to turn, which way to pursue his dreams, to the rising or the setting sun?

I used to say I was Kenyan, but people would just look at me expectantly. Relenting, I would mumble something about my grandparents being from India. An occasional colonial relic might jabber at me in Swahili or Hindi, and when I couldn't reply in kind I would look like a perfect idiot or simply like a liar.

I'm not a proper Indian, from India; nor a proper African, though I'm from there. And what kind of name is mine, especially when attached to a face dark as mine? What does it mean for me to not know my "own" tongue, and to be able to slip into the Jamaicanized cockney of an East London barrow boy? Or the jive of a Bronx B-boy? Should I be what you want? Why not be whatever I want?

Where am I on the slippery road between one place and another? Am I fully here or is part of me always elsewhere? Am I this? Am I that? I rarely ask such questions, though I face them on a daily basis. I shape-shift partly in response to and partly in revolt against what's expected of me. One day I'm Brazilian, another, Tahitian, or Maori,

Hawaiian. I even try Tasmanian. It's a game to ward off stupid questions—do-you-a-speak-a-Eng-lish?—and a way of refusing to be known.

VII.

I had a story with no beginning and no end. No past, no future, only the possibility of coming into being. A story, not so much recitation, but re-siting. Having changed places, stopped and restarted, this story is of the becoming, not just of the places—the changed from and the changed to—but of the changing; not just of the leaving and arriving, but of the passage itself.

In the beginning was before the word. How then to tell the story of this beforeness? Of my story before it is spoken, before it descends from the convolutions of the mind to the slippery slope of the tongue? Of the history that names me? And what of the history that misnames me?

How do I tell the story of what I believe to be my self—the differences and indifferences that I can't translate, so that whenever I open my mouth to speak it's always already of a middle with a missing beginning? All I can do is keep returning in hindsight, to middles, to beginnings, to what comes before:

Vibrations tingle my body; soothing then forceful. They gribble up my chest, up to my face and for a brief, ghastly moment my eyeballs bounce in their sockets. I'm pushed back against the seat but manage to turn my face towards the window and see the ground racing past. Abruptly, the vibrations stop, my eyes stilled. We're up. Off the ground. The world inside tips backwards the land outside falls away.

I push forward, face against the window. Roads tentacle in every direction, a maze of secrets. From up here, individuals are lost, each life a fleck of dust. Higher, trees and cars are bleached of color; higher, buildings become an indistinct fuzz of grays and browns. Higher, the main Nairobi-Mombasa road unravels like discarded string; higher, rivers and lakes glint silver, all other features little more than tonal disruptions against an overall haze. Higher still, all details disappear in washes of murky hues.

VIII.

I'm looking out at the ground below, 30,000 feet below says a crackling voice from an intercom or from inside my head; cruising at 500 mph it says, air temperature is -20. The meaningless numbers bear no relation to what my eyes tell me. I see fissures, crannies, gouges, lumps as far as where the world curves away. It could be a landscape: mountains and valleys, forests and plains. Or I could be a baby lying on my mother's breast, her body the extent of my world, laid out below me with its enigmatic geography: valleys and mountains, plains and forests.

I don't know how many hours later it is, but we've reached the coast. The Mediterranean, the voice says, surf frilling the strike of water and land with a ruffle collar. The plane slows to an immobile hover. I bathe my eyes in the turquoise sea beneath, then close them, floating in an orange afterimage. It feels like we've left the world.

The planet continues its lumbering revolutions; people are laughing, crying, wars are fought, babies born.

I wake with a start. The sound of the engines has changed, becoming more urgent. Seatbelts, the voice says. The plane tilts forward—Ladies and gentlemen, we shall be arriving at Heathrow Airport, London.

My stomach lurches with excitement. As if in response, the plane dips suddenly, plunging into clouds that could be the same as the ones over Nairobi. If I hadn't been told by the voice I would have thought that we had just gone in a circle, or the earth might have turned one way and we'd gone the opposite way so that we hadn't moved our position at all.

Clouds part in revelation: England, a patchwork of fields, each square hemmed neatly by hedges. A quilt of fables rushes up to greet me, of a land of glory and hope, of order and decency, of red letterboxes, of a white woman with a golden crown, of friendly blue bobbies.

As they say ... the lie of the land.

Bibliography

"63 migrants morts en Méditerranée : des survivants poursuivent leur quête de justice." Fédération internationale des ligues des droits de l'homme. www.fidh.org/La-Federation-internationale-des-ligues-des-droits-de-l-homme/droits-des-migrants/63-migrants-morts-en-mediterranee-des-survivants-poursuivent-leur-13483

Abbate, Janet. *Inventing the Internet*. Cambridge: The MIT Press, 2000.

Abdelmonem, Angie, Rahma Esther Bavelaar, N. Elisa Wynne-Hughes, and Susana Galán. "The 'Taharrush' Connection: Xenophobia, Islamophobia, and Sexual Violence in Germany and Beyond," *Jadaliyya*. March 1, 2016. www.jadaliyya.com/Details/33036

Abreu, Manuel Arturo. "We Need to Talk About Social Practice." *Art Practical*, March 6, 2019. www.artpractical.com/column/we-need-to-talk-about-social-practice/

Abu-Lughod, Lila. "Do Muslim Women Really Need Saving? Anthropological Reflections on the Cultural Relativism and Its Others," *American Anthropologist* 104, no. 3 (2003): 783–793.

Academy of Social Sciences, "Academy Adopts Five Ethical Principles for Social Science Research." 2015. www.acss.org.uk/developing-generic-ethics-principles-social-science/academy-adopts-five-ethical-principles-for-social-science-research/

Acquier, Aurélien, Thibault Daudigeos, Jonatan Pinkse. "Promises and Paradoxes of the Sharing Economy: An Organizing Framework," *Technological Forecasting & Social Change* 125 (2017): 1–10.

Adorno, Theodor W., *History and Freedom: Lectures 1964–1965*, translated by Rolf Tiedemann. Oxford: Wiley, 2014.

Agamben, Giorgio. "For a Theory of Destituent Power." February 5, 2014. www.criticallegalthinking.com/2014/02/05/theory-destituent-power/

Agamben, Giorgio. *The Coming Community*. Minneapolis: Minnesota University Press, 1993.

Agamben, Giorgio. "We Refugees." *Symposium: A Quarterly Journal in Modern Literatures* 49, no. 2 (1995): 114–119.

Agamben, Giorgio. *The Open: Man and Animal*. Stanford: Stanford University Press, 2004.

Agamben, Giorgio. *State of Exception*. Chicago: The University of Chicago Press, 2005.

Agamben, Giorgio. "Beyond Human Rights." *Social Engineering* 15 (2008): 90–95.

Agier, Michel. "Humanity as an Identity and Its Political Effects (A Note on Camps and Humanitarian Government)." *Humanity: An International Journal of Human Rights, Humanitarianism, and Development* 1, no. 1 (2010): 29–45.

Agier, Michel. *Managing the Undesirables: Refugee Camps and Humanitarian Government.* Cambridge: Polity Press, 2011.

Ahmed, Sara. *Strange Encounters: Embodied Others in Postcoloniality.* London: Routledge, 2000.

"AI Now Report." www.ainowinstitute.org/AI_Now_2018_Report.pdf

Alami, Aida. "Morocco Unleashes a Harsh Crackdown on Sub-Saharan Migrants." *The New York Times,* October 22, 2018. www.nytimes.com/2018/10/22/world/africa/morocco-crackdown-sub-saharan-migrants-spain.html

Alberro, Alexander and Blake Stimson, editors. *Institutional Critique: An Anthology of Artists' Writings.* Cambridge: The MIT Press, 2009.

Alduy, Cecile. "What a French novel tells us about Marine Le Pen, Steve Bannon, and the rise of the populist right." *Politico,* April 23, 2017. www.politico.com/magazine/story/2017/04/23/what-a-1973-french-novel-tells-us-about-marine-le-pen-steve-bannon-and-the-rise-of-the-populist-right-215064

Alexander, Jacqui. *Pedagogies of Crossing: Meditations on Feminism, Sexual Politics, Memory, and the Sacred.* Durham: Duke University Press, 2006.

Alioua, Mehdi and Charles Heller. "Transnational Migration, Clandestinity and Globalization: Sub Saharan Transmigrants in Morocco" in *New Mobilities Regimes in Art and Social Sciences,* edited by Sven Kesselring and Gerlinde Vogl. London: Ashgate Publishing, 2013.

Allen, Peter. "Alan Johnson praises French raid on Calais 'jungle'." *The Telegraph,* September 22, 2009. www.telegraph.co.uk/news/worldnews/europe/france/6218076/Alan-Johnson-praises-French-raid-on-Calais-jungle.html

Amoore, Louise. "Biometric Borders: Governing Mobilities in the War on Terror." *Political Geography* 25 (2006): 336–351.

Anarchist without Content, "Tiqqun Aprocrypha Repost." April 18, 2010. anarchistwithoutcontent.wordpress.com/2010/04/18/tiqqun-apocrypha-repost/

Andersson, Ruben. "A Game of Risk: Boat Migration and the Business of Bordering Europe." *Anthropology Today* 28, no. 6 (2012): 7–11.

Andersson, Ruben. *Illegality Inc.: Clandestine Migration and the Business of Bordering Europe.* Berkeley: University of California Press, 2014.

Andreone, Gemma. "Observations sur la 'juridictionnalisation' de la Méditerranée." *Annuaire Du Droit de La Mer* 9 (2004): 7–25.

Arendt, Hannah. "We Refugees." in *Altogether Elsewhere Writers on Exile,* edited by Marc Robinson. London: Faber and Faber, 1994 [1943].

Arendt, Hannah. *The Human Condition.* Chicago: The University of Chicago Press, 1998 [1958].

Arendt, Hannah. *On Revolution.* London: Penguin Books, 2006 [1963].

Arendt, Hannah. *The Origins of Totalitarianism.* New York: Harcourt, Brace, 1973 [1966].

"Asylgesetz (AsylG) in der Fassung der Bekanntmachung vom 2. September 2008 (BGBI. I S. 1789), das zuletzt durch Artikel 1 des Gesetzes vom 4. Dezember 2018 (BGBI. I S. 2250) geändert worden ist," *Bundesamt für Justiz.* December 4, 2018. www.gesetze-im-internet.de/asylvfg_1992/BJNR111260992.html

Austin, John L. *How to Do Things with Words,* edited by J. O. Urmson and Marina Sbisa. Cambridge: Harvard University Press, 1975.

Azoulay, Ariella. *The Civil Contract of Photography.* Cambridge: The MIT Press, 2008.

Azozomox and Duygu Gürsel. "The Untold Story of Migrant Women Squatters and the Occupations of Kottbusser Straße 8 and Forster Straße 16/17, Berlin-Kreuzberg," in *Migration, Squatting and Radical Autonomy*, edited by Pierpaolo Mudu and Sutapa Chattopadhyay. New York: Routledge, 2017: 114–128.

Bærenholdt, Jørgen Ole and Kirsten Simonsen. *Space Odysseys: Spatiality and Social Relations in the 21st Century*. Routledge, 2017.

BAK, *We are Here*, 2012/16. www.bakonline.org/person/we-are-here-2/

Baker, Daniel and Maria Hlavajova. *We Roma: A Critical Reader in Contemporary Art*. Utrecht: Valiz/BAK, 2014.

Balibar, Etienne. "The Nation Form: History and Ideology." *Review (Fernand Braudel Center)* 13, no. 3 (Summer 1990): 329–361.

Balibar, Etienne. "What we owe to the 'Sans-papiers'." *European Institute for Progressive Cultural Policies*. January 1996. www.eipcp.net/transversal/0313/balibar/en

Balibar, Etienne. "Is European Citizenship Possible" in *Cities and Citizenship*, edited by James Holston. Durham: Duke University Press, 1999.

Barad, Karen. *Meeting the Universe Halfway*. Durham: Duke University Press, 2007.

Bargu, Banu. *Starve and Immolate: The Politics of Human Weapons*. New York: Columbia University Press, 2014.

Bargu, Banu. "Another Necropolitics," *Theory & Event* 19, no. 1 (2016).

Bargu, Banu. "The Silent Exception: Hunger Striking and Lip-Sewing." *Law, Culture and the Humanities* 0, no. 0 (2017): 1–28.

Batycka, Dorian. "At Manifesta Artists Address Italy's Migrant Crisis." *Hyperallergic*, September 18, 2018. www.hyperallergic.com/459887/at-manifesta-artists-address-italys-migrant-crisis/

Bauder, Harald. "Why We Should Use the Term Illegalized Immigrant." *RCIS Research Brief*, no. 1 (2013): 1–7.

Baudrillard, Jean. *Simulacra and Simulation*. University of Michigan Press, 1994.

Bauman, Zygmunt. *Globalization: The Human Consequences*. Columbia University Press, 1998.

Becker, Carol, editor. *The Subversive Imagination: Artists, Society and Social Responsibility*. New York: Routledge, 1994.

Benjamin, Walter. *The Work of Art in the Age of Mechanical Reproduction*. London: Penguin Books, 2008.

Bennett, Jane. *Vibrant Matter: A Political Ecology of Things*. Durham: Duke University Press, 2009.

Bennett, W. Lance and Alexandra Segerberg. *The Logic of Connective Action: Digital Media and the Personalization of Contentious Politics*. New York: Cambridge University Press, 2013.

Bergson, Henri. *Matter and Memory*. Translated by Nancy Margaret Paul and W. Scott Palmer. Cambridge: Zone Books, 2005.

Berlant, Lauren. *Cruel Optimism*. Durham: Duke University Press, 2011.

Bernhard, Meg. "Spain was seen as welcoming refugees, but in North Africa it is cracking down." *Los Angeles Times*, March 8, 2019. www.latimes.com/world/europe/la-fg-spain-morocco-refugees-20190308-story.html

Betts, Alexander and Paul Collier. "Help Refugees Help Themselves." *Foreign Affairs* (November/December 2015). www.foreignaffairs.com/articles/levant/2015-10-20/help-refugees-help-themselves

Betts, Alexander and Paul Collier. *Refuge: Transforming a Broken Refugee System.* London: Penguin Books, 2017.

Bialasiewicz, Luiza. "Off-shoring and Out-sourcing the Borders of Europe: Libya and EU Border Work in the Mediterranean." *Geopolitics* 17, no. 4 (2012): 843–866.

Biemann, Ursula. "Remotely Sensed: A Topography of the Global Sex Trade." *Feminist Review* 80 (2005).

Bigo, Didier. "Security and Immigration: Toward a Critique of the Governmentality of Unease." *Alternatives* 27 (2002): 63–92.

Birrell, Ross. "Editorial: Jacques Rancière and The (Re)Distribution of the Sensible: Five Lessons in Artistic Research." *Art & Research: A Journal of Ideas, Contexts and Methods* 2, no. 1 (Summer 2008). www.artandresearch.org.uk/v2n1/v2n1editorial.html

Bishop, Claire. *Artificial Hells: Participatory Art and the Politics of Spectatorship.* New York: Verso, 2012.

Bishop, Claire. "Delegated Performance: Outsourcing Authenticity" *CUNY Academic Works,* 2012. academicworks.cuny.edu/gc_pubs/45

Black, Edwin. *IBM and the Holocaust.* Danvers: Crown Publishing Group, 2001.

Blunt, Alison. "Cultural Geographies of Migration: Mobility, Transnationality and Diaspora." *Progress in Human Geography* 31, no. 5 (2007): 684–694.

Bojadžijev, Manuela and Sandro Mezzadra. "'Refugee crisis' or Crisis of European Migration Policies?" *Focaalblog,* November 2015. www.focaalblog.com/2015/11/12/manuela-bojadzijev-and-sandro-mezzadra-refugee-crisis-or-crisis-of-european-migration-policies/

Bolongard, Kait. "Morocco offers fish for land." *Politico,* April 22, 2018. www.politico.eu/article/morocco-offers-fish-for-eu-recognition-of-its-claim-to-western-sahara/

Bolt, Barbara, Roger Alsop, Marie Sierra, Robert Vincs, and Giselle Kett. *Research Ethics and the Creative Arts.* Melbourne: Melbourne Research Office, 2010.

Borutta, Manuel and Sakis Gekas. "A Colonial Sea: the Mediterranean, 1798–1956." *European Review of History: Revue européenne d'histoire* 19, no. 1 (2012): 1–13.

Bourriaud, Nicolas. *Relational Aesthetics.* Paris: Les Presse Du Réel, 2002.

Boutang, Yann Moulier. *Economie politique des migrations clandestines de main-d'oeuvre: comparaisons internationales et exemple français.* Paris: Publisud, 1986.

Braudel, Fernand. *The Mediterranean and the Mediterranean world in the age of Philip II.* New York: Harper & Row, 1972–3.

Bredekamp, Horst. *Theorie des Bildakts* [*Theory of the Image-Act*]. Frankfurt: Suhrkamp, 2013.

Browne, Simone. *Dark Matters.* Durham: Duke University Press, 2015.

Brunwasser, Matthew. "A 21st-Century Migrant's Essentials: Food, Shelter, Smartphone." *The New York Times,* August 25, 2015. www.nytimes.com/2015/08/26/world/europe/a-21st-century-migrants-checklist-water-shelter-smartphone.html

Bulman, May. "The lost childhoods on Britain's doorstep: How growing number of families are waiting in tents to attempt dangerous Channel crossing." *The Independent,* December 1, 2018.

Bundesamt für Migration und Flüchtlinge. "Aktuelle Zahlen zu Asyl," November 2018. www.bamf.de/DE/Infothek/Statistiken/Asylzahlen/AktuelleZahlen/aktuelle-zahlen-asyl-node.html

Burns, Anne. "Discussion and Action: Political and Personal Responses to the Aylan Kurdi Images." *The Iconic Image in Social Media*, edited by The Visual Social Media Lab, 2015. www.visualsocialmedialab.org/projects/the-iconic-image-on-social-media

Butler, Judith. "Bodies in Alliance and the Politics of the Street." *Transversal*. September 2011. www.eipcp.net/transversal/1011/butler/en

Caccia, Beppe and Sandro Mezzadra. "What Can a Ship Do?" *Viewpoint Magazine*, January 7, 2019. www.viewpointmag.com/2019/01/07/what-can-a-ship-do/

Campana, Fahrinisa. "She arrived with nothing. Now this Iranian woman feeds Athens' homeless." *Middle East Eye*, February 28, 2019. www.middleeasteye.net/discover/she-arrived-nothing-now-iranian-woman-feeds-athens-homeless

Camuset, Gabrielle. Personal correspondence. May 24, 2019.

Carrera, Sergio. "A Comparison of Integration Programmes in the EU: Trends and Weaknesses." *Challenge Papers: The Changing Landscape of European Liberty and Security* 1, March 2006.

Carroll, Noël. "Art and Ethical Criticism: An Overview of Recent Directions of Research." *Ethics* 110, no. 2 (January 2000): 350–387.

Casas-Cortes, Maribel, Sebastian Cobarrubias and John Pickles. "Re-Bordering the Neighbourhood: Europe's Emerging Geographies of Non-Accession Integration." *European Urban and Regional Studies* 20, no. 1 (2013): 37–58.

Castles, Stephen. *Mistaken Identity: Multiculturalism and the Demise of Nationalism in Australia*. London: Pluto Press, 1988.

Cennetoğlu, Banu. *The List* website. www.list-e.info/liste-hakkinda.php?l=en

Césaire, Aimé. "Réponse à Depestre poète haïtien (Eléments d'un art poétique)." *Présence africaine*, avril-juillet, 1955.

Chadwick, Vincent. "Donald Tusk tells economic migrants: 'Don't come to Europe'." *Politico*, March 3, 2016. www.politico.eu/article/donald-tusk-tells-economic-migrants-dont-come-to-europe/

Chandler, Caitlin L. "Inside the EU's flawed $200 million migration deal with Sudan." *The New Humanitarian*, January 30, 2018. www.thenewhumanitarian.org/special-report/2018/01/30/inside-eu-s-flawed-200-million-migration-deal-sudan

"Charter of Fundamental Rights of the European Union. European Parliament, Council of the European Union, and European Commission. 2000/C 364/01," *Official Journal of the European Communities*, December 18, 2000.

Chatterjee, Partha. *The Politics of the Governed: Reflections on Popular Politics in Most of the World*. New York: Columbia University Press, 2004.

Chechi, Alessandro, Anne Laure Bandle and Marc-André Renold, "Case Venus of Cyrene—Italy and Libya." *ArThemis: Art-Law Centre, University of Geneva*. January 2012. plone.unige.ch/art-adr

Chouliaraki, Lilie and Tijana Stolic, Tijana. "Rethinking Media Responsibility in the Refugee 'Crisis': A Visual Typology of European News." *Media, Culture & Society* 39, no. 8 (2017): 1162–1177.

Chouliaraki, Lilie and Pierluigi Musarò. "The Mediatized Border. Technologies and Affects of Migrant Reception in the Greek and Italian borders." *Feminist Media Studies*, no. 17 (2017): 26–52.

Chrisafis, Angelique and Siddique, Haroon. "French Police clear the 'jungle' migrant camp in Calais." *The Guardian*, September 22, 2009. www.theguardian.com/world/2009/sep/22/french-police-jungle-calais

Chun, Wendy Hui Kyong. *Updating to Remain the Same*. Cambridge: The MIT Press, 2016.

Chun, Wendy Hui Kyong. "Virtual Segregation Narrows Our Real-Life Relationships." *Wired*, April 13, 2017. www.wired.co.uk/article/virtual-segregation-narrows-our-real-life-relationships

Clancy-Smith, Julia. *Mediterraneans: North Africa and Europe in an Age of Migration, c. 1800-1900*. Berkeley: University of California Press, 2010.

Clements, Paul. "The Recuperation of Participatory Art Practices." *International Journal of Art and Design Education* 30, no. 1 (2011): 18–30.

Clifford, James. *The Predicament of Culture: Travel and Translation in the Twentieth Century*. Cambridge: Harvard University Press, 1988.

Cohen, Kris. *Never Alone, Except for Now: Art, Networks, Populations*. Durham: Duke University Press, 2017.

Cole, Phillip. *Philosophies of Exclusion: Liberal Political Theory and Immigration*. Edinburgh: Edinburgh University Press, 2000.

Cole, Phillip. "On the Borders of Solidarity: An Ethical Perspective on Migration," *Eurozine*, August 12, 2016. www.eurozine.com/articles/2016-08-12-colep-en.html

Connolly, William E. *A World of Becoming*. Durham: Duke University Press, 2011.

"Convention and Protocol relating to the Status of Refugee." UN High Commission for Refugees, 2010 [1951/1967].

Coole, Diana and Samantha Frost. *New Materialisms: Ontology, Agency, and Politics*. Durham: Duke University Press, 2010.

Cote, Mark. "Technics and the Human Sensorium: Rethinking Media Theory through the Body." *Theory & Event* 13, no. 4 (2010): 1092–1311.

Cresswell, Tim. *On the Move: Mobility in the Modern Western World*. London: Taylor & Francis, 2006.

Cresswell, Tim and Tanu Priya Uteng. *Gendered Mobilities*. New York: Routledge, 2008.

Cresswell, Tim. "Towards a Politics of Mobility." *Environment and Planning D: Society and Space* 28, no. 1 (2010): 17–31.

"Culture: un film sénégalais cofinancé par la Côte d'Ivoire au Festival de Cannes" *News Africa*. May 23, 2019. www.news-africa.fr/2019/05/23/culture-un-film-senegalais-cofinance-par-la-cote-divoire-au-festival-de-cannes/19987/

Cubitt, Sean. "How to Connect Everyone with Everything." Blog post, August 13, 2014. seancubitt.blogspot.com/2014/08/how-to-connect-everyone-with-everything.html

Cubitt, Sean. *Finite Media: Environmental Implications of Digital Technologies*. Durham: Duke University Press, 2017.

Cuttitta, Paolo. "'Borderizing' the Island: Setting and Narratives of the Lampedusa 'Border Play'." *ACME: An International E-Journal for Critical Geographies* 13, no. 2 (2014): 196–219.

Cuttitta, Paolo. "Repoliticization Through Search and Rescue? Humanitarian NGOs and Migration Management in the Central Mediterranean," *Geopolitics* 23, no. 3 (2018): 632–660.

Cuttitta, Paolo. "Pushing Migrants Back to Libya, Persecuting Rescue NGOs: The End of the Humanitarian Turn." *Border Criminologies*, April 18, 2018. www.law.ox.ac.uk/research-subject-groups/centre-criminology/centreborder·criminologics/blog/2018/04/pushing-0

Danewid, Ida. "White Innocence in the Black Mediterranean: Hospitality and the Erasure of History." *Third World Quarterly* 38, no. 7 (2017): 1674–1689.

De Genova, Nicholas. "Migrant 'illegality' and deportability in everyday life." *Annual Review of Anthropology* 31, no. 1 (2002): 419–447.

De Genova, Nicholas. "Spectacles of Migrant 'Illegality': The Scene of Exclusion, the Obscene of Inclusion." *Ethnic and Racial Studies* 36, no. 7 (2013): 1180–1198.

De Genova, Nicholas, editor. *The Borders of "Europe": Autonomy of Migration, Tactics of Bordering*, Durham: Duke University Press, 2017.

De Genova Nicholas, Glenda Garelli and Martina Tazzioli. "Autonomy of Asylum?: The Autonomy of Migration Undoing the Refugee Crisis Script." *South Atlantic Quarterly* 117, no. 2 (2018): 239–265.

De Gruyter, Caroline. "Europa moet leren 'machtsdenken.'" *NRC.nl*. January 1, 2019. www.nrc.nl/nieuws/2019/01/08/europa-moet-leren-machtsdenken-a3184885

De Landa, Manuel. *Assemblage Theory*. Edinburgh: Edinburgh University Press, 2016.

De Leon, Jason. *The Land of Open Graves: Living and Dying on the Migrant Trail*. Berkeley: University of California Press, 2015.

Dearden, Lizzie. "Bangladesh is now the single biggest country of origin for refugees on boats as new route to Europe Emerges." *The Independent*, May 5, 2017. www.independent.co.uk/news/world/europe/refugee-crisis-migrants-bangladesh-libya-italy-numbers-smuggling-dhaka-dubai-turkey-detained-a7713911.html

Deleuze, Gilles and Félix Guattari. *A Thousand Plateaus: Capitalism and Schizophrenia*. Minneapolis: University of Minnesota Press, 1987.

Deleuze, Gilles. *Foucault*. Minneapolis: University of Minnesota Press, 1988.

Deleuze, Gilles, and Antonio Negri. "Gilles Deleuze in conversation with Antonio Negri." 1990. www.generation-online.org/p/fpdeleuze3.htm

Deleuze, Gilles. "Postscript on the Societies of Control." *October* 59 (1992): 3–7.

Deleuze, Gilles. *Difference and Repetition*. New York: Columbia University Press, 1994.

Deleuze, Gilles. *Negotiations, 1972-1990*. New York: Columbia University Press, 1997.

Deleuze, Gilles and Claire Parnet. *Dialogues II*. Translated by Hugh Tomlinson and Barbara Habberjam. London: Continuum, 2006.

Della Ratta, Donatella. *Shooting a Revolution: Visual Media and Warfare in Syria*. London: Pluto Press, 2018.

Democracy Now. "Trump Ramps Up Migrant Attacks, Says Soldiers Can Shoot Migrants," *Democracy Now*, November 2, 2018. www.democracynow.org/2018/11/2/headlines/trump_ramps_up_migrant_attacks_says_soldiers_can_shoot_migrants

Depledge, Duncan. "Geopolitical Material: Assemblages of Geopower and the Constitution of the Geopolitical Stage." *Political Geography* 45 (2013): 91–92.

Derrida, Jacques. *Politics of Friendship*, translated by George Collins. London: Verso, 1997.

Derrida, Jacques and Anne Dufourmantelle. *Of Hospitality: Anne Dufourmantelle Invites Jacques Derrida to Respond*. Translated by Rachel Bowlby. Stanford: Stanford University Press, 2000.

Derrida, Jacques. "Hostipitality." Translated by Barry Stocker and Forbes Morlock. *ANGELAKI: Journal of the Theoretical Humanities* 5, no. 3 (December 2000).

Deutscher Bundestag, "Schlussfolgerung aus der neuen Rechtsprechung zu verdachtsunabhängigen Personenkontrollen durch die Bundespolizei," *Drucksache* 19, no. 2151 (2018): 1–12.

Didi-Huberman, Georges. *Images in Spite of All: Four Photographs from Auschwitz*. Chicago: University of Chicago Press, 2008.

Didi-Huberman, Georges. *Peuples exposés, peuples figurants. L'Oeil de l'histoire*. Paris: Editions de Minuit, 2012.

Didi-Huberman, Georges. "From a High Vantage Point." *Eurozine*, October 12, 2018. www.eurozine.com/high-vantage-point

Easterling, Keller. *Extrastatecraft: The Power of Infrastructure Space*. London: Verso, 2014.

Eder, Jens and Charlotte Klonk, editors. *Image Operations: Visual Media and Political Conflict*. Manchester: Manchester University Press, 2016.

Eggers, Maureen Maisha, Grada Kilomba, Peggy Piesche, Susan Arndt, eds. *Mythen, Masken und Subjekte: Kritische Weißseinsforschung in Deutschland*. Münster: Unrast Verlag, 2005.

El-Tayeb, Fatima. *European Others: Queering Ethnicity in Postnational Europe*. Minneapolis: University of Minnesota Press, 2011.

Elden, Stuart. *The Birth of Territory*. Chicago: University of Chicago Press, 2013.

Eliasson, Olafur and Andreas Roepstorff. "Hosting the Spirit of *Green light*." *TBA21 Journal* (2017). www.tba21.org/journals/article/Hosting-the-Spirit-of-Green-light

Eliasson, Olafur. "Assembling a Light, Assembling Communities." *TBA21 Journal*. 2017. www.tba21.org/journals/article/Assembling-Light-Assembling-Communities

Elliott, Karla. "Caring Masculinities: Theorizing an Emerging Concept." *Men and Masculinities* 19, no. 3 (2016): 240–259.

Ellis-Petersen, Hannah. "Art of the state: how the Venice Biennale is tackling the refugee crisis." *The Guardian*, May 16, 2017. www.theguardian.com/artanddesign/2017/may/16/venice-biennale-refugee-crisis-nsk-tunisia

Eltagouri, Marwa. "26 teenage girls were found dead at sea. Italian officials wonder if they were killed." *The Washington Post: WorldViews*, November 7, 2017. www.washington post.com/news/worldviews/wp/2017/11/07/26-teenage-women-were-found-dead-at-sea-italian-officials-wonder-if-they-were-killed/?utm_term=.a41937ffa3ab

Enloe, Cynthia. *Bananas, Beaches and Bases. Making Feminist Sense of International Politics*. Berkeley: University of California Press, 2014.

Entous, Adam, Siobhan Gorman, and Julian E. Barnes. "U.S. Tightens Drone Rules." *Wall Street Journal*. November 4, 2011. www.wsj.com/articles/SB100014240529702 04621904577013982672973836

"The Emperor Exhibits his Temper." *The New York Times*, January 5, 1896.

Epkenhans, Michael, "Krupp and the Imperial German Navy, 1898–1914: A Reassessment." *The Journal of Military History* 64, no. 2 (April 2000): 335–369.

Esmeir, Samera. "Colonial Experiments in Gaza." *Jadaliyya*. July 14, 2014. www.jadaliyya. com/Details/27434/Colonial-Experiments-in-Gaza

Espinosa, Julio García. "For an Imperfect Cinema." *Jump Cut: A Review of Contemporary Media*, no. 20 (1979): 24–26.

"Escape from Libya: Europe is sending African migrants home. Will they stay?" *The Economist*. March 28, 2018. www.economist.com/middle-east-and-africa/2018/03/28/europe-is-sending-african-migrants-home-will-they-stay

Estrada-Cañamares, Mireia, "Operation Sophia Before and After UN Security Council Resolution No 2240 (2015)." *European Papers* 1, no. 1 (2016): 185–191.

European Commission, Twitter post, March 6, 2019, 3:21 a.m. www.twitter.com/EU_ Commission/status/1103254203387047938

European Commission. "A European Agenda on Migration. Communication from the Commission to the European Parliament, the Council, the European Economic and Social Committee and the Committee of the Regions. COM (2015) 240. Brussels, May 13, 2015."

European Commission. "EU Action Plan Against Migrant Smuggling (2015–2020): Communication from the Commission to the European Parliament, the Council, the European Economic and Social Committee and the Committee of the Regions. COM (2015) 285. Brussels, May 27, 2015."

European Commission. "EU Emergency Trust Funds for Africa," ec.europa.eu/trust fundforafrica/content/homepage_en

European Commission. "Eurosur," ec.europa.eu/home-affairs/what-we-do/policies/ borders-and-visas/border-crossing/eurosur_en

European Commission. "Migration and mobility partnership signed between the EU and Morocco." Press release. Brussels, June 7, 2013. www.europa.eu/rapid/press-release_IP-13-513_en.htm

European Commission. "Smart lie-detection system to tighten EU's busy borders." ec.europa.eu/research/infocentre/article_en.cfm?artid=49726

European Commission. "Speech by President Jean-Claude Juncker at the debate in the European Parliament on the conclusions of the Special European Council on 23 April: "Tackling the migration 'crisis'." April 29, 2015. www.europa.eu/rapid/press-release_SPEECH-15-4896_en.htm

European Commission Trade Helpdesk. "Trade Regime and General Product Safety." trade.ec.europa.eu/tradehelp/trade-regime-and-general-product-safety

European Council on Refugees and Exiles, "Transporter illégalement des migrants vous expose à une peine d'amende de 1.000.000 à 3.000.000 F CFA," June 23, 2017. Weekly Bulletin.

European Migration Network, "Ad-Hoc Query on Impact of false/forged documents in the immigration and asylum procedures." December 4, 2017. ec.europa.eu/home-af fairs/sites/homeaffairs/files/2017.1204_lu_impact_of_falseforged_documents.pdf

European Parliament and the Council of the European Union. "Directive 2013/33/EU of the European Parliament and of the Council of 26 June 2013, Laying Down Standards for the Reception of Applicants for International Protection (Recast)," *Official Journal of the European Union*, L 180/96, June 29, 2013.

European Parliament and the Council of the European Union. "Regulation (EC) No. 562/2006 of the European Parliament and of the Council of 15 March 2006 establishing a Community Code on the rules governing the movement of persons across borders (Schengen Borders Code)," *Official Journal of the European Union*, April 13, 2006 L 105/1–31.

European Parliament and the Council of the European Union. "Regulation (EU) 2016/1624 of the European Parliament and of the Council of 14 September 2016 on the European Border and Coast Guard and amending Regulation (EU) 2016/399 of the European Parliament and of the Council and repealing Regulation (EC) No 863/2007 of the European Parliament and of the Council, Council Regulation (EC) No 2007/2004 and Council Decision 2005/267/EC," *Official Journal of the European Union*, September 16, 2016, L 251/1–76.

European Union. "Regulations, Directions and Other Acts." www.europa.eu/european-union/eu-law/legal-acts_en

European Union Agency for Fundamental Rights. "Under Watchful Eyes: Biometrics, EU IT Systems and Fundamental Rights," Luxembourg: Publications Office of the European Union, 2018. fra.europa.eu/en/publication/2018/biometrics-rights-protection

Europol, "Experts meet to tackle document fraud as key factor in serious and organised crime and terrorism." September 13, 2017. www.europol.europa.eu/newsroom/news/experts-meet-to-tackle-document-fraud-key-factor-in-serious-and-organised-crime-and-terrorism

"EU's Frontex border force deploys teams to Albania to halt migrants." *DW*, May 22, 2019. www.dw.com/en/eus-frontex-border-force-deploys-teams-to-albania-to-halt-migrants/a-48823658

Fabian, Johannes. *Time and the Other: How Anthropology Makes its Object*. New York: Columbia University Press, 2014.

Fassin, Didier. *Humanitarian Reason: A Moral History of the Present*. Berkeley: University of California Press, 2012.

Feher, Michel. *Rated Agency: Investee Politics in a Speculative Age*. New York: Zone Books, 2018.

Felman, Shoshana. *The Scandal of the Speaking Body Don Juan with J. L. Austin, or Seduction in Two Languages*. Stanford: Stanford University Press, 2002.

FIDH-Migreurop-EMH. *Frontex Between Greece and Turkey: At the Border of Denial*. www.frontexit.org/en/docs/49-frontexbetween-greece-and-turkey-the-border-of-denial/file

Fischer-Lescano, Andreas and Gunther Teubner. "Regime-Collisions: The Vain Search for Legal Unity in the Fragmentation of Global Law." *Michigan Journal of International Law* 25 (2004): 999–1046.

Fitch, Nathan, "Smartphone Use on the Refugee Trail," *Ars Technica*, April 17, 2016. www.arstechnica.co.uk/video/2016/04/refugee-smartphone-use/

Forensic Architecture, editors. *Forensis: The Architecture of Public Truth*. Berlin: Sternberg Press, 2014.

Foucault, Michel. "The Subject and Power." *Critical Inquiry* 8, no. 4 (Summer 1982): 777–795.

Foucault, Michel. *The History of Sexuality, Volume 1: An Introduction*. New York: Vintage Books, 1990 [1976].

Foucault, Michel. *"Society Must Be Defended": Lectures at the Collège de France, 1975–1976*. Translated by David Macey. New York: Picador, 2003.

Foucault, Michel. *Security, Territory, Population: Lectures at the Collège de France, 1977–78*. New York: Palgrave Macmillan, 2007.

Foucault, Michel. *The Birth of Biopolitics: Lectures at the Collège de France, 1978-79*. New York: Picador, 2008.

Franklin, Seb. *Control: Digitality as Cultural Logic*. Cambridge: MIT Press, 2015.

Freedman, Jane, "Sexual and Gender-Based Violence Against Refugee Women." *Reproductive Health Matters* 24, no. 47 (May 2016).

Freedman, Jane, "Violences de genre et 'crise' des réfugié.e.s en Europe." *Mouvements* 93 (Printemps 2018).

"Libysche Küstenwache soll deutsche Fregatte bedroht haben." Süddeutsche Zeitung. November 26, 2017. https://www.sueddeutsche.de/politik/seenotrettung-libysche-kuestenwache-soll-deutsche-fregatte-bedroht-haben-1.3765900

Frontex. "Frontex opens first risk analysis cell in Niger." November 27, 2018. frontex.europa.eu/media-centre/news-release/frontex-opens-first-risk-analysis-cell-in-niger-HQIoKi

Frontex. "Information Management." frontex.europa.eu/intelligence/information-management/

Frontex Risk Analysis Unit. "Common Integrated Risk Analysis Model, Version 2.0." www.europa.eu/capacity4dev/file/21158/download?token=D9Gkxx6U

Frontex Risk Analysis Unit, "Risk Analysis for 2016," March 2016. data.europa.eu/euodp/data/storage/f/2016-04-06T124932/Annula%20Risk%20Analysis%202016.pdf

Frontex Risk Analysis Unit, "Risk Analysis for 2017." February 2017. frontex.europa.eu/assets/Publications/Risk_Analysis/Annual_Risk_Analysis_2017.pdf

Fusco, Alex. "The Futile Destruction of the Jungle in Calais." Open Democracy, November 17, 2016. www.opendemocracy.net/en/mediterranean-journeys-in-hope/futile-destruction-of-jungle-in-calais/

Galison, Peter. "The Ontology of the Enemy: Norbert Wiener and the Cybernetic Vision." Critical Inquiry 21, no. 1 (1994): 228–366.

Galloway, Alexander. Protocol: How Control Exists after Decentralization. Cambridge: The MIT Press, 2006.

Galloway, Alexander and Eugene R. Thacker. The Exploit. Minneapolis: University of Minnesota Press, 2007.

Galloway, Alexander. Laruelle: Against the Digital. Minneapolis: University of Minnesota Press, 2014.

Galan Julve, Susana Maria. "Risk-Taking Activism: Counter-Spaces Against Public Sexual Violence in Post-January 25 Egypt." PhD diss., Rutgers University, 2019.

Gammeltoft-Hansen, Thomas and Tanja E. Alberts. "Sovereignty at Sea: The Law and Politics of Saving Lives in the Mare Liberum." DIIS Working Paper (2010): 1–31.

Gaonkar, Dilip. "After the Fictions: Notes on the Phenomenology of the Multitude." e-flux 58, October 2014. www.e-flux.com/journal/58/61187/after-the-fictions-notes-towards-a-phenomenology-of-the-multitude/

Garrison, Tom. Essentials of Oceanography. Belmont: Brooks/Cole Cengage Learning, 2009.

Ghosh, Bishnupriya. Global Icons: Apertures to the Popular. Durham: Duke University Press, 2011.

Gibson, J. James. The Ecological Approach to Visual Perception, Boston: Houghton Mifflin Harcourt, 1979.

Gilroy, Paul. Postcolonial Melancholia. New York: Columbia University Press, 2005.

Gitelman, Lisa, editor. "Raw Data" Is an Oxymoron. Cambridge: The MIT Press, 2013.

Gitlin, Todd. "The Wild-Eyed Coverage of the Caravan." Columbia Journalism Review, October 29, 2018.

Giuffrida, Angela. "Arrests in Italy as 26 Nigerian women and girls found dead." The Guardian: World, November 7, 2017. www.theguardian.com/world/2017/nov/07/italy-investigating-deaths-of-nigerian-women-thought-to-have-been-murdered

Glare, Peter G.W. Oxford Latin Dictionary. Oxford: Clarendon Press, 2010.

Glick, Jeremy Matthew. "Aphoristic Lines of Flight." In *The Coming Insurrection: Ironies of Forgetting Yet Forging the Past—An Anamnesis for George Jackson—Situations* 4, no. 2. www.hunter.cuny.edu/english/repository/files/Aphoristic%20Lines%20of%20Flight%20J%20GLICK%20-1.pdf

Glissant, Edouard. *Une nouvelle région du monde: Esthétique 1.* Paris: Gallimard, 2006.

Glissant, Edouard and Patrick Chamoiseau. *Quand les murs tombent: L'identité nationale hors-la-loi?* Paris: Galaade Éditions, 2007.

Gould, Deborah. *Moving Politics: Emotion and ACT UP's Fight Against AIDS.* Chicago: University of Chicago Press, 2009.

"Greece: Refuge 'Hotspots' Unsafe, Unsanitary; Women, Children Fearful, Unprotected; Lack Basic Shelter." *Human Rights Watch,* May 19, 2016. www.hrw.org/news/2016/05/19/greece-refugee-hotspots-unsafe-unsanitary

Gregg, Melissa and Gregory J. Seigworth, editors. *The Affect Theory Reader.* Durham: Duke University Press, 2010.

Grieg, Ellen. "Interview with Banu Cennetoğlu," "Banu Cennetoğlu at Chisendale: 29 June–26 August 2018," Exhibition handout, Chisenhale Gallery, n.d., unpaginated. www.chisenhale.org.uk/wp-content/uploads/BC_Exhibition_Handout_FINAL-1.pdf

Grigoriadou, Sofia, interview by Suzana Milevska, Skopje, Macedonia, December 23, 2018.

Grosz, Elizabeth. "Geopower." *Environment and Planning D: Society and Space,* 30 (2012): 971–988.

Grün, Gianna-Carina. "Follow the money: What are the EU's migration policy priorities?" *Deutsche Welle,* February 15, 2018. www.dw.com/en/follow-the-money-what-are-the-eus-migration-policy-priorities/a-42588136

Guilfoyle, Andrew. "On being there to help: A critical reflection on discourse and something postmodern for the social inclusion of refugee communities." *Tamara Journal for Critical Organization Inquiry* 18, no. 2 (September 2009): 146–159.

Gürsel, Duygu. "The Emergence of the Enterprising Refugee Discourse and Differential Inclusion in Turkey's Changing Migration Politics," *movements: Journal for Critical Migration and Border Regime Studies* 3, no. 2 (2017): 133–146.

Gursel, Zeynep Deyrim. *Image Brokers: Visualizing World News in the Age of Digital Circulation.* Berkeley: University of California Press, 2016.

Hall, Stuart. *Race, the Floating Signifier.* Northampton: Media Education Foundation, 1996.

Hamilton, Andy. "Adorno and Autonomy of Art." *Nostalgia for a Redeemed Future: Critical Theory,* edited by Stefano Giacchetti Ludovisi and G. Agostini. Rome: John Cabot University Press, 2009.

Han, Sora Y. *Letters of the Law: Race and the Fantasy of Colorblindness in American Law.* Stanford: Stanford University Press, 2015.

Hannam, Kevin, Mimi Sheller and John Urry. "Editorial: Mobilities, Immobilities and Moorings." *Mobilities* 1, no. 1 (2006): 1–22.

Hansen, Mark. *New Philosophy for New Media.* Cambridge: The MIT press, 2004.

Hansen, Mark. *Bodies in Code: Interfaces with Digital Media.* New York: Routledge, 2006.

Haraway, Donna. "A Cyborg Manifesto: Science, Technology, and Socialist-Feminism in the Late Twentieth Century." In *Simians, Cyborgs, and Women: The Reinvention of Nature.* New York: Routledge, 1999.

Haraway, Donna. *Staying with the Trouble: Making Kin in the Chthulucene.* Durham: Duke University Press, 2016.

Haraway, Donna. "Tentacular Thinking: Anthropocene, Capitalocene, Chthulucene." *e-flux*, no. 75 (2016). www.e-flux.com/journal/75/67125/tentacular-thinking-anthropocene-capitalocene-chthulucene/

Haritaworn, Jinthana. *Queer Lovers and Hateful Others: Regenerating Violent Times and Places.* London: Pluto Press, 2015.

Harney, Stefano, and Fred Moten. *The Undercommons: Fugitive Planning and Black Study.* New York: Minor Compositions, 2013.

Harries, John, Linda Fibiger, Joan Smith, Tal Adler, Anna Szöke. "Exposure: the ethics of making, sharing and displaying photographs of human remains." *Human Remains and Violence: An Interdisciplinary Journal* 4, no. 1 (2018): 3–24.

Hartman, Saidiya. "Venus in Two Acts." *Small Axe* 12, no. 2 (2008): 1–14.

Hartman, Saidiya. "The Belly of the World: A Note on Black Women's Labors" in *Afro-Pessimism: An Introduction*, edited by Frank B. Wilderson III. Minneapolis: Racked & Dispatched, 2017: 80–96.

Hartman, Saidiya. "The Burdened Individuality of Freedom." In *Afro-Pessimism: An Introduction*, edited by Frank B. Wilderson III. Minneapolis: Racked & Dispatched, 2017: 31–48.

Hayles, N. Katherine. *How We Became Posthuman: Virtual Bodies in Cybernetics Literature and Informatics.* Chicago: University of Chicago Press, 1999.

Hayles, N. Katherine. *Unthought: The Power of the Cognitive Non-Conscious.* Chicago: University of Chicago Press, 2017.

Heck, Gerda and Sabine Hess. "European Restabilization Attempts of the External Borders and their Consequences." *HarekAct.* June 20, 2016. harekact.bordermonitoring.eu/2016/06/20/european-restabilization-attempts-of-the-external-borders-and-their-consequences/

Hegde, Radha S. *Mediating Migration.* Cambridge: Polity Press, 2016.

Hegel, Georg Wilhelm Friedrich. *Introduction to the Philosophy of History: with Selections from the Philosophy of Right.* Translated by Leo Rauch. Indianapolis: Hackett Publishing, 1988.

Heller, Charles and Lorenzo Pezzani. "Ebbing and Flowing: The EU's Shifting Practices of (Non-)Assistance and Bordering in a Time of Crisis." *Near Futures Online* 1, 2016. www.nearfuturesonline.org/ebbing-and-flowing-the-eus-shifting-practices-of-non-assistance-and-bordering-in-a-time-of-crisis/

Heller, Charles, Lorenzo Pezzani and Situ Research. *Report on the Left-to-Die Boat.* London: Forensic Architecture, 2012. www.forensic-architecture.org/wp-content/uploads/2014/05/FO-report.pdf

Heller, Charles and Lorenzo Pezzani. "A Disobedient Gaze: Strategic Interventions in the Knowledge(s) of Maritime Borders." *Postcolonial Studies* 16, no. 3 (2013): 289–298.

Heller, Charles and Lorenzo Pezzani. *Death by Rescue. The Lethal Effects of the EU's Policies of Non-Assistance.* Forensic Architecture, 2016. www.deathbyrescue.org/

Heller, Charles and Lorenzo Pezzani. *Blaming the Rescuers: Criminalising Solidarity, (Re)enforcing Deterrence.* Forensic Architecture, 2017. www.blamingtherescuers.org/

Heller, Charles and Lorenzo Pezzani. *Mare Clausum: Italy and the EU's undeclared operation to stem migration across the Mediterranean.* Forensic Architecture, 2018. www.forensic-architecture.org/wp-content/uploads/2018/05/2018-05-07-FO-Mare-Clausum-full-EN.pdf

Heller, Charles, and Lorenzo Pezzani. "Hostile Environment"(s): Sensing migration across weaponized terrains." in *Ways of Knowing Cities*, edited by Laura Kurgan and Dare Brawley. New York: Columbia Books on Architecture and the City, 2019.

Heller, Charles and Lorenzo Pezzani. "Contentious Crossings: Struggles and Alliances for Freedom of Movement Across the Mediterranean Sea." *South Atlantic Quarterly*, forthcoming issue (2019).

Heller, Charles, Lorenzo Pezzani and Maurice Stierl. "Disobedient Sensing and Border Struggles at the Maritime Frontier of Europe," *Spheres - Journal for Digital Cultures*, 4 (2017): 1–15.

Helmreich, Stefan. "Nature/Culture/Seawater." *American Anthropologist* 113, no. 1 (2011): 132–144.

Henry, Jules. "Homeostasis, Society, and Evolution: A Critique." *The Scientific Monthly* 6 (1955): 300–309.

Herscher, Andrew and Anooradha Iyer Siddiqi. "Spatial Violence," *Architectural Theory Review* 19, no. 3 (2014): 269–277.

Hess, Sabine und Bernd Kasparek. *Grenzregime: Diskurse, Praktiken, Institutionen in Europe.* Berlin: Assoziation A, 2010.

Hess, Sabine, Bernd Kasparek, Stefanie Kron, Mathias Rodatz, Maria Schwertl, and Simon Sontowski, editors. *Der lange Sommer der Migration. Grenzregime III.* Berlin: Assoziation A, 2017.

Higgins, Charlotte. "Banu Cennetoglu: 'As long as I have the resources, I will make *The List* more visible,'" Interview, *The Guardian*, June 20, 2018. www.theguardian.com/world/2018/jun/20/banu-cennetoglu-interview-turkish-artist-the-list-europe-migrant-crisis

Higgins, Charlotte. "Boat in which hundreds of migrants died displayed at Venice Biennale." *The Guardian* Art & Design Section, May 7, 2019. www.theguardian.com/artanddesign/2019/may/07/boat-in-which-hundreds-of-migrants-died-displayed-at-venice-biennale

Hodder, Ian. *Entangled: An Archaeology of the Relationships between Humans and Things.* Malden: Wiley-Blackwell, 2013.

Horii, Satoko. "The Effect of Frontex's Risk Analysis on the European Border Controls." *European Politics and Society* 17, no. 2 (2016): 242–258.

Human Rights Watch, "The EU General Data Protection Regulation." www.hrw.org/news/2018/06/06/eu-general-data-protection-regulation

Huyssen, Andreas. *After the Great Divide: Modernism, Mass Culture, Postmodernism.* Bloomington: Indiana University Press, 1986.

"ICS: Rescue of all persons at sea is a must." *World Maritime News.* October 29, 2015. www.worldmaritimenews.com/archives/141521/ics-rescue-of-all-persons-in-distress-at-sea-is-a-must/

"Immigration: Italy launches Mare Nostrum, 400 more saved." *ANSAmed.* October 15, 2013. www.ansamed.info/ansamed/en/news/sections/generalnews/2013/10/15/Immigration-Italy-launches-Mare-Nostrum-400-saved_9466386.html

Interact: European Regional Development Fund, "Interreg response to migration-related challenges working paper." June 2016. www.interact-eu.net/download/file/fid/3919

International Council on Human Rights Policy. *Irregular Migration, Migrant Smuggling and Human Rights: Towards Coherence*. International Council on Human Rights Policy, 2010. www.ichrp.org/files/summaries/41/122_pb_en.pdf

International Organization on Migration. "Overcoming Barriers: Human Mobility and Development." *National Institute on Aging*, 2005. oppenheimer.mcgill.ca/IMG/pdf/HDR_2009_EN_Complete.pdf

International Council on Human Rights Policy. *Irregular Migration, Migrant Smuggling and Human Rights: Towards Coherence*. 2010. www.ichrp.org/files/summaries/41/122_pb_en.pdf

Internet World Stats. www.internetworldstats.com/stats.htm

"Interview with Eyal Weizman." *International Review of the Red Cross* 98, no. 1 (2016): 21–35.

"It is time to end this migrant madness." *Daily Mail*. Comment Section. July 29, 2015. www.dailymail.co.uk/news/article-3179339/DAILY-MAIL-COMMENT-time-end-migrant-madness.html

"Italy seals Libya colonial deal," *BBC News*, August 30, 2008. news.bbc.co.uk/2/hi/7589557.stm

Jackson, George. *Soledad Brother: The Prison letters of George Jackson*. New York: Bantam Books Inc., 1970.

Jones, Bryony. "Calais 'Jungle': Demolition of Massive Migrant Camps Begins." *CNN*, October 25, 2016. www.cnn.com/2016/10/25/europe/calais-jungle-demolition-begins/index.html

Kalin, Walter. "Displacement Caused by the Effects of Climate Change: Who Will be Affected and What Are the Gaps in the Normative Framework for Their Protection?" *Brookings.edu*, October 10, 2008.

Kandel, Eric R. *In Search of Memory: The Emergence of a New Science of the Mind*. New York: W.W. Norton, 2007.

Kant, Immanuel, translated by Werner S. Pluhar. *Critique of Judgment*. Indianapolis, Ind: Hackett Publishing Company, 1987.

Kasparek, Bernard and Marc Speer. "Of Hope. Ungarn und der lange Sommer der Migration." *Bordermonitoring.eu*, 2015. www.bordermonitoring.eu/ungarn/2015/09/of-hope/

Kaufmann, Vincent. *Re-thinking Mobility: Contemporary Sociology*. New York: Routledge, 2017.

Keenan, Thomas. "Getting the Dead to Tell Me What Happened: Justice, Prosopopoeia, and Forensic Afterlives." *Forensis: The Architecture of Public Truth*, edited by Forensic Architecture. Berlin: Sternberg Press, 2014.

Kennedy, Merritt. "Italy Probes Deaths of 26 Nigerian Women and Girls at Sea." *NPR*. Nov 6, 2017. www.npr.org/sections/thetwo-way/2017/11/06/562335869/italy-probes-deaths-of-26-nigerian-women-at-sea

Keshavarz, Mahmoud and Eric Snodgrass. "Orientations of Europe: Boats, the Mediterranean Sea and the Materialities of Contemporary Mobility Regimes." *borderlands* 17, no. 2, 2018. www.borderlands.net.au/vol17no2_2018/kesharvarz&snodgrass_orientations.pdf

Kingsley, Patrick and Sima Diab. "Passport, Lifejacket, Lemons: What Syrian Refugees Pack for the Crossing to Europe." *The Guardian*, 2015. www.theguardian.com/world/ng-interactive/2015/sep/04/syrian-refugees-pack-for-the-crossing-to-europe-crisis

Knorr Cetina, Karin. "The Synthetic Situation: Interactionism for a Global World." *Symbolic Interaction* 32, no. 1 (2009): 61–87.

Kosuth, Joseph. *Art After Philosophy and After: Collected Writings 1966–1990*. Cambridge: The MIT Press, 1991.

Krauss, Rosalind E. *The Originality of the Avant-garde and Other Modernist Myths*. Cambridge: The MIT Press, 1985.

Kuntsman, Adi, editor. *Selfie Citizenship*. London: Palgrave Macmillan, 2017.

Kurgan, Laura. *Close Up at a Distance: Mapping, Technology and Politics*. New York: Zone Books, 2013.

La Chapelle Debout, Twitter post, May 19, 2019, 5:09 a.m. www.twitter.com/chapelle debout/status/1130083092029485056

Laqueur, Thomas W. *The Work of the Dead: A Cultural History of Mortal Remains*. Princeton: Princeton University Press, 2015.

Laplanche, Jean and Jean-Bertrand Pontalis. *The Language of Psycho-Analysis*. New York: W.W. Norton, 1974.

Laqueur, Thomas W. *The Work of the Dead: A Cultural History of Mortal Remains*. Princeton: Princeton University Press, 2015.

Larkin, Brian. "The Politics and Poetics of Infrastructure." *The Annual Review of Anthropology* 42 (2013): 327–343.

Larrabee, F. Stephen. "Russia, Ukraine, and Central Europe: The Return of Geopolitics." *Journal of International Affairs* 63, no. 2, (Spring / Summer 2010): 33–52.

"Last Groups to Leave for Britain As Sangatte Closure Looms." *UNHCR News and Stories*, December 13, 2002. www.unhcr.org/news/latest/2002/12/3dfa051b4/groups-leave-britain-sangatte-closure-looms.html

Latour, Bruno. "The Anthropocene and the Destruction of the Image of the Globe." Gifford Lecture, Edinburgh, 2013. www.ed.ac.uk/schools-departments/humanities-soc-sci/news-events/lectures/gifford-lectures/archive/series-2012-2013/bruno-latour/lecture-four

Laurent, Olivier. "See How Refugees Use Selfies to Document Their Journey." *TIME Magazine*. October 8, 2015. www.time.com/4064988/refugee-crisis-selfies/

"Legal action against Italy over its coordination of Libyan Coast Guard pull-backs resulting in migrant deaths and abuse." *Global Legal Action Network*. May 8, 2018. www.glanlaw.org/single-post/2018/05/08/Legal-action-against-Italy-over-its-coordination-of-Libyan-Coast-Guard-pull-backs-resulting-in-migrant-deaths-and-abuse

Lenner, Katharina and Lewis Turner, "Making Refugees Work? The Politics of Integrating Syrian Refugees into the Labor Market in Jordan." *Middle East Critique* (2018): 1–31.

Lillehammer, Hallvard. "Values of Art and the Ethical Question." *The British Journal of Aesthetics* 48, no. 4 (October 1, 2008): 376–394.

Lipsitz, George. "Academic Politics and Social Change." *Cultural Studies and Political Theory*, edited by Jodi Dean. Ithaca: Cornell University Press, 2000.

Lynes, Krista. "Between a Rock and a Hard Place: Performative Politics and Queer Migrant Activisms." *Ada: Journal of Gender, New Media and Technology* 14 (2018). www.adanewmedia.org/2018/11/issue14-lynes/

Lynes, Krista. "Drowned at Sea: What Haunts the Stories of Trafficked Women?" *Feminist Media Studies* 18, no. 6 (2018).

Lynes, Krista. "Decolonizing Corporeality: Teresa Margolles's Lively Corpses." *Social Text* 37, no. 4, 2019.

Macdonald, Sharon. "Contentious Heritage." *TRACES* 5 (April 2018): 6–7. www.traces.polimi.it/wp-content/uploads/2018/07/traces_mag_05_WEB.pdf

Manning, Erin. *Relationscapes: Movement, Art, Philosophy*. MIT Press, 2009.

"March in Lampedusa to honour victims of 2013 shipwreck." ANSA Med. October 3, 2018. www.ansamed.info/ansamed/en/news/sections/generalnews/2018/10/03/march-in-lampedusa-to-honour-victims-of-2013-shipwreck_66e17199-36d9-4b9b-a233-4d67f9a53be5.html

Marks, Laura U. *Enfoldment and Infinity: An Islamic Genealogy of New Media Art*. Cambridge: The MIT Press, 2010.

Marx, Karl. *Ökonomisch-philosophische Manuskripte*. Hamburg: Felix Meiner-Verlag, 2005.

Massey, Doreen. *Space, Place and Gender*. Minneapolis: University of Minnesota Press, 1994.

Massumi, Brian. *Parables for the Virtual: Movement, Affect, Sensation*. Durham: Duke University Press, 2007.

Massumi, Brian. "The Future Birth of the Affective Fact: The political ontology of threat." In *The Affect Theory Reader*, edited by Melissa Gregg and Gregory J. Seigworth. Durham: Duke University Press, 2010.

Matsuda, Mari J. "When the First Quail Calls: Multiple Consciousness as Jurisprudential Method." *Women's Rights Law Reporter* 14 (1992): 297–300.

Mayblin, Lucy. "Politics, Publics, and Aylan Kurdi." *The Iconic Image in Social Media*, edited by The Visual Social Media Lab, 2015. www.visualsocialmedialab.org/projects/the-iconic-image-on-social-media

Mbembe, Achille. "Necropolitics," *Public Culture* 15, no. 1 (2003): 11–40.

Mbembe, Achille. *On the Postcolony*. Berkeley: University of California Press, 2001.

McIntyre, Niamh and Mark Rice-Oxley. "It's 34,361 and rising: how the List tallies Europe's migrant bodycount," *The Guardian*, June 20, 2018. www.theguardian.com/world/2018/jun/20/the-list-europe-migrant-bodycount

McLagan, Megan and Yates McKee, editors. *Sensible Politics: The Visual Culture of Non-Governmental Activism*. Cambridge: The MIT Press, 2012.

McVeigh, Tracy. "Temperatures Plunge as Refugee Army Trudges Across Europe." *The Guardian*, January 24, 2016. www.theguardian.com/world/2016/jan/24/queues-refugees-lengthen-winter-descends-border-serbia

Médecins Sans Frontières (MSF), "MSF calls for large scale search and rescue operation in the Mediterranean." April 20, 2015. www.msf.org/article/msf-calls-large-scale-search-and-rescue-operation-mediterranean

Médecins Sans Frontières (MSF), "EU: your fences kill. Provide safe and legal passage." September 11, 2015. www.msf.org/eu-your-fences-kill-provide-safe-and-legal-passage

Merleau-Ponty, Maurice and James M. Edie. *The Primacy of Perception: And Other Essays on Phenomenological Psychology, the Philosophy of Art, History and Politics*. Chicago: Northwestern University Press, 2015.

Merriman, Peter. *Mobility, Space and Culture*. New York: Routledge, 2012.

Mezzadra, Sandro and Brett Neilson. *Border as Method, or, the Multiplication of Labor*. Durham: Duke University Press, 2013.

Mezzadra, Sandro and Beppe Caccia, "What can a ship do?" *Viewpoint Magazine*. January 7, 2019. www.viewpointmag.com/2019/01/07/what-can-a-ship-do/

Michalarou, Efi. "ART-PRESENTATION: The Mapping Journey Project." www.dream ideamachine.com/en/?p=11710

Mignolo, Walter. "Geopolitics of sensing and knowing: On (de)coloniality, border thinking, and epistemic disobedience" *Confero* 1, no. 1, 2013: 129–150.

"The Migrants' Files." www.themigrantsfiles.com

Migreurop. *Atlas of Migration in Europe: A Critical Geography of Migration Policies*. London: New Internationalist Publications, 2013.

Milevska, Suzana. "Participatory Art: A Paradigm Shift from Objects to Subjects." *Springerin* 12, no. 2 (2006): 18–23. www.springerin.at/dyn/heft_text.php? textid=1761&lang=en

Milevska, Suzana. "The Internalisation of the Discourse of Institutional Critique and the 'Unhappy Consciousness'" In *Evaluating and Formative Goals of Art Criticism in Recent (De)territorialized Contexts*, seminar proceedings, edited by Suzana Milevska. Skopje: National Gallery, 2009: 2–6.

Milevska, Suzana, editor. *On Productive Shame, Reconciliation, and Agency*. Berlin: Sternberg Press, 2016.

Milevska, Suzana. "'Infelicitous' Participatory Acts on the Neoliberal Stage." *p/art/icipate: Kulturaktiv gestalten* 07 (October 2016). www.p-art-icipate.net/cms/infelicitous-participatory-acts-on-the-neoliberal-stage/

Milevska, Suzana. "The Grammar and Politics of Commoning." *Commons as Work in Progress*. Trondheim: LevArt, (in print).

Milevska, Suzana. "Shameful Objects, Apologising Subjects: On Participatory Institutional Critique and Productive Shame." Paper presented at the conference "Narrating Culture(s) in Museums and Exhibitions," Leuphana University, Lüneburg, Sweden, January 18–19, 2018.

Milevska, Suzana. "Relations, Participations, and Other Dialogical Frameworks." *Dialogical Interventions*, edited by Martin Krenn and Gerald Bast. Berlin: Angewandte/De Gruyter, 2019.

Milevska, Suzana, editor. *Contentious Objects, Ashamed Subjects*. Exhibition Catalogue. Milan: Politecnico di Milano, 2019.

Minto-Coy, Indianna D. and Evan Berman. *Public Administration and Policy in the Caribbean*. London: CRC Press, 2015.

Miroff, Nick. "U.S. militia groups head to border, stirred by Trump's call to arms." *The Washington Post*, November 3, 2018. www.washingtonpost.com/world/national-security/us-militia-groups-head-to-border-stirred-by-trumps-call-to-arms/2018/11/03/ff96826c-decf-11e8-b3f0-62607289efee_story.html?utm_term=.d2e0639bf594

Mitchell, Katharyne and Matthew Sparke. "Hotspot Geopolitics versus Geosocial Solidarity: Contending Constructions of Safe Space for Migrants in Europe." *Environment and Planning D: Society and Space* (2018): 1–21.

Mitropoulos, Angela and Brett Neilson. "Exceptional Times, Non-Governmental Spacings, and Impolitical Movements." *Vacarme*. January 8, 2006. www.vacarme.org/article484.html

Mitter, Siddhartha. "What Does It Mean to Be Black and Look at This?" *Hyperallergic*. March 24, 2017. www.hyperallergic.com/368012/what-does-it-mean-to-be-black-and-look-at-this-a-scholar-reflects-on-the-dana-schutz-controversy/

Monzini, Paola, Nourhan Abdel Aziz, and Ferruccio Pastore. *The Changing Dynamics of Cross-border Human Smuggling and Trafficking in the Mediterranean*. New-Med Research Network. October 2015.

Moser, Caroline and Fiona C. Clark, editors. *Victims, Perpetrators or Actors? Gender, Armed Conflict and Political Violence*. London: Zed Books, 2001.

Moten, Fred. "The Case of Blackness." *Criticism* 50, no. 2 (Spring 2008).

Moten, Fred. "The Touring Machine (Flesh Thought Inside Out)." In *Plastic Materialities: Politics, Legality, and Metamorphosis in the Work of Catherine Malabou*, edited by Brenna Bhandar and Jonathan Goldberg-Hiller. Durham: Duke University Press, 2015.

Moyn, Samuel. *Not Enough: Human Rights in an Unequal World*. Cambridge: Harvard University Press, 2018.

Mozur, Paul. "One Month, 500,000 Face Scans: How China Is Using A.I. to Profile a Minority." *The New York Times*. April 14, 2019. www.nytimes.com/2019/04/14/technology/china-surveillance-artificial-intelligence-racial-profiling.html

Mudu, Pierpaolo and Sutapa Chattopadhyay, editors. *Migration, Squatting and Radical Autonomy*. London: Routledge, 2017.

Munster, Anna. *Materializing New Media: Embodiment in Information Aesthetics*. Hanover: Dartmouth College Press, 2006.

Nadeau, Barbie Latza, "Twenty-six young Nigerian migrant women laid to rest in Italy." *CNN: World*, November 17, 2017. edition.cnn.com/2017/11/17/europe/salerno-migrants-funeral/index.html

Nancy, Jean-Luc. *Being Singular Plural*, translated by Robert D. Richardson and Anne O'Byrne. Stanford: Stanford University Press, 2000.

Nancy, Jean-Luc. The Inoperative Community, edited by Peter Connor. Minneapolis: Minnesota University Press, 1991.

Nail, Thomas. *The Figure of the Migrant*. Stanford: Stanford University Press, 2015.

Nail, Thomas. *Theory of the Border*. Oxford: Oxford University Press, 2016.

Nail, Thomas. "We are Entering a New Epoch: The Century of the Migrant." *Aeon*, December 2016. www.aeon.co/ideas/we-are-entering-a-new-epoch-the-century-of-the-migrant

Nail, Thomas. *Being and Motion*. Oxford: Oxford University Press, 2018.

Nail, Thomas. "The Hordes Are Banging on the Gates of Europe?" *History News Network*. October 25, 2015. www.historynewsnetwork.org/article/160993

Nail, Thomas. *Theory of the Image*. Oxford: Oxford University Press, 2019.

Naukkarinen, Ossi. "Aesthetics and Mobility-A Short Introduction to a Moving Field." *Contemporary Aesthetics* 1, no. 1, 2005.

Neilson, Brett. "Between Governance and Sovereignty: Remaking the Borderscape to Australia's North," *Local-Global Journal* 8 (2010). mams.rmit.edu.au/56k3qh2kfcx1.pdf

Nevins, Joseph. "A Beating Worse than Death: Imagining and Contesting Violence in the U.S.-Mexico Borderlands." *AmeriQuests* 2, no. 1 (2005): 1–25.

Nevins, Joseph. *Operation Gatekeeper: The Rise of the "Illegal Alien" and the Making of the U.S.-Mexico Boundary*. New York: Routledge, 2002.

New Keywords Collective, "Europe/Crisis: New Keywords of 'the Crisis' in and of 'Europe.'" *Near Futures Online 1* (March 2016): 1–45. www.nearfuturesonline.org/europe crisis-new-keywords-of-crisis-in-and-of-europe/

Newman, Michael. "Médecins Sans Frontières-France: Tensions Arising from the "Migration" Projects." *Humanitarian Alternatives*, March 2019. www.alternatives-humanitaires.org/en/2019/03/25/medecins-sans-frontieres-france-tensions-arising-migration-projects/

Nielsen, Nikolaj. "Investigation exposed: How Morocco lobbies EU for its Western Sahara claim." *euobserver*. November 23, 2018. www.euobserver.com/investigations/143426

Nimako, Kwame and Glenn Willemsen. *The Dutch Atlantic: Slavery, Abolition and Emancipation*. London: Pluto Press, 2011.

Notes from Nowhere, *We Are Everywhere: The Irresistible Rise of Global Anticapitalism*. London; New York: Verso, 2003.

Nourhussen, Seada. "Macron vergat neokolonialisme." *Trouw*. July 13, 2017. www.trouw.nl/home/macron-vergat-neokolonialisme~ab31b791/

"Omar al-Bashir: Sudan's Ousted President." *BBC News: Africa*, April 11, 2019. www.bbc.com/news/world-africa-16010445

O'Sullivan, Simon. "The Aesthetics of Affect: Thinking Art Beyond Representation." *Angelaki: Journal of Theoretical Humanities* 6, no. 3 (2001): 125–135.

Padovani, Marcelle. "Les passeurs sont souvent des migrants auxquels on offre le passage gratis." *Le Nouvel Observateur*. November 3, 2015. www.nouvelobs.com/monde/migrants/20151102.OBS8685/les-passeurs-sont-souvent-des-migrants-auxquels-on-offre-le-passage-gratis.html

Pallister-Wilkins, Polly. "The Humanitarian Policing of 'Our Sea.'" *Border Criminologies Blog*, Faculty of Law, University of Oxford, 2015.

Panagia, Davide. *Rancière's Sentiments*. Durham: Duke University Press, 2018.

Panagiotidis, Efthimia and Vassilis Tsianos. "Denaturalizing 'camps': Überwachen und Entschleuningen in der Schengener Ägäis-Zone." in *Turbulente Ränder: Neue Perspektiven auf Migration an den Grenzen Europas*, edited by Transit Migration Forschungsgruppe. Bielefeld: transcript, 2007.

Papademetriou, Theresa. "European Union: Proposals to Establish a New European Border and Coast Guard." December 18, 2017. www.loc.gov/law/foreign-news/article/european-union-proposals-to-establish-a-new-european-border-and-coast-guard/

Papadopoulos, Dimitris, Niamh Stephenson and Vassilis Tsianos. *Escape Routes: Control and Subversion in the Twenty-First Century*. London: Pluto Press, 2008.

Papadopoulos, Dimitris and Vassilis S. Tsianos. "After Citizenship: Autonomy of Migration, Organisational Ontology and Mobile Commons." *Citizenship Studies* 17, no. 2 (2013).

Papastavridis, Efthymios. "Rescuing 'Boat People' in the Mediterranean Sea: The Responsibility of States under the Law of the Sea." *European Journal of International Law*. May 31, 2011. www.ejiltalk.org/rescuing-boat-people-in-the-mediterranean-sea-the-responsibility-of-states-under-the-law-of-the-sea/

Papastavridis, Efthymios. "The Right of Visit on the High Seas in a Theoretical Perspective: Mare Liberum versus Mare Clausum Revisited." *Leiden Journal of International Law* 24, no. 1 (2011): 45–69.

Parker, Cassidy. "The Missing Persons Task Team: Fleshing Out the Bones of the Apartheid Era," *The Cradle of Humankind*, June 20, 2016. www.maropeng.co.za/news/en try/the-missing-persons-task-team-fleshing-out-the-bones-of-the-apartheid-era.

Parks, Lisa. "Digging into Google Earth: An analysis of "Crisis in Darfur." *Geoforum*, 40 (2009): 535–545.

Parks, Lisa and James Schwoch, editors. *Down to Earth: Satellite Technologies, Industries, and Cultures*. New Brunswick: Rutgers University Press, 2012.

Parliamentary Assembly of the Council of Europe (PACE). *Lives Lost in the Mediterranean Sea: Who is Responsible? Report of the Committee on Migration, Refugees and Displaced Persons*. Strasbourg: Council of Europe, 2012. assembly.coe.int/Committee Docs/2012/20120329_mig_RPT.EN.pdf

Parliamentary Assembly of the Council of Europe (PACE). *The Interception and Rescue at Sea of Asylum Seekers, Refugees and Irregular Migrants*, 2011. assembly.coe.int/nw/ xml/XRef/Xref-XML2HTML-en.asp?fileid=18008&lang=en

Parliamentary Assembly of the Council of Europe (PACE). *The "left-to-die boat": Actions and Reactions*. Strasbourg: Council of Europe, 2014. assembly.coe.int/nw/xml/XRef/ Xref-XML2HTML-en.asp?fileid=20940&lang=en

Perraudin, Frances. "'Marauding' migrants threaten standard of living, says foreign secretary." *The Guardian*, August 10, 2015. www.theguardian.com/uk-news/2015/ aug/09/african-migrants-threaten-eu-standard-living-philip-hammond

Perkowski, Nina. "Deaths, Interventions, Humanitarianism and Human Rights in the Mediterranean 'Migration Crisis'." *Mediterranean Politics* 21, no. 2 (2016): 331–335.

Pessar, Patricia R. and Sarah J. Mahler, "Transnational Migration: Bringing Gender in." *The International Migration Review* 37, no. 3 (Fall 2003): 813–846.

Pettigrove, Glen. "Hannah Arendt and Collective Forgiving." *The Journal of Social Philosophy* 37, no. 4 (Winter 2006): 483–500.

Pezzani, Lorenzo. *Liquid traces: Spatial Practices, Aesthetics and Humanitarian Dilemmas at the Maritime Borders of the EU*. London: Centre for Research Architecture, Department of Visual Cultures, Goldsmiths University, 2015.

Pfeifer, Michelle. "Becoming Flesh: Refugee Hunger Strike and Embodiments of Refusal in German Necropolitical Spaces," *Citizenship Studies* 22, no. 5 (2018): 459–474.

Pickles, John, editor. *A History of Spaces: Cartographic Reason, Mapping and the Geo-Coded World*. London: Routledge, 2004.

Pickles, John, editor. *Ground Truth: The Social Implications of Geographical Information Systems*. New York: Guilford, 1995.

Pieper, Tobias. *Die Gegenwart der Lager. Zur Mikrophysik der Herrschaft in der deutschen Flüchtlingspolitik*. Münster: Westfälisches Dampfboot, 2008.

Plato. *Timaeus*. Translated by Peter Kalkavage, Second Edition, Focus, 2016.

Povinelli, Elizabeth. *Economies of Abandonment: Social Belonging and Endurance in Late Liberalism*. Durham: Duke University Press, 2011.

Probitz, Lin. "The Strength of Weak Commitment." *The Iconic Image in Social Media*, edited by The Visual Social Media Lab, 2015. www.visualsocialmedialab.org/projects/the-iconic-image-on-social-media

Puar, Jasbir K. *Terrorist Assemblages: Homonationalism in Queer Times*. Durham: Duke University Press, 2007.

Puar, Jasbir K. *The Right to Maim*. Durham: Duke University Press, 2017.

Rahman-Jones, Imran. "The History of the Calais 'Jungle' and how it's changed since 1999." *BBC*, October 24, 2016.

Rancière, Jacques. *Dissensus: On Politics and Aesthetics*. London: Bloomsbury Press, 2010.

Rancière, Jacques. "Ten Theses on Politics." *Theory and Event* 5, no. 3 (2001).

Rancière, Jacques. *The Politics of Aesthetics. The Distribution of the Sensible*. London, New York: Continuum, 2004.

Rancière, Jacques. "The Politics of Aesthetics." November 2006. roundtable.kein.org/node/463

Reinbold, Fabian. "Hallo Facebook, dieser Mann is kein Terrorist." *Spiegel Online*. January 19, 2017. www.spiegel.de/netzwelt/web/angela-merkel-ein-selfie-mit-folgen-hallo-facebook-dieser-mann-ist-kein-terrorist-a-1130400.html

Renzi, Matteo. "Helping the Migrants is Everyone's Duty." *The New York Times*. Opinion Section. April 22, 2015. www.nytimes.com/2015/04/23/opinion/matteo-renzi-helping-the-migrants-is-everyones-duty.html?_r=2

Rigo, Enrica. "Citizenship at Europe's Borders: Some Reflections on the Post-Colonial Condition of Europe in the Context of EU Enlargement." *Citizenship Studies* 9, no. 1 (2005): 3–22.

Rigo, Enrica. "Re-gendering the Border: Chronicles of Women's Resistance and Unexpected Alliances from the Mediterranean Border." *ACME: An International Journal for Critical Geographies* 18, no. 1 (2019): 173–186.

Ritaine, Evelyne. "Blessures de frontière en Méditerranée: Introduction." *Culture et Conflits* 99–100 (automne/hiver 2015): 11–24.

Roberts, Dan. "Sweet Brexit: What Sugar Tells Us about Britain's Future Outside the EU." *The Guardian*, Business Section. March 27, 2017. www.theguardian.com/business/2017/mar/27/brexit-sugar-beet-cane-tate-lyle-british-sugar

Roberts, Neil. *Freedom as Marronnage*. Chicago: University of Chicago Press, 2015.

Robinson, Marc, editor. *Altogether Elsewhere: Writers on Exile*. San Diego: Harcourt Brace & Company, 1994.

Ronzitti, Natalino. "The Treaty on Friendship, Partnership, and Cooperation between Italy and Libya: New Prospects for Cooperation in the Mediterranean?" *Bulletin of Italian Politics* 1, no. 1 (2009): 125–133.

Rothberg, Michael. "From Gaza to Warsaw: Mapping Multidirectional Memory." *Criticism* 53, no. 4 (2011): 523–548.

Römhild, Regina. "Reflexive Europeanization, or: Makings of Europe." In *TRACES* 5 (April 2018): 4–5. www.traces.polimi.it/wp-content/uploads/2018/07/traces_mag_05_WEB.pdf

Rowe, Victoria. "Armenian Women Refugees at the End of Empire: Strategies of Survival," in *Refugees and the End of Empire: Imperial Collapse and Forced Migration in the Twentieth Century*, edited by Panikos Pnayi and Pippa Virdee. London: Palgrave, 2011.

Ruffell, Alastair and Jennifer McKinley. *Geoforensics*. Chichester: Wiley-Blackwell, 2008.

Rygiel, Kim. "Bordering Solidarities: Migrant Activism and the Politics of Movement and Camps at Calais." *Citizenship studies*, 15.01, 2011, 1–19.

Said, Edward W. *Orientalism*. New York: Pantheon Books, 1978.

Said, Edward W. *Reflections on Exile and Other Essays*. London: Granta, 2012.

Sanchez, Gabriella, Rezart Hoxhaj, Sabrina Nardin, Andrew Geddes, Luigi Achilli, and Sona Kalantaryan. "A study of the communication channels used by migrants and asylum seekers in Italy, with a particular focus on online and social media," Luxembourg: Publications Office of the European Union, 2018.

Sassen, Saskia. *Expulsions: Brutality and Complexity in the Global Economy*. Cambridge: Harvard University Press, 2014.

Sassen, Saskia. *Territory, Authority, Rights: From Medieval to Global Assemblages*. Princeton: Princeton University Press, 2006.

Saucier, P. Khalil and Tryon P. Woods, "Ex Aqua: The Mediterranean Basin, Africans on the Move and the Politics of Policing." *Theoria: Journal of Social and Political Theory* 61, no. 141 (December 2014): 55–75.

Scheible, Jeffrey. *The Digital Shift: The Cultural Logic of Punctuation*. Minneapolis: University of Minnesota Press, 2015.

Schmitt, Carl. *The Nomos of the Earth in the International Law of the Jus Publicum Europaeum*. New York: Telos Press, 2003.

Schultz, Theodore W. "Investment in Human Capital," in *The American Economic Review* 51, no. 1 (March 1961): 1–17.

Schuppli, Susan. "Walk-Back Technology. Dusting for Fingerprints and Tracking Digital Footprints." *Photographies* 6, no. 1 (2013): 159–167.

Schuster, Liza. "Asylum seekers: Sangatte and the tunnel." *Parliamentary Affairs* 56, no. 3 (2003): 506–522.

Schwarz, Nina Violetta and Maurice Stierl. "Amplifying Migrant Voices and Struggles at Sea as a Radical Practice." *South Atlantic Quarterly*, forthcoming, 2019.

Scott, James C. *The Art of Not Being Governed: An Anarchist History of Upland Southeast Asia*. Cambridge: Yale University Press, 2010.

Scott, James C. *Seeing Like a State*. New Haven: Yale University Press, 1999.

Sekula, Allan. "The Body and the Archive." *October* 39 (1986): 3–64.

Sekula, Allan. "Photography and the Limits of National Identity," *Grey Room* 55, no. 31 (Spring 2014).

Sengupta, Somini, "U.N. Wants to Let Europe Use Military Force to Stop Migrant Smuggling Boats." *The New York Times*. Europe Section. May 6, 2015. www.nytimes.com/2015/05/07/world/europe/un-wants-to-let-europe-use-military-force-to-stop-migrant-smuggling-boats.html?_r=0

Sharpe, Christina. *In the Wake: On Blackness and Being*. Durham: Duke University Press, 2016.

Siddiqi, Anooradha Iyer. "On Humanitarian Architecture: A Story of a Border," *Humanity: An International Journal of Human Rights, Humanitarianism, and Development* 8, no. 3 (2017): 519–521.

Sigona, Nando. "Seeing double? How the EU miscounts migrants arriving at its borders." *The Conversation*, October 16, 2015. www.theconversation.com/seeing-double-how-the-eu-miscounts-migrants-arriving-at-its-borders-49242

Sparks, Ian. "9000 Calais migrants want to enter UK and they're so dangerous camp is police no-go zone." *Daily Express*. August 13, 2016.

Sparks, Ian. "Calais Jungle at 'breaking point" as number of migrants passes 9000 and camp becomes a 'major health and security risk." *The Daily Mail*, August 14, 2016.

Sparrow, Tom. *The End of Phenomenology: Metaphysics and the New Realism*. Edinburgh: Edinburgh University Press, 2014.

Spivak, Gayatri Chakravorty. "Subaltern Studies. Deconstructing Historiography." in Donna Landry and Gerald MacLean, editors. *The Spivak Reader*. London: Routledge, 1996 [1985].

Spivak, Gayatri Chakravorty. *A Critique of Postcolonial Reason: Toward a History of the Vanishing Present*. Cambridge: Harvard University Press, 1999.

Staff and Agencies, "Blunkett closes asylum 'loopholes'." *The Guardian*, April 12, 2002.

Starosielski, Nicole. *The Undersea Network*. Durham: Duke University Press, 2015.

Steinberg, Philip E. "Free sea." in *Spatiality, Sovereignty and Carl Schmitt: Geographies of the Nomos*, edited by Stephen Legg. London: Routledge, 2011.

Steinberg, Philip E. "Lines of Division, Lines of Connection: Stewardship in the World Ocean." *Geographical Review Geographical Review* 89, no. 2 (1999): 254–264.

Steinberg, Philip E. "Oceans." In *International Encyclopedia of Human Geography*, edited by Nigel Thrift. Oxford: Elsevier Science, 2009.

Steinberg, Philip E. "Of Other Seas: Metaphors and Materialities in Maritime Regions." *Atlantic Studies* 10, no. 2 (2013): 56–169.

Steinberg, Philip E. "Sovereignty, Territory, and the Mapping of Mobility: A View from the Outside." *Annals of the Association of American Geographers* 99, no. 3 (2009): 467–495.

Steinberg, Philip E. *The Social Construction of the Ocean*. Cambridge: Cambridge University Press, 2001.

Steward, Heather and Rowena Mason. "Nigel Farage's anti-migrant poster reported to police." *The Guardian*, June 16, 2016. www.theguardian.com/politics/2016/jun/16/nigel-farage-defends-ukip-breaking-point-poster-queue-of-migrants

Steyerl, Hito and Encarnación Gutiérrez Rodríguez, editors. *Spricht die Subalterne deutsch? Migration und postkoloniale Kritik*. Münster: Unrast Verlag, 2003.

Steyerl, Hito. *The Wretched of the Screen*. New York: Sternberg Press, 2013.

Stierl, Maurice. "A Sea of Struggle: Activist Border Interventions in the Mediterranean Sea," *Citizenship Studies* 20, no. 5 (2016): 561–578.

Stierl, Maurice. "A Fleet of Mediterranean Border Humanitarians." Antipode 50, no. 3 (2018): 704–724.

Stierl, Maurice. *Migrant Resistance in Contemporary Europe*. London: Routledge, 2019.

Stoler, A. L. "On Degrees of Imperial Sovereignty." *Public Culture* 18, no. 1 (2006): 125–146.

Strauch, Paul. "When Stopping the Smuggler Means Repelling the Refugee: International Human Rights Law and the European Union's Operation to Combat Smuggling in Libya's Territorial Sea." *The Yale Law Journal* 126, no. 8, June 2017.

Stryker, Susan. "Bodies of Knowledge: Embodiment and the Archival Imaginary." *Australian Feminist Studies* 25, no. 64 (2010): 105–108.

Suárez de Vivero, Juan Luis. *Jurisdictional Waters in the Mediterranean and Black Seas*. Brussels: European Parliament, 2010.

Tadiar, Neferti X. M. "City Everywhere." *Theory, Culture & Society* 33, no. 7–8 (2016): 57–83.

Tan, Monica. "Ai Weiwei poses as drowned Syrian infant refugee in 'haunting' photo." *The Guardian*, February 1, 2016. www.theguardian.com/artanddesign/2016/feb/01/ai-weiwei-poses-as-drowned-syrian-infant-refugee-in-haunting-photo

Taylor, Matthew and Patrick Wintour. "Calais crisis: Cameron pledges to deport more people to end 'swarm' of migrants." *The Guardian*, July 30, 2015. www.theguardian.com/uk-news/2015/jul/30/calais-migrants-make-further-attempts-to-cross-channel-into-britain

Tazzioli, Martina. "Calais After the Jungle: migrant dispersal and the expulsion of humanitarism." *Open Democracy*. June 20, 2017. www.opendemocracy.net/en/beyond-trafficking-and-slavery/calais-after-jungle-migrant-dispersal-and-expulsion-of-humanitarianis/

Tazzioli, Martina. "Crimes of Solidarity. Migration and Containment Through Rescue." *Radical Philosophy* 2, no. 1 (2018): 4–10.

Tazzioli, Martina. *Spaces of Governmentality, Autonomous Migration and the Arab Uprisings*. London: Rowman & Littlefield International, 2014.

Tazzioli, Martina. "The Desultory Politics Of Mobility And the Humanitarian-Military Border In the Mediterranean. Mare Nostrum Beyond the Sea." *REMHU: Revista Interdisciplinar Da Mobilidade Humana* 23, no. 44 (2015): 61–82.

Tazzioli, Martina. "When Rescue is Capture: Kidnapping and Dividing Migrants in the Mediterranean" *Open Democracy*. February 13, 2019. www.opendemocracy.net/en/beyond-trafficking-and-slavery/when-rescue-is-capture-kidnapping-and-dividing-migrants-in-mediterran/

Terranova, Tiziana. *Network Culture: Politics for the Information Age*. London: Pluto Press, 2004.

Thrift, Nigel. *Spatial Formations*. London: Sage,1996.

Ticktin, Miriam. "The Problem with Humanitarian Borders: Toward a New Framework of Justice." *Public Seminar*, September 18, 2015.

Tiqqun. "The Cybernetic Hypothesis." www.theanarchistlibrary.org/library/tiqqun-the-cybernetic-hypothesis

Torchin, Leshu. "'Ravished Armenia': Visual Media, Humanitarian Advocacy, and the Formation of Witnessing Publics," *American Anthropologist* 108, no. 1 (March 2006): 214–220.

Tosco Berlin. "Angela Davis: The Refugee Movement is the Movement of the 21st Century." *Vimeo*, 2015. www.vimeo.com/127986504

Travis, Alan. "Britain to accept 1200 migrants in Sangatte deal." *The Guardian*, December 3, 2002.

Trilling, Daniel. "Five Myths About the Refugee Crisis." *The Guardian*, June 5, 2018. www.theguardian.com/news/2018/jun/05/five-myths-about-the-refugee-crisis

Tsing, Anna. *Friction: An Ethnography of Global Connection*. Princeton: Princeton University Press, 2005.

Tufecki, Zeynep. *Twitter and Tear Gas*. Cambridge: Yale University Press, 2017.

Turin, Luca. *The Secret of Scent: Adventures in Perfume and the Science of Smell*. New York: Harper Collins, 2007.

United Nations Database. "Trends in International Migrant Stock: the 2008 Revision." *Eighth Coordination Meeting on International Migration*. 2009, esa.un.org/migration

UNHCR, "Desperate Journeys: Refugees and migrants arriving in Europe and at Europe's borders." January–December 2018. www.unhcr.org/desperatejourneys/

UNHCR, "Europe Situation." www.unhcr.org/europe-emergency.html

UNITED for Intercultural Action, "List of 35,597 documented deaths of refugees and migrants due to the restrictive policies of "Fortress Europe." www.unitedagainst refugeedeaths.eu/wp-content/uploads/2014/06/ListofDeathsActual.pdf

United Nations High Commissioner for Refugees (UNHCR), "Mediterranean boat capsizing: deadliest incident on record," April 21, 2015. www.unhcr.org/553652699. html

United Nations Human Development Report. *The Future of Migration: Building Capacities for Change*. IOM, Internat. Organization for Migration, 2010. www.iom.int/files/live/sites/iom/files/Newsrelease/docs/WM2010_FINAL_23_11_2010.pdf

United Nations Population Fund, 2015. *State of World Population 2015*. www.unfpa.org/migration

Urry, John. *Mobilities*. New York: Polity, 2007.

Urry, John. *Sociology Beyond Societies: Mobilities for the Twenty-First Century*. London: Routledge, 2012.

U.S. Geological Survey. "A World of Minerals in Your Mobile Device." *General Information Product* 167 (September 2016).

U.S. Intelligence National Council. "Global Trends 2030: Alternative Worlds." 2012. globaltrends2030.files.wordpress.com/2012/11/global-trends-2030-november2012. pdf

Van Dijken, Klaas and Abdulmoniem Suleiman. "De weg naar Europa loopt via Soedan." *Trouw* De Verdieping, January 24, 2018. www.trouw.nl/samenleving/de-weg-naar-europa-loopt-via-soedan~a5370778/

Vaughan-Williams, Nick. *Europe's Border Crisis: Biopolitical Security and Beyond*. Oxford: Oxford University Press, 2015.

Vermeulen, Maite and Leon de Korte. "Gewapend met migratiecijfers gooien we onze grenzen dicht. Maar die cijfers zijn onbetrouwbaar." *De Correspondent*. December 10, 2018.

Vis, Farida and Olga Goriunova. *The Iconic Image on Social Media: A Rapid Research Response to the Death of Aylan Kurdi*. Visual Social Media Lab. research.gold. ac.uk/14624/1/KURDI%20REPORT.pdf

Visual Social Media Lab. *The Iconic Image in Social Media: A Rapid Research Response to the Death of Aylan Kurdi*, 2015. www.visualsocialmedialab.org/projects/the-iconic-image-on-social-media

Vrasti, Wanda and Smaran Dayal. "Citizenship: Rightful Presence and the Urban Commons," *Citizenship Studies* 20, no. 8 (2016): 994–1011.

Walcott, Rinaldo, Twitter post, June 2, 2018, 12:12 p.m. www.twitter.com/blacklikewho/status/1002991281633542144?lang=en

Walters, William. "Foucault and Frontiers: Notes on the Birth of the Humanitarian Border" in *Governmentality: Current Issues and Future Challenges*, edited by Ulrich Bröckling, Susanne Krasmann and Thomas Lemke. New York: Routledge, 2011.

Walters, William. "Imagined Migration World: The European Union's Anti-Illegal Immigration Discourse." *The Politics of International Migration Management*, edited by Martin Geiger and Antoine Pécoud. London: Palgrave Macmillan, 2010.

Watenpaugh, Keith D. *Bread from Stones: The Middle East and the Making of Modern Humanitarianism*. Oakland: University of California Press, 2015.

Weber, Leanne and Sharon Pickering. *Globalization and Borders: Death at the Global Frontier*. London: Palgrave Macmillan, 2011.

Weizman, Eyal. "Introduction: Forensis." In *Forensis: The Architecture of Public Truth*, edited by Forensic Architecture. Berlin: Sternberg Press, 2014.

Welcome to Europe Network, "From Abolitionism to Freedom of Movement? History and Visions of Antiracist Struggles." Noborder lasts forever, Frankfurt am Main, 2010. conference.w2eu.net/files/2010/11/abolitionism.pdf

Whitehead, Alfred North. *Process and Reality*. New York: Free Press, 2014.

Whyte, Jessica. "Human Rights: Confronting Governments?" In *New Critical Legal Thinking: Law and the Political*, edited by Matthew Stone, Costas Douzinas and Rua Wall Illan. New York: Routledge, 2012.

Wiewiórowski, Wojciech Rafał. "Opinion on a notification for Prior Checking received from the Data Protection Officer of Frontex regarding the Processing of Personal Data for Risk Analysis (PeDRA)." July 3, 2015. edps.europa.eu/sites/edp/files/publication/15-07-03_risk_analysis_frontex_en_0.pdf

Winter, Yves. "Violence and Visibility." *New Political Science* 34, no. 2 (June 2012): 195–202.

Wood, Nicholas. "A Fake Macedonia Terror Tale That Led to Deaths." *The New York Times*, May 17, 2004. www.nytimes.com/2004/05/17/world/a-fake-macedonia-terror-tale-that-led-to-deaths.html

World Bank's World Development Indicators 2005: Section 3 Environment, Table 3.11. www.worldmapper.org/display.php?selected=141

World Tourism Organization, "World Tourism Barometer," Vol. 11, 2013. cf.cdn.unwto.org/sites/all/files/pdf/unwto_barom13_02_apr_excerpt_0.pdf

Winks, Christopher. *Symbolic Cities in Caribbean Literature*. New York: Palgrave Macmillan, 2009.

Xenos, Nicholas. "Refugees: the modern political condition" in *Challenging Boundaries*, edited by Michael J. Shapiro & Hayward Alker. Minneapolis: University of Minnesota Press, 1996.

Yuval-Davis, Nira. "What is transversal politics" *Soundings: A Journal of Politics and Culture* 12 (Summer 1999): 94–98.

Yuval-Davis, Nira. "Human/Women's Rights and Feminist Transversal Politics." *Transnational Feminisms: Women's Global Activism and Human Rights*, edited by Myra Marx Ferree and Aili Marie Tripp, editors. New York: New York Press, 2004.

Zablotsky, Veronika. "Governing Armenia: The Politics of Development and the Making of Global Diaspora," Ph.D. dissertation, University of California, Santa Cruz, 2019.

Zoubir, Zacharias. "A Vest That Fits All." *Commune*, Spring 2019. www.communemag.com/a-vest-that-fits-all/

List of Figures

Social and Cultural Studies

Ashley J. Bohrer
Marxism and Intersectionality
Race, Gender, Class and Sexuality
under Contemporary Capitalism

2019, 280 p., pb.
29,99 € (DE), 978-3-8376-4160-8
E-Book: 26,99 € (DE), ISBN 978-3-8394-4160-2

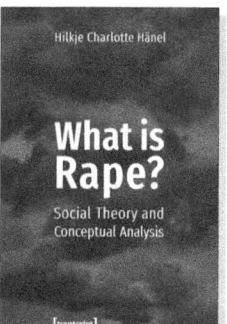

Hilkje Charlotte Hänel
What is Rape?
Social Theory and Conceptual Analysis

2018, 282 p., hardcover
99,99 € (DE), 978-3-8376-4434-0
E-Book: 99,99 € (DE), ISBN 978-3-8394-4434-4

Jasper van Buuren
Body and Reality
An Examination of the Relationships
between the Body Proper, Physical Reality,
and the Phenomenal World Starting from Plessner
and Merleau-Ponty

2018, 312 p., pb., ill.
39,99 € (DE), 978-3-8376-4163-9
E-Book: 39,99 € (DE), ISBN 978-3-8394-4163-3

**All print, e-book and open access versions of the titles in our list
are available in our online shop www.transcript-verlag.de/en!**

Social and Cultural Studies

Sabine Klotz, Heiner Bielefeldt,
Martina Schmidhuber, Andreas Frewer (eds.)
Healthcare as a Human Rights Issue
Normative Profile, Conflicts and Implementation

2017, 426 p., pb., ill.
39,99 € (DE), 978-3-8376-4054-0
E-Book: available as free open access publication
E-Book: ISBN 978-3-8394-4054-4

Michael Bray
Powers of the Mind
Mental and Manual Labor
in the Contemporary Political Crisis

2019, 208 p., hardcover
99,99 € (DE), 978-3-8376-4147-9
E-Book: 99,99 € (DE), ISBN 978-3-8394-4147-3

Iain MacKenzie
Resistance and the Politics of Truth
Foucault, Deleuze, Badiou

2018, 148 p., pb.
29,99 € (DE), 978-3-8376-3907-0
E-Book: 26,99 € (DE), ISBN 978-3-8394-3907-4
EPUB: 26,99 € (DE), ISBN 978-3-7328-3907-0

**All print, e-book and open access versions of the titles in our list
are available in our online shop www.transcript-verlag.de/en!**

GPSR Authorized Representative: Easy Access System Europe, Mustamäe tee
50, 10621 Tallinn, Estonia, gpsr.requests@easproject.com

www.ingramcontent.com/pod-product-compliance
Lightning Source LLC
Chambersburg PA
CBHW081653120626
46550CB00010B/2884